Mrs. Wm. Sprague.

THE

Court Circles of the Republic,

OR THE

BEAUTIES AND CELEBRITIES

OF THE NATION;

ILLUSTRATING LIFE AND SOCIETY UNDER EIGHTEEN PRESIDENTS; DESCRIBING THE SOCIAL FEATURES OF THE SUCCESSIVE ADMINISTRATIONS FROM

WASHINGTON TO GRANT;

THE DRAWING-ROOM CIRCLES; THE PROMINENT STATESMEN AND LEADING LADIES; THE BRILLIANT BELLES AND DISTINGUISHED VISITORS; THE PRINCIPAL ENTERTAINMENTS; FASHIONABLE STYLES OF DRESS; MANNERS; ETIQUETTE; ANECDOTES; INCIDENTS; ETC.; ETC.

Illustrated with Original Portraits, splendidly Engraved on Steel.

BY MRS. E. F. ELLET,

AUTHOR OF "THE WOMEN OF THE AMERICAN REVOLUTION;" "THE QUEENS OF AMERICAN SOCIETY," ETC., ETC.

WITH SKETCHES

BY MRS. R. E. MACK.

SOLD BY SUBSCRIPTION ONLY.

HARTFORD PUBLISHING CO., HARTFORD, CONN.

J. D. DENISON, NEW YORK; J. A. STODDARD & CO., CHICAGO, ILL.

GEO. P. HAWKES & CO., BOSTON, MASS.

1869.

ELECTROTYPED BY SAMUEL BOWLES AND CO.,
SPRINGFIELD, MASS.

TO

MRS. LEVI WOODBURY,

WHOSE INFLUENCE IN THE COURT CIRCLES HAS EVER BEEN SO
GRACIOUS, REFINING, AND BENEFICENT,
AND WHOSE BEAUTIFUL
HOME LIFE
IS A BLESSING TO ALL WHO KNOW HER,
THIS VOLUME

Is Admiringly and Affectionately Inscribed.

LIST OF ILLUSTRATIONS.

(ENGRAVED EXPRESSLY FOR THIS WORK.)

PREFACE.

LORD NAPIER remarked to a distinguished lady in Washington, that a book descriptive of Society in the National Capital ought to be written; and that a faithful record would give a better idea of the spirit and character of the period than any history. Except of the earliest "Republican Court," no attempt has been made to portray the social character of any administration. In this effort to supply a lamented defect, the necessary descriptions and sketches have been condensed as much as possible, and no memoirs have been included of men whose biographies have been elsewhere given to the public. The aim has been to exhibit statesmen, leading ladies, etc., in their drawing-room aspect, with only notices sufficient to illustrate their appearance and influence at special times. Thus mention is made repeatedly of the same persons under different administrations.

Imperfect as a brief survey must necessarily be, it will be found that a fair idea of an administration can be gained by a view of its fashionable life and every-day social habits. A great difference will be perceived in the terms of the Presidents, traceable in some degree to the influence of the Executive, but far more to those who surrounded him, and most of all to the ladies who ruled in the fashionable coteries, and gave the laws in assemblages, dress, and entertainments. The attention bestowed on these last may seem disproportionate to those who do not estimate their effect; those who remember the large share they occupy in the delineation of any period, will not charge the author with a frivolous taste in dwelling on them.

So vast a variety of sources of information have been consulted for this work, that a list of them would be tedious; and it will no doubt be more agreeable to the reader to be spared the enumeration. Letters and journals of the time have been especially used. In some cases access has been had to valuable family papers, throwing light on the subject illustrated.

The use of the term "Court-Circles," can hardly be censured, as it conveys exactly the meaning intended—the circles surrounding the President, and most conspicuous in the capital—and no other expression could be found to answer so well.

CONTENTS.

I. WASHINGTON'S ADMINISTRATION.

II. JOHN ADAMS' ADMINISTRATION.

III. JEFFERSON'S ADMINISTRATION.

IV. MADISON'S ADMINISTRATION.

V. MONROE'S ADMINISTRATION.

XII. TYLER'S ADMINISTRATION.

XIII. POLK'S ADMINISTRATION.

XIV. TAYLOR'S ADMINISTRATION.

XV. FILLMORE'S ADMINISTRATION.

XVI. PIERCE'S ADMINISTRATION.

The Court Circles of the Republic.

I.

WASHINGTON'S ADMINISTRATION.

Establishment of the First Presidential Court—Imposing Spectacle of the Inauguration—Brilliant Festivities in Honor of it—Arrival of Mrs. Washington and Mrs. Robert Morris—First Levee—The President's Equipage—Prominent Ladies and Statesmen—Dress of the President at his Official Receptions—Style of Ordinary Ones—Mrs Izard—Mrs. Knox—Alexander Hamilton—Robert Morris—Gouverneur Morris—Mrs. Burr—Attorneys and Divines in New York—Edmund Randolph—John Jay—Jefferson, Secretary of State—Charles Carroll of Maryland—The Misses White—Party at Mr. White's—The Best Dressed Gentleman—New Year's Calls—The President drawn by Six Horses to Federal Hall—Death of Franklin—Removal of the Capital from New York to Philadelphia—House assigned to the President—Brilliant Society—Mrs. Bingham and other Leaders of the Ton—Conspicuous Men of the Period—Foreign Visitors of exalted Rank—The Farewell Levee—Deportment in the Drawing-room a reflex of Temper in the Cabinet and Congress.

MRS. WASHINGTON is venerated as the earliest representative leader among the ladies prominent in the best society of the Republic. When the Chief was summoned by the nation to assume the duties of its Chief Magistrate, she came to form the establishment of the President at the seat of government.

In March and April 1789, the meeting of the first Congress under the Constitution took place, and the votes for the first President of the United States were opened and counted. Gen. Washington being notified of his election, left Mount Vernon for New York, greeted all along the way by the irrepressible enthusiasm of the people. Received with due honors at the Capital, he was conducted to his official residence, at what is now the corner of Cherry Street and Franklin Square. The imposing spectacle of the Inauguration took place with appropriate ceremonies in Federal Hall, April 30, 1789. The oath of office was administered by Chancellor Livingston. In the evening the city was brilliantly illuminated, and there was a display of fire-works. Afterwards rules were established for receiving visitors and entertaining company. At first a public intimation was given that the President would receive visitors on Tuesdays and Fridays, from two to three in the afternoon. Consulting friends, he adopted chiefly Mr. Hamilton's suggestions in social matters; and it was decided that the President should return no visits, and that invitations to dinner should be given only to official characters and strangers of distinction. The levees were held every Tuesday afternoon.

On the 7th of May a splendid ball was given at the assembly-rooms, at which the President and Vice-President appeared, with many members of both Houses of Congress, the foreign ministers, and distinguished citizens. The ladies were dressed with great taste and elegance, but little jewelry was then worn. Lady Stirling and her daughters, and her sister-in-law Mrs. Livingston, Mrs. Montgomery, Lady Christiana Griffin, Lady Temple, the Marchioness de

Brehan, Mrs. Clinton, Mrs. Duane the Mayoress, Mrs. Prevost the Bishop's wife, Mrs. Jay, Mrs. Hamilton, Mrs. Beekman, &c., were among the number. The next week the Count de Moustier gave a grand ball at his house in Broadway. Elias Boudinot described it as "a most splendid ball indeed." Mrs. Washington, accompanied by her grandchildren Eleanor Custis and George Washington Parke Custis, set out from Mount Vernon on the 19th of May, in her carriage, with a small equestrian escort. She was received with honors at every stopping-place, and was entertained in Philadelphia by Mrs. Robert Morris, and at Elizabethtown by the venerable Governor Livingston and his daughters. The President came here to meet her, in a splendid barge; and as they approached the battery, a salute of thirteen guns was fired; while crowds greeted the landing of the distinguished passengers. On the day after the arrival of Mrs. Washington a dinner was given at the President's, to Vice-President Adams, Governor Clinton, the Count de Moustier, Mr. Jay, General St. Clair, the Spanish minister, five Senators and the Speaker of the House. Mr. Wingate said it was the least showy dinner he had ever seen at that table. Washington said grace, and dined on boiled leg of mutton. After the dessert, a single glass of wine was offered to each guest, and when it was drunk, General Washington rose and the company adjourned to the drawing-room.

On the 29th of May, Mrs. Washington held her first levee; and they were continued every Friday evening from eight to ten o'clock. These receptions were marked by little ostentation or restraint, and were attended by all that was fashionable, elegant, or refined in society; but they were select and courtly, and not subject to the intrusion of the rabble. Mrs. Washington was careful to exact proper courtesies in her drawing-room. None were admitted to the levees but those entitled by official station, established merit, or suitable introductions; and full dress was required of all. A drawing-room sufficiently capacious in the President's house was plainly furnished; some pictures and ornaments, and the family plate, had been brought from Mount Vernon. The state coach was the finest carriage in the city, usually drawn by four horses; but always by six when it conveyed the President to Federal Hall. It was cream-colored and ornamented with cupids supporting festoons, with borderings of flowers around the panels.

The residence of the President was afterwards in Broadway near the Bowling Green. His office was on the first floor, opposite the drawing-rooms. The Vice-President had a beautiful rural residence at Richmond Hill.

In addition to the other ladies mentioned as guests at the ball, among the leading ladies of the metropolis were Lady Kitty Duer, Lady Mary Watts, Madame de la Forest, Mrs. John Langdon, Mrs. Tristram Dalton, Mrs. Knox, Mrs. Robert R. Livingston, the Misses Livingston, Mrs. Thompson, Mrs. Gerry, Mrs. McComb, Mrs. Edgar, Mrs. Lynch, Mrs. Houston, the Misses Bayard, Mrs. Livingston of Clermont, and many others. At his own official receptions Washington greeted his visitors with a bow, without shaking hands. He wore a black velvet suit, with white vest and yellow gloves, breeches, silver knee and shoe-buckles, and a long steel-hilted sword; a cocked hat in his hand. At his wife's levees he had neither hat nor sword, but conversed without restraint as a private gentleman. Mrs. Washington was about fifty-seven years of age when she opened the "Republican Court;" and she retained much of the grace of her earlier years.

The festivities that followed the inauguration—public and private—were interrupted by the ill-health of the President and the death of his venerable mother; so that he and Mrs. Washington participated in few gayeties during the winter that New York continued the national capital.

Several families who had held in the province a sort of baronial supremacy, were now eminent in public service or in private society; yet in social elegance the circles of New York were inferior to those of Philadelphia. New York continued to be the metropolis less than two years.

Mrs. Washington's decided disinclination to balls perhaps diminished the number given. But there were public amusements; an exhibition of wax-work is mentioned, and a review and sham fight; theatricals also had some encouragement, and private performances were sometimes given in the President's house. The wife of Robert Morris, the great financier, was usually at Mrs. Washington's right hand at her drawing-rooms; Mr. Morris having that post at her dinners. The refreshments at the ordinary levees were plain, consisting generally of tea and coffee with cake. It has been said that ice-creams were first introduced by Mrs. Washington. Mrs. Knox was a remarkable character of the time. She and her husband were said to be "the largest couple in the city." She was a lively and amiable leader of society, and his brilliant conversation and unfailing good humor brightened every circle. Many thought Mrs. Knox's co-operation and approval indispensable in the drawing-room or the ball-room. The house of the Secretary of War was the scene of munificent hospitality.

Mrs. Izard, of South Carolina, was about the age of Mrs. Adams. Her French descent, her marriage with a man of accomplishments and liberal fortune, her association with a brilliant society in London, Paris and Florence, fitted her to sustain her part with distinguished effect. Her beauty and wit made her universally admired.

Alexander Hamilton was a man of extraordinary genius, activity and knowledge. He was, of course, one of the most prominent men in the society of the period. He lived on the corner of Wall and Broad Streets, but built a beautiful country house—"The Grange"—on the island, a few miles from the city. He had a remarkably expressive face. He was under the middle size and thin, but erect and dignified. His hair was turned back from his forehead, powdered, and clubbed behind. His fair and rosy complexion, the play of his features lighted up with intelligence and vivacity, his sweet smile, attracted all who saw him. He had a mind of vast grasp, and was great either as a speaker or a writer. The originality of his views evinced the possession of genius. He was a frank, amiable, high-toned gentleman. His wife, the daughter of General Schuyler, was one of the most charming women of the time.

William Livingston, a most able representative of New Jersey, a forcible and elegant writer, was extremely plain in his dress and manner. Robert Morris was a native of England, but had lived in America since he was thirteen. Gouverneur Morris was the youngest son of Lewis Morris. He assisted Robert Morris in the superintendence of the finances.

One of the ancestors of Gouverneur Morris, who had been noted as a leader in Cromwell's army, came to New York, and purchased a thousand acres of land, with manorial privileges, in the vicinity of Harlem. The estate is still known as Morrisania. Gouverneur, born in 1752, was distinguished in the Revolutionary war, and eminently useful in his public life. He was sent as minister to France in 1792. A vein of eccentricity, with striking originality, marked his character; his commanding figure, expressive features, and emphatic articulation, with his superior intellect, made an impression on society. Madame de Staël remarked that he had "l'air tres imposant." He married a niece of John Randolph. The story went that he had invited a number of relatives to a Christmas dinner, and when the company was assembled, that he left the room and soon returned with his bride and a clergyman, who forthwith performed the marriage ceremony, to the astonishment of all, and the disappointment of those who expected to inherit the estate. While he was in attendance on Congress in Philadelphia, an accident caused the loss of his leg, and he had it replaced by a stump. On one occasion, when the cry of "aristocrat" was raised against him in the streets of Paris, for appearing in his carriage, when no such things were allowed by the mob, and the blood-thirsty crowd threatened his life—he coolly thrust his wooden leg out of the window, and cried out: "An aristocrat! yes—who lost his limb in the cause of American liberty!" He was not only allowed to proceed but vehemently cheered.

When a friend asked his son, a boy of four, if he had read Robinson Crusoe and Jack the Giant-killer? Morris said: "Tell the gentleman—no; but that you are acquainted with the lives of Gustavus Adolphus, and Charles the Twelfth of Sweden."

Intelligent crowds would hang in silent admiration on his eloquence; and servants would stop open-mouthed, dish in hand, to catch his table-talk. It was his rare fortune to be intimate with the leading spirits of two nations at a time of social and political convulsion, which brought into action the gifts and graces as well as the passions of humanity. His correspondence with Washington showed mutual respect and confidence. Once at a dinner party it was insisted that no one, however intimate, would dare take a liberty with the Chief. Gouverneur Morris foolishly accepted a bet that he would venture on the experiment. Just before dinner was announced, while the guests stood by the fire, in the midst of a lively chat, Morris clapped Washington familiarly on the shoulder. The Chief turned and gave him a look of such mild and dignified yet grieved surprise, that his friend shrank back repentant of his forgetfulness of respect, while the mirth of the company was instantly awed into silence.

A story was related in the Morris family, that while he was sojourning in Paris, the King noticed the remarkable resemblance which Gouverneur Morris bore his own royal family. One day during an audience, the monarch, after looking fixedly at the American statesman, exclaimed with energy: "The likeness is, indeed, too wonderful to be accidental!" immediately adding: "Pray, Mr. Morris—was your mother ever in France?"

With a low bow Morris instantly replied: "No—your majesty; but my father was!"

Mrs. Aaron Burr,—who had been Mrs. Prevost, the widow of a British officer, and had married Burr in 1782,—did not go into society. In 1789 Burr was only thirty-three. "He was small but well formed; with a handsome face, by some described as striking, and eyes jet black and uncommonly brilliant and piercing, with a manner singularly graceful, gentle and fascinating."

At this time the list of attorneys in the city comprised one hundred and twenty-two names; that of clergymen only fourteen. The legal learning and eloquence were then eminent; and the names of Duane, Hamilton, Jay, Kent, Troup, Lewis, the Livingstons, Morris, Hoffman and others, &c., are still remembered as ornaments to the profession. Dr. Linn, of the Reformed Dutch Church, was a fine scholar and a fervid, graceful orator. "The very good-tempered, gentlemanly and scholarly Dr. Provost," was bishop of the Episcopal Church, and was also much sought by his friends for his social qualities.

Sullivan thus described Mr. John Jay; "His height was a little less than six feet; his person rather thin, but well formed. His complexion was without color, his eyes black and penetrating, his nose aquiline, and his chin pointed. His hair came over his forehead, was tied behind, and lightly powdered; his dress black. The expression of his face was exceedingly amiable. When standing he was a little inclined forward, as is not uncommon with students long accustomed to bend over a table. His manner was very gentle and unassuming. His deportment was tranquil.

"History will assign to John Jay an elevated rank among the great; it will place him equally high among the pure and virtuous." He was born in New York in 1748. In 1779 he was appointed minister to Spain; in 1782 he was sent as one of the Commissioners to negotiate a peace with England. On the adoption of the Constitution, he was appointed Chief Justice of the United States, and resigned that office in 1795, to become Governor of New York.

It will be remembered that President Washington chose Mr. Jefferson to preside over the department of State. He had filled the office of minister plenipotentiary at the court of France, as the successor of Franklin. Alexander Hamilton was appointed Secretary of the Treasury; General Knox continued Secretary of War, as he had been under the confederation. Edmund Randolph of Virginia, was made Attorney General, and Samuel Osgood Postmaster

General. These heads of Departments of course aided to form the court society. Mr. Jay accepted the office of Chief Justice, and his colleagues were William Cushing, of Massachusetts, James Wilson of Pennsylvania, John Blair, and John Rutledge the eloquent statesman from South Carolina, with James Iredell, of North Carolina. The manners of Mr. Edmund Randolph and his agreeable conversation had caused him to be described as "the first gentleman of Virginia." He had succeeded Patrick Henry as Governor of that State. His figure was tall and imposing, and he always dressed elegantly. John Randolph, of Roanoke, was his relative, and in New York at the time; he was sixteen years of age, and very lank, awkward and ill-dressed; known to everybody, however, as a boy of ability, destined to play an extraordinary part in the world.

Sullivan described Charles Carroll, the Senator from Maryland, as rather small and thin, with very gracious and polished manners. He was a man of great accomplishments and rare abilities, and was universally respected and beloved. Several members of his family were with him during the second session of the first Congress in New York. Polly, his daughter, was already married to Mr. Richard Caton, an English gentleman. The Misses White—daughters of Henry White, were conspicuous in society, though of a loyalist family. Sabine says: "Madame White was a lady of great wealth, and her recollections of New York society were curious." An elderly gentleman who went one evening to a party at the house of Mr. White—in the winter of 1789–90—spoke rapturously of the young ladies—"so gay and fashionable, so charming in conversation, with such elegant figures." On this occasion he went with Sir John Temple and Henry Remsen, and was dressed "in a light blue French coat, with a high collar, broad lappels and large gilt buttons, a double-breasted marseilles vest, nankeen colored cassimere breeches, with white silk stockings, shining pumps, and full ruffles on my breast and at my wrists, together with a ponderous white cravat with a pudding in it, as we then called it; and I was considered the best dressed gentleman in the room. I remember to have waltzed a minuet with much grace, with my friend Mrs. Verplanck, who was dressed in hoop and petticoats; I caught cold that night from drinking hot port wine negus, and riding home in a sedan chair with one of the glasses broken."

The foreign ministers added little to society this season. Mr. Van Berckel represented the States General of the United Netherlands, and had just returned from Europe. The custom of making calls on New Year's day brought to New York by the Dutch and the Huguenots, was duly observed on the first of January, 1790; the principal gentlemen waiting on the President. Mrs. Washington's levee held in the evening was attended with unusual elegance. Contrary to usual custom, the visitors were seated, and partook of tea and coffee, and plain and plum cake. The President expressed his hope that the New Yorkers would never forget the cordial and cheerful observance of New Year's day.

The President came to Federal Hall in his chariot drawn by six horses, to open the second session, and delivered his speech in the Senate Chamber. He was dressed in a suit of cloth manufactured in Hartford. Many public dinners were given this winter; the President continuing his every Wednesday to members of Congress, ambassadors and eminent persons.

Mr. Jefferson, who had returned from France with his two daughters, and had rested some time at Monticello, came to New York, by a fortnight's journey from Richmond. He took a house in Maiden Lane, and was cordially received by the President and the citizens. The dinner parties made him at once familiar with them.

A gloom fell over society with the news of Franklin's death in Philadelphia. This occurred in April. The session, the last ever held in New York, was closed in August. Leaving the city to go to Virginia, General Washington never again returned to live there.

The best private house in the city of Philadelphia —that of Robert Morris—was taken by the corporation for the residence of the President, and some additions were made for the accommodation of the family. The stables would hold "twelve horses only," and there was a coach house for all the carriages. It was the determination of Washington to live in a style of the utmost simplicity and modesty consistent with the dignity of his official position. The rent of the house was settled at three thousand dollars a year. In no respect did the President deserve the charges of anti-republican state and splendor, made against him by political opponents. He himself wrote to Mrs. Macaulay: "Mrs. Washington's ideas coincide with my own as to simplicity of dress, and everything which can tend to support propriety of character without partaking of the follies of luxury and ostentation."

It was with reluctance that General Washington permitted his name to be used for a second Presidential term. Mr. Hamilton urged that his declining would involve great evils to the country at that crisis of affairs. The affairs of the national government were not yet firmly established, and much was to be dreaded if the venerated and beloved Chief refused to continue in office. The re-election was unanimous, and on the 4th of March, 1793, he again took the oath of office in the hall of the Senate.

There were not wanting enemies to the administration; and active among these was Philip Freneau, who was said to write under the dictation of Mr. Jefferson. The pretenses for attacks on the President were his reserved manners, and his not supporting some demand of the army. He and his friends were accused of a leaning towards a monarchical form of government. Washington had not yet learned to make bows to suit the democracy!

M. Genet was the first minister sent by the French Republic. The exhibitions of popular enthusiasm on his coming grew out of the sympathy felt by a growing party with those who had thrown off the yoke of royalty. Democratic societies were formed in imitation of Jacobin Clubs; and common forms of expression such as the title of "citizen" became rife in Philadelphia. Genet complained at seeing a bust of

Louis XVI. in the vestibule of the President's house; and his conduct was such, that General Washington at length procured his recall. Genet was a member of one of the first families of France, and a brother of the celebrated Madame Campan. He married Miss Cornelia Tappan Clinton, a daughter of the Governor of New York, and fixed his residence in this country.

The party opposed to the administration, of which Jefferson was the apostle, now began to exert an influence deemed formidable. The events of the French Revolution had given an impulse to the spirit of ultra democracy. It pervaded society, and formed the subject of conversation in public and private circles throughout the country. The old respectability of the nation continued to adhere to the party of which Washington was the founder and head. Mr. Jefferson was no longer Secretary of State, having retired from official connection with public affairs. Edmund Randolph took his place, and his was filled by William Bradford of Pennsylvania.

The cream of the cream of society graced Philadelphia at this period. The Duke de Lauzun said that in beauty, grace and intelligence, the women could not be surpassed. The gay Marquis de Chastellux had been enthusiastic in describing its dames and demoiselles. Mrs. William Bingham was a queen in the highest social circle. All that the United States contained illustrious in statesmanship, was assembled at the new capital. Dominie Robert Proud, Benjamin Chew, Edward Shippen, Dr. Rush, the facetious Judge Peters, the sage Rittenhouse, the humorist Francis Hopkinson, Bishop White, Charles Brockden Brown, were a few among them. The rules adopted by the President and Mrs. Washington for receiving company were nearly the same as in New York. Receptions were given by the President every other Tuesday, from three to four in the afternoon, in the large dining-room on the first floor. His hair was usually powdered and gathered behind in a silk bag, his coat and breeches were of plain black velvet, with white or pearl-colored vest, yellow gloves, a cocked hat in his hand, silver knee and shoe-buckles, and a long sword with a glittering steel hilt and scabbard of polished white leather. He rarely shook hands, but bowed to each visitor. The door was closed at a quarter past three; the gentlemen moved into a circle, and the President went round exchanging a few words with each; after which the visitors again came up, bowed and retired. At Mrs. Washington's drawing-rooms he did not consider the visits made to himself, and he appeared as a private gentleman, without hat or sword.

Mrs. Adams described the first levee, given on Christmas day. She went attended by her son, and met "the dazzling Mrs. Bingham and her beautiful sisters, the Misses Allen, the Misses Chew, &c." Miss Allen became Mrs. Greenleaf, and had the reputation of superb beauty. Mrs. Theodore Sedgwick had a charming face, and an air of refinement and elegance; "the magnificent Miss Wolcott from Connecticut, was the boast of gentlemen from the Eastern States; and Mrs. Knox, of course, was the observed of all observers." Miss Sally McKean boasted of the party as "brilliant beyond anything you can imagine; and though there was a great deal of extravagance, there was so much of Philadelphia taste in everything, it must have been confessed the most delightful occasion of the kind ever known in this country."

Dinners, balls, and gayeties of every description, followed each other during that memorable winter. At Mr. Bingham's and Mr. Morris's houses the dinners were sumptuous to a degree unrivalled by other social leaders. One of the citizens wrote to a friend abroad: "You have never seen anything like the frenzy that has seized on the inhabitants here; they have been half mad ever since this city became the seat of government; and there is no limit to their prodigality. The probability is that some families will find they cannot support their dinners, suppers and losses at loo, a great while." "There have been a good many delightful parties, and I have been at Chews, McKean's, Clymer's, Dallas's, Bingham's, and a dozen other houses lately. Among your more particular friends there is more quiet and comfort, and it is not impossible that the most truly respectable people are least heard of."

Mrs. Bingham was well fitted to lead in the fashionable world. She gathered around her assemblages of aristocratic distinction and unquestioned taste. Splendid in beauty, elegant in deportment, sprightly, winning, and charming in manners, she had additional gifts by which to enchant every one who came within the sphere of her influence. Her social pre-eminence is historical, and America has rarely seen one like her. With all her advantages, personal, social and external, she was not envied, for she had the spell to disarm jealousy, and to win the coldest heart. Her dress was marked by propriety and good taste; her entertainments were delightful; and her command of wealth, with her family connections, gave her additional advantages. Mrs. Adams wrote: "I have not seen a lady in England who can bear a comparison with Mrs. Bingham, Mrs. Platt, or a Miss Hamilton, who is a Philadelphia young lady."

Mrs. Bingham's cousin, Chief Justice Shippen, lived in Fourth Street; another cousin, Mrs. Harrison, opposite the Bingham mansion; other relatives and connections resided in the neighborhood; and she could fill her drawing-rooms with her own kin at short notice, at any time. Her style illustrated the highest refinement; and it formed a contrast with the simplicity of the circle in which Mrs. Washington was regarded as the queen.

Benjamin Chew was one of the most conspicuous men of that period. He was seventy, but preserved the distinguished air and high-bred courtesy of his youth; as did Edward Shippen, eight years his junior, now also called to a high judicial position. Dr. Rush was a resident of Philadelphia, but had little to do with the Presidential court. Judge Peters was a great favorite from his wit and facetiousness. Francis Hopkinson, the genial humorist, had remarkable powers of pleasing; the sage Rittenhouse, William Bartram, and John Fitch, inventor of the steamboat, were then in the capital. That man of profound sense, Bishop White, was then in his meridian, while Dr. Sproat touched the verge of human life; there were several other clergymen of high moral worth, though not possessed of extraordinary abilities. Charles Brockden Brown and Dr. Milnor were students, and John Randolph was the center of a club of boon companions from the Southern States, members of which were Eppes, who afterwards married Jefferson's youngest daughter, Thomas Marshall, a brother of the great chief justice; Robert Rose, who married Madison's sister; Rutledge of South Carolina, Bryan of Georgia, and many others.

Wansey, an English traveler, took breakfast with the President in June, 1794, and noticed the simple manners of the family. Mrs. Washington made tea and coffee, and there was sliced tongue, dry toast and bread and butter. Miss Eleanor Custis, a girl of sixteen, sat nearest the hostess, and next, her grand-son George. One servant, who wore no livery, waited on the table; and a silver urn for hot water was the only expensive piece of table furniture. The President was at that time in his sixty-third year, but looked rather younger than Mrs. Washington. She was short, robust in figure and very plainly dressed; her gray hair turned up under a plain cap. Some of her drawing-rooms were criticised by the democrats as "introductory to the paraphernalia of courts."

Mrs. Adams greatly eulogized the old theatre in Philadelphia, which was frequently visited by the families of the President and Vice-President. The new one was opened in 1794. The manager, Mr. Wignell, fitted up the house with luxurious elegance. Harwood, one of the actors, married Miss Bache, a grand-daughter of Dr. Franklin. Another, Fennel, entertained five generals at his house at one time, and was on intimate terms with Governor Mifflin.

Mrs. Whitlock, one of the actresses, was a sister of Mrs. Siddons. Wansey described the head-dresses of the ladies at the theatre as in the English style. The younger appeared with their hair flowing in ringlets on their shoulders. The gentlemen had round hats, coats with high collars, and many coats of striped silk.

Mr. Hamilton resigned the Secretaryship of the Treasury in 1795, being succeeded by General Wolcott. General Knox had also resigned, and had been succeeded by Colonel Pickering. Thus the original cabinet was entirely changed. Mr. John Jay had been sent in April 1794, as envoy extraordinary to the British Court. The British minister to this country was Mr. Hammond, a stout, rosy, handsome man, wearing a powdered wig, who had married one of the beautiful daughters of Andrew Allen, and had a country place near the city. Mr. Bradford, the Attorney General, had also a house in the country.

The discovery of some practices to compass the ruin of the administration, in which Mr. Randolph was involved, led to his enforced resignation. His "Vindication" contained violent abuse of Washington, which moved the Chief to such anger, that he was said to have uttered the strongest language, and brought his fist down on the breakfast table with such force as to cause a clatter with the cups and plates, to the alarm of Mrs. Washington and her family party, the Custises, Lewises, &c.

Fisher Ames made the greatest speech ever yet made in Congress, on the treaty negotiated by Mr. Jay. John Adams wrote of this speech: "Judge Iredell and I happened to sit together. 'How great he is!' says Iredell: 'How great he has been'! 'He has been noble,' said I. After some time Iredell breaks out with 'Bless my stars, I never heard anything so great since I was born!' 'It is divine!' said I; and thus we went on with our interjections, not to say our tears, till the end. Not a dry eye, I believe in the house, except some of the jackasses who had occasioned a necessity of the oratory. These attempted to laugh; but their visages grinned horrible ghastly smiles."

One of the ladies who remembered General Washington most accurately, was Mrs. Susan Wallace, the daughter of Mrs. Mary Binney, who lived nearly opposite the President. General Washington used to walk out every fine day, attended by his secretary, and dressed in black, with a cocked hat. The President's coach, light carriage and chariot, were all cream-colored, and painted with figures on the panels. Two horses were driven when the General went to church; four in going into the country; and six to the Senate. He had white servants, dressed in liveries of white with scarlet or orange trimmings. Mrs. Wallace—or Miss Susan Binney—was a young girl in the later years of Washington's administration. Her mother often visited Mrs. Washington, and when the latter returned the call, which was on the third day, her footman would run over, knock at Mrs. Binney's door, and announce his mistress, who would come over with Mr. Lear, the secretary. Susan thought the great lady's manners very pleasant and unceremonious, and like those of most Virginia ladies. Miss Binney married a nephew of Mr. Bradford the second Attorney General of the United States.

Mr. Richard Rush remembered the Chief going in person to open the session of Congress, by a speech according to his custom. His carriage was white, with medallion ornaments, and the liveries white turned up with red; for at that time the display of equipages was rich and varied. The carriage passed through an immense crowd, and when it stopped Washington stepped out and ascended the steps of the House of Representatives. Pausing on the upper platform, he turned and looked towards a carriage that had followed the lead of his own. He wore a suit of black velvet; his gray hair was powdered to snowy whiteness; he had a dress sword at his side, and his hat was in his hand. Every eye was riveted on him, and profound stillness reigned in the crowd; for every heart was full. Washington was waiting for his secretary, who came up and handed him a paper. As both entered the building the long repressed huzzas burst forth.

Many foreign visitors came during this administration to the United States, and distinguished refugees were driven here by the French revolution. As high-bred gentlemen they brought examples of courtly usages, useful to the rising generation. One of these illustrious exiles was Chataubriand, a nephew of Malesherbes. He came in 1790 and was two years in the country. Another was Count Andriani, of Milan, bearing to Washington an ode addressed to him by the great poet Alfieri. The Viscount de Noailles, a brother-in-law of La Fayette, was a visitor at Mrs. Washington's drawing-rooms, with his countryman M. Talon. When his means began to fail, Mr.

Bingham gave him some third story rooms in a building at the end of his garden. Here he gave a dinner to several noblemen, and the viands were cooked and served by Mr. Bingham's servants.

Those remarkable Englishmen, Thomas Cooper, Joseph Priestly and William Cobbett, began their career in this country in 1794, and were in society. Alexander Baring, afterwards Lord Ashburton, married the eldest daughter of Mr. Bingham. M. de Talleyrand sought refuge here in 1794. He brought letters from the Marquis of Landsdowne and Mrs. Church, a sister of Mrs. Hamilton. The appearance of this gentleman was as remarkable as his character. He "was very tall and had light hair, long and parted in front; his eyes were blue and expressive, and he had a sallow complexion; his mouth was wide and coarse; his body 'large and protuberant in front;' his legs were singularly small and his feet deformed. His manner was tranquil and watchful; and in some respects vulgar and repulsive. A woman in New York at whose house he dined frequently, said he would rest his elbows on the table and talk with his mouth full; he would cut the meat on his plate into small pieces, pierce them with his fork till its prongs were full, then thrust them into his mouth, and closing his teeth pull out the fork, leaving its freight in his capacious jaws."

M. Fauchet—afterwards Baron—had succeeded M. Genet as French minister. At the birthnight ball he was placed by the managers on the right hand of the President, which gave offence to the British minister and the Spanish commissioners. Mr. Adet, who superseded him, arrived in Philadelphia in the summer of 1795.

The Duc de la Rochefoucault Liancourt arrived in 1794. He was about forty-five. His immense estates had been confiscated; but he had some income. He was intimate in the families of Judge Chew and General Knox.

Louis Philippe d' Orleans, who had taught geometry in Switzerland under an assumed name, was sent to this country by Gouverneur Morris in 1796, and in Philadelphia lodged in a single room over a barber's shop. He gave a dinner to several distinguished gentlemen, and apologized for seating half of them on the side of a bed. He was about twenty-three, with a dark complexion, sunken eyes, and great dignity. He was intimate in Mr. Bingham's family, and was refused as a suitor to one of the daughters. His brothers, the Duke de Montpensier and the Count de Beaujolais, joined him the following year.

John Singleton Copely, son of the painter, was also known in society as a quiet gentleman with pleasing manners. The Duke of Kent was here at the same time. Mr. Liston succeeded Mr. Hammond as British minister, and arrived in May 1796. Mrs. Cushing, wife of the Judge of the Supreme Court, mentioned a dinner at the President's in April, 1795, in company with Mr. and Mrs. Hammond, and other eminent persons. Two of the foreign ladies, the wives of the Spanish and Portuguese ministers, were brilliant with diamonds. In June, 1796, Don Carlos Martinez, Marquis d' Yrujo, succeeded Jaudennes as Spanish minister. He married Sally McKean, daughter of the

Chief Justice of Pennsylvania, a celebrated beauty. Thus Philadelphia furnished wives for the envoys of France, England and Spain during this administration. Kosciusko came to this country, about the close of Washington's term, and met the Duc de Liancourt at the house of General Gates.

The ladies most intimate with Mrs. Washington were Mrs. Hamilton, Mrs. Knox, Mrs. Morris, Mrs. Stewart, Mrs. Powell, Mrs. Bradford, Mrs. Otis, Miss Ross, and others. The Duke de Liancourt spoke of Mrs. Knox with warm admiration, and also of her daughter and husband. He was their guest in Maine. Mrs. Otis was the wife of the Secretary of the Senate. Her son, the great orator, married Sally Foster in 1790. Mrs. Otis was remarkable for beauty, wit and vivacity. Mrs. Bradford was the daughter of Elias Boudinot. Mrs. Carroll was the daughter of Benjamin Chew, and with her sister, Mrs. Henry Phillips, was a great favorite with Washington. Mrs. John Eager Howard was an elder sister. Dolly Payne—afterwards Mrs. Todd—was one of the most charming, gay and fascinating women in the city, reigning some years as a courted belle. She married James Madison in 1794. Robert Harper had married a daughter of the elder Charles Carroll, and William Smith a sister of John Rutledge. Aaron Burr was now a senator, lived in style, and gave elegant entertainments. Mr. Jefferson also kept open house for his friends. Wolcott had a circle consisting in great part of New Englanders, and it was said to be a most intellectual society. Wolcott's youngest sister was a celebrated beauty, and married the eminent Chauncey

Goodrich. Mrs. Wolcott also was a lovely woman, of very graceful manners.

Josiah Quincy figured prominently in the society of the period, and was highly praised by Mrs. Adams. She playfully recommended him to pay his addresses to Nelly Custis, and adds that she thought him the first match in the United States. Mr. Jeremiah Smith, afterward one of the justices of the Supreme Court, dining at Mr. Wolcott's, was captivated by the loveliness of Miss Eliza Ross of Maryland. She became Mrs. Smith in due time. Eli Whitney, with his famous cotton-gin, was introduced to Wolcott about this time.

The last formal levee of the President was crowded with the beauty and fashion of the capital, and with many distinguished visitors. The day before the close of his administration, Washington gave a dinner to the President elect, the heads of departments, &c. Among the guests were Mr. and Mrs. Liston, the Marquis and Marchioness d' Yrujo, and the foreign ministers with their wives; Mr. and Mrs. Wolcott, Mr. and Mrs. Pickering, Mr. and Mrs. McHenry, Mr. and Mrs. Cushing, Mr. and Mrs. Bingham, Mr. Adams, Mr. Hamilton, Mr. Jefferson, and Bishop White. "During the dinner"—said the bishop, "much hilarity prevailed; but on the removal of the cloth, having filled his glass, the President rose and said: 'Ladies and gentlemen, this is the last time I shall drink your health as a public man. I do it with sincerity, and wishing you all possible happiness.' This put an end to all pleasantry, and forced the tears into many eyes."

Washington declined a third term of the Presidency, and published his dignified "Farewell Address" before the sixty-fifth anniversary of his birthday. Mrs. Washington accompanied him to his beloved retirement at Mount Vernon, with her grandchildren, Miss Eleanor Custis and George W. P. Custis. The son of La Fayette was his preceptor.

At that time deportment in the drawing-room was a reflex of temper in the Cabinet and the Senate; and styles of living and conversation were continually referred to as evidences of political tendencies. The statesmanship of Washington, Adams, Jay, Hamilton, Marshall, and their friends, was commented on by the social habits of their adherents, as well as that of Jefferson, Randolph, Giles, Paine, Madison, Monroe, and the other opposition leaders.

II.

JOHN ADAMS' ADMINISTRATION.

Mrs. Adams' Description of Her Philadelphia Residence—A Presidential Drawing-room—Mr. Adams at a Dinner at Mr. Bingham's—A Singular Incident—The Inauguration—Departure of General and Mrs. Washington—Character of Mrs. Adams—Presiding in the Executive Mansion—Gayeties of the City—Routs and Tea and Cards—Gambling customary at Parties—An honored Visitor in Mrs. Adams' Circle—Removal of the Capital to Washington—Descriptions of the "Wilderness City"—Mrs. Adams' Lively Picture—Inconveniences and Privations—Marcia Burns a noted Belle—Married to J. P. Van Ness—Samuel Dexter—Mrs. Adams in after Life.

IN the contest for the Presidency, Mr. Adams prevailed by a very small majority. Hence, Federalism was still ascendant in the national councils, though considerably depressed in those of some of the States. The tone given by Washington was maintained by his successor.

Mrs. John Adams, in a letter to her daughter Mrs. Smith, in November, 1790, describes her new residence in Philadelphia: "Bush Hill, as it is called, though there remains neither bush nor shrub upon it, and very few trees, except the pine grove behind it—is a very beautiful place. But the grand and the sublime I left at Richmond Hill:—the Schuylkill is no more like the Hudson than I to Hercules. By accident the vessel with our furniture had arrived the day before, and Briesler was taking in the first load into a house all green painted; the workmen there with their brushes in hand. This was cold comfort in a house, where I suppose no fire had been kindled for several years, except in a back kitchen.

"The next morning was pleasant, and I ventured to come and take possession; but what confusion! Boxes, barrels, chairs, tables, trunks, &c. The first object was to get fires; the next to get up beds; but the cold damp rooms, the new paint, &c., proved almost too much for me. On Sunday Thomas was laid up with the rheumatism; on Monday, I was obliged to give Louisa an emetic; on Tuesday Mrs. Briesler was taken with her old pain; and on Thursday Polly was seized with a violent pleuritic fever. And every day, the stormy ones excepted, from eleven till three the house is filled with ladies and gentlemen. Mrs. Bingham has been twice to see me. I think she is more amiable and beautiful than ever. Nancy Hamilton is the same unaffected affable girl we formerly knew. Mrs. Lear was in to see me yesterday, and assures me I am much better off than Mrs. Washington will be when she arrives; for their house is not likely to be completed this year. And when all is done, it will not be Broadway. If New York wanted any revenge for the removal, the citizens might be glutted if they would come here, where every article has become almost double in price and where it is not possible for Congress and the appendages to be half as well accommodated for a long time."

At the age of forty this daughter of a village clergyman and wife of a village lawyer had left her modest home at Braintree to mingle in the shows of a magnificent court, where her husband was ambassador, and where she maintained the social fame of her country. Her native abilities and habitual elevation of feeling and demeanor, supplied the want of that aristocratic cultivation illustrated in everything around her, and commanded a higher consideration for herself than the rank of the minister. She was four years in Paris and London, and had but recently returned, when the election of Mr. Adams as Vice-President summoned him to New York. Mrs. Adams was then in the maturity of her life and her mental powers. She joined her daughter, Mrs. Smith, in New York.

Again she wrote:

"On Friday evening last I went with Charles to the drawing-room. The room became full before I left it, and the circle very brilliant. How could it be otherwise, a constellation of beauties? Mrs. Bingham has certainly given laws to the ladies here, in fashion and elegance. Mrs. Powell, I join the general voice in pronouncing a very interesting woman. She is aunt to Mrs. Bingham."

"I have received many invitations to tea and cards in the European style, but have hitherto declined them on account of my health," &c.

In June, 1795, Mr. Adams wrote to his wife:

"Yesterday I dined at Mr. Bingham's with a large company. While at table a servant came to me, with a message from Mr. Law, who desired to speak with me in the ante-chamber. I went out to him, and found that he wanted to enquire of me concerning a young lady of amiable manners and elegant education, whom Mr. Law and Mr. Greenleaf had found in Maryland in great distress and a little disarranged, and brought with them to Philadelphia."

January 11, 1797:

"On Tuesday, when I waited as usual on Mrs. Washington, after attending the levee, she congratulated me very complaisantly and affectionately on my election to the Presidency, and went farther and said more than I expected. She said it gave them great pleasure to find that the votes had turned in my favor."

At the inauguration of President Adams, he wrote:

"Chief Justice Ellsworth administered the oath, and with great energy. Judges Cushing, Wilson, and Iredell were present. Many ladies. . . . I believe scarcely a dry eye but Washington's."

Chestnut Street, in the vicinity of Congress Hall was filled with an immense concourse on the day of Washington's final retirement and the inauguration of President Adams. It was the Fourth of March 1797. Mr. Adams, then sixty-one years of age, was dressed in a full suit of pearl-colored broadcloth, and wore his hair powdered. At eleven Jefferson took his oath as Vice-President before the Senate; at twelve Washington entered the crowded Chamber of Representatives, followed by Adams; both received with enthusiastic cheers. The new President being inaugurated, gave his address before the administration of the oath. "At the close of the ceremony" said President Duer, "as the venerable hero moved towards the door, there was a rush from the gallery that threatened the lives of those who were most eager to catch a last look. Some of us effected our escape by slipping down the pillars." As soon as Mr. Adams had returned to his residence, Washington made him a visit, cordially congratulated him, and expressed a wish that his administration might be happy, successful, and honorable. In the evening an entertainment was given by the principal citizens at the amphitheater. The leading public characters, including the foreign ministers, were present.

Mrs. Adams had written to her husband, Feb. 8th, 1797. On that day the votes for President were counted, and Mr. Adams, as Vice-President, was required to announce himself as President elect:

"You have this day to declare yourself head of a nation. 'And now, O Lord, my God, Thou hast made Thy servant ruler over the people. Give to him an understanding heart, that he may know how to go out and come in before this great people; that he may discern between good and bad. For who is able to judge this thy so great a people!' were the words of a royal sovereign; and not less applicable to him who is invested with the Chief Magistracy of a nation, though he wear not a crown, nor the robes of royalty."

"My feelings are not those of pride or ostentation upon the occasion. They are solemnized by a sense of the obligations, the important trusts and numerous duties connected with it."

The retirement of General Washington from the Presidency at the end of eight years, was the signal for the great struggle between the two political parties which had been rapidly maturing their organization during his administration. Mr. Adams' election was by a bare majority of the electoral college, and against the inclinations of one section even of that party which supported him. The open defection of that section at the next election, turned the scale against him, and elevated Mr. Jefferson.

Mr. Adams wrote, 9th March, 1797:

"The President and Mrs. Washington go off this morning for Mount Vernon. Yesterday afternoon he came to make me his farewell visit, and requested me, in his own name and Mrs. Washington's, to present 'their respects' to Mrs. Adams. I believe that I envied him more than he did me and with reason. The house is to be cleared and cleaned, and I am to go into it on Monday next if possible. I shall make a small establishment for myself, for the present, and wait your advice for ulterior arrangements."

Mrs. Adams appeared, as in other situations, the accomplished woman, the pure-hearted patriot, and the worthy partner of her husband's cares and honors. In her elevated position, her grace and elegance, with her charms of conversation, were rendered more attractive by her frank sincerity. Her close observation, discrimination of character, and clear judgment, gave her an influence that failed not to be acknowledged. Her buoyant cheerfulness and affectionate sympathy sustained the spirit of her husband, and it was her part in social life to calm agitations, heal the rankling wounds of pride, and pluck away the root of bitterness.

When Adams became President, Philadelphia was still the national capital; but in 1800, the seat of government was transferred to Washington, in the District of Columbia. The struggle of parties which had begun in the first President's term, became more violent in that of Mr. Adams; but the exemplary deportment of his wife went far to disarm even the demon of party spirit. She enjoyed universal esteem as well for the endowments of her mind as the correctness of her deportment; and the only form which personal malevolence or party malignity could assume to turn her virtues into weapons of annoyance, was that of occasional insinuations that she exercised over her husband an influence which extended even to measures of public concernment. Those who could not deny her tenderness and womanly grace, maintained that her chief distinction was a masculine understanding.

The social circles of the metropolis were nearly the same during the administration of Adams, as in the preceding one. The increasing virulence of party strife had some effect in disturbing the harmony of society.

Mrs. Adams wrote of the gayeties of Philadelphia: "I should spend a very dissipated winter if I were to accept one-half of the invitations I receive, particularly to the routs or tea and cards." There was a prevalent passion for gambling; and at one time it was not uncommon to hear that a lady or a gentleman had lost three or four hundred dollars at a sitting. Mrs. Adams pronounced the dancing "very good," but says of the etiquette: "It was not to be found." "Friendliness," she adds, "is kept up among the principal families, who appear to live in great harmony; and we meet in all places nearly the same company."

Josiah Quincy was one of the honored visitors of Mrs. Adams' circle. She wrote of him, on his arrival: "This young man is a rare instance of hereditary eloquence and ingenuity in the fourth generation. He comes into life with every advantage of family, fortune and education."

The site of Washington had been twelve years before designated as the future and permanent capital of the country; yet it remained in a very primitive state. Wolcott wrote to his wife: "There is one good tavern, about forty rods from the capitol, and several other houses are built or erecting; but I do not see how the members of Congress can possibly secure lodgings, unless they will consent to live like scholars in a college, or monks in a monastery, crowded ten or twenty in one house, and utterly secluded from society. There are few houses in any one place, and most of them small, miserable huts, which present an awful contrast to the public buildings. The people are poor, and as far as I can judge, they live like fishes, by eating each other. You may look in almost any direction, over an extent of ground nearly as large as the city of New York, without seeing a fence or any object except brick-kilns and temporary huts for laborers. There appears to be a confident expectation that this place will soon exceed any city in the world."

Gouverneur Morris wrote to a lady, a few months later:—"We want nothing here but houses, cellars, kitchens, well-informed men, amiable women and other little trifles of the kind to make our city perfect; for we can walk here as if in the fields and woods, and, considering the hard frost, the air of the city is very pure. I enjoy more of it than any one else; for my room is filled with smoke whenever the door is shut."

Mrs. Adams gave a still livelier picture, writing to her daughter. "In the city there are buildings enough, if they were compact and finished, to accommodate Congress and those attached to it; but as they are and scattered as they are, I see no great comfort for them. The river, which runs up to Alexandria, is in full view from my window, and I see the vessels as they pass and repass. The house is on a grand and superb scale, requiring about thirty servants to attend and keep the apartments in proper order and perform the ordinary business of the house and stables; an establishment very well proportioned to the President's salary. The lighting the apartments from the kitchen to parlors and chambers is a tax indeed, and the fires we are obliged to keep to secure us from daily agues is another very cheering comfort. Bells are wholly wanting; not one being hung through the whole house, and promises are all you can obtain. Yesterday I returned fifteen visits."

A letter dated Washington, November, 1800, says:

"Woods are all you see from Baltimore, until you reach *the* city, which is so only in name. No wood-cutters or carters to be had at any rate. We are now indebted to a Pennsylvania wagon to bring us, through the first clerk in the Treasury office, one cord and a half of wood, which is all we have for this house, where twelve fires are constantly required; and we are told the roads will soon be so bad it cannot be drawn. Briesler procured two hundred bushels of coal, or

MRS. ALEX. W. RANDALL.

Eng'd by H. B. Hall, N. Y.
from a Painting by S. W. Waters

Page 5[illegible]

we must have suffered. This is the situation of almost every person. The public officers have sent to Philadelphia for wood-cutters and wagons.". . . "The vessel which has my clothes and other matters has not arrived. The ladies are impatient for a drawing-room: I have no looking glasses but dwarfs for this house; nor a twentieth part lamps enough to light it; my tea china is more than half missing.". . . "You can scarcely believe that here, in this wilderness city, I should find my time so occupied as it is. My visitors,—some of them—come three or four miles. The return of one of them is the work of one day: most of the ladies reside in Georgetown, or in scattered parts of the city at two and three miles' distance. Mrs. Otis, my nearest neighbor, is at lodgings almost half a mile from me; Mrs. Senator Otis two miles." . . . "We have not the least fence, yard or other convenience without, and the great unfinished audience-room I make a drying-room of, to hang the clothes in. . . . Six chambers are made comfortable; two are occupied by the President and Mr. Shaw; two lower rooms,—one for a common parlor, and one for a levee-room. Up stairs there is the oval room, which is designed for the drawing-room, and has the crimson furniture in it."

Mrs. Adams made no claim to learning; though her reading had been extensive in the lighter departments of literature, and she was well acquainted with the poets in her own language. The soul shining through her words gave them their great attraction; "the spirit, ever equal to the occasion, whether a great or a small one; a spirit inquisitive and earnest in the little details of life, as when she was in France and England; playful, when she describes daily duties; but rising to the call when the roar of cannon is in her ears, or when she reproves her husband for not knowing her better than to think her a coward and to fear telling her bad news; or when she warns her son that she 'would rather he had found his grave in the ocean, or that any untimely death should crop him in his infant years, than see him an immoral, profligate, or graceless child.'"

One of the most admired belles in Washington at the commencement of the century was Miss Marcia Burns, the daughter of David Burns, whose estate, inherited from Scottish ancestors, had covered the site of the capital. Marcia lived with her widowed mother; and the extraordinary attractions of her person, manners and character drew a throng of admirers around the lovely heiress. She married John P. Van Ness, in 1802. She was prominent in Washington society fifteen years, and her house was the resort of a brilliant and distinguished circle. After the untimely death of her daughter, Mrs. Arthur Middleton, Mrs. Van Ness retired from the world, devoting her time to works of charity.*

Mr. Samuel Dexter was a member of the cabinet under the Presidency of John Adams. Mrs. Adams condoling with his wife after his death, calls him "a great man, fallen in the zenith of his glory; and in the estimation of his ancient friend, the ablest statesman of his age which his native State could boast. Such an assemblage of powerful talents rarely meet in one individual united to such an upright and independent mind, which soared above all low concerns, and was elevated beyond all selfish considerations and party views."

Mrs. Adams wrote Mr. Jefferson a kind letter of condolence from Quincy, in May, 1804. It was to her care his young daughter had been committed when she went abroad, and Mrs. Adams "recalled the tender scene of separation from me, when, with

---

*For memoirs of this lady and others of her family, see "The Queens of American Society."

the strongest sensibility, she clung around my neck and wet my bosom with her tears, saying, 'Oh, now I have learned to love you, why will they take me from you?'" This letter led to an overture for a renewal of former friendship, and to some mutual explanations. But Mrs. Adams was not easily mollified, and the correspondence was closed with her feelings apparently unappeased by the concessions of one who had been a political adversary. Of Mrs. Adams it was said: "Her lofty lineaments carried a trace of the Puritan severity. They were those of the helmed Minerva, and not of the cæstus-girdled Venus. Her correspondence uniformly exhibits a didactic personage, a little inclined to assume a sermonizing attitude, as befitted the well-trained and self-reliant daughter of a New England country clergyman, and a little inclined, after the custom of her people, to return thanks that she had no lot or part in anything that was not of Massachusetts. Perhaps the masculineness of her understanding extended somewhat to the firmness of her temper. But, towering above, and obscuring these minor angularities, she possessed a strength of intellectual and moral character, which commands our unqualified admiration. When her New England frigidity gave way and kindled into enthusiasm, it was not like "light straw on fire," but "red-hot steel." "Had Mr. Adams been the victor and Mr. Jefferson the vanquished, half the advances made by the latter would have sufficed. The overthrow of a President had not then been made a common occurrence; circumstances rendered the downfall of Mr. Adams personally irritating and humiliating, and Mrs. Adams felt morbidly for her husband."

Mrs. Adams lost none of the imposing features of her character in the decline of life. A visitor at Quincy described Mr. Adams as of sound mind and heart, though trembling as with palsy. He joked and laughed heartily, and talked freely about everything and everybody; seeming a vast encyclopedia of written and unwritten knowledge, which gushed out on every topic, and was mingled with lively anecdotes and sallies of humor. His carelessness of language suggested anything but pedantry: in short, the brave old man was as delightful as he was commanding in conversation. While the guest was enjoying the interview, an aged and stately woman came in, and he was introduced to Mrs. Adams. Her cap of delicate lace surrounded features still exhibiting intellect and energy though possessing no beauty. She was dressed in pure white, and there was that immaculate neatness in her appearance which gives to age almost the sweetness of youth. With less warmth of manner and sociability than Mr. Adams, she was gracious, and her occasional remarks betrayed intellectual vigor and strong sense. Her serenity and benign cheerfulness continued to the last; the shadows of a life full of changes never deepened into gloom; and she was still a messenger of blessing to all within her influence. In 1813, she lost her only daughter, Mrs. William S. Smith. Mrs. Adams died, seventy-four years of age, in October, 1818.

III.

JEFFERSON'S ADMINISTRATION.

The two great Parties—The Widow Skelton—The Musical Courtship—The Bridal Festivities—The Snow-storm—Jefferson's Equipage—Fashions in Dress—The Inauguration—Absence of Court Ceremony—Vain Protest of Ladies against the abolition of Levees—Social Etiquette—Complaint of the British Minister of uncivil Treatment—Tom Moore's Indignation and Abuse of Americans—Burr's Treason—The President's Courtesy—The old Man at the Ferry—The Kentuckian won over—Josiah Quincy's Experiences—Why the Barbers were Federalists—Personal Appearance of Jefferson and Madison—Hospitality at Monticello—"Country Gentleman" Style of Living—Domestic Life of the Ex-President—Illustrative Anecdotes—Death of Jefferson—Interesting Case of Virginia Murray—Character of John Randolph—His Declamation and piquant Wit—The Irishman who sought his Acquaintance—Amusing Anecdotes.

As events rolled on, one circumstance and another conspired to mark more distinctly the lines between the parties of the day, and at the period of the election of the third President of the United States, they were very clearly defined throughout the Union, under the names of Federalists and Democrats. In the first class were included Washington, Hamilton, Jay, Pickering, Ames, Marshall, and others like them; the last enrolled in its list Jefferson, Burr, George Clinton, Madison, and many more throughout the States.

"Jefferson's influence" said an English writer, "was greater than that of any other President except Washington; and the reason is, that his convictions went along with the national mind." Jefferson married, January 1, 1772, Mrs. Martha Skelton. She was the widow of Bathurst Skelton and the daughter of John Wayles of "The Forest" in Charles City County. Wayles was an Englishman and had been three times married; his last wife was Mrs. Martha Epes, widow of Llewellin Epes, of Bermuda Hundred. Martha Wayles was born in 1749, and married Skelton in 1766. Her husband lived but two years. The widow, scarcely advanced beyond her girlhood, was distinguished for beauty, accomplishments, and solid merit. She was slight, but exquisitely formed, a little above the medium hight. Her complexion was brilliant; her large expressive eyes were a soft, rich hazel; her luxuriant hair was golden auburn. She walked, rode, danced, with inimitable grace and spirit; she sang, and played the spinet and harpsichord, (the musical instruments of the ladies of that day in Virginia) with admirable skill. She was also well read and intelligent; she conversed agreeably, had excellent sense and a lively play of fancy, and possessed a disposition frank, ardent, and impulsive. She had proved herself a true daughter of the Old Dominion in housewifery, and was a clever business woman. With these traits, added to rank and wealth, it is not wonderful that she was a favorite in society, and that her hand was sought by wooers far and near.

Tradition has preserved an anecdote, that on one occasion two of Mrs. Skelton's admirers chanced to meet at the door of her house, and were shown into a room where they heard her harpsichord and voice, accompanied by Mr. Jefferson's violin and voice, in a touching song. They listened for a stanza or two, and then, convinced of the hopelessness of their errand, took their hats and retired. Another and less probable version of the story is, that the *three* wooers met on the door-stone, and agreed to "take turns," and that the interview should be decisive; that Jefferson led off, and that during his trial, the others heard the music that settled the point!

The bridal festivities at the "Forest" were worthy of Virginian hospitality. Rev. Mr. Davis, the officiating clergyman, and Rev. Mr. Coutts, shared the fees, and douceurs to fiddlers and servants occupy a page of the pocket account-book. The bride and bridegroom, when they set out for Monticello, had a light snow-storm; and, as they advanced up the country, had to leave the carriage, which stuck in the snow, and proceed on horseback. They stopped a short time at Blenheim, eight miles from Monticello, the seat of Col. Carter, where an overseer lived. At sunset they pursued their way through a mountain track, the snow from eighteen inches to two feet deep. They arrived at Monticello late at night, the fires all out and the servants retired to their own houses. It was a dreary welcome for the bride.

The only part of the house then habitable was a small pavilion. Part of a bottle of wine, found on a shelf behind some books, served the newly married couple both for fire and supper. But their sunny tempers found all a source of diversion, and the dreariness was banished by song and merriment. The next day the snow was three feet deep. At this time Jefferson drove only a phæton and two horses; though the grandees drove six, and the middlemen four. Jefferson always had magnificent horses. When his saddle horse was led out, if there was a spot on him that did not shine like a mirror, he rubbed it with a white handkerchief; and if this was soiled, the groom was reprimanded. Mrs. Jefferson died in September, 1782.

The fashions of the commencement of the century in female dress, were significant. In June, for a head-dress, a hat of white muslin was turned up in front and ornamented with white ostrich feathers; a bow of white ribbon fixed to the top of the crown, hung down behind. Also a cap of pink crape and white lace; a bunch of flowers in front, and one ostrich feather. A hat of chip and crape was made in the melon form, and ornamented with a rose and flower in front. A cap of lace was thrown carelessly over the head, and confined with a lace ruff which passed under the chin. The favorite colors were lilac, pea-green, pink and buff. Turbans, with white ostrich feathers, were generally worn in dress. Pearls were preferred in necklaces.

After Jefferson's election, he was anxious that the ceremonies of his inauguration in the new Capitol at Washington, March 4, 1801, should be as few and simple as possible. But the feelings of his friends, who had flocked to the city—then almost a wilderness, and difficult of approach—would not permit him to go unattended to the Senate chamber to take the oath of office. An English eye-witness said: "His dress was of plain cloth, and he rode on horseback to the Capitol without a single guard, or even servant, in his train; dismounted without assistance, and hitched the bridle of his horse to the palisades."

On his entering the Senate chamber, Burr, who had already taken the oath of office, gave up his chair, and took his seat on the right. On the left sat Chief-Justice Marshall, who administered the oath; but two imposing figures were absent—the late President of the Senate and the late Speaker of the House of Representatives. Mr. Adams had abruptly left the city early in the morning; and Sedgwick's absence was unexplained.

After Mr. Jefferson had delivered his inaugural address, listened to by the usual crowd of officials, friends and spectators, he was sworn into office by the Chief Justice. On the 6th March he wrote to John Dickinson: "The storm through which we have passed has been tremendous indeed. The tough sides of our Argosie have been thoroughly tried. Her strength has stood the waves into which she was steered with a view to sink her. We shall put her on her republican tack, and she will now show, by the beauty of her motion, the skill of her builders."

The day before, the President had nominated James Madison, Secretary of State; Henry Dearborn of Massachusetts, Secretary of War; and Levi Lincoln of Massachusetts, Attorney General. In May, Albert Gallatin of Pennsylvania, was appointed Secretary of the Treasury; Samuel and Robert Smith of Maryland, successively occupied the post of Secretary of the Navy; Gideon Granger of Connecticut, being appointed Postmaster General.

Albert Gallatin was a man of profound logical and clear understanding; his forte lay in political economy, and particularly in the figures, statistics, and philosophy of finance. He did not consider the Treasury Department a huge turtle to constantly lay eggs in the sand to feed those carnivorous political birds which might otherwise flesh their hungry beaks in the carcass of the administration. Nor did he consider it like the turtle of the mythology of certain Indian tribes, which carries the world on its back. His integrity was above suspicion; and in every respect he was singularly adapted to execute the precise line of policy the new President desired to carry into the Treasury Department.

Jefferson was anxious that the American court should be like its government, characterized by simplicity and dignity. A foreign functionary who had a high idea of his own importance and was a great stickler for etiquette, which Mr. Jefferson detested, went one morning to pay him a visit of ceremony; he found the philosopher deliberately drawing on his boot, and prepared with a shoe-brush to give it a polishing touch with his own hands.

The foreign ambassador was shocked at the sight of so degrading an occupation in the ruler of America. The President apologized for his negligence in not being prepared for the honor of his visit; stating that he was not aware of his intention to call on him, and that, being a plain man, he did not like to put his servants to unnecessary trouble. The ambassador retired entirely satisfied in his own mind that no government could long exist, the head of which was his own shoe-black and under which so little attention was paid to etiquette.

Jefferson wrote to his daughter—May 28th, 1801—to urge expedition in her preparations for removal to Washington. He says: "Mr. and Mrs. Madison stayed with me about three weeks till they could get ready a house to receive them. This has given me an opportunity of making some acquaintance with the ladies here. We shall certainly have a very agreeable and worthy society. It would make them as well as myself very happy could I always have yourself or your sister here." He had already declared, among the established points and maxims of his administration, that "Levees are done away." His two public days for the reception of company were the first of January and the fourth of July; when his doors were thrown open to all who chose to enter them. At other times all who wished were permitted to call upon him.

Some of the fashionables—chiefly ladies—had come to the conclusion that the abolition of levees was inexpedient. Accordingly, they mustered in force, at the usual time, at the presidential mansion. The President soon returned from his ride on horseback, and learning what an extraordinary number of ladies had called, and at once comprehending their motive, he went immediately, hat in hand, spurs on, and soiled with dust, into their midst. He expressed himself overjoyed at such a happy coincidence; and never had he been seen so cordial and attentive; allowing no one to go without urging her to stay longer. The fair visitors finally departed, laughing heartily at the result of their experiment. It was never repeated.

It was one of the regulations of the social etiquette agreed on by the President and his Cabinet, that residents should pay the first visit to strangers, and first comers to later comers, except in the case of foreign ministers, who were to pay the first visit to the ministers of the nation. All who were brought together in society were esteemed on a perfect equality. The families of foreign ministers were to receive the first visit from those of the national ministers, and from other residents. No title being admitted, those of foreigners gave no precedence, nor did any difference of grade among the diplomatic members. To maintain this principle of equality, and prevent the growth of precedence out of courtesy, the members of the executive were to practise and recommend an adherence to the ancient usage of the country—of gentlemen in mass giving precedence to the ladies in mass in passing from one apartment into another.

Washington at this time was considered unhealthy, even for acclimated Virginians, for more than two months of the autumn. During August and September, people had to take refuge in climates rendered safer by their habits and confidence.

The birthday of Mr. Jefferson was never publicly known till after his death. He refused every proposal to have it celebrated as an anniversary, not wishing "to transfer the honors and veneration for the great birthday of our Republic to any individual."

It was touching to see how constantly, in the midst

of public business, Mr. Jefferson's heart turned to his absent daughters. His letters to them prove this. He made two visits every year to Monticello: a short one in early spring, and a longer one in the latter part of summer; always stopping at Edgehill, where Mrs. Eppes, his youngest daughter, lived. She was in delicate health for some years and died in April, 1804. She had been, shortly before, carried to Monticello in a litter borne by men. Her father, left alone for some hours after her death, was found with the Bible in his hands. He who had been so often and so harshly accused of unbelief, in his hour of intense affliction sought and found consolation in the sacred volume.

The two daughters had visited the President in Washington in the winter of 1802–3. The younger never went there again; but Mrs. Randolph, with her children, passed some time there in the winter of 1805–6. Mrs. Eppes was singularly beautiful; and she was high-principled, just and generous. Her temper was mild, but saddened by ill health in her later years. Her sister possessed inexhaustible sweetness, kindness, patience and self-devotion, being superior in native powers of intellect. Jefferson was loved by both daughters with the utmost devotion, and they considered his affection as the great good of their lives. Mrs. T. Eston Randolph, the sister of the one who married Jefferson's daughter, was an exemplary and admirable woman.

Mr. Jefferson felt his child's death with terrible keenness. He wrote to his friend Gov. Page: "Others may lose of their abundance; but I of my want, have lost even the half of all I had. My evening prospects now hang on the slender thread of a single life."

The British minister, Mr. Merry, complained to Mr. Josiah Quincy of uncivil treatment received from President Jefferson. On presenting his credentials, he asked Mr. Madison, the Secretary of State, to introduce him officially, and was accompanied by him on the day and hour appointed, to the mansion house. The ambassador wore his full official costume, as the etiquette of his place required. They found the hall of audience empty, and Mr. Madison led the way to the President's study, through an entry, in which they met Mr. Jefferson, and in this narrow space the presentation was made. The President was "not merely in an undress, but actually standing in slippers down at the heels, and both pantaloons, coat and under-clothes indicative of an indifference to appearance." Mr. Merry regarded the whole scene as prepared and intended to be disrespectful to him and the sovereign he represented. This occurrence was talked of by the opponents of the President to his disparagement, as if he sought unduly the gratification of the democracy.

The Irish poet, Tom Moore, wrote to his mother from Baltimore in June, 1804: "I stopped at Washington with Mr. and Mrs. Merry for nearly a week. They have been treated with the most pointed incivility by the present democratic President, Mr. Jefferson; and it is only the precarious situation of Great Britain which could possibly induce it to overlook such indecent, though at the same time petty hostility. I was presented by Mr. Merry to both the Secretary of State and the President."

This "hostility" was thus manifested: Mr. and Mrs. Merry were invited to dine at the President's, and when dinner was announced, Mr. Jefferson chanced to be standing by and talking with Mrs. Madison, at some distance from Mrs. Merry. He escorted Mrs. Madison to the table, and the angry ambassador deemed it the next thing to an insult, making such a stir about it that Mr. Madison wrote to Mr. Monroe, who had succeeded Mr. King as minister to England, apprising him of the facts, to enable him to answer an expected call of the British government for official explanations! Monroe got his first information from a friendly British undersecretary; and he was delighted: for not long before, the wife of an English undersecretary had been given precedence over his own wife, and under similar circumstances. But no call was made for explanations, and Mrs. Merry tossed her head without shaking the peace of two nations. Merry, however, never forgot the "incivility," though he and his friends knew that, by an express regulation at the executive palace, all etiquette in respect to official precedence was formally abolished. Mr. Monroe often told the story, and a better one of amusing circumstances that took place at an official dinner, where he was ranked below the ministers of sundry German States "about half as big, by Jove, Sir! as our county of Albemarle." From the time of that offense against her dignity, Mrs. Merry avoided the Presidential mansion; and her husband only went there officially. The President felt a good-natured wish to put an end to this frivolous matter; and he inquired of the Swedish ambassador if Mr. and Mrs. Merry would accept an invitation to a family dinner. The invitation was sent written in the President's own hand. The minister replied by addressing the Secretary of State to know whether he was invited in his private or his official capacity; if in the one, he must obtain the permission of his sovereign; if in the other, he must receive an assurance in advance that he would be treated as became his position.

Tom Moore, then twenty-four years old, had as yet published nothing which had crossed the Atlantic but "gentle Little's moral song," and Mr. Jefferson had no idea that he stood in the presence of the young Catullus of his day. Standing in his height of six feet two and a half inches, the President looked down on the perfumed little Adonis, spoke a word to him and gave him no further attention. Moore, after this unflattering reception, fell to lampooning the President and almost everything American. Some of his scurrilous attacks fell into the hands of Mr. Burwell, formerly the President's private secretary, who carried them to Mrs. Randolph. The gentle Martha was roused by such insults from a man who had been introduced into society and patronized by the British minister. They were indignant, and agreed that it was proper to place the matter before the President. This was done at Monticello, while Jefferson was reading in his library. He glanced through the obnoxious passages pointed out, looked at his daughter and his friend and burst into a clear, hearty laugh, in which they joined after a moment of reflection.

When Moore's Irish melodies appeared years afterwards, and the book was put into Jefferson's hands, "Why this," he said, "is the little man who satirized me so!" He read on: he had always sympathized with the Irish patriots: and presently exclaimed: "Why, he *is* a poet, after all!" Henceforth the bard of Erin shared with Burns the hours of the retired statesman.

The President was sixty-two when his second inauguration took place, on the 4th of March, 1805. That autumn was made a memorable epoch in American history by the treasonable projects of Aaron Burr. One of Burr's counsel was Henry Clay, chosen United States Senator in November, to fill the vacancy occasioned by the resignation of Adair. His talents, address and popularity were even then acknowledged, and the star of his professional and political greatness had begun to beam splendidly on the western horizon. Another of Burr's friends was Luther Martin of Maryland, described as an able, but coarse man, with violent and unrestrained passions.

One day the President and his eldest grandson were driving in a carriage. A stranger slave in the road took off his hat and bowed to them; Jefferson according to his invariable custom, touched his hat and bowed. The grandson made no return to the salutation; and Jefferson turning to him said, "Thomas, do you permit a slave to be more of a gentleman than yourself?"

About 1807, while on a visit at his home, the President accompanied two of his nephews on horseback to Charlottesville. He invited two or three gentlemen of that place to dine at Monticello, and returned homeward, Mr. Jefferson and the young men a little in advance. A shower had fallen, and when they came to Moore's Creek, the water was up to the saddle-girths. A Western countryman was sitting on the bank with a saddle in his hands. He waited till all the party had entered the stream but Mr. Jefferson, and then asked him for a ride across. The President reined up to a stone, bade him mount, and carried him to the opposite bank. The party in the rear, in a few moments overtaking the pedestrian going on at a sturdy pace, asked him why he let the young men pass and asked the elder gentleman to carry him over. "Wall," replied the Kentucky man, "if you want to know, I'll tell you. I reckon a man carries yes or no in his face. The young chaps' faces said no; the old 'un's said yes."

"It isn't every man that would have asked the President of the United States for a ride behind him," observed the other. "You don't say that was Tom Jefferson, do you!" cried the Kentuckian, adding, "He's a —— fine old fellow any way." Then he burst into a loud laugh, and said: "What do you suppose my wife Polly will say when I get back to Boone County, and tell her I've rid behind Jefferson? She'll say I voted for the right man!"

One day the President, riding along the bank of the Rivanne, saw a ragged old man waiting at a ford opposite. He rode across, took him up behind and brought him over. On another occasion, riding towards Washington, he overtook a working man of respectable appearance, on foot. To draw up and salute him was an habitual civility. A conversation on political topics ensued, and the man strongly censured certain acts of the administration. Finally he alluded to some of the gross personal stories of Callender against the President. "Do you know Mr. Jefferson personally?" asked the equestrian. "No, nor don't want to," replied the other. "But is it fair play to repeat such stories, and then not dare to meet the subject of them face to face?"

The man was a Kentuckian—a country merchant, and at the word "dare" he promptly responded; "I will never shrink from meeting Mr. Jefferson if he comes in my way."

"Will you go to his house to-morrow, and be introduced to him, if I will meet you there!" "I will," was the reply: and the President rode on. Next day the stranger sent in his card at the palace. When he saw the President, he said "I have called, Mr. Jefferson, to apologize for having said to a stranger——" Here the President laughingly interrupted him with—"hard things of an imaginary personage, who is no relation of mine!" All attempts at explanation were laughingly parried, and animated conversation on another subject was introduced. When the servant announced dinner, the President insisted on his staying. Afterwards this Kentuckian used to caution his young people not to be too free in talking with strangers, while he and his family were fiery Jeffersonians.

Josiah Quincy wrote in Washington: "My wife was the ornament and attraction of my establishment. She was admired for her manners and mind, was most kindly received by Mrs. Madison at the palace, and enjoyed the society and friendship of a select circle—among whom were the families of Peter, Lee, Teacle, Smith, Tayloe, Cranch, &c." Mr. Quincy described the city as exceedingly dull and "distracted with every species of personality and violence." A senator told Mr. Goodrich that at this time all the barbers in Washington were federalists, because the leaders of that party in Congress wore powder and long queues, which were dressed, of course, every day. The democrats wore short hair, or small queues, tied up carelessly with a ribbon. One day a barber who was shaving the senator, suddenly burst out against the nomination of Madison by the democratic party. "What Presidents we might have, sir! Look at Daggett, of Connecticut, and Stockton, of New Jersey, with queues as big as your wrist, and powdered every day, like real gentlemen as they are! But this little Jim Madison, with a queue no bigger than a pipe-stem! Sir, it is enough to make a man foreswear his country!"

The Presidential election of 1808 was conducted with extreme heat, particularly in the Eastern States. Jefferson and Madison were friends. The latter was in the full meridian of manhood at fifty-eight; Jefferson at sixty-six had not passed the mellow autumn of old age. His visitors at Monticello were numerous and often intrusive. Strangers would plant themselves in the passage between his study and dining-room, waiting for him to pass to his dinner. A woman once broke a window-pane of the house with her parasol, to get a better view of him. When sitting in the shade of his porticoes, to enjoy the cool evening air, parties of men and women would approach within a dozen yards. In 1810, the house servants, including children, were thirty-seven. The general mode of traveling at that time in Virginia was on horseback, or by carriages drawn by at least two horses; and servants generally accompanied travelers. Mrs. Randolph, who presided over the domestic establishment at Monticello, once said she had been called on to provide beds over night for fifty guests.

Martha Jefferson used to relate how once, when traveling with her father, they came to a ferry, and found the two boatmen engaged in a violent quarrel. They took the travelers on board, and rowed silently to the middle of the stream; when the contention broke out afresh. The boat drifted swiftly towards some dangerous rapids. Mr. Jefferson spoke to them calmly; then sternly; then he suddenly started up with "a face like a lion," and, with a hand on each of the boatmen, bade them in tones of thunder, row for their lives, or he would pitch them into the stream. They did pull for their lives, till they reached the shore.

It will be remembered that Jefferson expired on the 4th of July, 1826, the first semi-centennial anniversary. Hundreds of miles away, John Adams' last sands too were running out.

The interesting case of Virginia Murray has never been mentioned in history. Her father, Lord Dunmore, was colonial governor of Virginia. Her letter to President Jefferson, tells the story:

"SIR,—I am at a loss how to begin a letter in the which I am desirous of stating claims that may long have been forgotten, but which

I think no time can really annihilate, until fulfilment has followed the promise. I imagine that you must have heard that during my father's, the late Lord Dunmore's, residence in America, I was born, and that the Assembly, then sitting at Williamsburg, requested I might be their god-daughter, and christened by the name of Virginia; which request being complied with, they purposed providing for me in a manner suitable to the honor they conferred upon me, and to the responsibility they had taken on themselves. I was accordingly christened as the god-daughter of that Assembly, and named after the State. Events have since occurred which in some measure may have altered the intentions then expressed in my favor. These were (so I have understood) that a sum of money should be settled upon me, which, by accumulating during my minority, would make up the sum of one hundred thousand pounds when I became of age. It is true many changes may have taken place in America, but *that fact* still remains the same. I am still the god-daughter of the Virginians. By being that, may I not flatter myself I have some claims upon their benevolence, if not upon their justice? May I not ask the gentlemen of that State, especially you, Sir, their Governor, to fulfil in some respects the engagements entered into by their predecessors? Your fathers promised mine that I should become their charge. I am totally unprovided for; for my father died without making a will. My brothers are married, having families of their own; and not being bound to do anything for me, they regard with indifference my unprotected and neglected situation. Perhaps I ought not to mention this circumstance as a proper inducement for you to act upon; nor would I, were it not my excuse for wishing to remind you of the claims I now advance. I hope you will feel my right to your favor and protection to be founded on the promises made by your own fathers, and in the situation in which I stand with regard to the State of Virginia. You will ask, Sir, why my appeal to your generosity and justice has been so tardy? While my father lived, I lived under his protection and guidance. He had incurred the displeasure of the Virginians, and he feared an application for me then would have seemed like one from him. At his decease I become a free agent. I had taken no part which could displease my god-fathers; and myself remained what the Assembly had made me—their god-daughter, consequently their charge. I wish particularly to enforce my dependence upon your bounty; for I feel hopes revive which owe their birth to your honor and generosity, and to that of the State whose representative I now address. Now that my father is no more, I am certain they and you will remember what merited your esteem in his character and conduct, and forget that which estranged your hearts from so honorable a man. But should you not, you are too just to visit what you may deem the sins of the father upon his luckless daughter. I am, Sir, your obt., etc.,

"VIRGINIA MURRAY,

"*Trafalgar Place, Opposite Cumberland Gate, Oxford Road, London.*"

This letter was forwarded to Mr. Monroe, then Governor of Virginia. Mr. Monroe submitted the touching appeal to the Legislature of the State; but it does not appear that any action resulted, or that the pledge of the Colonial Assembly was regarded as binding.

One of the most remarkable characters in American history and society was John Randolph of Roanoke. It is probable that his peculiarities gave a degree of extraneous and scenic effect to his speeches. "His pride, his isolation, his rich appointments, his claims to a baronial family consequence, his aristocratic assumption of superiority, his capricious and dangerous temper, all set him apart, and made him a popular marvel. There was something in his general aspect which reminded one of his lineage from the royal Powhattan. His eye was piercingly brilliant. His invective was tremendous; it scorched and consumed its victim like fiery rain. It was when passion mounted to its zenith that his intellect threw out its finest coruscations like meteoric showers. His gaunt frame, his cadaverous countenance, a voice shrill yet strangely sweet at times, an eye that seemed gifted with power to read the secrets of the heart—were accesories to his forcible oratory. He pointed his sarcasm by extending his long, thin elfish forefinger towards the offender, keeping it quivering till the climax of his scorn was reached, when it rested immovably, as if at that moment the death shot flashed from it to the victim's heart."

Randolph was once opposing a motion for an appropriation for the public buildings. He rose, and in his shrill, clear voice, moved to refer the subject to the committee on *unfinished* business. A workman in the gallery, irritated at the opposition to what was to constitute his support, cried out in a voice something like Mr. Randolph's: "And I move, Mr. Speaker, that the gentleman be referred to the *same* committee." This retort upon the ill-formed orator set the whole house in a roar. The sergeant-at-arms was despatched to arrest the offender; but he had disappeared.

An Irishman just arrived in the country was anxious to become acquainted with the eccentric orator of Roanoke. He undertook to introduce himself, and approached him with—"Have I the honor of addressing the distinguished American orator, Mr. Randolph?" "That is an honor I allow only to those with whom I am acquainted," replied Randolph, in his sarcastic tone. After some conversation, he asked the Irishman how long he had been in the country. He replied: "I have been but a short time in the country; have had the honor to be introduced to General W., Colonel B., Major C. and numerous other officers. Your revolutionary war, Mr. Randolph, must have been very unfortunate; indeed, I may say, disastrous, for it seems to have cut off *all the privates,* and left nothing but officers behind." Randolph was so much pleased with his remarks that he invited him to call and see him at his lodgings.

Randolph's first and only love was unfortunate. The lady was Miss Ward, of Wintapeke. For thirty years the statesman worshiped the idol of his youth, and no other image was ever enshrined in his heart. He had a great abhorrence of debt. On one occasion, in Congress, he suddenly interrupted himself in a speech on some other subject, and exclaimed: "Mr. Speaker, I have discovered the philosopher's stone! It is this, Sir: Pay as you go! Pay as you go!" In a letter he says: "The muck-worm whose mind knows no other work than money-keeping or money-getting, is an object of pity and contempt. I hold it essential to purity, dignity and pride of character that every man's expenses should bear a due relation to his means and prospects in life." One day, while he was speaking, the Speaker began privately to write a letter. Randolph perceived it, and stopped short in the middle of a sentence. The Speaker, presently aroused by the stillness, inquired whether the honorable gentleman from Virginia had finished his speech. "Mr. Speaker," returned Randolph, in his high falsetto voice, and pointing his long forefinger, "I was waiting until you had finished that letter."

His last speech in the Senate, and the master effort of his life, was in reply to Rufus King on the Missouri question. He referred to the new member as "the member from Maryland:" and then pausing, as if not certain, added, "I believe he is from Maryland." This implied doubt amused Mr. Pinkney, who went over to Mr. Randolph's seat, introduced himself, and assured him that he *was* "from Maryland." They became close friends afterwards; and Randolph in announcing his death, called him "the boast of Maryland, and the pride of the United States."

His device to put down Barnabas Bidwell, a Massachusetts lawyer and an active democratic politician, was curious. Randolph at Bidwell's maiden speech, was dressed in his usual morning costume,—his skeleton legs cased in tight-fitting leather breeches and top boots, with a blue riding coat, the thick buckskin gloves from which he was never parted, and a heavily loaded riding whip in his hand. After listening attentively for about a quarter of an hour, he rose deliberately, settled his hat on his head, and walked slowly out of the House, striking the handle of his whip emphatically upon the palm of his left hand, and regarding poor Bidwell as he passed him with a look of insolent contempt.

On one occasion, John Randolph resorted to a curious and novel stratagem to gain the attention of the House. After midnight, when most of the members had composed themselves to sleep as they best might, Randolph began to utter a disconnected farrago of long words, apropos to nothing in the universe. Gradually the whole House awoke, and looked with wondering eyes upon the orator, supposing him mad. His purpose thus answered, he turned suddenly on an honest Dutch member from New York, who never ventured anything more than a zealous yea or nay; pointed his slow, unmoving finger at him, and cried in his shrill, deliberate tones: "And now, Mr. Speaker, the honorable gentleman from New York denies the truth of what I have been saying!" "Good gracious!" sputtered forth the mystified Dutchman; "Mr. Speaker, I have done nothing of the kind!" The House, now thoroughly aroused, shook with inextinguishable laughter.

Love of opposition and change was a disease of his organization. He followed Jefferson devotedly for years, and then broke off on a trifling provocation. He loved Mr. Madison, and soon fiercely hated and denounced him. He was enthusiastic in his admiration of Monroe, and afterwards poured out contemptuous epithets upon him. He was one of the earliest supporters of Gen. Jackson, and one of the first to abandon him. He insulted Mr. Clay in the Senate, fought with him; and then rushed in a dying state across the country as fast as his horses could be driven, to be reconciled to him. He clung to Macon, Tazewell, and a little knot of friends through all; but had one of them been elected President, Randolph would probably have denounced him within six months of his inauguration. Jefferson was his first and longest official love.

IV.

MADISON'S ADMINISTRATION.

Condition of the City of Washington—Heterogeneous Elements of Society—Mrs. Madison's Influence—Accession to the Presidency—Beauty and Fashion at the Drawing-rooms—The Office Seeker satisfied with old Clothes—First Visit of William C. Preston to the White House—A Bashful Boy—The Grace and Beauty of the Hostess—Her maternal Claim to the Lad—His Introduction to the Belles—Miss Mayo (afterwards Mrs. Scott) and Miss Coles—The Cavalier made useful—Domestic Habits of the Rulers—The raw Youth at the Reception—Remarkable Statesmen of the Time—The War with Great Britain—Details of Dr. Beans' Adventure—Francis Key to the Rescue—"The Star-Spangled Banner"—The News of Peace—Brilliant Party and queenly Beauty of the Hostess—Court Etiquette towards Foreigners.

Mr. Madison, being appointed Secretary of State, removed to Washington with his family in April, 1801. The metropolis was then almost a wilderness. The President's house stood unenclosed on a piece of waste, barren ground, separated from the Capitol by a marsh. The incomplete building stood amid rough masses of stone and other materials, and was half hidden by venerable oaks. Thick groves of forest trees, with wide plains, and here and there a house, were to be seen on every side. The proprietors of the grounds retained their rural residences and habits of living; while the new-comers brought the manners and customs of their respective states: Mr. Madison those of Virginia, Mr. Gallatin of Pennsylvania, Gen. Dearborn of Massachusetts and Robert Smith of Maryland. Never were more heterogeneous elements for society brought together. There were no established fashions; no sympathy of tastes and habits; no bond of union growing out of previous acquaintance. The motley company was thrown into intimate relations, while each felt strange and uncomfortable, and the necessity of mutual aid taught them to feel for each other. On account of the absence of Jefferson's daughters, Mrs. Madison always presided in the President's house when ladies were among the visitors, and a liberal hospitality was exercised. Next to the President's, the house of the Secretary of State received most company. The charming hostess was so frank and cordial in her manners, that her frequent parties were thoroughly enjoyed. Not only the governmental officers, the Senators, Representatives and citizens, but the foreign ministers and strangers from every part of the world, came to her receptions, and mingled with a cordiality, freedom and gayety rarely to be found in social assemblages. No bitter political animosities could show themselves in the atmosphere of this genial home. Even persons hostile to each other, who avoided a meeting elsewhere, would come to Mrs. Madison's house forgetful of their causes of disagreement, subdued by her gracious urbanity and spirit of conciliation to moderation and forbearance. The dinners were always abundant and sumptuous, more, however, in the Virginian style than in the European. For eight years this gentle influence exercised its sway, and the civilities received and reciprocated were productive of excellent effect. The regulation of social intercourse devolved upon Mrs. Madison in her double hostess-ship; yet it does not appear that misconstruction or envy ever assailed her. She won the admiration and approbation of all. Though she saw a continued round of company, her dress was simple and her house was plainly furnished. She economized in these matters, while her hospitality and charity were bounteously liberal.

The canvassing for a President to succeed Mr. Jefferson, roused the spirit of competition and party prejudice. Political intrigues infused their bitterness into the intercourse of society, and as the partisans of the several candidates did not scruple to employ calumnies, attacks were made on Mr. Madison, and his lovely wife. The lady met these assaults with a mild serenity which went far to disarm turbulent injustice.

At the ball given to celebrate the inauguration of Mr. Madison, Jefferson received him and Mrs. Madison, who "looked and moved a queen." She wore buff-colored velvet, with pearl ornaments, and a Paris turban with bird-of-paradise plume. The manager brought her the first number in the dance, which she declined, as she never danced; and it was presented to her sister. It was the wish of Mr. Madison that the civilities of his house should be extended even to his rancorous opponents, and he looked for the cessation of hostilities when the popular excitement should subside. The chiefs of the different parties continued to receive the frank and graceful attentions of Mrs. Madison, in the circles where she presided. Thus kindly feelings were cultivated, even with the leaders of opposition, till a popularity was won which the statesman's cold manners and lofty reserve might have failed to gain. The eight years' residence of this illustrious pair in Washington, had made them troops of friends who rejoiced when the day arrived for Mr. Madison's inauguration. The oath was administered by Chief Justice Marshall, March 4, 1809. Madison wore a plain suit of black. Every face beamed with smiles of gratulation, and every hand was stretched out in cordial greeting. Ex-President Jefferson sat on the right hand of the new Chief Magistrate. The removal of the Madisons to the President's house gave general satisfaction in society; for it was foreseen that the mansion would be the center of a gay and brilliant circle. Dinner parties were given every week; and a drawing-room was opened,—where the beauty and fashion of the capital found a scene appropriate for display. The strict ceremonials and formal etiquette of Mrs. Washington's court were banished, as interfering with social enjoyment. No requisitions were made beyond those prevailing in private drawing-rooms, and the dignity of high station never imposed dullness. To Mrs. Madison all justly attributed these agreeable regulations.

The mother of James Madison, Eleanor Conway, in her day added largely to the attractions of social life. Mr. Madison was kind, gentle and conciliating. He was annoyed, like all his successors, by applications for office. An illiterate man from the far West applied for the governorship of one of the Territories. The President could not oblige him. He next, though he could scarcely read, asked for a judgeship, and renewed his application for every vacancy, finally saying: "Since your excellency cannot grant me an office, I shall esteem it a favor if you would just give me a—— a pair of your old breeches." Mr. Madison immediately gave him an order on a tailor for a suit of clothes.

William C. Preston, in his unpublished journal, gave an account of his first visit to President Madison in Washington. He was about eighteen years old. When he went to call at the White House, he was painfully shy and awkward.

"I and my conductor proceeded in the hack in utter silence. The appearance of the house and grounds was very grand. There was a multitude of carriages at the door; many persons were going in and coming out; especially many in gaudy regimentals. Upon entering a room where there were fifteen or twenty persons, Mr. Madison turned toward us, and the General said, presenting me, 'My young kinsman, Mr. Preston, who has come to present his respects to you and Mrs. Madison.' The President was a little man with a powdered head, having an abstracted air and a pale countenance, with but little flow of courtesy. Around the room was a blaze of military men and naval officers in brilliant uniforms. The furniture of the room, with the brilliant mirrors, was very magnificent. While we stood, Mrs. Madison entered—a tall, portly, elegant lady, with a turban on her head and a book in her hand. She advanced straight to me, and, extending her left hand, said: 'Are you William Campbell Preston, the son of my old friend and most beloved kinswoman, Sally Campbell?' I assented. She said: 'Sit down, my son; for you are my son, and I am the first person who ever saw you in this world. Mr. Madison, this is the son of Mrs. Preston who was born in Philadelphia.' The President shook hands with me cordially. 'General Wilkinson,' said Mrs. Madison, addressing a gentleman who seemed to have been dipped in Pactolus, 'I must present this young gentleman to our distinguished men—Captain Decatur, Mr. Cheves; and yet, after all, you would as soon be presented to the young ladies,' turning to three who entered at this moment, 'Miss Maria Mayo, Miss Worthington and your kinswoman Miss Sally Coles. Now, young ladies, this young gentleman, if not my son, is my protegé, and I commend him to your special consideration. With you, he shall be my guest at the White House as long as he remains in the city. I am his mother's kinswoman, and stand towards him in the relation of a parent.' All this was performed with an easy grace and benignity which no woman in the world could have exceeded. My awkwardness and terror suddenly subsided into a romantic admiration for the magnificent woman before me.

"Thus suddenly and strangely domesticated in the President's house, I found myself translated into a new and fairy sort of existence. Edward Coles was private secretary to the President, a relation, a thorough gentleman, and one of the best-natured and most kindly-affectioned men it has ever been my good fortune to know. He was an inmate of the house, as were Miss Mayo, afterwards Mrs. General Scott, and Miss Coles, afterwards Mrs. Andrew Stevenson. These ladies were experienced belles, used to reigning over a multitude of willing subjects. They soon turned me to account; made me useful as an attendant; were entertained by my freshness—perhaps amused at my greenness. I rode with them, danced with them, waited on them, and in a short time they created or developed in me a talent for thread paper verses, on which they levied contributions. When I met Mrs. Scott in New York, she gracefully, and even touchingly, alluded to one of these half-extempores, which, with the tact that made her so admired, she had remembered for thirty years."

Thus appointed cavalier to two belles, Mr. Preston was swept into a current of fashionable dissipation. The country at the time was in the agony of the war, and Madison's position was painful and difficult.

"His labors were incessant; his countenance was pallid and hard; his social intercourse was entirely committed to Mrs. Madison, and was arranged with infinite tact and elegance. He appeared in society daily, with an unmoved and abstracted air, not relaxing, except towards the end of a protracted dinner, with confidential friends. Then he became anecdotal, facetious, a little broad occasionally in his discourse, after the manner of the old school. His most confidential companion was a Mr. Cutts, a kinsman of his wife, whom General Jackson afterwards removed from office. This gentleman habitually recounted to the President, over a glass of wine, the news, gossip and *on dits* of the day. Mr.

Madison listened with interest to his details, frequently interposing questions in a dry, keen way, and, as it seemed to me, directing his inquiries more to personal matters than to things of real importance. He showed more interest in hearing about General Marshall, as he called the Chief Justice, than in regard to any one else, frequently asking, 'What does General Marshall say about such and such matters?' For the diplomatic corps (I forget who they were) he habitually, and somewhat ostentatiously, expressed the most thorough contempt. Mrs. Madison told me the necessities of society made sad inroads upon his time, and that she was wearied of it to exhaustion. As she always entered the drawing-room with a volume in her hand, I said: 'Still you have time to read.' 'Oh no,' said she, 'not a word; I have this book in my hand—a very fine copy of Don Quixote—to have something not ungraceful to say, and, if need be, to supply a word of talk.' She was always prompt in making her appearance in the drawing-room, and when out of it was very assiduous with household offices. She told me that Mr. Madison slept very little, going to bed late and getting up frequently during the night to write or read; for which purpose a candle was always kept burning in the chamber. When not in company, he habitually addressed Mrs. Madison by the familiar epithet of 'Dolly,' under the influence of which the lady, and on no other occasion, relaxed the deliberate and somewhat stately demeanor which always characterized her. I was a gay young man, favorably received and considered in consequence of being in the White House and a pet of Mrs. Madison's, she being universally beloved and admired. When I knew her in after life, widowed, poor and without the prestige of station, I found her the same good-natured, kind-hearted, considerate, stately person that she had been in the heyday of her fortunes. Many of her minor habits, formed in early life, continued upon her in old age and poverty. Her manner was urbane, gracious, with an almost imperceptible touch of Quakerism. She continued to the last to wear around her shoulders a magnificent shawl of a green color. She always wore a lofty turban, and took snuff from a snuff-box of lava or platina, never from gold. Two years before her death, I was in a whist party with her, when Mr. John Quincy Adams was her partner, and Lord Ashburton mine. Each of the three was over seventy years of age.

"My gay residence in Washington, which my father considered a part of the education he had prescribed for me, gave me a very decided turn for gay society. However, I was soon thrown into a comparatively solitary way of life, at least removed from the fascinations of fashion and dissipation. Having flashed and floated along this bright current for four or five weeks, I returned to my remote village of Abingdon, Va., making the journey of four hundred miles on horseback; thus having time, during the solitary ride through the mountains, to recover from the gay and exciting scenes through which I had passed."

At dinner Mrs. Madison always took the head of the table; Mr. Madison the middle, and one of his secretaries the bottom. Her memory was so good that she never forgot a name, and would address each of her guests, though just introduced with twenty others, as if she had known them for years. She was a magnificent looking woman in the drawing-room. Her stately and Juno-like figure towered above the rest of the ladies. When she found a timid young girl, she would attend to her most assiduously, conduct her to the piano, and remain with her till she became more at her ease. At one of her receptions, a tall, dangling youth, fresh from the backwoods, made his appearance, and took his stand against a partition wall. He stood in that position like a fixture for half an hour, and finally ventured to take a cup of coffee, which it was then the custom to hand around. Mrs. Madison's keen eye had noticed his embarrassment, and she wished to relieve it. She walked up and addressed him. The poor youth, astounded, dropped the saucer on the floor, and unconsciously thrust the cup into his breeches pocket. "The crowd is so great"—remarked the gentle lady—"that no one can avoid being jostled. The servant will bring you another cup of coffee. Pray, how did you leave your excellent mother? I had once the honor of knowing her, but I have not seen her for some years." Thus she continued, till the poor youth felt as if he were in the company of an old acquaintance. He took care, secretly and soon, to dislodge the protuberance in his pocket.

Washington Irving, visiting Washington, was presented to Mrs. Madison by Mr. Herman Knickerbocker as his "cousin-german—Mr. Dietrich Knickerbocker." Mr. Robert Walsh had introduced him to Josiah Quincy as "a young gentleman of New York."—Quincy wrote that he "left Washington with the feelings of a man quitting Tadmor in the wilderness, where creeping things had possession."

Mr. Gaillard was a senator from South Carolina and had been so from 1804. Urbane in his manners, amiable, patient and firm, he made an excellent presiding officer in the Senate. He was of a Huguenot family. Crawford was a man of almost gigantic proportions, and, though not graceful, the effect of his presence was imposing. Napoleon remarked it when he was ambassador at the Imperial court, and complimented the Americans present on the grand air of their representative. Mr. Lowndes was one of the galaxy of brilliant young men sent by South Carolina, with Calhoun and Cheves, to the House of Representatives at the beginning of the war of 1812. When he rose to speak, the members, quitting their distant seats, would gather close about him, with the attention of affectionate confidence. Virtue, modesty, benevolence, patriotism were his, with a sound judgment, and mild persuasive eloquence; his manners were gentle, cordial and engaging. It was he who expressed the sentiment, that the Presidency was an office neither to be sought nor declined. He died at the age of forty-two. William Pinkney, too, fell in the plenitude of his strength, and on the field of his fame, under the double labors of the Supreme Court and the Senate. In his day he was thought the first of American orators; and he loved the admiration of the crowded gallery. His forte lay in his logic and power of argument; he drew on imagination, and laid great stress on action and delivery.

The Clay of 1812,—in the flush of early ambition, —was gallant, chivalrous; the boast of Kentucky, the idolized Speaker of the House. The magic of his lofty presence, the persuasive power of his magnetic voice, none could forget. His impassioned oratory was like the rush of a whirlwind. Yet the fervid Kentuckian could not pretend to the compact style, the clear method, or the massive logic of Calhoun.

Francis Key—author of the "Star Spangled Banner,"—lived in Georgetown in 1810. Dr. Beans of Marlborough, a surgeon in the United States army, was attending the sick soldiers when Commodore Barney's flotilla was attacked. The British army, on their march to Washington, bivouacked on the plantation of Dr. Beans, who though detesting them, treated the officers with true Maryland hospitality. A few days after their departure, while he was at dinner with some friends, a slave brought the news that the British were marching back to their boats. Full of glee, Dr. Beans' party went to a spring on the estate, with lemons, whiskey &c., to drink to the confusion of "perfidious Albion." Three tired English soldiers, coming for water, were made prisoners by the patriotic American gentlemen, and marched off to the county gaol. The men were missed from the ranks, and a detachment sent in search of them, traced them to Marlborough, where the terrified inhabitants betrayed who were their captors. The men were recovered; Dr. Beans was seized at midnight, placed in his night-dress on the bare back of a mule, and taken, closely guarded, to the troops; thence he was sent to Admiral Cockburn's ship, and thrown into rigorous confinement. The whole country was aroused, and as soon as steps could be taken, Francis Key, the intimate friend of Dr. Beans, was sent by President Madison with a flag of truce to get him exchanged. When Key reached the British fleet at North Point, they were about to attack Baltimore; and though he was courteously received and invited to dine with Cockburn, he was informed that he must remain on board till after the bombardment of the city. He shared his friend's uncomfortable quarters that memorable night; at sunset seeing the "Star Spangled Banner" waving proudly from the ramparts of Fort McHenry. When the day dawned after that night of battle, lit at intervals by the lurid flash of exploding bombs, and made fearful by the thunders of cannon, the mist was too dense to discover if "the Flag," or the red-cross of St. George waved from the Fort, in the direction of which the two watched through the port-hole, trembling with suspense. Presently there was a ripple in the water, a soft sough in the fog; and like magic it rolled away, revealing the American flag still floating defiantly from its staff

MRS. E. F. L. ELLET.

TAKEN IN 1850

Engraved by H. S. Hall. N. Y.

above the ramparts! The patriots fell on each other's breast, weeping for joy. Mr. Key then drew a letter from his pocket, and on its back pencilled the first stanzas of the celebrated national song. This only authentic account of the incident was furnished by the grand-niece of Dr. Beans, the distinguished poetess, Mrs. Dorsey of Washington.

The war, spreading desolation along our coasts, brought ruin to the national capital. When the British forces were approaching Washington, the President went with his friends to join General Winder and hold a council of war. The heroism displayed by Mrs. Madison, who refused to leave the city till she could see her husband safe, has been often recorded. In the private house where the President lived after those disastrous events, his wife still received their guests with hospitality, and made them happy as before. The news following the glorious defence of New Orleans by General Jackson, of the advent of peace, was borne to Washington by the slow process of travel by horses and carriages from New York. Late in the afternoon of the 14th February, 1815, came thundering down Pennsylvania avenue a coach and four foaming steeds, in which was Mr. Henry Carroll, the bearer of the treaty of peace between the American and British commissioners. The carriage was followed by cheers and congratulations as it sped towards the office of the Secretary of State—James Monroe—and thence to the President's house. Soon after dusk, the members of Congress and others presented themselves, the doors standing open. The drawing-room was crowded, Mrs. Madison doing the honors, the observed of all observers, in the meridian of her life and queenly beauty. She represented the feelings of the statesman who was in grave consultation with his official advisers. Her face was radiant with joy as she exchanged congratulations with her visitors upon the happy change in the aspect of public affairs, dispensing hospitalities with unrivalled grace. Her sisters, Mrs. Cutts and Mrs. Washington, were much admired in society.

President Madison had the old school elegance of manners, and abounded with information. He was rather taciturn in public, without being didactic or frigid. Among private friends his conversation was delightful and humorous, and in small and confidential circles he blazed out into unrestrained facetiousness and occasional brilliant flashes of wit. A friend once visited him at Montpelier, when he was confined to his bed by severe indisposition. When his family and guests sat down to dinner, the invalid desired the door of his room left open, "so that he could hear what was going on." Every few moments he called out in a feeble but humorous voice, "Doctor, are you pushing about the bottles? Do your duty, Doctor, or I must cashier you!"

President Madison died in 1836, at the advanced age of eighty-six, his mind clear and active to the last, and occupied with solicitous concern for the safety of the Union, of which he had been one of the great founders. Moderation, purity, temperance, virtue in everything, were the characteristics of his life and manners, and he was one of the purest of public men.

V.

MONROE'S ADMINISTRATION.

Monroe a Representative of an Age prolific in Great Men—The Eulogy of Peyton and Adams—The Old Man at the Polls—Inauguration of Monroe—His Cabinet—The Dress of the Period—"The Last of the Cocked Hats"—Curious Reminiscence at the first Levee—Monroe's Character—Madison's Anecdote of the Dutchmen—Henry Clay a rising Man—Calhoun in his Youth—Men of Note—Judge Marshall—William H. Crawford—Thomas H. Benton and Others—The Quarrel of the British and French Ministers at a Court Dinner—Lighting of the Executive Mansion—Extinction of the Federal Party—Mrs. Monroe and her accomplished Daughters—Mr. Crawford's Rebuff by the President—Female Society in Washington—Letter of Lord Holland introducing two young Gentlemen of Rank—The Presidential Campaign—Disinterestedness of Monroe—Letter of La Fayette—His Offer of Aid declined—The Grandchildren of Monroe—Mr. and Mrs. Gouverneur—Sketch of Mrs. Wingate.

COLONEL PEYTON said: "Mr. Monroe is a noble representative of an age prolific in great men; men who had passed the ordeal and been chastened by the fires of a revolution on principle. Men whose ambition was nurtured on wholesome food, and who, as De Tocqueville, the great political philosopher of France, remarked, would have been intellectual giants in any period of the world. Coming forth from a revolution in which they had pledged to each other and to the cause 'their lives, their fortunes, and their sacred honor,' they set to work earnestly and honestly to put in motion and give efficiency and success to what they had created at so much cost of blood and treasure. It was in the midst of such men, surrounded by such circumstances, breathing such an atmosphere of self-sacrificing virtue and heroic devotion, that Mr. Monroe learned his first lessons and had stamped upon him the glorious impress of the age." From presiding over the commonwealth of Virginia as governor, Monroe was called to a seat in the United States Senate. Then as Minister Plenipotentiary to the courts of France, Spain and England, when our government was just settling upon its foundations, and all its relations as one of the family of nations had to be arranged, and when the disturbing causes of the French Revolution had disjointed every thing in the old world, and the position of a minister could only be filled by a man of experience, ability, and courage.

John Quincy Adams wrote: "Mr. Monroe strengthened his country for defence by a system of combined fortifications, military and naval; sustaining her rights, her dignity and honor abroad; soothing her dissensions and conciliating her acerbities at home; controlling by a firm though peaceful policy the hostile spirit of European alliance against republican South America; extorting, by the mild compulsion of reason, the shores of the Pacific from the stipulated acknowledgment of Spain; and leading back the imperial autocrat of the North to his lawful boundaries, from his hastily asserted dominion over the Southern Ocean. Thus strengthening and consolidating the federative evidence of his country's union, till he was entitled to say, like Augustus Cæsar of his imperial city, that he had found her built of brick, and left her constructed of marble."

"I will vote for James Monroe!" exclaimed an aged man, brought to the polls at the warmly contested election; "his grandfather befriended me when I first came into the country." The same noble spirit of benevolence which prompted the grandfather to receive a helpless stranger in his home, might be traced in the descendant, who pledged his property for the credit of the nation. Mr. Monroe had been made Secretary of State by President Madison, in 1811. It was an important and awful crisis. Monroe came on board the ship of state just before she plunged into the midst of her perils. The resignation of the Secretary of War threw upon him the additional duties of that department. When, from the low state of the national credit and the exhausted condition of the treasury, it was impossible to raise funds for the defence of New Orleans, Monroe, with a patriotic devotedness worthy of the brightest epoch of Grecian fame, pledged his own individual credit as subsidiary to that of the nation. He was inaugurated as President of the United States, on the 5th of March, 1817. He and the Vice-President were escorted by a large cavalcade to Congress Hall, where the Ex-President, the Judges of the Supreme Court, and the Senators were assembled. They attended him to the portico, where he delivered his address. After the oath of office was administered by Chief Justice Marshall, military salutes were fired. The day was a beautiful one, and the vast assemblage testified their respect and kindly feeling.

The President appointed John Quincy Adams Secretary of State, and William H. Crawford for the Department of the Treasury. Mr. Calhoun was afterwards made Secretary of War, and B. W. Crowninshield of the Navy. In his tour through the country Monroe was greeted with general enthusiasm. The barge fitted up for his reception at Philadelphia, was lined and trimmed with crimson velvet, and rowed by sixteen oarsmen dressed in scarlet vests, with white sleeves and trowsers. The President wore a dark blue coat, with buff vest, doeskin buff-colored breeches, and top boots. He had on a military cocked hat of the fashion of the Revolution, with a black bowed ribbon worn as a cockade. He was the last of the Presidents who adhered to this old-fashioned style of dress, as small-clothes and their accompaniments were soon afterwards discarded. In some of the journals he was called "the last of the cocked hats." At the first levee given by President Monroe, when he was surrounded by a crowd, he heard a voice outside the throng shout; "Ah, Jemmy Monroe! Jemmy Monroe! you feel finer than you did the day I picked you up from the battle-field of Trenton, with a Hessian bullet in your shoulder!" The speaker was unable to make his way to the President; but the latter soon discovered him to be old Mr. Coryell, to whose house he had been carried wounded from the field, and where he remained till he was able to take his place as aid to Lord Stirling.

It was owing to his conciliatory and tranquillizing

influence—the effect of deep and calm mental power—that the party spirit which had been so fierce and disturbing, was laid to rest. "The era of good feeling" was inaugurated, by his wise management and his personal manners. On the 7th July 1817, he dined with Mr. Adams, and after dinner, accompanied by the other guests, made an afternoon visit to Mr. Quincy. Mr. Monroe's exterior was grave and mild. He was tall and well formed, and had a manner marked with dignity and ease, without any of the acquired graces of a man of society. He was prudent, plodding, generous and patriotic, and though one of the least splendid, the most fortunate of statesmen. Few persons ever knew him intimately who did not love him. There was a downrightness, a manliness, a crystal-like integrity in his conduct, which constantly grew upon associates. Jefferson's frequent remark that he was so perfectly honest, that "if his soul were turned inside out, not a spot would be found on it," has become historic. Mr. Madison said that his countryman had not generally appreciated his solid but not showy understanding. His extreme generosity, not only to the numerous members of his family dependent on him, but to friends, contributed to his impoverishment. He and Madison often addressed the people each in his own favor. On one occasion they met at a church. There was a nest of Dutchmen in that quarter, whose vote might probably turn the scale. Service was performed, and then they had music with two fiddles. When it was all over, they made speeches to the people, keeping them standing in the snow. They stood it out very patiently; seem-

7

ing to consider it a sort of fight, of which they were required to be spectators. Madison had to ride in the night twelve miles to quarters, and got his nose frost-bitten.

Mr. Goodrich was in Washington in the winter of 1819–20. Mr. Tompkins was Vice-President; Judge Marshall was at the head of the Supreme Court; Clay was Speaker of the House. The two most noted members besides him, were William Lowndes of South Carolina and John Randolph of Virginia. The clouds were then mustering for the tempest that followed the application of Missouri for admission; "poor unheard Missouri" as Clay called her—she being then without a representative. His tall, towering form, his long, sweeping gestures, his musical yet thrilling tones, made a deep impression.

"Mr. Calhoun," Quincy said, "is quite a young man compared with Mr. Adams, and has much personal beauty; he is tall and finely made, neither spare nor robust; his movements are light and graceful; his complexion is dark; his features are handsome and animated, with brilliant black eyes. In his countenance all the manly virtues are displayed, with shining benevolence. In his manners he is frank and courteous. In Washington as well as elsewhere, Mr. Calhoun is held as a model of perfection. M'Lean is apparently older than Calhoun; in person he is tall and spare; his complexion is fair, his countenance mild and pleasing, his fine blue eyes beaming with good nature, revealing the benevolence of his heart. His manners are those of an accomplished gentleman. General Brown, General in Chief of the United States army,

Judge Thurston, General Van Ness, Messrs. Brent and Carroll, all gentlemen of wealth and distinction, reside in Washington." The appearance of Lowndes was remarkable. He was six feet two inches high, slender, bent, emaciated, and of feeble frame. His complexion was sallow and dead, and his face almost expressionless. His voice was low and whispering. Yet he was the strong man of the House; strong in his various knowledge, his comprehensive understanding, his pure heart, his upright intentions. Rufus King at that time held the highest rank in the Senate for able statesmanship, combined with acknowledged probity and great dignity of person, manner and character; Harrison Gray Otis, too, stood very high, and William Hunter, of Rhode Island, noted for his agreeable presence and his great conversational powers; with William Pinkney, of Maryland, the most distinguished lawyer of that era; a large, handsome man, dressed somewhat foppishly—often in a white waistcoat and white top-boots; and Mr. Macon, of North Carolina, a solid, farmer-like man, greatly esteemed for combining a sound patriotism with a consistent political career. The general aspect of the Senate was that of dignity, sobriety and refinement. There were more who had the marks of well-bred gentlemen than at the present day.

Judge Marshall was still in the full vigor of his career. He was tall and thin, with a small face, expressive of acuteness and amiability. His personal manner was eminently dignified; yet his looks did not give the idea of his great abilities and lofty moral qualities. William H. Crawford was one of the few men who, having a great fame, became greater as he was more closely examined. In stature he was a head and shoulders above the common race, and justly proportioned, with manly features and open countenance, frank and cordial manners and fluent and impressive conversation. When he was a member of Monroe's cabinet, the array of eminent men was thick; historic names of the expiring generation were still on the public theatre, and the distinguished of the new generation were entering on it. He had served in the Senate during Madison's administration, conspicuous in that body, then pre-eminent for its able men. He spoke forcibly and to the point, with a ready and powerful elocution, and was "the Ajax of the administration." Senatorial debate was then of a high order—a rivalship of courtesy as well as of talent: and Crawford was invaluable in the Senate; but a man of head and nerve was wanted to represent the United States at the French Court, and Madison selected Mr. Crawford, who was in Paris when the great Emperor fell, reappeared, and fell again. From this high, critical post he was called by Monroe to be Secretary of the Treasury. He was the dauntless foe of nullification.

Chief Justice Marshall still presided over the supreme Court, associated with Justice Story, Justice Johnson, of South Carolina, Justice Duval and Justice Washington, of Virginia. The friends of popular representative institutions might contemplate their administration with pride and pleasure, and challenge comparison with any government in the world.

The agitating question of the session of 1820–21,

was the admission of the State of Missouri. The question of restricting slavery had been compromised the session before; the "compromise" being the work of the South, sustained by the united voice of Monroe's cabinet and the Southern Senators. Mr. Clay was the author of the final settlement of the Missouri controversy by the actual admission of the State. The session was also remarkable as being the first at which any proposition was made in Congress for the occupation and settlement of our territory on the Columbia River—the only part then owned by the United States on the Pacific Coast.

Thomas Hart Benton, who was thirty years a Senator, was born in North Carolina, March, 1782; the son of Colonel Jesse Benton and Ann Gooch, of a colonial family in Virginia. He was cousin to the wife of Henry Clay, who was Lucretia Hart. His mother was a woman of fine intellect, matured by reading and observation, and of great moral worth, elevation of character and ardent piety. The hospitality of the times brought her into acquaintance with the prominent men of the Revolution. Colonel Benton was one of the first Senators sent from the State of Missouri. All the departments of the Government then appeared to great advantage in the personal character of their administrators. Mr. Monroe was President, Governor Tompkins Vice-President; John Quincy Adams, Secretary of State; William H. Crawford, Secretary of the Treasury; John C. Calhoun, Secretary of War; Smith Thompson, Secretary of the Navy; John McLean, Postmaster General; William Wirt, Attorney General. The Senate presented a long list of eminent men known by their services in the federal or State governments, and the national representation was of great weight and efficiency.

At a court dinner given to the diplomats by the President, Sir Charles Vaughan, the British minister, found himself seated opposite the Count de Serrurier, the ambassador from France. The differences between these two countries had not a little influenced the feelings of their representatives. Several times Vaughan noticed that the French minister bit his thumb when he made a remark; and at last his irritation found vent in the question—"Do you bite your thumb at me, Sir?"—"I do," was the Count's unhesitating reply. Vaughan instantly left the table and went out into the hall, promptly followed by his antagonist. Both drew their swords, and the swords were crossed. Mr. Monroe, who had come after them, drew his also; but it was to throw theirs up. He then called his servants, ordered the gentlemen into separate apartments, and sent for their carriages to convey them home. When this was done, he returned to his remaining guests, and finished dinner. Early the next morning the two ministers sent apologies for their unbecoming behavior, and their difference was amicably settled.

"The east room" was the play-room of Mr. Monroe's daughters, and was then in an unfinished state. The streets of the capital were often in so bad a condition, that it was common to see several four-horse wagons stalled in front of the house. At every reception given by the President, the lighting of the mansion by wax lights cost one hundred dollars. This expense is now saved by the gas, which, as well as the coal, is furnished by the government. All Mr. Monroe's silver plate was his own property, and bore his initials. It was purchased of him by the government, and used in the White House till Van Buren's time.

Mrs. Adams wrote to Judge Vanderkemp in January, 1818: "When President Monroe was in Boston upon his late tour, encompassed by citizens, surrounded by the military, harassed by invitations to parties and applications innumerable for office, some gentleman asked him if he was not completely worn out. To which he replied, 'Oh no; a little flattery will support a man through great fatigue.'"

Monroe's re-election was with scarcely the show of opposition. The Federal party had ceased to exist. The leading aspirants to the Presidency were members of the cabinet, and were reluctant to oppose their chief. All the previous Presidents except Adams had served two terms, and the general opinion was that not to elect one to a second term would be equivalent to a condemnation of his conduct in the first. The defeat of John Adams, in 1800, had been spoken of as "an interruption of his administration," and was regarded as a disgrace as well as a defeat. The political calm that had followed the election of Jefferson lasted some twenty years, during which time the Federal party was annihilated. Then the Jeffersonian influence seemed to have spent its force. The older politicians, invested with revolutionary associations, were passing from the stage, and the second generation of public men had acquired experience and celebrity.

Mrs. Monroe was an elegant and accomplished woman; a model of all that is charming in the feminine character, with a dignity of manner peculiarly befitting her elevated station. She was Miss Elizabeth Kortright, a native of the city of New York. She and her two sisters were beautiful girls, belles of New York during the Revolutionary war, and courted by both American and British officers. One of the sisters was married to Nicholas Gouverneur; another to Mr. Hylager, a wealthy West Indian. Elizabeth was ridiculed and reproached by her young friends for having passed by so many brilliant and dashing adorers, to choose a plain and quiet member of Congress. When she accompanied Mr. Monroe to Paris, she was called "la belle Americaine," and entertained the best society at her residence, with grace and ease. Her eldest daughter Eliza was educated in Paris at Madame Campan's establishment, and became the second wife of Judge George Hay, of Virginia, a distinguished member of the bar in Richmond. Their daughter Hortensia was a very beautiful girl. A daughter of Judge Hay by a former marriage—Mrs. Samuel Ringgold—was one of the family circle at the White House. Hortensia married Lord Rogers of Baltimore.

Maria Monroe was one day in her father's office, during his Presidency, when William H. Crawford came in, urging something on Mr. Monroe which he wanted time to consider. Crawford insisted with vehemence on its being done at once; saying, at length, "I will not leave this room till my request is granted." "You will not!" exclaimed the President, starting up and seizing the poker. "You will *now* leave the room, or you will be thrust out." Crawford was not long in making his exit. Maria was married at the White House to Samuel L. Gouverneur, the nephew of Mrs. Monroe; Nicholas, his father, having married Miss Kortright. These ladies dispensed the hospitalities of the Presidential mansion, and exercised a favorable influence on Washington society. The court circle in Monroe's administration still had the aristocratic spirit and elevated tone which had characterized the previous administrations. Its superiority was universally acknowledged, and nothing vulgar entered its precincts. Elegance of dress was absolutely required. On one occasion Mr. Monroe refused admission to a near relative who happened not to have a suit of small-clothes and silk hose in which to present himself at a public reception. He was driven to the necessity of borrowing for once.

Mrs. Monroe died at Oak Hill, Virginia, the residence of her husband, and her grave was shaded by a large pine tree in the garden. Her daughter Maria was laid beside her in 1850; Mrs. Hay died in Paris, and was buried in Pere la Chaise.

The female society at Washington during the administration of Monroe was essentially Southern. Virginia, proud of her Presidents, sent forth her brightest flowers to adorn the court circle. The wealth of the sugar and cotton planters, and of the vast wheat-fields of the agricultural States, cultivated by negroes, enabled Southern Senators and Representatives to keep their carriages and liveried servants, and to maintain great state. Dinners and suppers with rich wines and the delicacies of the season, had their persuasive influence over the minds as well as the appetites of the entertained. A few of the richer members from the North vied with Southern members in their style of living and entertainments; but so inconsiderable was their number, that they furnished only exceptions to the rule. John D. Dickinson, a member of Congress from the Rensselaer District, (N. Y.,) a man of wealth, was one of these. His daughter became the wife of Ogle Tayloe of Washington.

After his second election as President, Monroe made a journey through the Northern and Eastern States and saw many of his old companions in arms as objects of charity. One broken old man who had once been a gallant officer, as well as a scholar and a merchant, came to pay his respects, and conversed with the President with the freedom of an old friend. Mr. Monroe noticed his scanty wardrobe, though he uttered no complaint. At Hanover, in New Hampshire, he visited Mrs. Wheelock, and reminded her of the time when, a sprightly maiden, she had prepared the surgeon's bandages for the wounded Lieutenant Monroe, on the morning of the battle of Trenton. The grave statesman and the elderly lady were reminded of the changes time had made, as they talked of the incidents of that memorable day.

Mr. Monroe's military education, and the intrepidity and decision he had learned as a soldier were of great use to him in public life. The half century in which he was an actor on the great stage of human affairs, was eventful in the history of nations. His imperturbable serenity was an excellent thing for a diplomatist, and often of service to an executive officer. He was never dazzled nor deluded by imagination. Ages may pass before one more fortunate will be found in the Presidential chair of the American republic.

Lord Holland wrote to Mr. Monroe in January 1824, introducing four young English gentlemen, Mr. Wortley, Mr. Stanley, Mr. Labouchere, and Mr. Dennison, who were taking a tour of pleasure and curiosity to the United States. His lordship continues:

> "Such a deviation from the common line of travels hitherto in fashion with young men of their rank has excited no little sensation in London, but receives the warm approbation of all thinking and sensible men. Should it become a precedent for others, the two freest (I am afraid I might say the only two free) countries upon earth will derive mutual advantages from those destined to acquire influence, in each cultivating acquaintance and friendship with one another in early life. The balance, indeed, is likely to be greatly in our favor; for in the present state of all our neighboring courts, hitherto the common markets for fashionable opinion, all love of liberty and all popular feeling which we can retain for our own consumption must be of our own growth, or imported from your side of the Atlantic. There is no such commodity on the Continent of Europe."

Of those young men, Mr. Wortley belonged to a branch of the Stuarts, and was a lineal descendant of Lady Mary; Mr. Stanley was heir to one of the oldest names and largest estates in the British empire—Lord Derby's, and had commenced his career in the House of Commons with the prospect of brilliant success. Labouchere was the nephew of Mr.

Baring. Lord Holland understood the advantage to them of an acquaintance with the free institutions of the United States, and an introduction to the President. He adds:

"I know not whether they will find you still at Washington, discharging your useful and honorable functions as President, or retired from your labors; and I hardly know which to wish for their sakes. In either case I envy them the satisfaction of conversing with you. . . . I can assure you with the utmost sincerity, that among the pleasantest reflections on the events of my public life, is the circumstance of having been brought in contact with one who was destined by his fortune and his virtues to fill the Presidency of the greatest republic now in the world in a way honorable and advantageous to his country, beneficial to the common interests of freedom, and not unworthy of the great man who was first elevated to that most glorious of situations. Accept, my dear Sir, my congratulations on the just commendations which are everywhere bestowed on your late administration, and my thanks, as a friend of freedom and a citizen of the world, for the example which you have given, and the manly and benevolent policy you have pursued." *

As the Presidential election of 1824 approached, great popularity accrued to De Witt Clinton by the completion of the Erie Canal in New York State; exciting a great appetite among public men for that kind of fame. The steam-car had not then been invented; but "internal improvement," was the cry everywhere. In the summer of 1824, General La Fayette came under an invitation from the President to revisit the United States, and his progress through the States was a triumphal procession. He found three of his old associates ex-Presidents—Adams, Jefferson and Madison; another, Monroe, in the Presidential chair. He was sent home the following year

* MS. letter.

as the country's guest, by its new President, Mr. Adams.

An eminent statesman of Virginia, who was a Senator in Congress in the first term of Washington's administration and in the last term of Monroe's, was John Taylor "of Caroline." He died at the close of 1824. He gave his time to his farm and his books when not called by an emergency to the public service. His character was announced in his looks and deportment, and in his uniform senatorial dress; the coat, waistcoat and pantaloons of the same "London brown" and in the cut of a former fashion; beaver hat with ample brim, fine white linen, gold-headed cane, used for support when bending under the heaviness of years. "He seemed to have been cast in the same mould with Mr. Macon, and it was pleasant to see them together, looking like two Grecian sages." He belonged to that constellation of great men which shone so brightly in Virginia in his day, and whose light spread through the boundaries of the civilized world.

The Presidential campaign of 1824 was not the less exciting for the long lull in the political firmament. The question of the succession had been the great topic of conversation during the last three years of Mr. Monroe's term. The Secretary of the Treasury, William Harris Crawford, was the heir apparent of the Virginia dynasty, and the "regular" candidate of the Republican party. Next to him the most prominent one was John Quincy Adams, Secretary of State. A third was John C. Calhoun, Secretary of War, then but forty-one years of age, and a different man from him who in his later years, as Miss Martineau said, lived among his peers in "intellectual isolation," "a spectral statesman, gaunt and grim, coming out of the past to repeat the maxims of other ages." Wirt wrote of him in 1824: "Calhoun is a most captivating man. His is the very character to strike a Virginian: ardent, generous, high-minded, brave, with a genius full of fire, energy and light; a devoted patriot, proud of his country, and prizing her glory above his life."

Colton, the biographer of Henry Clay, mentioned a party given by John Quincy Adams on the 8th January, 1824, in honor of General Jackson. The President, foreign ambassadors, members of Congress and many distinguished persons, were present; but General Jackson was the star of the evening, with Mrs. Adams on his arm, presenting him to the guests.

Mr. Crawford was struck with paralysis in August, 1823, and was removed to a cottage near Washington, where he was visited only by his confidential clerk and his nearest friends. The canvass for the Presidency raged on; hotels and drawing-rooms being thronged by the votaries of fashion and the satellites of the different champions.

On the morning of March 16th, 1824, Jackson was notified by the President to attend him, and be presented with the medal voted him by Congress in 1815. This was presented in the presence of the heads of departments and their ladies, the ladies of the executive mansion, etc. Monroe visited Nashville during his Presidency, and General Jackson was among those who welcomed and escorted him. They entered the room at a grand ball, arm in arm, the General in his newest uniform; while on Monroe's other side walked General Carroll, also a man of lofty stature.

The administration of Monroe closed March 3d, 1825; and after laying down the burden of State cares, he retired to his home in London County, Virginia. For a few years only had he the society of his beloved wife in this pleasant retreat. She was taken from him, and the widower went on a visit to New York. Here his failing health was watched by filial solicitude and tenderness. After the close of Monroe's second term, he commenced to reap the bitter fruits of a life devoted to the best interests of his country, regardless of his own. As a private citizen, he emerged from all his successive public trusts with poverty as the emblem of his purity and the badge of all his public honors. In the death of his devoted wife in September, 1830, he realized that his cup of earthly sorrow was full to the brim. She had adorned every public position he ever held, with enviable graces of person and mind. She had nobly participated in all his troubles, and with her sudden loss all the hopes of his declining years faded rapidly.

La Fayette wrote to Mr. Monroe in 1828, when he was depressed by the failing health of his wife:

"The papers have confirmed my fears of your pecuniary situation being still worse than I had for a long time apprehended. Under those circumstances, there is great need of her and your fortitude. My feelings on every account it were superfluous to express. The settlement of your claims has been left open. May the actual session finish what the last one has begun!

"In the meantime, my dear Monroe, permit your earliest, your best, and your most obliged friend to be plain with you. It is probable that, to give you time and facilities for your arrangement and mortgage, might be of some use. The sale of one-half of my Florida property is full enough to meet my family settlements and the wishes of my neighbors. There may be occasion for a small retrocession of acres, in case of some claims on the disposed of Louisiana lands—an object as yet uncertain, at all events inconsiderable; so that there will remain ample security for a large loan; for I understand those lands are very valuable, and will be so to a great extent after the disposal of a part of them. You remember that in a similar embarrassment I have formerly accepted your intervention. It gives me a right to reciprocity. Our friend Mr. Graham has my full powers. Be pleased to peruse the inclosed letter, seal it, and put it in the post-office. I durst not send it before I had obtained your approbation. Yet, should it be denied, I would feel much mortified. I hope, I know you are too much my friend not to accept what, in a similar case, I would not an instant hesitate to ask." *

The enclosed letter was a power-of-attorney to Mr. Graham, to mortgage the lands mentioned. Mr. Monroe declined accepting the offer, and returned the power-of-attorney to General La Fayette.

Mr. Monroe left three grand-children, of whom the youngest was Mr. Samuel L. Gouverneur. The duties of administrator of President Monroe devolved on him. He published, in 1867, a work composed by Mr. Monroe in his later years, entitled "The People the Sovereigns," a comparison of the government of the United States with those of other republics. This work has excited much attention both in this country and abroad, and Mr. Bancroft considers it worthy of the closest study of statesmen and diplomatists. Mr. Gouverneur, at the outbreak of the Mexican war, was commissioned in the 4th Regiment of Artillery, and ac-

---

* MS. letter.

companied General Scott from Vera Cruz to the city of Mexico. He served with distinction, and was brevetted for gallant conduct at the battles of Contreras and Cherubusco. At the close of the war he resigned, and subsequently was United States Consul at the port of Foo Choo, in China. He remained there till the commencement of the civil war, when he returned to this country, and now resides in Frederick City, Md. His wife, who was Miss Marion Campbell, is the daughter of Judge Campbell, formerly Surrogate of New York. She is the sister of Mrs. Eames of Washington, and is a most lovely and accomplished woman.

Mrs. Julia C. Wingate was a celebrity in the court society during Monroe's administration. She was a daughter of General Henry Dearborn, whose long life of seventy-eight years, filled with patriotic services to his country, terminated in 1829. He was a distinguished Revolutionary officer, and served with honor at Bunker Hill, Ticonderoga, Monmouth, Yorktown and elsewhere. In 1801 he was appointed Secretary of War and served through both terms of President Jefferson's administration. In 1812 he received the appointment of Senior Major-General of the American army. In 1822 he was sent as minister to Portugal. During his residence at the capital, he and other foreign ministers were instrumental in saving the King and his court, from a conspiracy of the Queen and her son Don Miguel. As an expression of his gratitude the King conferred orders of distinction upon all the foreign ministers, except General Dearborn, whom the law of his country forbade to accept any; to him he presented his miniature set with large solitaire diamonds. It is now in the possession of his grand-daughter Mrs. Charles Quincy Clapp. The wife of General Dearborn was remarkably gifted and cultivated in mind and person, and eminently fitted to grace her position. Under the influence of such parents, their daughter grew to womanhood. At eighteen she was married to General Wingate, whose name is honorably identified with the early history of Maine. She accompanied him to Washington, where they resided in General Dearborn's family. The resources of Mrs. Wingate's brilliant mind were here called forth, with the exercise of her extraordinary conversational powers. These, with her attractive person, dignified though captivating manners, and genial disposition, rendered her society eagerly sought after. She was the ornament and the pride of every circle in which she appeared.

In Washington, at that time, society was represented by the best specimens of beauty, intelligence and refinement in the country. Mrs. Wingate's cordial but unostentatious hospitalities rendered her home attractive to the most gifted. She was an intimate friend of Mrs. Madison, and enjoyed the esteem of all the distinguished personages at the seat of government. She was in Washington at the time of General La Fayette's visit to this country. On the occasion of his visit to Portland, General and Mrs. Wingate gave him a brilliant morning reception.

Willis, in his History of the distinguished lawyers of Maine, has placed upon record an incident illustrative of Mrs. Wingate's character. "In 1806, when party spirit was raging like a pestilence, and the whole community was divided into Federals and Democrats, Mrs. Wingate, who was one of the most beautiful women that Maine ever produced, was desirous of giving a genial welcome to her numerous acquaintance in her new house. Cards were issued, the drawing-rooms were filled, and ladies and gentlemen of both parties there met face to face. But the elegant and fascinating hostess was almost overwhelmed with anxiety and despair to observe that there was no conversation; there were no smiles nor kind looks at each other. What could she do? how could she make her friends happy? A bright thought suddenly sprang from her warm heart. 'Wingate,' as she always called her husband, 'send for Terpsichore; let us have music and dancing.' It was done. The instruments struck up; hands and feet were soon in lively and graceful motion. Though few and short were the sentences exchanged, Federalists and Democrats long remember that happy evening." In the last years of her life she enjoyed, as ever, the society of her friends, and her recollections of the memorable time spent in Washington were clear and full of interest. She remembered particularly the visit of some French gentlemen at her father's, in Maine, where they remained for several days, and mingled freely with the citizens of the town. After their departure, no little surprise was created by the announcement of her father that the strangers were Talleyrand and Louis Philippe, then traveling *incog.*

Mrs. Wingate was deeply religious, and was noted for her charities and her sympathy with the unfortunate. A descendant of this distinguished family is Mrs. Winthrop G. Ray, mentioned here before her time, as she was one of the most admired visitors to Washington in the reign of President Pierce. She is the niece of Mrs. Levi Woodbury. Colonel Charles Quincy Clapp, the father of Georgiana Wingate Ray, was the great-nephew of Mrs. John Hancock, and married Octavia Wingate, the only daughter of Mrs. Julia C. Wingate. Her uncommon personal beauty rendered her irresistible. Her presence was an inspiration to the students at Bowdoin College, when she attended their annual exhibitions. At a private ball in Boston, where Harvard University was represented, complimentary couplets, printed on cards in Greek and Latin, with her name, attested the general admiration. Their eldest daughter, Julia, a celebrated beauty, and highly gifted, married John Bryce Carroll, a gentleman of rare endowments, and highly connected in Virginia. Miss Georgie, the youngest daughter, was noted for sprightliness and wit, with a piquant, original, charming grace. At one of the reunions at Colonel Clapp's hospitable mansion in Portland, where the broad hall was a splendid picture-gallery, the author, Henry William Herbert, improvised a poem celebrating the loveliness and gifts of the ladies of the family—

———"A wreath of beauties such as ne'er
Of king or kaiser graced the courtly sphere." *

---

* The poem closes thus:

For who can mark the fleet expression rise,
So fraught with soul in Minna's glorious eyes?
Who look upon the clear and sparkling grace,
That crowns the young Francesca's fairy face?
Who catch the gems that fall, so careless cast
From Anna's lips so fluent and so fast,

MRS. WINTHROP G. RAY.

Engraved by H. B. Hall N. Y.

Georgiana was married to Mr. Winthrop G. Ray, of New York, a grandson of Samuel Gray, one of the most eminent and prosperous merchants and ship-owners of Boston. Mr. and Mrs. Ray passed the first winter after marriage in New Orleans, where the bride received much attention from Henry Clay, an old friend of the family, and other distinguished persons. She afterwards spent much time in Washington, where her cousin Mrs. Montgomery Blair, and other relatives resided, and where she was the acknowledged ornament of the best circles. Her home is in the city of New York. There she has been for several years a leader in society, the brilliant gatherings in her drawing-rooms being often described in newspapers. The companionship of a young and lovely daughter, whose charms and graces have early won celebrity, of late has added to the attractions of Mrs. Ray's house. She is herself in the prime of

---

So free and fearless ?—she for whom one breast
In the far forest of the boundless West
Beats worthily ?—who see, so young and fair,
Sarah beside her—sweet and kindred pair,
Fit sisterhood ? Who marvel at the state
Of queenly Julia, merrily sedate,
Serenely courteous, and superbly bright?
Who look upon the quick and flashing light
That leaps from Georgiana's every feature—
Most artless, innocent, bewitching creature?
Who gaze on Sarah's soul entrancing face,
All woman mirthfulness and woman grace;
Her self-curled locks, and eyes whose azure hue
Mocks the most lovely heaven's most lovely blue?
Who can behold, and dream that seven like these,
Bloom on the softer shores of Southern seas?
Tis done! tis done! the high emprise is gained,
The minstrel's task is o'er, his end attained—
Francesca, Minna, Sarah, Julia, Ann,
Georgiana, Sarah,—match them if you can!

Minna was Mrs. Montgomery Blair; Francesca, Mrs. Fry; Anna, Mrs. Bigelow; Sarah, Miss Chaddock; Julia, Mrs. Carroll; Sarah, Mrs. Herbert; Georgiana, Mrs. Ray.

lovely womanhood, and her bright beauty is rendered more bewitching by her sprightliness and quick, though always good-natured wit. Something sparkling and original always appears in her conversation; perfectly unstudied and impulsive, illuminating every subject or placing it in an amusing light, and carrying the sympathies with her by the entertainment afforded. She is the life of every circle; and so noble is her heart, so full of kindly charity, that her vivacity never wounds. Many of her off-hand jeu d'esprits are repeated as capital sayings; but they have no sting beyond the gentlest rebuke for self-conceit, presumption or pride of wealth. Her unostentatious charities are known to recipients far and wide, and often have her indignant sarcasms been leveled at the worldly spirit that neglects merit where the gifts of fortune are denied. For what is termed "snobbishness"—the meanness that courts riches and distinction, while doing injustice to talent obscured by poverty—her high-hearted scorn is always shown. In her generous, chivalric nature, as well as in her personal and mental charms, there are few women like Mrs. Ray.

VI.

JOHN QUINCY ADAMS' ADMINISTRATION.

Jefferson's Opinion of Adams—His previous Career—Dress in the Senate—As Secretary of State—Mrs. Adams—Her Influence on Society—Personal Appearance of Adams—Anecdotes—Levee after the Counting of the Electoral Votes—Meeting between the President and Jackson—The Inauguration—Re-opening of the old Controversy of Parties—Duel between Clay and Randolph—The Gossip discreet for once—Effects of early Rising—New Year's Receptions—The Congressional Library a Lounging-place—Etiquette at Presidential Parties—Party at the British Minister's—Brilliant one given by the Secretary of War—Remarks of a Belle of Jefferson's days—Description of the "Court of the younger Adams"—Soiree given by the Dutch Minister—Randolph's Praise of Poverty—Prominent Statesmen and reigning Belles—The Premier's last Party for the season—Mrs. Secretary Porter—Mr. Clay's Party—Character of Mr. Adams.

JEFFERSON'S feelings towards the younger Adams were purely amicable. He had a high opinion of his integrity and ability, particularly as a writer; but sometimes distrusted his temper and judgment. He said in 1816 or 1817: "Monroe showed his usual good sense in appointing Adams. They were made for each other. Adams has a pointed pen; Monroe has judgment enough for both and firmness enough to have *his* judgment control." Adams was Minister Plenipotentiary and Envoy Extraordinary to the Court of St. James. He had been connected with the government many years; was a federalist of the old school and head of that party after the death of General Hamilton. In dress and manners he was a model of courtly refinement. He always appeared in the Senate in full dress; short small-clothes, silk stockings and shoes; and was habitually observant of all the courtesies of life. When Adams accepted the post of Secretary of State under Mr. Monroe, his wife took leave of Europe, where she had passed the greater portion of her life amid a succession of astonishing events. It devolved on her to make the house of the Secretary an agreeable resort to the multitudes of visitors that thronged the capital during the session. A large diplomatic corps and a distinguished set of public men, not then divided by party lines in the usual manner, rendered the society of that time and of Mrs. Adams' house memorable for its pleasantness. For a brief time sectional animosities relented, personal denunciation was suspended, and the jealous rivalry for political honors was smoothed over, if not quite covered, by the polish of social life. During the eight years in which Mrs. Adams presided in the house of the Secretary of State, she excluded none on account of political hostility. Her aim was to amuse and enliven society, and her success was admitted to be complete. When the violence of partisan warfare increased during the great contest for the Presidency, Mrs. Adams became inclined to adopt habits of greater seclusion. When the result made her mistress of the Presidential mansion, her health began to fail her so much that though she continued to preside upon occasions of public reception, she ceased to appear at other times, and began to seek the retirement she preferred.

Miss Louisa Catherine Johnson, who became the wife of John Quincy Adams—was born, educated, and married in London. She was the daughter of Joshua Johnson. In advanced age, her children were accustomed to call her "Madame," and their father "The President." The utmost deference was systematically paid to both parents. In person she was petite, with lively manners, very fluent and brilliant in conversation. Mr. Adams was then about fifty, of middling stature, robust make, and with every indication of a vigorous constitution. His complexion was fair, his face round and full and expressive of intellect; his eye black, and of such keenness that it pierced the beholder. While Secretary of State, he had from constant use, a weeping eye. But it could not be said, "He gave to misery all he had—a tear." A collection was once made to defray the funeral expenses of a man who had been in prosperous circumstances. The friend who went soliciting contributions among officers of high rank in the government found little encouragement. He was recommended to call on Mr. Adams. "On that iceberg!" he exclaimed. "It would be folly." However, he finally went to see Mr. Adams. He looked over the paper, took out his pocket-book, and handed the young man in silence, two notes of twenty dollars each.

On the 9th February, 1825, after the formal opening of the electoral packets, it was announced that Mr. Calhoun had been elected Vice-President; that no one had received a majority of electoral votes for the Presidency, and that the House of Representatives had then to elect a President from the three highest candidates, Jackson, Adams and Crawford. The Senators retired. The roll of the House was called by States; the vote of each State was deposited in a box, and placed on the table. The tellers, Daniel Webster and John Randolph, proceeded to open the boxes and count the ballots. The election of Mr. Adams was announced by Mr. Webster. Mr. Monroe gave a Presidential levee that evening, to which all Washington rushed. Goodrich relates that in the course of the evening Mr. Adams and General Jackson unconsciously approached each other in the throng. Suddenly the persons around, seeing they were about to meet, stepped aside and left them face to face. General Jackson had a handsome lady on his arm. The two looked at each other for a moment, and then Jackson moved forward, stretched out his long arm, and said, "How do you do, Mr. Adams! I give you my left hand, for the right, as you see, is devoted to the fair; I hope you are well, sir." Mr. Adams took the hand, and said with chilling coldness: "Very well, sir; I hope General Jackson is well?" It was curious to see the western planter, the Indian fighter, the stern soldier, who had written his country's glory in the blood of the enemy at New Orleans, genial and gracious in the midst of a court; while the old courtier and diplomat was stiff, rigid, cold as a statue! It was the more remarkable from the fact that, four hours before, the former had been defeated, and the latter was the victor, in a struggle for one of the highest objects of human ambition. Judge Breckinridge thought the repulsive manner of Mr. Adams in public, owing partly to natural reserve, partly to the diplomatic habit of dismissing all expression from his countenance, derived from his position abroad. "Knowing his natural warmth of disposition, I was surprised when I saw him, as the Chief Magistrate of the nation receive a splendidly dressed personage glittering in gold and feathers, with a formal coldness that froze like the approach to an iceberg." After the inauguration, the multitude rushed as usual, to the White House to congratulate the new President; General Jackson prominent in the throng. He was among the earliest of those who took the hand of the President, and their looks and deportment towards each other were a rebuke to that bitterness of party spirit which can see no merit in a rival, and feel no joy in the honor of a competitor. General Jackson, as the oldest Senator present, had that morning administered to Mr. Calhoun the oath of office. The choice of Mr. Adams by the House of Representatives had been brought about through the influence and exertions of Mr. Clay.

Mr. Adams' cold apathetic manner often created unpopularity. When he was a candidate for the Presidency, his political friends persuaded him to attend a cattle show. Among the persons introduced to him, was a respectable farmer of the vicinity, who said, "Mr. Adams, I am very glad to see you. My wife, when she was a gal, lived in your father's family; you were then a little boy, and she has often combed your head." "Well," replied Mr. Adams in his harsh way, "I suppose she combs yours, now." The poor farmer slunk back. In the House of Representatives, one day he attacked Mr. Wise with great bitterness, and in allusion to the Cilley duel, spoke of him as coming with "hands dripping with blood." There was a terrible "yarring" tone in his voice, which seemed to thrill the listeners with horror, rather towards Mr. Adams than the object of his reproaches.

With the elevation of Mr. Adams, the old controversy, supposed slain at his father's defeat, was reopened, and Federalism appeared living and rampant. The long, bony finger, the piercing screech of John Randolph, were raised in execration of the delusions thus revived. Randolph had an old grudge against the name and race of Adams, and he called the President "John the Second." He remembered when, in but school-boy days, his brother was spurned by the coachman of the Vice-President for coming too near the arms emblazoned on the escutcheon of the carriage. In one of his fierce harangues, he spoke of the union of Adams and Clay as the "coalition of Blifil and Black George: of the puritan and the blackleg;" a remark which caused the famous duel between Clay and Randolph in 1826.

On the 4th of March, 1825, John Quincy Adams delivered his inaugural address and took the oath of office administered by Chief Justice Marshall in the capitol. His cabinet was composed of able and experienced men; Mr. Clay, Secretary of State; Richard Rush of Pennsylvania, recalled from the London Mission to be Secretary of the Treasury; James Barbour of Virginia, Secretary of War; Samuel L. Southard of New Jersey, who had been Secretary of the Navy under Monroe, continuing in that office; and McLean and Wirt occupying their places.

Mr. Randolph's duel with Mr. Clay took place in April, on the right bank of the Potomac, in Virginia, Mr. Clay's bullet knocking up the gravel behind Mr. Randolph, who fired in the air. The combatants then shook hands, Mr. Randolph saying jocosely, "You owe me a coat, Mr. Clay"—the bullet having passed through the skirt of his coat. To which Mr. Clay replied, "I am glad the debt is no greater." Benton pronounced this "the highest toned duel he had ever witnessed." A gentleman noted for love of gossip—Mr. Ned Wyer—had come dashing upon a group in the street with the news that the two statesmen had gone to fight. They had not recovered from their astonishment when Clay himself joined them; and, as he did so, he called out, "For mercy's sake, tell me one thing! Does Ned Wyer know what I have been about? If he does, it is all over town, and Mrs. Clay will be frightened into fits!" It happened for once, however, that the newsmonger had been discreet, and his prudence in the matter restored him to the favor of Mrs. Adams, who had treated him coolly for some time because he had introduced at one of her select parties the wife of a member not very particular in her conduct.

President Quincy carried one of his virtues to excess—early rising. He rose so early in the morning that he scarcely had sleep enough; so that when he sat down during the day for ten minutes, he was very likely to fall asleep. John Quincy Adams was also addicted to excessive early rising. One day these two distinguished men went into Judge Story's lecture-room to hear him read his lecture to his class in the law school. The Judge received the two Presidents with his usual politeness, placed them on the platform by his side, in full view of the class, and then went on with his lecture. In a very few minutes both the Presidents were fast asleep. The Judge paused a moment, and, pointing to the two sleeping gentlemen, said, "Gentlemen, you see before you a melancholy example of the evil effects of early rising." This remark was followed by a shout of laughter, which effectually roused the sleepers, after which the Judge resumed his discourse.

On New Years' day it was customary for the President to receive all sorts of company. They walked up, presented themselves—if with ladies also to Mrs. Adams—stalked about through the numerous apartments, tried to catch the refreshments which went scudding round on the heads of the servants, and then went home to tell what they heard, saw and did. "Mr. Adams," said a visitor, "was punished for more than two hours. He stood in the center of the center-room, and most pathetically shook hands the whole time. In the ladies' corner it was all chat, flutter and graceful bowing. In the hall a band was planted, to keep the nerves of the company in a proper degree of agitation. The corps diplomatique appeared, each in his own national costume."

The library of Congress, though far from being completed, was a delicious morning lounge, and frequented by all the fashionables of both sexes. There was much amusement in looking over the pamphlets published about 1801, when the first great civil revolution took place, and the marginal notes in Jefferson's small, round, delicate hand-writing. Towards the last of January the President gave his third drawing-room for the season. By a rule of fashion, every *second* levee was considered exclusively fashionable; why, there seemed no reason but the caprice of the gay world. This levee was very splendid, crowded, delightful and uncomfortable. Commencing at seven in the evening, it continued to nearly eleven. The three front rooms were brilliantly lighted with lustres, and the company entered at the eastern gate, passing through the large hall where hats, greatcoats and servants were deposited. At the soirees of the Secretaries, dancing was allowed, with card-tables, backgammon, or chess; but at the President's there was nothing but talking, squeezing, promenading, bowing, drinking coffee and sipping liqueurs. The Secretary of State, the Mayor of the city, and many Jackson men from the west were present. Every one seemed looking for something he could not find, except the Lady President, who, from her life and apparent gayety, appeared perfectly satisfied with the scene. Around a table many of the promenaders would linger a moment, pledge themselves in coffee or cordials, gaze in the mirrors, and then saunter after more compliments. Many of the western members would sit down and rest themselves on the superb sofas; observing that when backwoodsmen get fatigued, they always take a seat on the first stump they meet. The leaders of the ton were the very *élite* of the principal cities of the Union. "Last week was

Clay's Wednesday night, and this week has been the President's drawing-room; on both occasions it was a perfect jam. Clay's night was distinguished for some brilliancy, some beauty, plenty of politics, execrable music, and a solitary cotillion varied with an occasional waltz. On the 9th January, 1829, a party was given by Mr. Vaughan, the British minister, which excelled anything that had taken place that season. Mr. Vaughan was a bachelor, and admitted to be one of the most polished of that species. Another brilliant party was given at the house of the Secretary of War. Of all the sparkling festivities of the foreign legations, the gala at Baron M. Krudener's, was of surpassing effect. The wit and beauty were more brilliant than had yet bewildered the pleasure-seeking society of the national capital. The married ladies were the most admired belles. One of them was moralizing over the degeneracy of modern times. The halcyon days of Jefferson! the glorious, the republican days, when the mind shone forth in its pure unstudied richness, beyond the power of embroidery, lace, perfumes, and the accomplishments of modern music and dancing-masters. Whip-syllabubs were not then in fashion, ice-creams were unknown, and a thousand villanous compounds had not been invented. Jefferson restored the simplicity which should forever characterize the court of a free people. In his days, there were no 'drawing-rooms,' no waltzing, no fashionable mobs where death stalked abroad in the shape of bonbons and confectionery. Jefferson was always at home, from Monday till Saturday. Whoever called at the Presidential mansion, the sage would welcome him in his own simple benevolent manner. What a contrast—the court of the younger Adams! the gay drawing-rooms of the prince of diplomatists! The 'drawing-room night' in the court circle was Wednesday; then all the worshipers of his Presidential Highness, arrayed in their costliest, approached the mansion at the hour of eight. Entering a large door, the fair visitors passed through a spacious hall dimly lighted with a couple of lamps hung between the columns in the center. This was the common promenade for cooling themselves. By a door they were ushered into the presence-chamber, where the President and Mrs. Adams were encircled with brilliancy and beauty. A regiment of western visitors crept along the carpet, and made an attack on the outskirts of the crowd. Then came a throng of beauties from the Hudson; and Virginia and the South contributed their share. They moved forward the De Witt Clinton of the Old Dominion, who in the moment of gayety throws aside his canals and railroads without remorse, and becomes the politest, easiest, gayest, wittiest, and most enchanting bachelor that adorns the court of the second Adams. Then come the fine single gentlemen, the flutterers on the edges of society, the butterflies, the Venetian coloring of the gay world." The cake, coffee, ice-creams, sangaree, negus, and other hot and cold liqueurs, cost the President about fifty dollars a night. "The cabinet dinners are the grand affairs, where wines and delicious viands are congregated, and the fair sex are not admitted. Dancing is to be found in abundance at private parties. The lady mayoress, by the way, is one of the prettiest dancers of the age. You must not imagine that we dance at the President's drawing-room." In after years it was remarked: "Society in Washington ought to give the tone to the whole country. It did so during Mrs. Adams' enchanting, elegant and intellectual regime. For elegance, refinement, taste, purity, talent, beauty and worth, the fashionable circle Mrs. Adams drew around her was far superior to that which has appeared at any period since."

A last soiree was given by the Dutch minister and his wife. Their house was esteemed the most intelligent of the legations, and was usually animated and brilliant. A Dutch belle from New York, was conspicuous for dress and beauty; also a lovely, unaffected girl from Baltimore. "The heir apparent" had just been married and had come out in royal style at the last levee. That virtuous and patriotic man, Mr. Macon, called by Jefferson "the last of the Romans," had fixed the term of his political existence at seventy, and touched that age in 1828, in the middle of a third senatorial term, and in full possession of all his faculties. He resigned his honors as he had won them: meekly, unostentatiously; and after nine years at home, died in 1837. His was a long, noble and exalted career. A soldier in the war of the Revolution, he had served his country in legislation forty years; being senator under Madison, Monroe and Adams, and in the intervals of public duty working in his fields at the head of his slaves, and receiving at his hospitable home all guests, from the President to the day laborer. He had two daughters—accomplished ladies, who married polished gentlemen;

one of them, William Martin; the other William Eaton of Roanoke. He always wore a dress of the same material, cut and color—superfine navy blue, of the fashion of the Revolution; with fine linen, a cambric stock, fine fur hat, and fair top boots outside the pantaloons. He would wear no man's honors. Complimented on the report on the Panama mission which he, as chairman of the committee on Foreign Relations, had presented to the Senate, he replied—"Yes, it is a good report; Tazewell wrote it." Benton called him "the Cincinnatus of America." William Wirt died at sixty-two, having reached a place in the first line at the Virginia bar, where there were such lawyers as Wickham, Tazewell and Watkins Leigh; with a place at the bar of the Supreme Court, where there were such jurists as Webster and Pinkney. He had been attorney-general of the United States under Monroe. In youth he had been near falling into a fatal habit, but he retrieved himself, touched by the noble generosity of her who afterwards became his beloved wife; and he grew to be the model of every domestic virtue, with genius acknowledged by all. He died during the term of the Supreme Court—his revered friend Chief Justice Marshall still presiding, and Webster paid to his memory the tribute of justice and affection.

On the morning of the Fourth of July, 1826—only three of the fifty-six signers of the Declaration of Independence remained alive; in the evening there remained but one—Charles Carroll of Carrollton, Maryland. He had filled high offices in public life, had enjoyed the gifts of fortune and health, and lived in honor amid "troops of friends" to the age of ninety-six; then he passed away, the last of a noble band of patriots.

In the administration of John Quincy Adams men were not removed from office on account of their political opinions. He would not consent to do it even when warned that he would lose a re-election in consequence. He expected, however, to hold his place eight years, according to time-honored usage: and to be succeeded by Mr. Clay, as previous Secretaries of State had succeeded their chiefs. The renomination of General Jackson went against this theory. Mrs. Jackson's health was precarious, and having her mind fixed on religious matters, she strove to turn the General's in the same direction. One Sunday on the way to church, she entreated him to renounce the world, and join her at the sacred feast of the Communion. He answered that such a change would then be attributed to the desire of political effect. "Once I am clear of politics," he added, "I will join the church."

The spring of 1828 set in with great rapidity and beauty. The last week in March the atmosphere was balmy and delicious, the fields beginning to look green, the ladies to become restless, and the poor, harassed members to get sick of the tariff. That discussion still drew its slow length along. Some mixed up the Presidential question with it. Mr. Barnard of New York, in an oration on wool and woolens, showed himself a good speaker. He had caught some of the attitudes of Mr. Randolph, and used the white handkerchief rather gracefully. The fashionable season now approached its termination. The last drawing-room had been thinly attended, though several of the reigning belles were present. The star of every coterie for two weeks past had been a young lady from New Orleans. A famous *bas bleu* from the land of pan-cakes was shining in rivalry, her raiment studded with ten thousand Greek crosses, she having a true Greek accent, and looking the Sappho of the age. There was also the wealthy and magnificent Florida belle, Mrs. White, with a numerous train of admirers—a dozen orange blossoms in her hair, the mild light of the gazelle in her dark eyes, and her bust cased in glittering silver—languishing through the crowd, who retired to the right and left to permit her to pass. If met, said an admirer, walking through an orange grove in Florida, or beside one of the limpid lakes amid the eternal spring, she would instantly become an object of worship.

"Last week the Premier gave his last party for the season. The ladies were arrayed in their costliest habiliments, and the night was extremely brilliant. Soft and sweet and linguable Salem was there in all her Attic simplicity of taste and tongue and tasselated ringlets. Albany was brilliant and dashing; but what words can describe brilliant, black-eyed Baltimore, or the gay, spirituelle brunette of Georgetown! 'Can't you take cream like a gentleman?' asked a sharp-faced, fair Pennsylvanian of a Brutus who was swallowing it contrary to rule. In another quarter was one talking of the great men and great events he had seen. He had shaken hands with Jackson, eaten beefsteak with Adams, tasted pork and molasses with Webster, sipped eggnogg with Wright of Ohio, walked across the street with Van Buren, talked jokes with Clay, nodded familiarly to Everett, danced with Pennsylvania, feasted with Vermont, perambulated with New York, gallanted the Salem witches, and knew every secret of diplomacy better than Clay, and financiering than Senator Barker. Red Jacket has made no inconsiderable sensation among the fashionables. Some days ago he was sauntering round the rotunda, and, gazing listlessly on the several paintings which are going to destruction as fast as damp walls can carry them, his attention was called to a piece of carved work representing the landing of Penn and his treaty with the Delawares. Red Jacket examined it, then, with a mixture of melancholy and indignation, observed to the interpreter in his native language, that "Father Penn had not left them land enough to shoot a rifle over."

At the beginning of April, Mr. Randolph made his appearance. "After the tediousness of a month's dry siege upon sheep, molasses, hemp and whiskey, the reopening of his mouth was the opening of a honeycomb," enjoyed by the few fashionables who were determined to stay as long as Congress sat. The reply he gave to Tristram Burgess of Rhode Island, was one of the best hits of the session. Tristram was one of the famous midnight judges manufactured by John Adams, a reverend looking old gentleman, with a portion of the talent, the respectability and the wealth which was the boast of the old federalists. One of his florid harangues closed with a violent philippic against all foreigners and aliens. Rising to reply, Mr. Randolph pleaded guilty of a bias towards aliens, of no less than thirty years' standing, from the day he heard the eloquent and learned gentleman from Louisiana (Edward Livingston) deliver a speech against John Adams' alien law. The alien and sedition laws were the Castor and Pollux of that administration. "I see," he continued, "whence comes the bitterness of the gentleman from Rhode Island against the aliens. It is the ghost of the departed alien law. We—John the Second—have no longer the right to remove the aliens out of the country at our nod. Why, I say, does not the gentleman move to reënact the alien law?"

Tristram Burgess' most vindictive, true blue federal feelings were roused when he mentioned the name of Dr. Thomas Cooper of South Carolina, whom he called "a British renegado," though naturalized nearly thirty years. Every democrat knew what Dr. Cooper had suffered under the Presidency of the first Adams. He was then residing in the interior of Pennsylvania, and wrote on public affairs, and especially against some unpopular measures. For this, Dr. Cooper was arraigned before a court of federalists, and a jury, acting under the famous sedition law. He was fined and imprisoned. After that period Dr. Cooper acted with the democratic party. He became the President of the South Carolina College in Columbia, S. C.

There were at this time in Washington three daily papers: the National Intelligencer, the National Journal, and the Washington Telegraph. The first had been for years the organ of the administration, and had carried in its train its influence and patronage, and the patronage of Congress. The Journal was a mere echo to it, and both presses had been enlisted against the election of General Jackson.

A very bold innovation was made in December, upon the rule of fashion. "The famous east room has been thrown open and the dance introduced. This never has been done at the President's levee since the close of the last war. The inauguration ball will be a tremendous affair. Last Monday Mrs. Secretary Porter gave her first party. Mrs. Porter is charming, and entirely takes the lead of all the gay contemporaries of the day, now in the capital. She has been the possessor of great personal beauty, and is remarkable for an air of dignity with which her fine figure well corresponds. She sustains the administration with her spirit, her cleverness, and her versatile talents. She is perfectly acquainted with every political man, and Clay himself would not hesitate to take a lesson from her judgment. Her position as one of the most popular and influential of the court circle at Washington, was gained by her noble, sympathizing nature, and the charm of a naturalness of manner, which set others at ease in her society. In the midst of Washington gayeties this elegant Mrs. Porter said she had chiefly worn for a whole winter one black silk dress—varying cap and collar to suit different occasions." "Mr. Clay's first party for the season was held last night. Heretofore this has been considered the leading soiree, but it now falls back and takes its position behind that of the wife of the

Secretary of War. Mr. Clay says he is very much pleased with the election of General Jackson: it has afforded him much relief; and after the 4th of March, he mounts his horse, crosses the mountains, and turns farmer in Kentucky. Little Wright, of Ohio, it is said, is to be called to the bench in that State. Ichabod Bartlett, of New Hampshire, who was so well dressed last year by John S. Barbour, has cast his eye upon Governor Woodbury's seat in the Senate, if the latter should be called to Jackson's cabinet; he is therefore preparing the way by a resignation of his present seat. The English embassy is going to give Mrs. Adams a splendid ball on New Years' evening."

At another period of Mr. Adams' life, an observer wrote of him; "Adams was accustomed, when President, to rise early every morning (his habit through life) and walk from the President's house to the capitol, around the capitol square and back again, before breakfast; a distance of about four miles. This he did occasionally long afterwards, but the weakness consequent upon age and sickness, compelled him to betake himself occasionally to a carriage—a very plain affair. His habits were regular and his industry untiring. No event occurred that he did not note down in a diary kept for that purpose. He was thus prepared, if assailed, with facts known to himself, but perhaps forgotten or imperfectly remembered by his assailant. He had the appearance of great frigidity; and was seldom on terms of familiarity with any; but his feelings were warm and excitable, and when a member of the House, he manifested those feelings somewhat too frequently."

The issue of a jeu d'esprit called "The Adams Catechism, for the use of Noble Families and Good Society," created no little excitement in social circles. The sentiments were all inferences or quotations from the writings of Mr. John Adams. One or two may serve as a specimen:

"There is not in the whole Roman history so happy a period as that under the Kings." "By Kings and kingly power is meant the executive power in a single person." "Question: What is the duty of a 'practised statesman?' Answer: Not to be palsied by the will of his constituents."

A social imbroglio grew out of some remarks by the President's son at a drawing-room, which several ladies chose to resent. They retreated to a sofa in an adjoining room, and requested one of their attendants to call their carriage immediately. Mr. Adams protected his son, and the occasion was made the ground of embittered political hostility. The newspapers rang with the affair. People again remembered the equality of all persons in Jefferson's administration, and that the same principles had prevailed under the benignant reign of Mrs. Madison, continuing their influence to the close of Monroe's Presidency.

VII.

JACKSON'S ADMINISTRATION.

Jackson's Election by an overpowering Majority—Death of his Wife—His Inauguration—His Cabinet—Scandal about Mrs. Eaton—The Suitor for the President's Pipe—Conspicuous Men—Ladies of the White House—Webster's Oratory and the Farmers—Albert Gallatin and his Compeers—Description of Georgetown—Excursion to Norfolk—Fanny Wright as a Lecturer—Specific to change Negroes to white Persons—Festivities of the Capital—Jackson's celebrated Toast at a Dinner—Refusal of the Ladies to visit Mrs. Eaton—A Philadelphian who thought the Senate's rising was in Honor of him—Changes in the Cabinet—Party at Pointdexter's—Descriptions and Anecdotes of General Jackson—Threatening of Nullification—Mr. Clay and Mr. Calhoun—Death of John Randolph—His Character and last Hours—Visit of the Portuguese Minister to the President.

General Jackson was brought into office by an overpowering majority, and after a series of strong party excitements. The man of the people, he commenced his career in the war of the Revolution, when it was an honor and a pride to be a military chieftain. He was appointed by Washington, District Attorney for Tennessee, and afterwards a Judge of the Supreme Court; filling with credit seats in the House of Representatives and Senate of the United States; and in civil stations displaying strength of mind, firmness, and integrity, giving him claims to the character of a sound and able statesman. In the dark hour of peril to the country he rendered the most valuable services; he penetrated the wilderness, overcame the savage allies of our enemies, and consummated the great work by the memorable battle of New Orleans. No man but Washington ever rendered more important services. It was in his election that the old Democratic party expected to achieve its former power, union and triumph. Pennsylvania, that great pillar of the party, was firmly devoted to him; Virginia, North and South Carolina, Georgia, and several of the Western States, were equally firm; while in New York the opposing party claimed its head-quarters.

Some of the Nashville ladies were secretly preparing for Mrs. Jackson a magnificent wardrobe, to be worn at the White House. But she was to wear other robes before the accession of her husband. Her disease had been aggravated by the cruel aspersions cast on her, and in a few days she died, at the age of sixty-one. The bereaved husband was compelled to set out on his journey to Washington as President elect. His nephew accompanied him, and Mrs. Donelson, who was to preside in the Executive mansion, assisted by a beautiful and accomplished niece. The new President had a triumphal progress, and in Washington received hundreds of visitors at his rooms in the Indian Queen tavern. General Jackson's delicate attention to Mrs. Adams, and his request that she would use the Presidential mansion as long as she chose, were noticed. It was thought strange that Mr. Adams had not called on the President elect on his arrival in Washington.

A point of etiquette was discussed by the Adams leaders, and it was generally allowed that as far as regarded the forms of society and its conventional rules of etiquette—the moment the votes were counted before the Senate and the House, the President elect became the center of society. It thus became the duty of the President *de facto* to call and make him the usual compliments.

The Fourth of March, 1829, was ushered in by a grand national salute, and between ten and twelve the hum of voices and the din of life pervaded every avenue of the metropolis, the concourse of citizens and visitors choking the way to the capitol, and universal greetings and acclamations cheering the man who had triumphed over the arms and the hearts of his enemies. The procession, accompanied by hundreds of carriages, moved slowly to the senate chamber. At half-past eleven the President elect was received and conducted to his chair in the senate room; a vacant chair being set for the ex-President; the ministers and members of foreign legations were in full costume on the left, and the chairs and couches in the lobbies resplendent with beauty and fashion. As the General came forth between the columns of the portico, all hats were off at once, and the dark tint which usually pervades a mixed mass of men, was turned into the bright hue of ten thousand upturned and exultant human faces. The peal of shouting rent the air, and seemed to shake the very ground. For the last time, Chief Justice Marshall administered the oath of Presidential office. The crowd followed the President from the capitol to the

White House. Judge Story said, "The reign of King Mob seemed triumphant." Orange punch had been made by barrels full, and as the waiters opened the door to bring it out, a rush was made, the glasses were broken, the pails of liqueur upset, and general confusion prevailed. Wine and ice-cream could not be brought out to the ladies till tubs of punch were taken from the lower story into the garden, to lead off the crowd from the rooms. It was mortifying to see men with boots heavy with mud, standing on the satin-damask covered chairs to get a sight of the President.

Mr. Van Buren was appointed Secretary of State; Samuel D. Ingham of Pennsylvania, Secretary of the Treasury; John H. Eaton, Senator from Tennessee, Secretary of War; John Branch of North Carolina, of the Navy; Mr. Berrien of Georgia, Attorney General; Major William T. Barry of Kentucky, Postmaster-General. General Duff. Green was supposed to have considerable influence with the President; and Amos Kendall was taken into his confidence and began his long official career. Major Lewis, and Major Donelson the private secretary, were of importance in Washington society, and Colonel Webb of New York was supposed to be kept advised of the secrets of the White House. The episode of Mrs. Eaton, and the controversy in which the iron will of General Jackson came into conflict with the obstinate determination of the fair leaders of fashion and was forced to succumb, are well known. Major Eaton had married Mrs. Timberlake, with General Jackson's warm approval. When he was taken into the cabinet, the ladies of the other members were alarmed at the prospect of having to receive one whose name was associated with scandal into their charmed circle. Major Eaton was a stout, good-humored, agreeable man, extremely easy and cordial in his manners. His wife was said to be a strikingly beautiful and fascinating woman, all grace and vivacity. Her rooms were the resort of the ultra partisans of Jackson, and from the General's earnest defence of her, it was supposed that her favor was the indispensable preliminary to preferment.

A confidential clerk of Mr. Van. Buren's illustrated his diplomacy by mentioning that one morning when he called, he found him writing, and was presently told to read the letter and say what he thought of it. "I will tell you what I think, Mr. Van Buren," he answered, "if you will tell me what it is about." "Then it will do: it will answer," said the Secretary, folding the letter.

One day when President Jackson was smoking in his private office, a member of Congress, who had set his heart on a foreign mission, having obtained a clue to one of the General's weaknesses, came in and begged as the greatest favor, one of his pipes as a relic for his old father at home. The General, laughing, rang the bell and ordered two or three clean ones. "Excuse me," said the member, "but may I ask you for the very pipe you have just been smoking!" When the General was about to empty it of the ashes, he was again interrupted with "No, General, don't throw out the tobacco, I want the pipe just as it left your lips." He folded it carefully in paper, thanked the giver, and left the room. In less than a month he started on his mission, and "it was that pipe that did the business for him."

One of General Jackson's friends, invited to dine with him, mentions that every guest was provided with two forks; one of steel, the other of silver. The President adhered to the primitive metal.

Postmaster-General Barry seemed to possess extraordinary abilities, active business habits and exact knowledge of men and things. He was rather above the ordinary stature, but thin in face and form. With an extremely modest deportment, he maintained strong indications of energy. His voice was melodious, and his conversation fluent and to the point. He was called a great orator. Mrs. Barry was frank, yet lady-like, free from affectation, with a fine person and agreeable manners. Major-General Macomb, lately promoted to the command of the army, while Generals Gaines and Scott were his competitors, was young in appearance, and frank and unreserved in manner. He seemed disposed to yield to others rather than assume any superiority in consequence of his high military rank, modestly waiting for any place at the table, or in the train of the President. Majors Donelson and Hays, nephews of the President, were good-looking, stout young men, above the ordinary height, and well-proportioned, with manly and modest deportment; just such men as General Jackson might be supposed to attach to his person. Major Donelson was named Andrew Jackson, after the President. Mrs. Donelson was beautiful, dignified, and very gracious in demeanor. Her only son, a lovely boy of three years old, was the pet of his uncle the President. Indeed all the children received the notice of the Chief Magistrate; even the little barefooted boys had cause to know his regard for children.

Miss Eustice, a niece of the President, was admired for her unaffected and easy deportment. The two Commodores Rodgers and Warrington were excellent specimens of navy officers; both possessing that sound judgment and good common sense notion of things which mark the practical man. General Gibson, an old companion in arms of General Jackson, should not be passed unnoticed. He was one of the modest, discreet, sensible men, who, without much parade, think deeply and do a great deal. He was a universal favorite, especially with the ladies. Young Van Buren, the son of the Secretary of State, was described as having a youthful and manly appearance that gave great interest to his situation, and as possessing extensive and varied knowledge. There was nothing supercilious about him; but on the contrary a modesty becoming his years, and an intelligence beyond the ordinary acquirements of young men. Mrs. Jackson was the wife of the General's adopted son and private secretary, and a very pretty woman, but seemed to prefer the tranquillity of domestic life to the glare and splendor of official rank. The idea was unfounded that any jealousy existed between her and Mrs. Donelson in relation to the favor of the President.

Mr. Monroe died in the first term of the administration of President Jackson. Chief Justice Marshall died in Philadelphia in July, 1835, having been Chief Justice of the Supreme Court of the United States thirty-five years; presiding, as Randolph said "with native dignity and unpretending grace." He had solid judgment and great reasoning powers; an acute and penetrating mind, with manners and habits to suit the purity and sanctity of the ermine. Seen by a stranger, he would be taken for a modest country gentleman, ready to take the lowest place in company; closely observed, he would be seen to be a gentleman of finished breeding and winning conversation.

William B. Giles of Virginia also died during Jackson's Presidency. He was esteemed by Randolph the Charles Fox of our House of Representatives: the most accomplished debater in the country. Macon was wise, Randolph brilliant, Gallatin and Madison able in argument: Giles was the ready champion, always ripe for the combat. He was a gentleman in manner and heart, and intimate with all the eminent men of his day. Describing the three great Senators in Jackson's Presidency, Mr. Goodrich said: "They were all of remarkable personal appearance: Webster of massive form, dark complexion, and thoughtful, solemn countenance: Clay tall, of rather slight frame, but keen, flexible features, and singular ease and freedom in his attitudes, walk and gestures: Calhoun tall, erect, and rigid in form, his eyes grayish blue, and flashing from beneath a brow at once imperious and scornful. Clay, Calhoun and Pinkney, King, Dwight and Daggett, stand as high examples of personal endowment in our annals; yet not one approached Mr. Webster in the commanding power of their personal presence. There was a grandeur in his form, an intelligence in his deep, dark eye, a loftiness in his expansive brow, a significance in his arched lip, beyond those of any other human being I ever saw." Two old farmers, who listened to an oration by Webster, sat with their mouths open from beginning to end. When it was over, they rose, and drawing a long breath, one said to the other: "Well, that was good; every word seemed to weigh a pound!"

Others were grouped as "John Taylor of Caroline, an able Virginian statesman, the personification of old-fashioned dignity and courtesy; Albert Gallatin, a dark, swarthy man, whose eye seemed to penetrate the souls of all who approached him; Henry R. Storrs, one of the ablest debaters of his day; General Hayne, the gallant jouster with Mr. Webster; Burgess of Rhode Island, a man of prodigious powers of sarcasm, who made even John Randolph quail; Silas Wright of New York, ever courteous, ever smiling—a giant in strength, conquering his antagonists with such good humor as to reconcile them to defeat."

Mr. Goodrich dining with Mr. Forsyth, met Mr. Benton, Isaac Hill, John M. Niles, and others. After the ladies had retired to the parlor, some of the gentlemen lingered at the table. Mr. Forsyth was in the parlor, receiving them as they came from the dining-room. Benton, Hill and Niles, came at last; Hill, who was lame, said good-night and went to the door; Benton, an old courtier, paid his respects to the ladies, beginning with Mrs. Meigs, the mother of Mr. Forsyth: Niles, in approaching the ladies, was seized with a panic of bashfulness. Pulling out a red bandanna handkerchief, he gave a loud blast upon his nose, shot out of the door, and effected his retreat.

In May, 1829, the Hon. Louis McLane was in Washington, preparing to proceed to England. His daughter came with him, to remain with the ladies of the President's family. Mr. James A. Hamilton was performing the duties of Under Secretary of State, or rather Chief Clerk of the State Department. Washington Irving was very intimate in the family of Mr. McLane, and sent messages to the minister's wife so frequently, that an idea of her elevated character may be formed from his expressions of regard and admiration.

Mrs. Louis McLane was the daughter of Robert Milligan, and married the son of Allan McLane, of Delaware, in 1812. After being sent as minister to England in 1829, he had charge of the Treasury and State Departments. One of their daughters married General Joseph Johnson; another the grandson of Alexander Hamilton.

Neither Van Buren nor the President had ever been placed in situations where they could have made themselves familiar with all the papers belonging to the Department of State, and the details of business connected with our foreign relations. It had been different with other Presidents. Washington had Mr. Jefferson, who began his political career with the commencement of all our republican institutions. He had helped to frame the constitution, and had been a foreign minister shortly after it went into operation. Jefferson was made President after being thus drilled in all our foreign affairs. He was familiar with the business of the Department of State and with our foreign relations. He selected Mr. Madison, who had the same familiarity with both home and foreign affairs. Madison selected Mr. Monroe, who had also been a foreign minister. Mr. Monroe chose Mr. Adams, who had been a foreign minister for a long time. After serving eight years in the Department of State he was made President. He selected Mr. Clay, to whom he could impart his knowledge of the papers and the details of the office. The first two Presidents had assisted in laying the foundation of the Republic. The four following ones had all served in the Department of State and could render any assistance to a newly appointed minister. General Jackson only had not the advantage of familiarity with offices. Besides this, Mr. Van Buren had to fit out more foreign ministers, than any Secretary of State had ever done in the same time. He had to furnish three or four with instructions on most important subjects. His proving himself equal to the great occasion, tested his character, and his fertility in resources.

In January, 1830, there were three Presidents of the United States at Washington—Monroe, Adams and Jackson. Mr. Adams had taken up his residence there on account of the mildness of the climate and the ill health of some of his family. Mr. Monroe was on his way home from the Virginia Convention, full of years, sorrow and disease.

"Who that has ever visited Georgetown, our sister city, has not admired the beauty of her situation! Sailing up the majestic Potomac, the town is presented to you on the north, rising hill over hill, and displaying the extended rows of streets, and further on the beautiful moss-covered grounds and variegated foliage that enclose its rear; the seventh and highest hill crowning the amphitheatre around the town. Approaching by the Fredericktown road, the town appears compact below, the Potomac seen for ten or twelve miles. In a further range the eye takes in the city of Washington, with the White House, the Capitol, and the public buildings on one side of the river, and Alexandria on the other, about seven miles below. The setting sun shining on the windows of Georgetown, gives it the effect of an illuminated city."

In July, the President went with a party to Norfolk. There were his private secretaries, Majors Donelson and Hays, Mrs. Donelson and Miss Eaton, the Secretary of War and his wife, the Secretary of the Navy and his daughters, the Misses Branch, the Postmaster-General and his wife, Major-General Macomb and his daughter, Lieutenant Van Buren, aid-de-camp to General Macomb, General Bernard of the Board of Engineers, Commodores Rodgers and Warrington of the board of Navy Commissioners, and others, in all about fifty. The steamer took the party down the Potomac to Alexandria, where crowds on the wharf saluted them; cannons were fired from the ships and the artillery companies saluted from the head of the docks.

After a reception of visitors at the landing, the vessel proceeded to Fort Washington, a fortification opposite Mount Vernon; the commandant, Major Mason, received the President with due honors, and conducted the party into the Fort. The ladies were entertained by Mrs. Mason and the wives of the other officers. The party proceeded to Old Point Comfort, where they landed the next afternoon. Colonel House, the commandant of Fortress Monroe, came with other officers to welcome them. The concourse of visitors was very great, and the display of fireworks very entertaining. Hon. Mr. Branch—the Secretary of the Navy—was tall and well-proportioned, graceful in his gestures and affable and kindly in his manners. His daughters possessed a full share of beauty and accomplishments, with retiring modesty.

Miss Fanny Wright, about this time, had attracted much public attention by her lectures, given in the principal cities. She was undoubtedly one of the most singular women of the age. Possessing intellectual powers of the first order, and fervid eloquence, undaunted in the advocacy of her views, and reckless of public opinion, in an ignorant age she might have stirred up disturbance, and shaken society to its foundation. Among the warm admirers of her eloquence were Ming, Blatchley, Tom Skidmore and other originators of the "Military Hall" party. They took advantage of the excitement produced by her lectures to avow their own bold principles. A scientific quack issued an advertisement to the ladies and gentlemen of color, offering to them a newly invented chemical agent, warranted to wash them white in six hours. Dinah, one of Miss Wright's favorite disciples, exclaimed, on hearing of it, "Guy, massa, spose eberybody's skin white as yellowbaster, what den! Guy, massa, Massa Wilberforce and de phillanthreefists no care one cent about us after dat. Hah! we all no better dan de white people den!" The following extract is from a private manuscript letter:—

"WASHINGTON, Feb. 18th, 1830.

. . . . "The 22d comes next Monday. Wonderful preparations are making: the theatre to be converted into a spacious ball-room, and most beautifully ornamented; the upper row of boxes to be enclosed as a supper-room, &c.; tickets five dollars. There are two other balls on the same evening; one at Carusi's at one dollar per head, and another at the Masonic Hall. General Harrison arrived here last Friday. Colonel Torrens is expected in a day or two. You know they say he is engaged to Miss Vail. Expectation waits on tip-toe the result of their meeting. What a loss she would be to Washington, she being one of the most accomplished of our ladies!

"We are almost destitute of beaux this winter. Our neighbor, the Baron, and his secretary, seem to be among the most highly esteemed. There were parties every evening last week. At Mrs. Dickens' on Monday evening; she has Miss Bainbridge passing the winter with her. At Lieutenant Williams' on Tuesday evening. In that very small house next Lieutenant Turnbull's, they gave five hundred invitations. On Wednesday evening Madame Huygens appeared in all her glory in a very full, light-colored silk dress, a very broad blonde flounce around the bottom, and an immensely high and broad head-dress, composed of blonde, feathers and flowers. The new Mexican minister made his first appearance there, accompanied by the Secretary of Legation and Mr. Rivafinoli, decked out in all his orders. Mrs. O'Sullivan was also there, looking sweetly amiable upon all who approached her. Mr. Van Buren was very attentive to her, as, I believe, he always is. Miss Temple and Miss Duer seemed the reigning stars of the evening. Waltzing is getting more in vogue every day. . . . Mrs. White of Florida, he (Mr. Harding), has taken in a royal purple velvet mantle trimmed with fur; it is very pretty, but wants her intellectual expression.

"Feb. 28th.—Last evening I made my first appearance in the world of fashion. We went first to a small party at Mrs. Rush's; found her seated at the tea-table, which was spread with a variety of silver articles and some very beautiful china. One of the most conspicuous guests was Mr. Rivafinoli, an Italian by birth; but having resided in almost every other country, he seems to have acquired a little manner from each. He is engaged here to examine the country about Fredericksburg, and work the gold mine there. At nine o'clock we went to Baron Krudener's little party. We were received in the front parlor down stairs, and danced in the back room, and in the little portico we had a very neat supper. The Kerrs and Munroes were there. There were two brides—Mrs. Augustus Pleasanton (a runaway match, she being a rich heiress from Philadelphia) and Mrs. Hays. . . . The Baron danced a cotillion with Mrs. Commodore Stewart's little daughter. Mr. Krehmer was out of spirits, perhaps because Miss Duer did not arrive until after ten o'clock, she having just returned from a dinner party at Mr. Calvert's. Miss Silsbee wore a yellow satin dress, trimmed around the bottom with two rows of old-fashioned black lace, such as our grandmothers wore in times of old; then there was a row of the same around her belt, her sleeves and the neck of the dress. Mrs. Silsbee had a white muslin dress, white satin bodice with a very low point before, and a large white satin cape close around the throat and falling over the shoulders. There is a great dearth of beaux.

"March 7th.— . . . . We had a large dinner-party yesterday. Some of your friends were here, such as Mr. Vaughan, Barons Krudener and Stackelberg, Count de Menou, Mr. Van Buren, Mr. Rush, President Adams, &c. Mr. Van Buren had an immensely crowded house at his ball on Friday evening. Miss Easten made her first appearance there, having been in mourning all winter. The Secretary of War and lady were there. They were also at Mr. Vaughan's ball last Monday. I have never yet met with *her* this winter; Count de Menou told me that he should not invite her. He has given verbal invitations for Tuesday evening.

"What do you think of Mr. Alexander's having been offered five hundred dollars for your picture by a young gentleman, who promised never to divulge the secret that he had it in his possession! He said he would have a case made for it with a strong lock and key, and no one should ever suspect that he had it. Mr. A. refused most decidedly.

"JULIA M. D. T."

It had been a custom in Washington for twenty years to celebrate the birthday of Thomas Jefferson

—April 13,—as the apostle of Democracy. General Jackson being regarded by his party as the great restorer and exemplifier of Jefferson's principles, it was desired to celebrate the festival in 1830 with more than usual eclat. The President, Vice-President, Cabinet, and many leading men were invited to a grand banquet. It was a subscription dinner. General Jackson gave a volunteer toast that electrified the country and became historical: "Our Federal Union: it must be preserved." This sentiment was received by the public as a proclamation from the President to announce a plot against the Union and summon the people to its defence.

Notwithstanding the President's vindication of Mrs. Eaton, the ladies of Washington refused to receive or visit her. Mrs. Donelson braved her uncle's anger, and was sent back to Tennessee, with her husband, for her contumacy; not returning for six months. Mr. Van Buren, a widower, who had no daughters, called on Mrs. Eaton, and made parties for her. He induced Mr. Vaughan, the British minister, and Baron Krudener, the Russian minister—both bachelors—to do the same, and she occupied the post of honor at the President's side, at a grand dinner given in the palace. But all availed nothing; the female leaders of the ton were inflexible; their opposition rent society into sets, introduced discord into the cabinet, and finally led to its dissolution.

Mr. Francis P. Blair of Kentucky was engaged to edit a paper which should be the government organ. He was slight in person, retiring and quiet in manner and amiable in character. When he first came to

Washington in obedience to the summons, he was almost moneyless, with only a frock coat, and had a great gash on the side of his head from an overset in the road. Going to dine with the President, he found a company of ambassadors and other high functionaries, superbly dressed, in the east room. "The tails of his uncomfortable frock coat hung heavily upon the stranger, who shrunk into a corner abashed. The President sought him out, placed him at his right hand, and completely won his heart. Thus sprang the Globe into existence."

On May, 1830, a soi-disant leader in the fashionable world went to Washington. He wished to see the Senate, and made his entrance at the side door, at the very moment the full, rapid tones of the Vice-President were heard—saying: "The Senators in favor of the motion will please to rise."

Half the Senate rose as the man of fashion was entering. "Gentlemen" he cried—"pray don't rise! do be seated." Again rose the voice of the Vice-President, putting the negative of the question. The other portion of the Senate rose. This mark of condescension overwhelmed the leader of the ton. "Why, really, gentlemen," he said, "you do me too much honor; let me beg you to be seated." When he returned to the banks of the Schuylkill, he told his friends that the Senate of the United States was composed of the politest gentlemen he had ever seen.

At the time of General Jackson's election, four gentlemen who stood preëminent in the political ranks, were indicated for the succession: Clay and Webster, Calhoun and Van Buren: the first two political opponents of the General; the two latter his friends. Van Buren retired from the cabinet, received the appointment of minister to London, and immediately left the United States. On the evening of the day when the news of his rejection as minister was heralded in London, he was at a party at Prince Talleyrand's, the representative of the new King Louis Philippe. He received distinguished attentions; apparently gave himself no trouble about what had happened; came home, was taken up by the people and elected successively Vice-President and President.

The changes in the cabinet took place in 1831. Edward Livingston of Louisiana agreed to accept the post of Secretary of State. Louis McLane was recalled from England for the Treasury; Judge White of Tennessee was selected for Major Eaton's place; and Mr. Levi Woodbury was to be Secretary of the Navy. Judge White declined the post offered him; and a new man was summoned to the councils, Lewis Cass, Governor of the Territory of Michigan, who became Secretary of War. Roger B. Taney was made Attorney General.

The session commencing in 1831 was the great one of Jackson's administration, and the most exciting and important one held since the earliest years of the Republic. Mr. Parton says truly that illustrious names, great debates, extraordinary incidents, momentous measures, combined to render it memorable.

General Jackson's hospitality at Washington was as liberal as it had been at the Hermitage, though it compelled him to eke out his salary by drawing on his farm proceeds, and to pay for many dinners with his cotton crop. An English writer described him as tall, bony and thin, with erect military bearing, and "a gamecock-look all over him." Energy marked the lines of his face, and he had a penetrating and sage look. "His eye is of a dangerous fixedness, deep-set, and overhung by bushy gray eyebrows; his features are long, with strong, ridgy lines running through his cheeks; his forehead is seamed, and his white hair, stiff and wiry, brushed obstinately back, and worn with an expression of bristling bayonets. In his mouth there is a redeeming suavity when he speaks; but the instant his lips close, a vizor of steel would scarcely look more impenetrable. His manners are dignified, and have been called high-bred and aristocratic by travelers; they are the model of republican simplicity and straightforwardness."

Nicholas P. Trist of Virginia, who had married one of Jefferson's grand-daughters, was at one time General Jackson's secretary, and much attached to him. Mr. Buchanan used to relate how a daughter of Charles Carroll, returning from a residence in England, where she was admitted into the circles of the highest aristocracy, called on President Jackson at an hour he had appointed. Going a few minutes before, Mr. Buchanan found the President at work in his office, and not dressed or shaved. He reminded him of the expected visit; the General retorted by saying he "once heard tell of a man in Tennessee, who made a fortune by minding his own business!" He then left the room, and in a few minutes walked into the parlor as neat in appearance as if he had passed hours at the toilet.

The storm of Nullification threatened the Union. A letter dated January, 1833, says, at Washington, "Dark and portentous are the clouds which overshadow our land. Deep and settled anxiety is depicted in the countenance of every thinking man. To-morrow Congress will be called upon by a report from the Judiciary Committee of the Senate to surrender to General Jackson the use, at his discretion, of all the civil, naval and military force of the nation."*

The coalition formed between Mr. Clay and Mr. Calhoun in 1833 was pronounced by Benton "only a hollow truce," and kept alive by their mutual interest. The rupture took place in a few years, in open Senate; and it became a question between them which, with respect to General Jackson and Mr. Van Buren, had the upper hand of the other. Mr. Calhoun declared he had Mr. Clay down on his back; that he was his master. Mr. Clay retorted, "He my master! I would not own him for the meanest of my slaves."

A newspaper correspondent thus gives a *jeu d'esprit*, which he designs to be significant of tendencies at the capital at this crisis:—

"I know that Mr. Webster dined the other day at the White House, in company with Isaac Hill, and that the dishes were so cooked in the French style that neither the great man from the Bay State nor the great man from the Granite State could eat much. I argue from all this that the coalition between President Jackson and Mr. Webster is perfect. Indeed, Mr. W. sat by General Jackson at table, and they conversed confidentially! The other day I saw Mr. Calhoun and Mr. Clay shake hands and smile complacently upon each other; from which I have no doubt that Mr. Calhoun is trying to conciliate Mr. Clay, and bring him over to a coalition, and the South and the West against the North and New England. I know that Edward Everett, the other evening, went to the theatre to see Miss Fanny Kemble, and that Mr. Livingston stood up in the pit almost the whole evening. I know that Mr. Bankhead asked Mr. Clay and the Kembles to dine with him, and that Mr. Clay was wonderfully pleased with Miss Kemble. I suspected from all this that Mr. Bankhead was about to bribe Mr. Clay to surrender the American system to British interests; and as Mr. Clay was at this moment a disap-

The so-called "Compromise" designed for the relief of both, was managed by outside politicians.

John Randolph of Roanoke died at Philadelphia in the summer of 1833. It was in that city that he had commenced his brilliant parliamentary career, under the first Adams. For more than thirty years he had been the political meteor of Congress, blazing with splendor undiminished. After a flow of wit and classic allusion for hours at a time, a friend remarked: "He has wasted intellectual jewelry enough here this evening to equip many speakers for great orations." After his return from the Russian mission, and when he was in full view of death, a friend heard him read the chapter in the Revelations on the opening of the seals, with great power and beauty of voice and delivery, and depth of pathos. At the opening of the sixth seal, he stopped; laid the book open on his breast as he lay on his bed, and began a discourse on the beauty and sublimity of the Scriptural writings.

---

pointed politician, he imagined a dinner might bring him over, or, if not, that British gold could be added. I know that Mr. McDuffie wears an outer garment not so elegant as it might be. I know that at M. Serrurier's party Mr. Webster carried on a long flirtation in a cluster of young ladies. I know that Washington Irving is here somewhere, but none of us will ever find him out. I know that John Quincy Adams and Henry Clay talked together an hour the other day, very earnestly, from which I infer that great mischief is brewing. I know that Mr. Livingston gives elegant dinners, and that his wines are the best in the city. I know that Mr. Calhoun is a very fast walker and a very fast talker; few can keep up with him, either in the one or the other. I know that Mr. Ward is the chief beau in Congress, and is a great favorite with the ladies. I know that Senator Benton and Editor Blair walked together up to the Capitol the other day, and that both talked very earnestly about something. I know that Mr. Pointdexter drives in fine style four cream-colored horses. I know that the *bon ton* is divided into two great parties; one contending that Miss Fanny Kemble has grossly slandered the Americans, and the other doubting the assertion, or arguing that, as she is a woman, she ought to be treated well on the stage, &c."

According to Baillie Peyton, when McLane was Secretary of State, a new minister arrived from Lisbon, and a day was appointed for him to be presented to the President. The hour was set, and McLane expected the minister to call at the State department: but the Portuguese had misunderstood Mr. McLane's French, and he proceeded alone to the White House. He rang the bell, and the door was opened by the Irish porter, Jimmy O'Neil. "Je suis venu voir Monsieur le President," said the minister. "What the deuce does he mean! muttered Jimmy. "He says President, though, and I suppose he wants to see the General." "Oui, oui," said the Portuguese, bowing. Jimmy ushered him into the green room, where the General was smoking his corn-cob pipe with great composure. The minister made his bow to the President, and addressed him in French, of which the General did not understand a word. "What does the fellow say, Jimmy?" said he. "De'il knows, sir: I reckon he's a furriner." "Try him in Irish, Jimmy," said Old Hickory. Jimmy gave him a touch of the genuine Milesian, but the minister only shrugged his shoulders with the usual "Plait il?" "Och!" exclaimed Jimmy, "he can't go the Irish, sir. He's French to be sure!" "Send for the French cook, and let him try if he can find out what the gentleman wants." The cook was hurried from the kitchen, sleeves rolled up, apron on, and the carving-knife in his hand. The Minister seeing this formidable apparition, and doubting he was in the presence of the Head of the Nation, feared some treachery, and made for the door, before which Jimmy planted himself to keep him in. When the cook, by the General's order, asked who he was, and what he wanted, and he gave a subdued answer, the President discovered his character. At this juncture McLane came in, and the minister was presented in due form. It is said General Jackson always resented allusion to this incident.

Some time in Jackson's second term the celebrated Gaines suit was commenced. This case is the most remarkable one in the history of American jurisprudence. Myra Clark was born in New Orleans—the only child of the wealthy aristocrat—Daniel Clark, and became a very beautiful girl. She was taken away in her childhood after her father's death, by persons interested in claiming the property to which she was the lawful heiress, and was brought up to womanhood in ignorance of her real parentage and her rights. Three months before her marriage with Mr. Whitney, her first husband, a discovery was made of the mysterious circumstances of her birth and history, and her title to the possession of millions—by her father's last will naming her sole legatee, and by her heiress-ship as his only legitimate child. With the aid of her husband she entered on the prosecution of her claims with an earnestness and perseverance without parallel, undismayed by obstacles and embarrassments that might have appalled the most heroic. Her faith knew no faltering and her courage shrank from no sacrifice. She was not actuated by a desire for wealth so much as a determination to vindicate the honor of her parents and the stainlessness of her birth. After many years of labors long foiled, of heroic sacrifices, and of a struggle that would have exhausted the vigor and even hopes of an ordinary person, rising from every partial defeat with strength renewed, and re-entering on the strife with a firm reliance on the justice of her cause, Myra Clark Gaines achieved a victory that commanded the admiration and sympathy of the whole country. The Supreme Court of the United States decided the case in her favor, against the city of New Orleans and other incumbents on her property. The Supreme Court of Louisiana, recognizing the justice of her claim, ordered the last will of Daniel Clark—charged to have been fraudulently destroyed—to be admitted to probate and executed. But though invested with an unquestionable title to an estate of millions, the law's delay and vexatious suits continued to interpose between her and the fruits of her well-earned victory; while the civil war postponed her possession of her own. With patience unabated and heroic hopefulness, she waited for the resumption of the jurisdiction of the Supreme Court of the United States over appeals from Louisiana. She ought now to enjoy her success without further legal contention. But with a whole city in opposition and hundreds of purchasers whose titles are invalidated by her paramount right, there are still difficulties to overcome.

MRS. MYRA CLARK GAINES.

VIII.

JACKSON'S ADMINISTRATION.

Party at Secretary Woodbury's—Social Etiquette—The President crowded from his own Table—Popular Churches—Mr. Cass's Party—New Year's Levee—Amos Kendall—Mrs. Florida White—Presidential Ball and Supper—Mrs. Huntington—Mrs. Johnston—Mrs. Benton's Coteries—Miss Cora Livingston—Memoir of Mrs. Benton—Her Succor of a poor Girl—The mad Woman's attempt to kill her, to save her from the Ills of Life—Mr. Benton's timely Interposition—Mrs. Benton's Liberation of her Slaves—Curious scene of the Execution of the Expunging Resolution—"Spat" between Mr. Buchanan and Mr. Clay—Society and Manners in Washington—Etiquette of Parties—Amusing Account of a fashionable Soiree—The rough Kentuckian and his "Jane"—The deaf foreign Minister and the Belle—Nicholas Biddle—Tableau party in Georgetown—The eccentric Secretary of the Navy—Gorgeous Fancy Ball—First attempt at a Masquerade—Mrs. Forsythe's Parties—Mrs. Woodbury's—Brilliant one in Baltimore—Miss Martineau and her Tube—Santa Anna—Scene in the Gallery—Judges of the Supreme Court—Scene in the Library—The Big Cheese—Amusing Anecdotes of Jackson's Determination—Memoir of Mrs. Edward Livingston—Memoir of Mrs. Levi Woodbury.

"WHAT the Secretaries are to do with the ten thousand applications for the freedom of their drawing-rooms, I cannot imagine," was the exclamation of a visitor at the close of 1835. The gay season opened with a party at Secretary Woodbury's. The lady presided with great dignity and grace. Several dashing belles from Baltimore, Alexandria and Georgetown, were present. The President had a long consultation with the ladies of the several high departments, and came to the conclusion to change the etiquette of the season. The custom of dining the members had fatigued the old hero, and the promiscuous assemblage of the levees annoyed him. The evening before Christmas he gave a splendid ball and supper, to a select invited company. The guests assembled at nine, the ball was in the east room, the supper ready in the west room by eleven, and the company dispersed before half-past twelve. The fashionables were delighted with this party. "A little set of exclusives is now formed under the immediate patronage of the President, who has set himself to the grand object of separating the true and acknowledged fashion and rank of the community from contact with those who are not exactly of the right sort. The social institutions of Washington have too long, in his estimation, borne a resemblance to the political institutions of the country, and admitted respectable persons from every quarter of the country, without a very rigid scrutiny into their pretensions as people of fashion. The system is now to be changed. The scale established by the President is peculiarly arbitrary; for instance, clerks with three thousand dollars salary are invited; those of two thousand are excluded. On Friday the public New Year's levee is to be held; and to that the Irish laborers, &c., are to be admitted, in their shirt sleeves, as heretofore." "Andrew the First will give an exclusive ball and supper, once a fortnight, hereafter, till the weather is too hot for dancing and squeezing." Again: "The President has determined to give no more 'exclusives.' The last one was a shocking exhibition. The members of Congress brought ladies, and members came from every part of the city and vicinity without invitation, and pushed their way in. Sixteen hundred persons were computed to have been present, and, of course, the rooms were crowded to suffocation. The President handed Mrs. Forsythe to the upper room; but the mob rushed past him, and excluded him from the table. 'Well,' said he, very properly offended, 'this is the first time that I was ever shut out from my own table, and it shall be the last.'"

Mr. Cass had given a splendid party at his residence to close the year, attended by all the fashionables. The New Years' levee at the President's was densely crowded; all the foreign ambassadors, consuls and chargés being there in their brilliant costumes, army and navy officers in full uniform, members, citizens, etc. The President, flanked on either side by Webster and Van Buren, looked the picture of happiness. Amos Kendall was present, but none of the clerks of his department. The levee closed at two, to the regret of many, who knew this was the last levee of the season, and that to the private parties which are henceforth to be the order of the day, they cannot be admitted.

"Mrs. White, of Florida, is here, and report says she intends introducing a new style of everything. She has but lately returned from France, and there is no doubt that she will bear the palm from all party givers."

Early in February General Scott, in Florida with

General Clinch, General Curtiss, General Gaines and General Macomb, called for five thousand men to carry on his operations against the Indians. Major Van Buren—son of the Vice-President, was appointed Scott's aid-de-camp. The General informed the gallant Major that he might sometimes be obliged to sleep out in the swamps all night, and that therefore he had better provide himself with a suit of India rubber. Accordingly Major Van Buren got himself equipped from head to foot; remarking to the shop man: "I am going to Florida, and may want a few more yards of your cloth for sheets; if so, I will get my father to frank them to me." The incredulous ladies declared they would wear all the scalps sent home by the Major, and, like Beatrice, eat all the Indians of his killing. On the 11th February, General Jackson gave a magnificent ball and supper: the whole palace being thrown open, and music, dancing and flirtation enlivening the scene. All the leading opposition members were present, except the nullifiers. The President was in high spirits. He had got the news of the adoption of the expunging resolutions by the Virginia House of Delegates.

The lady usually called Mrs. "Florida White," because her husband, Colonel White, represented Florida, was celebrated for her magnificent beauty and intellectual accomplishments, throughout the Gulf States. She was Ellen Adair, the daughter of Governor Adair, of Kentucky. Her sister, Mrs. Benjamin F. Pleasants, was also greatly admired in Washington society. These were two of the seven daughters of Governor Adair, all of whom were women of mark for beauty and talents. Mrs. White's cousin, Mrs. Fitzhugh, was a courted belle in Washington in 1842. She was tall and splendidly proportioned, possessing a commanding dignity of mien, with faultless grace in every movement. She was fair, with blue eyes, and her dark brown hair fell in heavy waves almost to her feet. Refined intelligence illumined her beautiful face; her eloquence in conversation was fascinating, and the elegance of high breeding harmonized in her with feminine gentleness. She was the daughter of Dr. Rudd, of Kentucky. Her second husband was Mr. E. M. Huntington, Commissioner of the general land office in Washington. President Tyler offered him the position of Judge of the United States Court in Indiana.

The house of Mrs. Josiah S. Johnston, of Louisiana, was noted for its hospitality. Edward Livingston was not only an associate of Johnston in their public career, but an intimate friend; and their friendship was never interrupted. Mrs. Johnston's second husband was Henry D. Gilpin, of Pennsylvania, who became Solicitor of the Treasury and Attorney General after the election of Van Buren to the Presidency. Richard Henry Wilde, of Georgia, was prominent for some time in the society of this period. His poetical genius, and literary accomplishments, rendered him distinguished.

One of the most admired belles in Washington during General Jackson's administration was Miss Cora Livingston. She married Thomas Barton, who went as Secretary of Legation with Mr. Edward Livingston on the mission to France; was left as Chargé des Affaires when Livingston returned, and came to the United States in 1836, bringing water for the fire between Jackson and Louis Philippe. The beautiful Mrs. Ashley—afterwards Mrs. Crittenden, was also the star of the most brilliant circles, and Miss Octavia Walton from the South, was a celebrity for her gifts and accomplishments.

The coteries of Mrs. Thomas H. Benton were always composed of the most distinguished persons in Washington. Chief-Justice Marshall, Mr. Randolph, Chief-Justice Taney, Mr. Mason of North Carolina, Mr. Archer, Mr. Van Buren, and many others, with her own relatives, formed her select circles, which were historical in this administration. She was the daughter of Colonel James McDowell, and related to half the first families of Virginia.

Mrs. Benton came to Washington soon after her marriage, and for more than twenty years was one of the most distinguished members of its society. Mr. Benton's position as leader of the powerful and victorious Democratic party, and her own as belonging to one of the most prominent Virginia families, added to the influence exercised by her own force of character and the rare vigor of her mental faculties. Mr. Benton was one of the fortunate public men in whose homes the domestic altar is a sacred fact and not a figure. The repose and strength gained in such a home makes so much a part of the power of a man's public life, that it should not be omitted in speaking of him. The families of both were connected with the most noted in the State, the Prestons, Madisons, Peytons, Randolphs, &c. Many members of Mrs.

Benton's family were conspicuous in the country's history. She first entered society in Richmond while General James Preston was Governor of Virginia; and everything bore the stamp of its English origin, the conservative feeling being very strong in the neighborhood of the young lady's home. Yet her mind, gifted with rare force, saw for itself, and convictions gained strength which governed her own life and shaped the principles and fortunes of her children. Accustomed to the most liberal hospitality in her father's house, spending every summer at the then chief watering-place of the country—the White Sulphur Springs, while the winters were passed in Richmond—traveling to and fro in her own carriage imported from London—a big, yellow chariot lined with red morocco, christened Cinderella's pumpkin by the next generation—with maid and men-servants, harness and saddle horses—endowed with health and high spirits, having no experience of grief or want to give her insight into the needs of others,—there came to this young heart the conviction that there must be another side to the repulsive tales she had heard associated with "liberal views." Her marriage took place at the time Missouri was admitted as a State, and the law was made providing against the extension of slavery beyond its borders. In all that belonged to large and humane measures Mrs. Benton took part, and brought her influence and talents to bear especially on the subject that had forced itself on her mind—the emancipation of the negro race. Prominent southerners of that time looked to gradual emancipation and colonization. Chief-Justice Marshall, Mr. Randolph, Mr. Macon of North Carolina, Francis Key, and Mr. Pinckney of Maryland, William C. Preston of South Carolina, Mr. King of Alabama, and Dr. Linn of Missouri, were among those anxious for such a remedy for an evil felt to be growing and threatening. Mrs. Benton not only gave her slaves their freedom, but a support till they were able to maintain themselves. Colonel Benton sanctioned this not only from conviction, but for "the honor he bore his dear ladye." He refused the bequest of a plantation and slaves from a brother who died in Louisiana.

Mrs. Benton had other sacrifices to make for conscience sake. She was one of nine Presbyterians who met for worship over a saddler's shop in St. Louis, then a mere village settled by French and Catholics, to whose prejudices the newer settlers conformed. The form of religious service to which Mrs. Benton attached herself was esteemed vulgar, but she gave to its support her position, wealth, talents, and her example of true piety. Her charities and co-operation in all good works left such an abiding impression, that in the early part of the civil war, many contributions of clothing, wine and other comforts for the hospitals, were sent to her daughter Mrs. Fremont, with a line or message to say they were not sent, to the wife of an "Abolition officer," but to the daughter of Mrs. Benton, who in her day had helped all without distinction of religion.

Thus passed this useful and brilliant life—alternating between her early home in Virginia, and her winter home in Washington; with visits to her house in St. Louis, and with her husband in New Orleans—for some twenty years. In person Mrs. Benton so closely resembled Girard's portrait of Madame de Staël, that it is held by her family as better than those taken from life of herself.

In the early part of her married life she received the shock which caused her years of ill health, resulting at last in her death. She had succored a poor girl, who became crazed by shame and sorrow, and had procured her admission to the lunatic asylum in Stanton. When discharged as harmless though incurable, the poor creature haunted the neighborhood of Mrs. Benton's home, delighted to receive the presents brought for her on the annual visit. One day the demented woman came into the house to see "Miss Betsey," as she called Mrs. Benton, and found her asleep in her room. In her jangled brain stirred the thought that it would be an act of love and gratitude to the dear young lady to kill her as she slept, and save her from her own agonized experience —a father's curse when her child should be born, expulsion from her home, and desertion by him she had loved too well. Mr. Benton in the next room heard a whispering, sobbing sound, and came into his wife's chamber just in time to arrest the heavy bough of a tree which the maniac had lifted to dash it with all her strength on the sleeper's head. Mrs. Benton started from slumber to take in her danger at a glance: the descending bough, the interposition of her husband, the mad woman struggling furiously in his grasp; and the effects of the fright were most disastrous. The death of the delicate child born soon afterwards, her own lengthened sufferings, and the terrible jar to her nerves, gave a downward turn, that ended in the complete breaking down of the nervous system. Yet the noble principles and acts of her life continued to sustain her husband. Her numerous acts of charity will never be known: but the poor who came to her funeral, the men in high position who standing by the dead said to her daughter—"But for her I was a lost man. What I am now I owe to her admonitions and encouragement:"—the women who acknowledged her aid, helping them through the dark hours when suicide or desperate bravado seemed their only resource—helping them back to unquestioned security of reputation—all testified to her Christian upholding of those who fall. Her faithful colored servants, too, who remained with her on wages, were witnesses that neither wealth nor worldly honors, nor mental powers nor the attractions of society, had won her to live for herself. She often referred to Jeanie Deans' words to the Queen of England,—"It's not what we hae done for ourselves my leddy, but what we hae done for others, will help us then." Mr. Benton, too, called to mind the Baillie's saying,—"Some men were ower gude for banning, and ower bad for blessing—like Rob Roy"—particularly when he gave his opinion that "party was too tremendous an engine to use against a poor clerk whose salary was all that stood between his family and starvation, and too small a consideration where the national honor was involved."

Those two sayings embody the ruling principles of those two noble lives—so harmoniously united that one cannot be written separate from the other.

On the night of the passage and execution of the expunging resolution, Mrs. Benton, anxious for the safety of her husband, and knowing him obnoxious to the Bank party, was near him in the Senate chamber. It was the last scene of a seven years' contest with that great moneyed power. When the Secretary of the Senate began to perform the expunging process, a storm of hisses, groans and vociferations arose in the gallery over Benton's head. The presiding officer ordered the gallery cleared; but Benton opposed the order, bidding the sergeant-at-arms seize only the Bank ruffians, and pointing one out. The ringleader was seized and brought to the bar. General Jackson gave a grand dinner to the "expungers" and their wives; and being too weak to sit at table, with the company, placed the "head expunger" in his chair and withdrew to his sick chamber.

Commodore Rodgers, the great naval commander who died early in Van Buren's administration, was then prominent. His form and face were those of the naval hero. He was at the head of the American navy, but did not see the rank of admiral established in our naval service. Mr. Rives was an easy, graceful, fluent speaker. He never dealt in sarcasm or invective, always treating his opponent with the courtesy of a gentleman. He was in consequence esteemed by both parties; though not much liked by the ultras. Mr. Clay's eloquence was described as that of Jupiter Tonans; the fearless independence of his mind being always discernible. Experience, he once said, quoting Coleridge, "is like the stern lights of a ship, to most men; illumining only the way it has passed."

On the 29th March, "Andrew Stevenson, minister to England, was in the House to-day looking remarkably well and in good spirits. He is to go out as soon as a national ship can be got in readiness to convey him."

On the 1st April, "Mr. Buchanan and Mr. Clay had what the Yankees call a bit of a spat. Mr. Buchanan had spoken of his adventure at a certain battle, in which he came too late to do any active service; but Mr. Clay tried to show that the gentleman's age could not have been at that time more than twelve, and wished the ladies in the gallery were more numerous, to hear the exploits of such a youth. Whereupon Mr. Buchanan blazed out in wrath. Mr. Clay was cool as an ice-house, and the Senate and galleries were convulsed with laughter."

An observer wrote: "The soirées of the Secretaries usually commence from nine to ten; all the apartments being thrown open; from seven to nine hundred are invited, though generally not more than half that number attend. The host and hostess stand in the drawing-room to receive the company. Dancing, conversation, and cards, are the amusements of the evening; the first left to the young people; the elder and middle-aged participating in the latter. A small band of musicians is stationed in the ball-room, where the young girls and beaux are conversant with the 'poetry of motion.' Light refreshments circulate through the different apartments. At about eleven the guests partake of a collation or supper;

about three they begin to retire, and at four the lights are extinguished. At the soirée of a Secretary, entering about ten, I wound my way into another room and found a diminutive woman gaudily attired, hanging on the arm of the Secretary of the Navy, who is six feet high and whose pantaloons were somewhat deficient in length. 'Dear me!' exclaimed the little Miss; 'What a crowd! I really never saw anything like it in Jersey. Don't you think it's enough to make one faint?' The Secretary smiled and observed that it would be very inconvenient to faint there, as water was an article that could not be had at a party in Washington. 'Pray who' asked the young lady, 'is that strange looking man with the dirty black mustache, talking to that enormous lady in black velvet?' 'That is one of the representatives of the Northern Bear, the great autocrat of all the Russias.' 'Is it possible! Well, on a closer inspection, I don't think him so very frightful after all,' and they moved off, that the young lady might be introduced, leaving me alongside of a tall, gawkish looking young man, whom I soon ascertained to be the Earl of S——, a young Scotchman, who had come to visit some land he owned in America. He was very silent and awkward, and seemed to be under the special guardianship of the British minister, and a Scotch attaché. The sound of music produced a rush towards the ball-room, where I found myself stationed behind a lady of no particular age, most absurdly and fantastically arrayed. She was the sister of the host's wife. The waltz was in favor, and the various couples whirled round with such bewildering gyrations, I was almost dizzy with merely looking on. 'I declare!' cried the lady above-mentioned, 'I begin to feel the effects of old age.' She was about forty, and no doubt expected her attendant cavalier to contradict her; but he was half choked with a piece of pound cake, and could not have managed to utter a compliment.

"'How I envy that lady hanging on the arm of the Vice-President,' continued the lady. 'Pray who is she?' asked the gentleman. 'She is a kind of female clerk in one of the public offices. Her father has acted the Vicar of Bray so admirably as not only to keep himself in office, but his whole family; they have realized an income from the public crib of about six thousand dollars a year. Not less than six of them go to every party during the winter; never failing to make a deep impression on the ice creams and confectionery. That one believes her beauty of the Spanish style; and she endeavors to dress and act the Spanish belle; but it won't do. The less she says the better; for when she keeps her mouth closed, it is impossible to find out the small capital on which she trades.'

"'Indeed, I think you are inclined to be somewhat satirical this evening,' remarked the gentleman.

"'Not in the least,' replied the belle of forty; and she gave a killing toss of her head, that threw a long, straggling, artificial curl into one of her eyes; which so affected her vision, she immediately withdrew to apply some palliative to her injured organ. Their place was supplied by a couple fresh from the country; a rustic pair invited by some accident. The beau, a tall, strapping Kentuckian, had taken a saucer of frozen Roman punch, which he had never tasted before. He had no sooner put it into his mouth than he exclaimed; 'I swar, Miss Jane, this beats julep all to nothing; who ever thought of chawing rum!' The servant stopped near him with a tray on which stood a pyramid of candied oranges. Peering at it with great curiosity, he took hold with his fingers, and broke off a large piece, which stuck to his fingers so tenaciously, that, finding he could make nothing of it, he thrust it into his pocket, and began to suck his fingers to clear them from the adhesive substance. Miss Jane had helped herself to an ice-cream and sundry comfits in large quantities. Presently their attention was caught by a fashionable dance—the Mazurka—just commenced.

"'Well, I'm shot if that don't beat Burke,' cried the Kentuckian. 'There's a fellow that looks like Walk-in-the-Water—kneeling to a lady, while the rest get round him like a parcel of Indian squaws! I'm smashed if they haven't been taking lessons from the Osages.' A clapping noise called my attention to the dancers, now arranged in two lines extending the whole depth of the room, and I saw the Scotch attaché stamping with his feet, and clapping his hands, as if he thought he was dancing the Highland Fling. The whole man was in motion. One of the members was denouncing the exhibition, and saying he would sooner witness a parcel of Choctaws or Winnebagoes perform the war dance. Entering another less crowded apartment, I saw a pretty girl and a young naval officer seated on a sofa, discussing Baron Krudener's party and a belle in Turkish costume who had tried her arts to captivate the old diplomat, seemingly determined to live and die a bachelor. But she talked French and showed her white teeth to him in vain. His deafness compelled her to scream her soft nothings into his ear to the occasional annoyance of the company. 'Baron,' in her most bewitching tone, 'I should like to waltz.' '*Oui, oui,*' responded the Baron, '*il fait fort chaud:* very hot, warm, *oui.*' 'I am not speaking of the heat, but of dancing,' ventured the belle, a little louder. '*Oui,* she is *tres jolie,* I 'ave say so to her.' 'Baron, you *will* not hear me.'

"'Oh, dat mamselle is certainement var pretty; but she 'ave bad teeth. I 'ave told her she was pretty in spite of her teeth! ha ha!' and with this stale joke he moved off, to the mortification of his companion. Stimulated by champagne, the chargé at length became so amorous, that in the ecstacy of the moment, he exclaimed to his fair companion: 'I vil bite your chin off.' The next subject was a lady who came to Washington as an heiress and was pronounced a belle, till it was ascertained that she is one of a family of six children.

"'Tired of gossip, I followed the crowd into the supper room, and was again beside an honorable member, doing justice to the viands and champagne: bolting down oysters, pheasant, tongue, &c., and moistening them with copious libations. Another member asked—'why he was like a clerk?' 'Because he is fond of salary.' 'But why is his mouth like Athens?' 'Because it is the centre of Greece.' The strapping Kentuckian had found his way in without his fair companion, and seemed ready to devour everything. 'Mister'—he began, 'I'll thank you for a piece that thar duck.' 'It's a pheasant,' replied the other. 'A pheasant! what—that thar? you're makin' game of me.' 'But you shan't make game of me! will you be helped to the wing or the leg?' 'I'll take both.' The whole fowl was handed to him, then he cried—'Waiter, I'll thank you for a glass of that cider.' 'It is champagne, sir,' said the servant smiling. As he tossed off the glass, he exclaimed, 'I'm smashed if this don't beat old Kentuck' all to shivers! Give us another glass, mister, I could drink this here truck all day.'"

"'Pray who is that making such formal preparations for a regular siege to the good things?' asked a member, pointing to a little man with a broad face and a smile on it. 'You might tell, from the manner in which he provides for himself, that he is the chairman of the Committee of Ways and Means.' 'And that round-faced, jolly-looking personage making love to the Sherry, Madeira, &c.?' 'The chairman of the Committee on Foreign Relations.' 'And to what Committee do you belong?' 'I am a member of the Committee of the Whole. The Speaker has sometimes wished to put me on the Committee of Unfinished Business; but I have always begged off; and so, if you please, we will finish our last bottle of champagne.'

"In the dancing-room I saw a fine looking woman elegantly dressed, leaning on the arm of a Senator, and surrounded by gentlemen eager to pay her attention; a chaplet of roses rested on her head, and she handled an ivory fan with skill and effect. I was told the attachés and other foreigners sought her society because she could speak their own languages. 'She has a soirée every Monday,' said my informant, 'but allows no dancing and wishes her parties to be considered merely conversaziones.'

"It was now two o'clock, and going into the dressing-room, I found the tall Kentuckian in a dreadful pother about the loss of his cap, which he said he had given a servant to take care of in that room. 'I say, mister, ain't that thar my cap you've got in your hand! I'm smashed if some scamp hasn't made off with my cap!' and he tore up the pile of hats, cloaks and caps like a dog scraping loose earth.

'A lady waits for you,' said the servant. 'Tell Miss Jane I can't go without my cap, and I'm shot if I don't have it in spite of all natur.'

"Such is a sample of the fashionable soirées of Washington."

Ever since General Jackson came into office and developed his opinions and theories on the currency, Mr. Biddle had been the effective head of the opposition to his administration; sometimes in secret, sometimes openly. Webster, Calhoun, Clay and others were merely powerful instruments set in motion by the great magician in Philadelphia, as a counterpart to the art with which the great magician of New York —Martin Van Buren—moved the President and his cabinet at Washington. The master spirits of the two opposing parties for the last eight years, now flung aside each his silver veil, and appeared in the arena armed and equipped. Both were powerful, original, and remarkable men; perhaps without an equal in their peculiar traits of thought. In the summer of 1833 Mr. Biddle was seen coming out of the Mansion House in Philadelphia, and said to an acquaintance—smiling in his half-sarcastic, half-earnest way: "I have just been paying my respects to Mr. Van Buren. One magician should always treat another with courtesy when he passes through his dominions." Mr. Van Buren was then holding a levee at Head's.

Reuben M. Whitney was handled severely by Wise and Peyton in the House of Representatives; and he was accustomed to retort with similar epithets. Mr. Wise was called an imitator of Randolph, and was at this time rather young, though his hair was sprinkled with gray. He was bold, fearless and independent, high-minded and patriotic. Not so highly cultivated as the orator of Roanoke, he had not his ferocity of spirit, with equal energy and a better regulated disposition. His style was more vituperative than satirical; his illustrations were not classical, though often felicitous. He quoted more from the Bible than the poets or classical writers, yet was sometimes irreverent.

An amusing fancy ball was given in January, 1837, by a matron anxious to work her way into fashionable society. There were kings and queens, shepherds and shepherdesses, &c., in all manner of ludicrous costumes; and a fat, blowsy-faced "Virgin of the Sun," said to be the mother of ten children. An Hibernian dressed as Shylock told her she was brilliant as the sun itself. At a party given in Georgetown by a colonel who liked to imitate European fashions, tableaux vivants were introduced. The figures sat in a rich and spacious frame, and resembled a life-sized picture. The wife of a clerk in one of the offices appeared as a bandit's bride; another lady of magnificent rotundity in the costume of a sylph.

Santa Anna was expected hourly in Washington and it was thought his coming was to persuade Congress to recognize the independence of Texas. At this period it was not usual for the Executive to visit or attend parties, though he might give as many as he pleased. It was expected that one of Mr. Van Buren's sons would be married, and would reside in the palace with his father after his accession.

Colonel Johnson had no personal dignity, and was not fluent; but was clever and amiable. He, as well as the President elect, seemed fascinated with the performances, at the theatre, of Miss Clifton. That magnificent creature was quite a Patagonian, and "small men were always more pleased with large women than with little ones." One of the first attempts to get up a masquerade in Washington was by a Major of marines, assisted by the boarders in a fashionable establishment. A gentleman went in the dress of Diogenes. He was reminded that he had forgotten his lantern and that it required "a stronger blaze than that of a lantern to find out an honest man in these days." An apparent Hibernian enquired, "which of these ladies is the masther of ceremonies?" and when the presiding lady stepped up to him, he introduced himself as "Dennis O'Lary, from Cork, in the county of Dublin in the south of Ireland, and have a cousin in the Herald office in London."

The parties at Secretary Forsythe's were noted. At Secretary Woodbury's evenings Mrs. Woodbury's suavity and ease of manners were generally admired; as well as her exceeding grace of deportment. She possessed great beauty of face and form, and was said to resemble Mrs. Madison, one of the most popular women in society. She always put strangers at their ease, and was particularly attentive to the awkward and embarrassed. The British minister, Mr. Fox, "never makes his appearance at the soirées. He is a perfect oddity. The Secretaries have all left their cards at his residence; but he has not returned a single call, and is therefore not invited to the parties. Mr. Fox is the first barbarian that ever England sent to a civilized court."

A distinguished lady of fashion in Baltimore, Mrs. Meredith—gave a party at the Assembly Rooms which was attended by all the beauty, taste and fashion of Baltimore and Washington. It was given on "Twelfth Night," and the curious olden ceremony was introduced of cutting the cake and contending for the ring imbedded among the sugar plums. The Assembly rooms were fitted up with great magnificence. Miss Meredith "looked a fairy in fairy land." Her elegance, grace, and peculiar naïveté, were greatly admired. Mrs. T. Oldfield was charming and fascinating, and, with Mrs. N. P. Willis, was conspicuous in the reel. Mrs. Skinner was dressed in a very beautiful though old-fashioned style. Miss Ackerman and her sister from the South, had many distinguished men in their train. Miss Traverse was a brilliant beauty, Miss Belt a perfect Hebe; Miss M. Patterson

—of a race that adorned the highest ranks of the British court—was elegantly attired; Miss Carroll too; and her name and lineage were a passport. Among the debutants were two lovely daughters of Judge Magruder. Miss C. Barney called to mind the lovely Rowena, and Miss E. Gilmore's smile was bewitching.

The cake was placed on a table in the supper room. Scores of lovely girls and expectant gentlemen were crowding around it, eager to obtain the prize. "I've got only a plum!" cried one. "I've eaten the whole slice, but there's no ring," exclaimed another. At last there was a burst of merriment, and a soft hand, that of the mayor's daughter, held up the prophetic ring. J. P. Kennedy, one of the principal literary men, was there; also Major Van Buren, said to be engaged to a western lady, whom he had seen blooming somewhere among the prairies, during his Black Hawk expedition. There was also Judge Thompson, of the Supreme Court, Mr. West, the son of Lord Delamar, Mr. Dangerfield, and others.

"The President's palace was closed to the fashionables this whole session, in consequence of the indisposition and death of Mrs. Donelson. The theatre and concert were the resort of the *beau monde;* the fashionables holding back for a splendid fancy ball, to be given by the patroness of the blondes. The ladies sometimes made a great noise in the gallery, and were now and then called to order, or requested to be less talkative. While Colonel Bell was Speaker of the House, he sent up a messenger to inform a party of ladies and gentlemen who sat in front of the chair, that their courtship must be carried on in a lower key or elsewhere, if they did not wish him to be acquainted with it. Miss Martineau was in the gallery one day, and surrounded by a crowd of such as thought they derived importance from her company. She was unfortunately deaf, and used a silver trumpet, applied to her ear when she wanted to hear what was said to her. The noise in her immediate circle was considerable. The rough door-keeper came to her and told her she must make less noise. Miss Martineau immediately applied the tube to her ear. "You needn't put that 'ere thing to your ear; you make noise enough without it," growled the old Cerberus, to the amazement of the illustrator of the principles of political economy.

When the gallery of the House had been fearfully crowded, at the trial of Judge Peek, a little chunk of a man had got wedged into one corner, and apprehensive of being smothered, he made a desperate attempt to get out, crying lustily for egress.

"Order!" shouted the marshal. The burly little prisoner still endeavored to make his way to the door, repeating the cry, "let me out."

"Order in the gallery!" again thundered the marshal. "If you don't keep order, I'll turn you out." "That's just what I want!" screamed the little man. "Let me out or turn me out, I don't care which." The whole gallery and chamber were in a roar.

The most gifted of the delegation from Ohio was Mr. Corwin. He astonished the House by his eloquent speech against the bill reducing the Tariff in January of this year. Mr. William C. Preston, in the Senate, exhibited his usual splendor of declamation and rhetorical coloring. His declamation was thought by some too artificial. General Ward was called "The Chesterfield of the House," and George IV. could not have made a more condescending bow than he, to everybody he met.

Mrs. R. M. Whitney's party was a splendid affair, and the refreshments were abundant. The ex-President, Heads of Departments, Foreign Ministers, Mr. Fox excepted, and members of Congress, were among the guests. Mr. C. C. Cambreling was conspicuous, and pronounced superior to his great model, Julius Cæsar, in his three Cs: for he might have said "I came, I caught, I conquered." Mrs. Cambreling was noted for grace and suavity of manners.

The chamber occupied by the Supreme Court had now become a place of fashionable resort. It was then immediately under the Senate chamber, and lighted from the east. The Judges wore robes; the clerk of the court was a pompous appendage to the bar, dealing in the grandiloquent style. Each Judge was furnished with a handsome mahogany desk surrounded by a plain railing, and a mahogany arm-chair covered with velvet. A desk was set apart near the clerk's table for the Attorney-General, and cushioned sofas were placed on each side of the room for the audience. Judge Baldwin, among those who occupied the bench, was a Pennsylvanian, plain in his manners, social in his habits and amiable in his disposition. He treated the rich and the poor, the humble and the exalted, with equal courtesy and kindness. While a member of Congress, it was said of him, as once of Sheridan, he always, "hit the House between wind and water." He was a sound lawyer, and exceedingly popular. Judge McLean was in person tall, well-formed, and graceful; sedate, grave and modest; regular in his habits, temperate in all things, laborious and indefatigable in the discharge of every duty. He made up by industry for the want of quickness. His judgment was never warped by prejudice, nor led into error by the imagination. He never allowed feeling to enter into his legal investigations; though it was indicated by acts of benevolence and generous sympathy. His mind was more logical than metaphysical, and he liked demonstration better than speculation.

A newspaper writer described at a party: "That tall, narrow-faced, but good-looking man—the Chief-Justice of the Supreme Court. He and I, some thirty years ago, were small lawyers in a small county court in Maryland, satisfied with the humblest fee for wear and tear of intellect; and now he is at the head of the highest judicial tribunal in the United States. When I first knew him he had an impediment in his speech, which he still retains, but to a much less extent. He was exceedingly modest, retiring and unassuming. As he rose at the bar his ambition became inflamed, and he plunged into the vortex of party politics, and became a federal demagogue in a State where democracy had the ascendency. He devoted his days and nights to his profession; was made Attorney-General; was appointed Secretary of the Treasury;—and finally was elevated to the Chief-Justiceship of the Supreme Court of the United States, in the place of one 'whose like we ne'er shall see again.'

"That gentleman of medium size and intelligent countenance, with gray hairs, and 'spectacles on nose' is his associate, and should have been the Chief Justice. Judge Story is a man who, like Blackstone, commenced life as a poet, and published a volume on Solitude. He is a fine *belles lettres* scholar, writes well on all subjects, and is profoundly versed in the science of jurisprudence. His mind is acute, penetrating, and comprehensive, not too refining and metaphysical, but by the application of analysis arriving at just conclusions and reaching truth by the process of sound logic. Though his arduous judicial functions require much of his time and attention, he is noted in the various walks of literature and science. He relaxes his mind by strolling amid the groves of the Academy, or reposing in the bower of the muses."

A delegation of the chiefs of the Sac and Fox tribes of Indians was in Washington on business in February. They were a wild, ferocious-looking set, in dirty blankets, their faces daubed with red paint and their heads ornamented with feathers.

"I sat the other day by a group of ladies in black; one about forty, with a very intelligent and animated countenance. On her right sat a much older woman. The first listened to Colonel Bell, who was then speaking, with intense interest, appearing absorbed in the subject he was discussing. Her companion threw out an observation now and then in the Irish accent, which evinced real knowledge of the world, and of men and things in Ireland. Curran, Grattan, Phillips, Fitzgerald, Lady Morgan, &c., were sketched with accuracy and fluency.

"'Who are those ladies?' I said to my fair young friends, the Misses ——, who had just come in.

"'One is the wife of the ex-Speaker of the House, a lady of fine sense and feeling; the other is the widow of the celebrated Wolfe Tone, the mother of young Wolfe Tone, and the mother-in-law of the daughter of Sampson. She is a remarkable woman, and her career in life has also been remarkable. She is now Mrs. Wilson, and, I believe, again a widow; a lone woman in this wide world, and in a foreign land.'

"'And what fine-looking woman is that in a colored dress to our left, so dignified and conversational?'

"'That is the wife of the late candidate for the Presidency, Mrs. H. L. White, a lady of good understanding, agreeable manners, and no little ambition.'"

There were two parties every night in February, 1837. Washington presented a continual scene of speaking by day, and dancing and feasting by night. Among the distinguished guests, was Power the actor, who, after despatching his theatrical duties, was wont to relax himself among the fashionables, abandoning the Irish gentleman on the stage for the Irish gentleman in society. The whole world assembled on the 8th February to witness the ceremony of counting the electoral votes for President and Vice-President. It took place at noon in the Hall of Representatives.

It had been officially announced, through the Globe that the President's big cheese was to be distributed among those who pleased to visit him on the birthday of Washington. The Senate adjourned at an early hour, the volunteer companies turned out and the inhabitants of the three cities of the District, of all ranks and conditions, repaired to the Palace. The Presidential mansion was crammed.

The cheese was certainly enormous, and about twice the weight of the mammoth one sent to Jefferson. It had been surrounded by a belt, on which had been painted the words applied to Jackson by Branch, "The Greatest and the Best," with his own sentiment, "The Union must be preserved."

"By the powers," said a raw Irishman, taking an enormous mouthful of cheese, "it may be the greatest, but it's far from bein' the best."

A lady asked what animal it was intended to represent on the cloth that covered the cheese. Some one said, the cow from the milk of which it was made. Another cried, "The cow! The donor, in his letter to the President, said it was made by two hundred and sixty cows."

The old President stood shaking hands with, and receiving the salutations of his numerous visitors as long as he could stand. The east room, splendidly furnished, and looking like a fairy palace, was crowded, and the company was emphatically *mixed*, a curious mixture of democracy and aristocracy. At one moment one was knocked against the wall by a sturdy hack-driver and his fat spouse, and at the next pressed by a lovely creature, under the protection of a foreign minister; at one moment the scent of eau-de-cologne and otto of roses was deliciously inhaled, and the next the smell of garlic and odor of brimstone assailed the olfactories. "At a levee a few years ago," said one, "Sir Charles Vaughan rolled up to the Palace in his carriage, in his court dress, to pay his respects to the President; but he saw such a crowd of all sorts and descriptions pushing into the Executive Mansion, that he cried out roughly to his coachman to drive home, 'This is too —— democratic for me!'"

"Bless his old heart!" cried a portly woman, wedged into one corner of the splendid room, and dressed in all the colors of the rainbow, "How sorry I shall be when he goes away. My darter Eberline has been to visit the Gineral several times, and shook hands with him twice. She says how he spoke to her so kind and affectionate, she could almost have hugged the dear old man. And did you not observe how he smiled when he shook hands with me! I vow he's the most agreeablest old man I ever seen. But don't you think there's a wast deal of wulgarity here to-day?"

"In this administration," said her escort, "these mixtures are allowed. For my part, I always likes genteel society, and abominates what is vulgar."

"And so does I," said the lady with a toss of her head.

At the door was a splendid barouche, which had been presented to General Jackson. It was made entirely of the wood of the old frigate Constitution.

Captain Isaac Phillips, a worthy and respectable officer of the navy, had been peremptorily dismissed by the elder Adams, for permitting a British frigate to muster on deck the crew of an American sloop-of-war under his command, for the purpose of impressing British subjects. He applied to General Jackson to appoint him to office in consideration of his persecution by Adams; and said the gentleman now holding the appointment of navy agent at Baltimore had held it many years. "That proves him worthy of confidence," replied the General. Captain Phillips then remarked that the incumbent was rich and did not require the office. "Then" replied the hero, "he has no inducement to be dishonest;" the General all the while calmly smoking his pipe, his feet resting on the mantel-piece. The Captain resolved to make a last desperate effort. "I have an aged wife," he pleaded, "we are fast declining into the valley of the shadow of death in wretched poverty; this little office would give us the comforts of life, and speed our downward path to the tomb." The General dropped his feet to the floor, laid his pipe on the table, called for pen and ink, wrote a note and handed it to Captain Phillips.

"Here is an order for your appointment; take it to the Secretary of the Navy. If this little office is not necessary to the comfort of its possessor, and will make yourself and your aged wife happy, you shall have it." Captain Phillips took the note to Governor Branch, but was informed it came too late; that Mr. James Bealty, of Baltimore, had been recommended by political friends of the administration; that his nomination was before the Senate and that he would not recall it. Phillips returned to the President and told him the result. "He won't recall it?" exclaimed Jackson. "Then, by the ——, I will! Mr. Secretary, fill up a nomination for Captain Isaac Phillips; carry it to the Senate Chamber, recall the nomination of James Bealty, and substitute the one for Isaac Phillips." In a few days the Captain received his commission. Presenting himself to Governor Branch for instructions, he expressed his gratitude. "You owe me nothing," said the Governor, "I did all in my power to prevent it. General Jackson rules in all and over all."

The distinguished statesman Louis McLane, who was minister to England, then Secretary of the Treasury, then Secretary of State, winning the confidence and respect of all who associated with him, eminent in ability, and most competent to judge of the ability of others, averred that General Jackson was a greater man than any member of his Cabinet. He withered and annihilated every man who dared oppose his iron will. He buried in the tomb of the Capulets that leviathan, the Bank of the United States; that distinguished financier, that truly honest and upright man, Nicholas Biddle, dying of a broken heart. Grief had slain him: his poverty vindicating his integrity.

General Jackson's prejudices were indomitable. On one occasion his influence was solicited in favor of the Baltimore and Ohio railway, and it was urged that benefits would accrue to the rich valley of the Mississippi by the facility of intercourse with the Atlantic border. "Sir," he answered, "it is a rebellion against Providence. If it had been designed that the produce of the western world should find its market on the shores of the Atlantic, the great rivers of the West would have flowed in that direction."

The social brilliancy of General Jackson's administration was generally acknowledged, and will long be remembered. In no city in the Union could there be found a more polished and refined society than in Washington at this period. Foreigners of high rank, citizens of wealth, men of the most distinguished intellect and learning, with ladies the most lovely and refined, were assembled there during the congressional terms. The constant presence and association of such persons naturally gave a tone and polish to the manners of the place not to be found to the same extent in other cities. Some thought the manners of the gentlemen artificial and affected, allowing the women, however, natural tact, with much grace and elegance.

Fashionable society in the capital, then as now, was accessible to all who pleased to enter it. There was no aristocracy of wealth to form an exclusive circle or present a barrier to the less affluent. Many families depended upon government for the means of subsistence, and the only difference among them arose from the difference of income which they received, which, of course, governed their manner of living and regulated their expenditures. Example had its effect in Washington, as it has in all other communities. The President opened his drawing-room periodically for the reception of those who pleased to visit him on those occasions. The heads of departments and bureaus, foreign ministers, &c., gave dinner and evening parties during the session to members of Congress, strangers of distinction, &c., on a visit to the capital; and this was followed up to an almost ruinous extent by the subordinate officers of government, clerks and citizens, who thought they must become a part of the fashionable circle. To the soirées of the secretaries and others, invitations were sent out usually about eight or nine days in advance, and, of course, no one was expected to go who was not an invited guest. An invitation, however, was easily procured by a stranger who had any standing in society, by leaving his card before the soirée was given. The hotel books were regularly examined, and invitations were sent to the stranger or foreigner of note newly arrived. Lions were as eagerly sought after in Washington as in the circles in London. A constant requisition was made upon members of Congress; they were the life of all companies, and a necessary ingredient in the composition of fashionable parties. Some of them, who were at first exceedingly rough, contrived to throw off the awkwardness and rusticity of former habits, and mingled freely in society. As a man's standing and consequence were tested by the figure he made in fashionable circles, every one was anxious to be initiated, and to play his part as conspicuously as possible. These efforts to be classed with the fashionables were attended with expenses which the circumstances of but few could justify. A carriage, servants in livery, fine furniture, splendid apparel—especially among the women, who were as passionately fond of dress as in other cities—good wine, and all the other "pride, pomp and circumstance of glorious" fashion had to be procured. The man who attended parties was expected to give them, and in striving to keep up appearances insolvency was too often the result. Some, however, were very sagacious in maintaining their rank. They lived sparingly, and except when they gave parties or were invited to them, observed the strictest economy.

A writer of the day described the bachelor Secretary of the Navy as: "not in the least bellicose, very close in his private matters, and not inclined to be profuse in his public expenditures. In this particular he bears a strong resemblance to another Secretary of the Navy, who filled the office some twenty years ago. He boarded with a lady who kept a boarding-house near Georgetown, and always dined with a small flask of wine containing about half a pint, from which he was wont to help himself, but asked no one else at the table to join him. When he had finished his dinner he carried off his precious casket, to be reproduced at the succeeding repast. The present Secretary also boards; is in the habit of going to all the parties to which he is invited, but seems to have conscientious scruples about giving any himself. His pantaloons, like his speeches, are always too brief, and his coat, like his reports, too long. When a member of the Senate, he never failed to advocate the duty on iron, having iron works himself; and he was said to be the most ironical speaker in that body. He is tall, and the wags say he is very lofty and elevated in his notions."

Mrs. Edward Livingston was so preëminent in Washington society, that no apology is made for the introduction of an authentic sketch of her life; no memoir of her having ever before been published.

Mrs. Edward Livingston was born in the Island of St. Domingo in the year 1782. She was descended from a French family of which several members have distinguished themselves in literature and politics. Her grandfather Pierre Valentin D'Avezac de Castera was of the ancient family of the Seigneurs of Avezac in Neboussau, but of the younger branch, that of the Seigneurs of Castera, settled in Bigorre. Pierre Valentin himself was a younger son. His father, who reserved for this son's only patrimony, some ecclesiastical benefices which he possessed in the Diocese of Tarbes, destined him for the Church, and sent him to Paris to study at the Sorbonne. When prepared to take orders, young D'Avezac showed inclinations little in conformity with his father's intentions; and to escape the ecclesiastical profession, he suddenly embarked for Martinique in the year 1748, and thence went to St. Domingo. His talents and perseverance soon gave him prominence among the inhabitants of the Island. He held successively military and legal offices of importance under the colonial government, and having finally become a planter, showed in the cultivation of his lands, ability that gave him great influence. He proposed the construction of a canal for the purpose of fertilizing the beautiful valley of the Fond, and, in the absence of a professional engineer, undertook himself to have it made by his own slaves. He had to contend with difficulties and embarrassments to accomplish his purpose, but these were settled to his honor by the intervention of the Comte d'Argout, Lieutenant Governor, and the award in judgment of the Prince de Rohan, Governor-General of the Island.

D'Avezac had married, in the year 1752, Marie Thérese de Linois, a near relative of the vice-admiral of that name. By her he had five children, of whom the second son was the father of Mrs. Livingston. Jean Pierre Valentin Joseph D'Avezac de Castera was born in 1756 at St. Domingo. He was one of the Deputies elected in 1790, by the great planters in St. Domingo, to form the famous Assemblée Générale of St. Marc, that undertook to resist the spreading of the revolutionary spirit of France into the colonies. The Deputies, eighty-five in number, embarked on board the "Léopard" for Paris, to encounter the storm. On arriving at Brest they were received with enthusiasm, but when they reached Paris, the national assembly treated them as aristocrats and took sides with their adversaries. On their return to St. Domingo they continued their opposition to the revolutionary ideas, in the colonial assembly. But the insurrections of the mulattoes received encouragement from the party then dominant in France, and the planters were obliged to seal with their blood the cause they had espoused. D'Avezac had two sons killed in expeditions in which they commanded detachments sent against the insurgents. His younger brother and his brother-in-law were made prisoners and shot at Léogane by the mulatto general, Rigaud. He himself, exhausted by vain efforts in the cause of order against anarchy, sought refuge in exile with his family. By his marriage with Marie Rose Valentine Genevieve Tallary de Maragon, he had remaining but four children. The eldest son, Auguste, was afterwards well known as United States Chargé d'Affaires to the Hague for many years. Louise D'Avezac, (later Mrs. Edward Livingston) was the eldest daughter. Her mind developed at a very early age. Her father, in surrounding himself with all the refinements of European luxury unusual in the Island, had collected a large library to which the child was allowed access. She learned to read, no one could tell how. Mrs. Livingston in speaking of this in after life used to relate that one day while her mother was at her toilet undergoing the elaborate process of having her hair dressed and powdered according to the fashion then prevailing in France, she had taken up a glittering pomatum jar and read off aloud the label on it. Her father, who at that moment entered the room, was amazed at finding the little girl had spared them the trouble of teaching her to read. From that time books were her passion. Fortunately her instincts led her to all that was elevated in literature, for no one guided her in any way. Plutarch's heroes became the objects of her girlish enthusiasm. The classics, ancient and modern, in prose and in verse, were greedily devoured, and these treasures, appropriated by her memory, were retained through life to extreme old age, for she never forgot what she had acquired in that plantation library. Her brother Auguste, nearly her own age, shared in these tastes. Whenever one of the two was consigned for some youthful misconduct, to the dark closet reserved for juvenile delinquents in all countries, the other would crouch at the door before the *chattiére,* (an opening which it was the custom to leave under doors for the egress of cats), with a Virgil, a Tasso, a Racine or some other work equally above their years, and reading aloud the magic pages, charm away the solitude of the captive within. The sports of these children partook of the same spirit. They would enact whole scenes improvised from the Iliad, the Eneid or the Jerusalem Delivered, and the little girl was by turns Helen, Dido or Clorinda. For a long time she was the only daughter of her parents. She was consequently taught with her brothers, and shared in the instructions of their tutor until the young men were sent off to college in France, according to the custom of the Island. She was then left to finish her education by herself. It was in her early home also, that she first learned to love the works of nature. Her father's estate was beautifully situated, and tropical vegetation gave a peculiar character to the scene. The house was very spacious; her father had lavished his great wealth upon it and adorned it with European taste and elegance. Terraces bordered with orange trees, surrounded the dwelling, from which the eye wandered down the long rows of cocoa-nut trees which formed the avenue of entrance to the place.

At the age of thirteen Louise married Monsieur Moreau de Lassy, a French gentleman of fortune. He took her to Jamaica to reside, having there large estates. But this union did not last long. At eighteen she was a widow, and returned to St. Domingo to live with her parents. The revolutions on the Island soon followed, and her father left it to prepare a refuge for his family in Norfolk, Virginia. But immediately after his arrival there he fell ill and died of yellow fever, broken-hearted at the ruin of the once flourishing colony. Her mother clinging to the hope of better days, believed she could best serve the interests of the family by remaining as long as she could on the plantation. It was thought best that Madame Moreau, then so young and beautiful, should not run the risk of remaining too long amidst the dangers that surrounded her. She therefore accompanied her aged grandmother who had determined upon immediate emigration. The party was completed by an aunt with two unmarried daughters, and Madame Moreau's little sister, a child six years of age. Those who knew Mrs. Livingston will remember hearing her narrate this episode of her early history in her own peculiarly graphic style. She would describe the English frigate hovering round the Island, offering means of escape. A time had been appointed to receive the fugitives on board. They found their way to the shore by night through a dense forest. There they lay concealed, waiting with breathless anxiety for the boat which was to come to their rescue. At day-break they heard footsteps approaching, crunching the dry twigs. In their despair they drew closer and closer together, to receive the death blow. A dog now came bounding upon them in an ecstasy of joy. Then the branches which surrounded them were cautiously parted, and they heard the well-known voice of a faithful slave, saying in the French idiom of the St. Domingo negroes: "Mistress, are you there? Don't be afraid, it is I, bringing you some food. The boat will not be here until night." They waited throughout that long weary day until it came to a close, and the shadows of evening deepened upon the Island. A small boat was then seen coming for them from the frigate. It reached the shore; they all got in, and the sailors began to row off again making direct for the ship. Just then a party of negroes came in sight. Maddened at the escape of their prey, they fired a volley and killed the old grandmother, who was holding in her arms Madame Moreau's little sister.* The child, though bespattered with blood, was providentially uninjured, but the faithful slave who had brought them food and aided in their escape was not so fortunate. A shot from the shore stretched him out lifeless beside his aged mistress. Reaching at last the French frigate, the diminished party was taken safely to Jamaica. Thence they embarked in a schooner, ready to sail, as it happened, for New Orleans. The schooner was so small and crowded that the passengers lay in heaps all over the deck. It was impossible to move after once getting on board. In addition to this, a contagious disease broke out, of which several persons on board died. The voyage was prolonged by adverse winds and storms. At last, however, they reached New Orleans, where many exiles from St. Domingo had already preceded them, thankful for the preservation of life, almost all they had left them. New Orleans was at this period in a state of transition. It had passed not long before from the hands of Spain into those of France, and had just been purchased by the United States. The population was motley, tinged with the various national characteristics of successive possessors. Spaniards, French, Americans and the native Creoles, combined to make up this community of easy and primitive manners. The old settlers were not yet reconciled to the last change of rulers. Prejudices almost amounting to superstition made them regret the past and dislike innova-

* Afterwards married to Judge Carleton of the Supreme Court of Louisiana.

tions of every sort. Every accident was attributed to the mismanagement of the Americans, and this idea was carried so far that there is a tradition of a public ball given about this time and interrupted by a sudden earthquake. This roused the ire of a gallant old Creole gentleman present, who was heard to proclaim, in a stentorian voice, "Ce n'était pas du temps des Espagnols et des Français que le plaisir des dames était ainsi troublé!"

The D'Avezac family met with the kindest reception on all sides, and their courage under such reverses of fortune, excited general admiration. Madame Moreau established herself with her aunt, her two young cousins and her little sister, in a small and humble dwelling. They were fortunate in the devotion of several slaves who followed them in their flight, enabling them to avoid the necessity for such domestic drudgery as their habits and education little fitted them for. In the beginning, the sale of some jewels of value, which they had succeeded in bringing away with them, enabled them to live. But the time soon came when the younger members of the family were obliged by their handiwork to provide for the daily maintenance of their parents. Mrs. Livingston in after years spoke of this with great pleasure. Never, she would say, had we been happier or lighter-hearted. After the mornings passed over her sewing, she would make her simple toilet, and radiant in youth and spirits, would pass the evenings gayly with her cousins in the midst of such social enjoyment as could be found around them. The proverbially aristocratic beauty of the women of St. Domingo was exemplified by the remarkable appearance of the young émigrées. Their presence imparted a new lustre to the simple old ball-room, where the society of New Orleans assembled weekly, without ostentation or extravagance, for amusement and dancing. These balls, though called public, were scarcely so in reality. The whole company knew each other, and met by common consent, admitting none but those of their own circle. Orange flower syrup and eau sucré were the sole refreshments. Carriages were unknown in those primitive days. Even to go to the balls, ladies walked in their satin shoes, preceded by a slave carrying a lantern, which was necessary on account of the dark streets. When it rained or the weather was bad, the ball could not take place. This was announced by a crier, to the sound of the drum, a signal understood by all that the ball was postponed until the next fair evening.

It was at one of these primitive entertainments that Madame Moreau first met Mr. Edward Livingston. He had recently come from New York to establish himself in the new domain secured to the United States chiefly through the ability of his brother, Chancellor Livingston. Mr. Livingston was a widower. He had left his two children in New York with their relations. Although he was twenty years older than Madame Moreau, she soon appreciated his noble intellect, and above all things the goodness so characteristic of this distinguished man. On the other hand he was not slow to discover that beauty and grace were not the only gifts which nature had lavished on the young widow. They were married on the 3d of

June, 1805. One of Madame Moreau's young cousins was at the same time united to the son of one of the most esteemed citizens of New Orleans. The double wedding took place at midnight in the chapel of the Ursuline Convent, (an old building still extant in New Orleans.) Madame Moreau having recently lost her venerable aunt, the ceremony was private and but few were present to witness it. But the place, the hour and the circumstances, made it most impressive. The chapel dimly lighted with wax tapers, and sweet with the perfume of June flowers; the nuns behind their grating, unseen, yet revealing their presence by their chants; the brides, both beautiful and one surpassingly so; no one who saw her could ever forget her. And above all, the remembrance of the vicissitudes they had experienced, and the haven of rest they had found, all combined to inspire the eloquence of the priest officiating. L'Abbé de Espinasse's address on the occasion left no one unmoved.*

When the family of émigrés left the chapel it was not to return to the modest home where they had all lived and labored together. From that time the little household was broken up. Mrs. Livingston's mother, who had some time previously come to New Orleans, now accompanied her to her new home, taking with her also her younger daughter. The husband of the young cousin likewise took his bride and her sister to his house. The exiles had found a country and their destiny was fixed. The country of her

* Thirty years afterwards, when Mr. Livingston was United States' Minister at Paris, he received a letter from this gifted ecclesiastic, then promoted to a bishopric in one of the French provinces.

adoption soon became also that of Mrs. Livingston's affections. She did not like even to remember that she had ever had another. The English language was acquired by her with wonderful rapidity. Although she always retained a foreign accent, her fluency and elegance of diction were very remarkable. She had the gift of eloquence, in English as well as in her native tongue. She soon made herself mistress of the new literature which opened before her, and her conversation, choice in its expressions but never pedantic, gave evidence of her familiarity with the best English authors. Her husband guided her himself in this new field of knowledge. She soon became interested in all his pursuits, whether literary, professional or personal. Such was his opinion of her judgment and good taste, that he was never satisfied with any composition which had not received her approval. Mrs. Livingston laughingly compared herself to Molière's old woman upon whom he tried the effect of his dramatic compositions, But she was far from playing the part of a mere listener. Her criticisms, freely offered, were almost always accepted. When Mr. Livingston had been engaged in any suit of importance, involving property or life, he was always met on his return from the courts at the street door, (even when detained until the middle of the night,) by his anxious wife, flying to learn the results of a trial, the merits of which had been previously discussed with her. Her interest in his cases was intense. When the cause was a criminal one, and Mr. Livingston had been unable to save the life of the client he believed innocent, Mrs. Livingston would be days recovering from her disappointment. She had imbibed her husband's views on the inviolability of human life, and would weep bitterly over the fate of the unfortunate being who was doomed. But Mr. Livingston, proverbially successful in those criminal cases which called forth all his sympathies and talents, generally returned home triumphant. Mrs. Livingston used to say never did her heart swell with such grateful pride as on these occasions of rejoicing to both.

New Orleans now became the home of several of her relations, attracted there after her marriage. Her brother Auguste D'Avezac, and her uncle Jules D'Avezac, the latter called by his talents to preside over the first college New Orleans boasted of, were inmates of her home. The domestic circle was a charming one. Mr. Livingston had been the providence of the family. Often in summer, literary readings would enliven the breakfast table, set out in the broad piazza shaded by orange and fig-trees. There M. Jules D'Avezac, whose genius for poetry was no ordinary one, would bring a canto of his translation of Marmion into French verse. Mr. Livingston, the better to judge of its merits, would take the original. This translation of Marmion was afterwards sent by the author to Sir Walter Scott, who was much pleased with the muse that repeated his songs in another hemisphere. The president of the college also found time to employ his pen on more serious labors, Mr. Livingston having selected him as the most competent person to translate into French the Penal Code, to which Mr. Livingston owes his European celebrity. But to return to the breakfast table from which we have wandered. Auguste D'Avezac's brilliant conversational powers are still remembered by all who knew him. Anecdote after anecdote would be told by him with peculiar wit and humor. Other literary friends would drop in, and the circle widen. Mrs. Livingston shone the presiding genius of her table, ever considerate of others, and possessing in an eminent degree the gift of drawing out the talents of her guests, and making them appear to the best advantage. The conversations which sprung up spontaneously in such an atmosphere, were instructive without pedantry, witty without malice, gay and refined. In the evening the balcony, (the southern reception-room in warm weather,) was the resort of every stranger of distinction who visited New Orleans. Scarcely any Frenchmen arrived there without bringing letters from La Fayette to his friend Mr. Livingston. The Lefevre Desnouettes, the Lallemands, the La Kanals and a host of others, enjoyed the easy and refined hospitality of the Chartres Street house. The distinction of manner and brilliant powers of its mistress carried them back in imagination to their own Parisian salons.

About this time war with England was declared. The story of General Jackson's first dinner in New Orleans is worth recording. He arrived unexpectedly. Mrs. Livingston had for that day invited a party of fashionable ladies to a grand dinner, and she was somewhat annoyed at the contretemps when Mr. Livingston announced to her that he had met the General and asked him to join their party. With the ideas prevailing in what was still, in manners, a French province, an American General from the far West seemed a poor acquisition to the entertainment. Mrs. Livingston thought it necessary to prepare her friends for what they had to expect. Great therefore was the surprise when General Jackson entered the room. Innate dignity, chivalric courtesy, perfect self-possession, marked him as one whom nature had fashioned into the gentleman. Taking in all this with a glance, it was with renewed pride in her adopted country and its generous institutions, that Mrs. Livingston took the General's arm to be led in to dinner.

A few days after this, the inhabitants of New Orleans were listening to the sound of battle raging close at hand. From Mr. Livingston's position and the friendship existing between himself and General Jackson, his house was the place where all flocked to hear the latest news. Another circumstance caused it also to be considered a place of refuge among the ladies. After the battle of the 23d of December, while escorting a party of wounded prisoners who were being conveyed to the hospital, Mr. Livingston observed among them a young officer whose appearance interested him. He obtained permission from General Jackson to take him home, where he was left during his illness to the care of Mrs. Livingston. Major Graves was insensible when brought to the house. He was placed in the best room, and every kindness and attention were lavished on him. He used to say that he never could forget his sensations of amazement and gratitude when on recovering his senses, he found himself in this comparative elysium, with beautiful women surrounding him and watching over him. For all in the house had eagerly joined Mrs. Livingston in doing what they could for the sick stranger. Other prisoners had now been brought into the city. Some conspiracy, fancied or real, caused General Jackson to issue an order that all such persons should be sent back at once to the camp hospital. Major Graves was still in too critical a condition to be moved without risk. Mrs. Livingston went herself to General Jackson. She asked permission to retain him, pleading that it was the only return she would desire for the services of her family. Her husband, step-son, two brothers and a future brother-in-law were all there engaged in the defense of their country and personally devoted to the General. Her eloquence prevailed, and she kept her prisoner, the only one allowed to remain in the city. The roof that sheltered him was now supposed to be invulnerable. When the noise of the cannon gave notice that fighting was going on, women and children flocked to Mrs. Livingston's for safety. Major Graves, who had become much attached to the family, would at such times, listen to the sounds with anxiety, advising Mrs. Livingston to leave the city at once should it be taken, and never to remain in the power of any conquering army. He could promise to die for them, he said, but not to protect them; his presence under those circumstances would be of no avail. There was however no necessity for protection; the victory was ours. Many years after this, in the latter part of her life, when Mrs. Livingston was a great invalid, confined to her bed in Philadelphia, a card was brought to her. It was that of Major Graves. Passing through the United States, he had heard where Mrs. Livingston was and had called. The memory of her former kindness had never been effaced from his mind.

Shortly after the war, New Orleans was visited by the yellow fever. During these epidemics, Mrs. Livingston formed part of a society of ladies who went about nursing the helpless victims of this terrible disease. She took pleasure in these offices of charity, for which she was fitted by a natural aptitude to take care of the sick. With her it was a labor of love.

When still young, Mrs. Livingston was fearful of falling into a weakness common among women, of concealing her age. She therefore gave a dinner to which she invited many friends and acquaintances. When all were assembled, she requested them to drink her health, adding: "To-day I am thirty; if I should be tempted to forget it, you must remind me of it."

She had but one child, upon whom she lavished extraordinary maternal devotion, hardly ever suffering her to be out of her sight. Her daughter had scarcely reached girlhood, when Mrs. Livingston assumed the simplest matronly attire. Ever afterwards she seemed rather displeased than flattered when allusions were made before her, to her own still remarkable personal appearance. All self was merged in her daughter. This lovely girl was a celebrated belle in Washington.

In 1822 Mr. Livingston left New Orleans to enter political life as member of Congress from Louisiana. He afterwards exchanged his seat in the House for one in the Senate. This was in turn relinquished for the office of Secretary of State, which he resigned in 1833 to go to France as Minister. During these ten years, Mrs. Livingston spent all her winters in Washington. When she first went there Mr. Monroe was President. Mrs. Monroe was lady-like, gentle and dignified in manner. It was difficult to imagine that anything could disturb the placid serenity of her countenance. Discriminatingly courteous, she seemed born to adorn the high position she occupied. Around her were grouped Mrs. Adams, the gifted wife of the then Secretary of State, whose features sparkled with intelligence; Mrs. Richard Rush, polished and refined, a model of native elegance; Mrs. Hays, the daughter of Mr. Monroe, who at Madame Campan's in Paris, had become intimate with Hortense Beauharnais, after whom she named her beautiful daughter.* There were also many others of note.

After the death of Commodore Decatur, Mrs. Decatur had retired to Kalorama, her country-place, in the vicinity of Washington. There she received, at her select evenings, all the most agreeable as well as prominent persons in Washington. When Mrs. Adams became mistress of the White House, her literary tastes and range of thought were bonds that drew Mrs. Livingston and herself together, notwithstanding the different politics of their husbands. Washington society at that period could boast of many remarkable women. Among others, Mrs. Van Renneslaer, the wife of the Patroon, as he was still called, was distinguished for her matronly beauty, cultivated mind and dignified manners. Mrs. Stevenson, the wife of the Speaker, did not require beauty to charm her listeners.

---

* Afterwards married to Mr. Lloyd Rogers of Maryland.

General Jackson's accession to the Presidential honors made Mrs. Livingston still more prominent. The friendship that existed between Mrs. Livingston and the President, as well as her being the wife of the Secretary of State, gave her a position she was well calculated to fill. Mr. Livingston left to her the entire direction of the household, confident of those powers which infused taste and elegance into every arrangement. She had a special gift in giving entertainments of every description. Her manner of doing the honors was particularly fascinating. Even political animosity was subdued into politeness, by her tact and kindness. Mrs. Livingston became very intimate with the ladies of the diplomatic corps, effectually aiding her husband in his cordial relations with the European representatives. Her house was the nucleus as it were of foreign society in Washington. The duty of doing the honors of the White House having devolved on General Jackson's young niece Mrs. Donelson, she was assisted and guided by Mrs. Livingston. Mrs. Donelson was unaffected and gentle, with an agreeable and lady-like appearance.

In those days, as in New Orleans, Mr. Livingston discussed all the serious affairs which came before him with his wife. In one of his letters, he speaks of the high value he placed upon her judgment on every occasion. When he accepted the place of Minister to France, he left all the arrangements for departure to her; his own time thus reserved for the affairs of the country. His reception in Paris was a source of great satisfaction to his wife. A Frenchwoman herself, she had never before seen France. Her mind was fully prepared for the intellectual and social feast before her. Nevertheless she remained faithful in her devotion to her adopted country. She did not even like to explain how she came to speak the language so purely, and when complimented about it, would simply say that in the United States all women of education spoke French. The dignity of the country she represented was above all things dear to her, and she never permitted a word detrimental to it, in her presence. The Prussian Ambassador in Paris one day spoke of Washington as a village, and turning to Mrs. Livingston asked her what was its population. To which she answered courteously but with a smile: "à peu prés celle de Potsdam." On another occasion there was some difficulty about certain rights claimed by foreign ministers for the wives of the secretaries of legation. M. de St. Maurice, whose duty it was to settle these points of etiquette, expressed surprise that Mrs. Livingston, coming from a republic, should attach any importance to such things. To which she answered: "nous devons y mettre l'importance que vous y attachez vous même." She not only gained her point with M. de St. Maurice, but the additional consideration due to one who knew her rights and enforced them, great or small, never for a moment neglecting what was due to her country. Mrs. Livingston was appreciated at the court of Louis Philippe by the most distinguished men of the day, such as Guizot, Mignet and Villemain, who were all confréres of Mr. Livingston at the French Institute. M. de Marbois was an old friend of his, whom he had

MRS. TULEY.

(VIRGINIA)

Engd by H.B. Hall, N.Y.

known in the United States. He was so aged and infirm, that to join the circle in Mrs. Livingston's salon, he would be carried there by his valet de pied, who would place him in an arm-chair for the evening. Once seated, he would delight every one by conversation full of interest, information and benevolence. Chateaubriand was also frequently there, but he too was old and broken. The Duc de Broglie was then Minister of Foreign Affairs. Mrs. Livingston's intercourse with Madame de Broglie was more than official. They saw each other often, and always met on Sunday at the little Protestant chapel in the Rue Taitbout. Here the most celebrated ministers of the Reformed Church of Geneva preached. Reserved seats were not known in this simple place of worship, and the daughter of Madame de Stael sat on a straw chair, which she found occupied by some one else if she arrived too late.

Mrs. Livingston was on a most agreeable footing with the royal family. The Queen and Madame Adelaide liked to receive her without ceremony in their circle of intimates, and she greatly admired the dignified character and goodness of the Queen. It was of Queen Marie Amelie that General La Fayette said: "Quand á la reine, c'est une aristocrate." The impress of high birth and breeding marked her unmistakably. She never forgot her rank, but that rank was never made oppressive to others.

While Mr. Livingston was minister, his warm and constant friend from childhood, General La Fayette, died. Livingston was not present at his obsequies, being at the time, absent in Holland with his wife.

The impression she produced there delighted her brother Auguste D'Avezac, then the United States Chargé d'Affaires at the Hague. The brother and sister met, and perhaps recollected the strange fate which had brought them from their readings by the Chattiére in St. Domingo, to fulfilling destinies they had little dreamed of, in their days of childhood!

The mission to France was terminated by events on which it is useless to dwell here. On Mr. Livingston's return to the United States he retired to Montgomery Place on the Hudson. This country-seat he had inherited from his sister Mrs. Montgomery, the widow of General Richard Montgomery, who fell at Quebec. He loved the place dearly. It was not many miles from Clermont, where he was born. Here he had habitually spent his summers, after winters of toil in New Orleans or Washington. Here too he proposed to pass the remainder of his life; surrounded by a host of kindred scattered along the banks of the river. He had now renounced public life and wished to give his remaining years to literary pursuits, in the midst of the family circle so dear to him. But Providence willed it otherwise. He passed but one summer in his country home after his return from Europe. A sudden and violent illness terminated his career of usefulness on the 23d of May, 1835.

From that time Mrs. Livingston returned to the world no more. She resided for half the year at Montgomery Place, which was left to her by her husband. Her winters were passed with her daughter in Philadelphia and afterwards in New York. Her health, always delicate, had begun to fail while she was in France, and she now became a confirmed invalid. Her passion for books contributed greatly to while away the long hours of her sick-room. Again and again she returned to the classics which she had loved almost from infancy. She constantly read history with delight, devouring with the eagerness of youth all new publications worthy of her notice. The scope of her mind was manifest from the variety and character of the books that surrounded her. As she advanced in years, her appearance was singularly striking. Notwithstanding continued sufferings, the hand of time was not laid heavily on her, and she retained to an uncommon degree, traces of that beauty which in her youth, had been so celebrated. Her dress was deep black, with a high standing collar and close widow's cap. Her hair, with scarcely a white thread visible, was parted over a soft feminine brow, still fair and smooth. Her eyes were undimmed by age, and her noble countenance reflected her thoughts and beamed with intellect, dignity and kindly feeling. "Like a light within a vase the spirit shone through the outer temple."

For twenty-five years Mrs. Livingston's life was one of constant suffering, which she bore with Christian patience and submission. She was, even in the midst of pain, the least selfish of human beings, always occupied in doing something for others, most considerate not only towards her friends and equals, but with her dependents and inferiors in station. The memory of her kind acts is still fresh among the poor who lived in her neighborhood. The close of her life was as quiet and peaceful as the beginning had been stormy and eventful. Years glided by without landmarks. Her enjoyment of nature was a great boon to her. When no longer able to walk she was wheeled about her grounds and gardens in an invalid's chair, enjoying every breath of mountain air, every view, every flower, with a zest given to few in the fullness of health and spirits. For a quarter of a century, during her long widowhood, to the close of her life, Mrs. Livingston was a member of the Methodist Church. She had been drawn to it by the simplicity and fervor of its mode of worship. She died at Montgomery Place on the 24th of October, 1860, at the advanced age of seventy-eight years.

Another lady whose social influence was abiding, was the wife of Hon. Levi Woodbury of New Hampshire. Her father was the Hon. Asa Clapp of Portland, Maine; her mother was a descendant of the ancient family of De Quincey. Carefully educated, with fine natural parts, Miss Clapp came into society with more than ordinary éclat. Her uncommon personal charms, united to polished manners, grace and kindliness, attracted every one. When yet a schoolgirl, she was called on, in the absence of her mother from home, to preside at the reception of President Monroe and suite at her father's mansion, and won encomiums for her good taste and graceful deportment. After their marriage, Judge and Mrs. Woodbury settled in that delightful old town, Portsmouth, for two centuries the capital of the Province, and subsequently the sovereign State of New Hampshire; and retaining more of that high tone, and social elevation which clings naturally around an old capital, than is often found on this continent. In the autumn succeeding his marriage, Judge Woodbury was elected Governor of the State, and entered on a long career of political life. The graceful ease with which his young wife presided at the executive mansion, threw a charm over the usual stiffness of official intercourse. When his term had expired, Governor Woodbury was elected Senator in Congress; and a large part of his time was thenceforward necessarily spent in Washington. Mrs. Woodbury accompanied him, and entered metropolitan society. History lingers on those days: the standard of statesmanship was high; the old school polish still existed. The Senate and the House held a body of brilliant men, whose acquirements and wit set off their solid merit; and who exercised on the public mind a potent influence, not surpassed by any succeeding generation of public men.

The Corps Diplomatique also formed a bright ornament of that society, and with the leading members of the Executive, the Judiciary, Army, and Navy, and a few distinguished unofficial families, made up in those days, a charming social circle, not too large for acquaintance and friendship, the tone of which was unusually high. It was the rare charm of Washington society that its male element was composed of so many distinguished men, who combined rare intellectual powers with wide-spread observation. The ladies of the families represented the culture and beauty of all sections of our country.

It was then the usage for members of Congress who were agreeable to each other, to form themselves and families into "messes," having a table in the boarding-house, or hotel where they lived. In this way friendships were cemented or formed, and many of the messes acquired a special reputation from the talents and polish of the associates. Often has Mrs. Woodbury related casual anecdotes, or bonmots, of some of the messes to which she and her husband belonged in Washington at that time. And it seemed like another age, to hear the brilliant Verplanck, the great conversationist Tazewell, the metaphysical Calhoun, the eccentric Randolph, and his no less distinguished rival Burgess, sparkle and flash as freshly as if they were of to-day. It was in those times that the great Jackson party formed itself in Congress, which for over thirty years held the affections of the people of the United States, despite the eloquence and popularity of Clay, the sagacity and ponderous power of Webster, and their many able friends. "Fort Jackson" by which this, perhaps the most brilliant of the "messes," was known, derived its name from its political predilections, and was especially celebrated for witticisms. On the breaking up of President Jackson's first Cabinet, Mr. Woodbury was invited to a seat, as Secretary of the Navy, and removed to Washington; continuing through General Jackson's, and Mr. Van Buren's Presidential terms in the Cabinet, but after one or two years, as Secretary of the Treasury.

Questions of etiquette arise as necessarily in a Republican Administration, as in a court; and usages become established. The ladies of General Jackson's second Cabinet were noted for their refinement and taste, as well as for the harmony that prevailed amongst them; and this rendered their efforts to give social distinction to their receptions eminently successful. The question of precedence at State dinners, between the cabinet and foreign ministers, was started by the French minister, and after much discussion it was decided by the President, that the precedence should be given to his cabinet. This rule was adhered to during his term. The Count Serrurier and his wife were so annoyed at the decision that they declined invitations. The dinners at the White House during General Jackson's time, were marked by the growing preference for continental usages over the stiff English ceremonial previously in vogue. While in Mr. Adams' administration the guests departed after coffee, now they lingered after leaving the table, terminating the dinner with a soirée. At the "Drawing-rooms" it had been customary to have supper tables, and the entrance was permitted to all; but the growing population and the vast crowds who flocked to these occasions rendered the custom insupportable; and towards the last of his administration the President was obliged to give up the habit of offering refreshments. It has never been resumed. Many remember the surging crowd which rushed at, and stripped the salvers in the corridors, long before they reached the salons. General Jackson frequently made informal visits to the family of Secretary Woodbury, and showed the kindliness of his heart by the pleasure he took in chatting with the children; winning their affection as truly as he had the devotion and respect of their parents. Mrs. Woodbury sustained her social duties with unyielding patience. It is easy to say, she was popular, but it is not enough; her house was delightful for its social reunions. The private receptions for friends were most agreeable, and no events were ever permitted to interfere with them. In those unpretending weekly soirées the fascination of her manners and the charm of her conversation were most conspicuous and appreciated. They were not political, and the guests were not confined to those in public life; artists and men of merit always found there a kindly welcome. One of the journals of that time, says: "If, as has been said, some are born to command, Mrs. Woodbury seems born to please. Portland may justly feel pride in the recollection that she is a native of that city." Another writer, speaking of those gathered at the Secretary's: "The foreign legations were there too, with their embroidered coats, and I could not but feel proud as an American, when glittering in their stars and badges, they approached the fair hostess, that so splendid a specimen of American beauty, amiability, and politeness should welcome and receive them in this land of Republicanism."

At the close of Mr. Van Buren's administration, Mr. Woodbury again entered the Senate. In 1844, Mr. and Mrs. Woodbury and family, were present on board the man-of-war Princeton, when the accidental bursting of the twelve inch "big gun" hurled Secretaries Upshur and Gilmer, Commodore Kennon, Mr. Maxy, and several other gentlemen into eternity; besides wounding many, including Senator Benton. Fortunately, Mrs. Woodbury and daughters, although invited to take a position near the gun as it was about to be fired, in order to witness the ricochet of the shot on the water, declined doing so and escaped unhurt.

In 1845, her husband was appointed to the bench of the Supreme Court of the United States, which seat he held until his death in 1851; at that time he was a prominent candidate for the Presidency. During this long association with Washington society, and amid the rancor arising from party strife, Mrs. Woodbury never indulged in its bitterness; the arrows of her wit were never dipped in gall. She possessed a cultivated taste for modern classics, and was especially familiar with the writings of the most gifted women of France, England and America. She had also that eloquence du billet, formerly so much admired, and her letters to her friends were of that pointed and piquant style, of which Madame de Sevigné is considered the founder. The loss of her husband was a serious blow; but Mrs. Woodbury was left surrounded with affectionate children, for whom the duties of life were still to be performed. She had four daughters, whose gifted minds and personal advantages made them eminently successful in society. The eldest child, Charles, is a lawyer, lately United States Attorney for Massachusetts. Her daughter Mary married the Hon. Montgomery Blair, Postmaster General under President Lincoln. Frances married Archibald H. Lowery of New York; Virginia the Hon. G. V. Fox, Assistant Secretary of the Navy, and subsequently the Special Envoy to the Emperor of Russia, with the congratulatory resolutions of Congress on his escape from assassination. The youngest, much celebrated as a belle, Miss Ellen, is still unmarried.

Mrs. Woodbury was never ambitious of social distinction; neither her cultivated tastes, nor the attractions of court life abroad, were able to tempt her across the ocean. It was because of her objections, that her husband refused the mission to Spain, tendered him in 1831, by General Jackson; and again in 1845, the mission to England offered him by President Polk. A true American matron, the love of home duties was strongest in her heart, and it required but little exercise of her powers of abnegation to refuse what many fair ladies would have deemed a golden opportunity to breathe the atmosphere of courts, and gaze on royalty at advantage. Wearied with formal society, she embraced the opportunity, as her children were settled in life, to withdraw herself more and more into the domestic circle; and to sympathize with, and see the great world of society through them. Visiting them in the winter, and having them cluster around her in the summer, at her own lovely home, her life glides harmoniously along; her eyes are bright, her form is erect, and her step as elastic as in youth. She takes exercise on foot and in the saddle. The ready repartee springs as gaily as of yore to her lips, and the young love to draw around one who has neither lost her power to please, nor her quiet enjoyment of social intercourse. Influenced by a sense of duty in the daily walk of life, love and respect gather around her from neighbors, family, friends and Christ's poor. She was ever free from envy; possessing intelligence and benevolence. In the symmetry of her character, no marked contrasts strike the observer. It would be difficult to analyze the qualities to which Mrs. Woodbury owed her remarkable success and popularity. Esteemed as she was and is, for a thousand virtues and accomplishments, by a wide circle of friends and acquaintances, and all her acquaintances *must* be her friends—noted for the union of personal charms with solid judgment, perfect taste, and the graceful ease acquired by constant association with the best society, there is something more that constitutes the subtle attraction for which she is distinguished. It is partly her invariable calmness and the moderation of her nature, inspiring confidence; partly her generous consideration at all times for others. She is a lovely study for all who appreciate the highest and gentlest qualities of womanhood. But though we cannot say in what the spell consists, it will be well for all women to emulate the virtues of such a character.

IX.

VAN BUREN'S ADMINISTRATION.

The new President's wifeless Condition a Difficulty to meeting the Claims of Society—Mrs. General Macomb's splendid Party—Ladies conspicuous for Fashion and Beauty—The Rival Generals—The Inauguration, and Ball—Noted Men of the Time—" Connecticut Niles"—Indian Delegation—Calhoun and Preston—Mrs. Madison's Return to Washington—The Diplomatic Corps—Scene in the Gallery—Exciting Scene in the House—New Year's Receptions—Mrs. Adams and Mrs. Madison—Hugh Legare—The Jam in the Galleries—Mrs. Kendall's Party—Mrs. Paulding—Mrs. General Scott—Mrs. De Witt Clinton—Mrs. Gales—Mrs. Seton—Mrs. Dickens—Mrs. Macomb—The Cilley Duel—Scene at Mrs. Towson's Party—Calhoun, Clay and Webster in Competition—Mrs. Schaumburg—The Prince de Joinville—Brilliant Party at M. Bodisco's—Scene at a Presidential Levee—Vespucci at a Cabinet Dinner—The White House on Fire—A "Locofoco Jam"—Madam Calderon's Musical Party—Mr. Preston—The Birthnight Ball, and Catastrophe of the Chandelier—Grand Closing Fete—Clay and Van Buren—Marriage of M. de Bodisco—The Chinese Mandarin at the Spanish Minister's Party.

Martin Van Buren learned his principles from Jefferson. He was a student at law in the office of William P. Van Ness, who was the friend and second of Aaron Burr in his duel with Hamilton. Burr was then at the height of his career,—was Vice-President, lived in great style, and dispensed a lavish hospitality. He was struck with the talents, energy and diligence of the handsome country youth, who imbibed some of his political tactics. Some sanguine spirits hoped that Mr. Van Buren's accession to the purple might give a new polish aud a higher tone to society. He had a taste for the graceful things of life. A letter writer said: "The court of Mr. Van Buren will be the most elegant that ever was got together in Washington. Mr. Van Buren himself will not marry, but his son will soon lead to the altar the accomplished and beautiful daughter of the Patroon of Albany. Arrangements are making among several distinguished ladies to create an era in the fashionable soirées of Washington. The star of New York is in the ascendant; the wit, the beauty, the grace, the genius of New York ladies are about to change the social face of the capital."

It seemed desirable to close the season with as much brilliancy as possible. The wife of the Major-General of the armies of the United States—Mrs. Macomb—gave her second party about the middle of the month. The General was described as "equally graceful in the ball-room and the field. He is neither a laggard in love nor a dastard in war, but prefers the sound of a lady's lute to the music of the drum. He has also been smitten with literary ambition, and has produced a tragico-comico-melodramatic piece, 'Pontiac,' which was brought out on the boards of the Washington theater. Mrs. Macomb is a leader in fashionable society, but attends church regularly. She is the daughter of a clergyman who formerly lectured to a congregation in Georgetown. Under the droppings of his sanctuary she grew up, and retains her early impressions. She gives splendid parties with a military air about them, and goes to soirées, but not to balls, having some religious scruples on that head. Among the married ladies Mrs. Bass was the most magnificently attired. She wore in her turban an aigrette, said to have cost ten thousand dollars. The other elderly ladies seemed to have a passion for birds of paradise. As two of them moved their heads to greet each other, the tails of the birds came in contact, and bobbed about like a cork in the water on the line of an angler. Among the oddities was a widow from Annapolis, literally covered with tinsel, which she called jewelry, and loaded with finery. A young girl from Delaware wore a head-gear of red ribbons, with a scarlet silk bodice, a muslin fly which came down to her knees, trimmed with scarlet, and under it a frock of the same material and trimming! Mrs. Gales—the exclusive, wore a scarlet velvet, and moved a goddess. One pretty young girl was noticed who was said to be the future daughter-in-law of the new President. Mr. Van Buren was said to be devoted to a lady from Baltimore, a widow of considerable beauty. But the lady protested that there was no truth in the rumor."

Colonel Benton was at the time in Washington and seldom went into society unaccompanied by his wife. Mr. Van Buren wore his honors meekly, often riding on horseback along the avenue with his son, taking off his hat and bowing gracefully to all he met. Mr. Adams moved on the footwalk alone, without looking at any one. The expiring throe of gayety for the season was given in a musical and tableaux party. The performers were amateurs, and the violin, flute and clarionet, with the piano, accompanied the voices. One of the company remarked that it had been talked of among the fashionables, to adopt the Italian custom, and entertain a party at the new theater. General Scott was observed as a majestic and noble-looking man. It was remarked that the two generals did not appear to assimilate. One lady said, "The one dislikes what most men pursue,—*Gaines;* the other, though a descendant of a Caledonian, hates the *Scott.*"

A lady who came to attend the splendid ball to be given on the night of the inauguration was Mrs. Bayard, the grand-daughter of Charles Carroll, of Carrollton, and the wife of a Senator. She had an intelligent and lovely countenance, and bore herself well. A noted worshiper of Bacchus, and a brawler, had a piece of hickory made into a cane and waited upon President Van Buren to present it. The new President told the militia major that he never used a cane. "It will be of more service to yourself, major," added he, with an icy smile.

On the evening before the inauguration, which closed the administration of Jackson, the ladies were permitted to come on the floor of the House with their escorts, and the assemblage was magnificent. Many of the members gave up their seats to them, and instead of grave representatives, one might see the ornamental head-gear of the ladies; plumes waving between the lights, and bonnets of various colors. Groups were seen here and there, some seated on sofas, some in the recesses of the windows, some standing behind the scenes, and others promenading, without paying the least attention to the important affairs of the nation, and only listening when Peyton or Wise rose to address the House.

The day of the inauguration, 4th of March, 1837, was bright and clear, but very cold. At an early hour Pennsylvania avenue was crowded with a moving mass of all colors, sizes, ranks and sexes, bending their way to the Capitol. Mass after mass rolled onward till the space in front of the grand staircase of the eastern portico was filled. This staircase and the floor of the portico, were crowded with women; group pouring in upon group, shivering in the cool and frosty air. The oath of office was administered by Chief Justice Taney.

The inauguration ball was designed to surpass in splendor all that had preceded it. The managers were gentlemen of high official rank and young men of fashion. The indication of their authority was a piece of white ribbon, decorating the lapel of their coats. The saloon was very large and was prepared with some expense, but was illuminated by sperm candles instead of lamps, and not so brilliantly as it might have been. The ball was somewhat aristocratic, as the price of admission was ten dollars; yet it was considered crowded. The President and Vice-President made their appearance about ten, and were led up the room to an elevated platform by two of the managers. They there received the congratulations of the company. All the heads of departments and the chief officers of the government, the most respectable citizens, distinguished strangers, and the resident diplomatic corps in the costumes of their nations, were present.

The military and naval officers wore their respective uniforms.

The first sermon was preached in the Capitol in September, 1837, by Rev. T. Fisk of Charleston, South Carolina. In that month Congress was in session, and the galleries were again thronged with auditors of both sexes. Mr. Calhoun was active with his plan for regulating the finances of the government, and eloquent in the exposition of his views. A new orator—John Sargeant of Philadelphia, came into notice. He was a small man, with not a prepossessing face or appearance; but every eye turned on him when he rose. Presently members began leaving their seats, and moving towards the spot where he stood. All was silence, so that one might have heard a pin drop. The voice of the speaker was weak and husky; his manner was cool and collected.

Among noted men of that time Colonel Bell was not inferior in intellect to any in the country. "His conception is rapid, his judgment sound, and his memory tenacious. He decides promptly and generally correctly. He always does justice to the subject he is handling, and brings to it a mind invigorated by reflection. His temperament is melancholy, and he appears absent and abstracted when not engaged in debate or conversation. His feelings are generous and elevated, and his heart is noble and manly."

Mr. Niles—Connecticut Niles—was thus described: "He is about five feet eight, leans forward, is ill-shaped, has red hair that stands up in front and curls all over his head; he frowns incessantly and has a sort of barrel cough peculiarly disagreeable to the hearer. His face is protuberant and wrinkled. Around his neck he girts a white handkerchief tied behind, which gives an expressive projection to his chin. On his rounded shoulders hangs a black coat which fits him badly; his vest is of black satin, and his black breeches are of cloth or cassimere. He crosses his hands behind his back when in an argument; and often slaps his thigh with his right hand as if to enforce what he says. He stands directly in front of his desk, and turns his head frequently to the right and left, so as to let his eyes fall upon Senator Benton on one side and Senator Rives on the other. He must belong to the temperance society; for he drank, during his speech, six tumblers of water, doubtless to keep cool his rising eloquence and prevent it from overflowing the Senate."

In September the delegation of Sioux Indians were invited to meet the Secretary of War, Joel R. Poinsett, and a council was held in Dr. Laurie's church, instead of the war office, or the President's house. The natives attended in their costume of a blanket daubed with red paint, with red leggins and all sorts of head dresses. They listened to an address from Secretary Poinsett.

In October it was written: "Mr. Preston outdid himself to-day. Even they who knew him best were astonished. Calhoun's speech was a mere school-boy's essay to that of his colleague. Nobody had dreamed that Mr. Preston was a political economist; but his discourse to-day has undeceived even his friends. He marched up to the subject with a fearlessness that would have made your heart leap within you had you heard him. He took up the subjects of currency, of money, of exchange, of manufactures, of buying and selling, of credit in all its forms, of banking, and handled them with all the ease that a master mechanic would his tools. The perfect command he has over language enables him to do what others would not dare to attempt. . . . . The breach between Calhoun and Preston is all the talk here. On Saturday the latter made a long and eloquent speech in opposition to his colleague. Duff has opened his battery upon Preston, but Duff is in the last stage of decrepitude, and flutters like an expiring cock. Calhoun will carry but few with him, and it is believed his career is at an end. Black Hawk and his son are the only lions in the city at present. The people are rushing in crowds to see them. There is a member of the lower house from Alabama, worth a trip to Washington to get a sight of. He is about five feet ten inches high. His legs resemble inverted old-fashioned churns. I should guess his weight to be not less than five hundred pounds. They say he is a man of some sense; he certainly carries great weight of character with him. This elephantine legislator would not disgrace old Jack Falstaff. He is the great point of attraction. The ladies can't imagine how the poor fellow can live."

In October of this year, Mrs. Madison returned to live in Washington, after an absence of twenty-three years. A visit to her was thus described:—"I took her to be between sixty and seventy years of age. The same smile played upon her features and the same look of benevolence and good nature beamed in her countenance. She had lost the stately and Minerva-like motion which once distinguished her in the house of the President, where she moved with the grace and dignity of a queen; but her manner of receiving was gracious and kind, and her deportment was quiet and collected. She received all visitors with the same attention and friendly greeting. She remarked that a new generation seemed to have sprung up. 'What a difference,' she said, 'twenty years makes in the face of society! Here are young men and women who were not born when I was here last; whose names are familiar to me, but whose faces are unknown. I seem to have suddenly awaked after a dream of twenty years to find myself surrounded by strangers.' 'Ah, madam,' remarked one of the ladies, 'the city is no longer what it was when you were the mistress of the President's house! Your successors have been sickly, tame, spiritless and indifferent. The mansion you made so charming and attractive, is now almost inaccessible. The present incumbent has no female relative to preside, and seems to be so much absorbed in party politics, that he will scarcely open the house to those who wish to see it. The very tone of society has been affected by these changes. At one time, such was the bitterness of party feeling, that no visits were interchanged between those belonging to the administration and those in the opposition. Almost all the oldest citizens are now excluded from office, and brawlers, broken merchants, disbanded officers, and idle young men have been put in their places.

But the society is beginning to improve, and the

fashionable of all parties mingle more harmoniously. Foreigners now, as in your day, are all the go. A poor attaché, a gambling minister, a beggarly German baron, or a nominal French count, is preferred to the most substantial and accomplished citizen, among the young women at this court.' "

Mrs. Madison smiled at this picture, and spoke with much feeling of the former condition and appearance of the city.

After Christmas, it was said: "The Attorney General, to avoid giving parties, has taken lodgings, and quitted housekeeping. Secretary Dickerson is an old bachelor, and has a good excuse. Secretary Forsythe is too poor to afford the expense, and finds he can get along as well without them. Secretary Woodbury is waiting till after the holidays, when he will probably entertain as usual. Of the foreign diplomatic corps I know of none except M. Pontois, who is likely to entertain this winter. Fox is an old bachelor, who dines at twelve o'clock at night, and breakfasts at one the next day. He hates the sight of women, and eschews their society. He is fond of mutton, but seldom invites Mouton to his table. He is a solitaire, who, though he does not forget all, is 'by all forgot.' His few servants threaten to leave him, as they do not like leading the life of an owl:—sleep all day and work all night."

A scene in the gallery was reported by a witness:

"'Did you hear Menifee on this question?' asked one.

"'Yes, what do you think of him!'

"'That he is a young man of fine talents; destined

to take a high stand in the House. Clay says he is the first young man in the nation, and his speech to-day will give him a high reputation. Kentucky is rich in talent. Clay and Crittenden in the Senate are unequalled, and this young man will yet rival them in the walks of eloquence.'

"'Have you heard Hoffman?' 'Yes; he is very clever, and with a little industry would become a very prominent member. He speaks well, and is noble-hearted, courteous and fearless. Preston paid him a high compliment when he made his first speech.'

"'Speaking of Preston, Calhoun seems to have left him.'

"'Yes, and has destroyed himself. He has thrown himself under a falling party, and will be crushed beneath it.'

"'His State will sustain him, I have no doubt, and his opinions will be found to be correct.'

"'Never. He is the victim of blasted ambition, and will never rise again.'

"I moved towards another group of gentlemen and ladies, who were speaking of Wise and Gholson.

"'Do you think there will be a duel?' enquired a young Virginian. 'I trust not,' replied an elderly gentleman. 'But I regret to see both parties apparently so desirous of pitting these two men against each other. They are both fiery and hot-headed. The vitriolic blood of the South bubbles up in the veins of each upon the least provocation, and they seem unable to control their tempers.' 'Poor dear soul!' sighed an elderly belle in the group, 'it would be a monstrous pity to have Mr. Wise shot. He is such a bold and independent man, and makes such interesting speeches.' An old Jackson lady remarked: 'I am sure he would be no great loss if Mr. Gholson were to kill him; and I would rather hear him speak than a thousand Wises. But what a noise that man yonder is making. How shocking! to come here to sleep!'

"'Why do they keep the gallery so dark!' asked a black-eyed girl. 'Because,' was the gallant reply, 'the Speaker thinks the light from the radiant eyes of the fair quite enough without artificial illumination.'"

At the close of the year, Calhoun was still "the leader of the Southern party in the House, and wishes to be so of both Houses. But Wise, too, has thrown himself in front on this great Southern question, and takes the lead from him in Virginia, for the purpose of aiding Clay, whom Calhoun is maneuvering to defeat." One among many scenes like the following may be illustrative: "On the allusion of Mr. Slade (a member from Vermont) to 'the Alton tragedy,' a simultaneous movement was made throughout the House. Legaré attempted to get the floor, but was resisted by his friends, who used all their force to keep him down. Slade all the while was declaiming against the slaveholder and the slaveholding States. Wise, who at least has the appearance of a madman, was so infuriated that his clenched fist was making its way through every obstacle that came within his reach. Imagine this picture! Slade in the centre, inflaming the Southerners by his violence of speech; on his right some twenty or thirty, and here and there a group arguing 'What should be done?' On the other side of the House, greater excitement is manifested. Wise is appealing to Bell 'to assist in allaying the excitement'—himself so excited that his countenance has undergone a thorough change—his eyes darting fire, his nostrils distended, the muscles of his face so strongly marked, that it were not impossible to take hold of them; his hands clenched and his whole frame convulsed from top to toe. Some few members are now hanging around the marble pillars, with long and serious faces. The messenger boys are in front of the Speaker's desk, holding each other's arms in breathless silence. The Speaker, standing up, crying out for 'Order! order! order!' his face as pale as a sheet. Strangers are pressing into the galleries, and all there partake the excitement of the scene below. 'Who is that speaking in the midst of the group on the left?' inquired a stranger.

"'It is the eloquent Legaré, trying to get the eye of the Speaker.' A blow is heard on the desk. It is from Wise, who, no longer able to control his feelings, is making a call for 'the Southern Delegation to leave the hall.'

"'Agreed! agreed!' from fifty voices. 'Where shall we go?' 'To the committee room for the District of Columbia.' A general rush followed this annunciation; but the tempest within was still raging with increased violence. Adams rose, and begged his friend Mr. Slade not to be alarmed—he had seen such storms before. The Speaker's hammer was playing away on the desk, but to no effect; Slade still going on.

"Robertson—'One remark, Mr. Speaker.'

"Slade—'I claim the floor. I ask leave to read a paper I hold in my hand.'

"The Chair—'The gentleman will take his seat.' Here a hundred were on the floor, addressing the chair at one time.

"'Is not the gentleman from Vermont declared out of order?'

"Chair—'He is. Order—order! Take your seat.'

"Slade—'I propose to read this paper.'

"Turney—'I object to the gentleman proceeding at all.'

"The Chair—'Sir, take your seat.'

"Slade—'Not till I have read this paper.'

"Chair—'The rule is imperative. Sit down.'

"Slade, still on his feet—'Mr. Speaker——'

"Chair—'Sit down.'

"'I move an adjournment,' from twenty.

"Slade—'I demand the yeas and nays upon that motion.'

"Adams to Slade—'Go on—go on!'

"Cries of 'order,' and 'question. To adjourn 106, against 63. Notwithstanding the house was adjourned, none of the members left it. An announcement was made that the Southern Delegation was organized, and requested the friends of the Union to meet them in the committee room."

Parties were given by the different factions. Mrs. Woodbury was eminently fitted to adorn social reunions. She was handsome, graceful, courteous and fascinating, attentive and hospitable, and dressed with great taste. She had a lovely and accomplished daughter then not old enough to be brought out. At this time there was a considerable accession of foreign beauty. The President held a levee on New Years' day, said to be the finest first of January ever known in Washington. Mr. Van Buren, with his usual smile, stood in the center, supported on the right by the Marshal of the District, and on the left by a gentleman well known in fashionable society. The visitors after paying their respects, retired into the east room. There Henry Clay was seen escorting a tall, majestic woman, Mrs. Bell, the wife of the ex-Speaker. Clay received the congratulations of all who passed, in the easy, democratic style for which he was remarkable. This room extended the whole depth of the house north and south, opening on a terrace running to the east, from which is presented a beautiful view of the Potomac and the country on either side. The foreign ministers were all in their court dresses, and the military and naval officers in their uniforms. The dresses of the Russian and French attachés were splendid.

A gentleman complimented by the name, "Sir Thomas Humbug," and "Old P. Q."—the impersonation of the Previous Question,—were conspicuous; one crying out "Mornin', Sar!" continually, in a nasal twang. The Vice-President was planted near the main entrance. A dark-eyed, yellow-faced man was pointed out as connected with him by marriage; a Senator, who always talked loudly and vociferously from being accustomed to bawl to his team in the backwoods. Major General Scott looked splendidly. He towered above the rest of the company like a giant among pigmies. His Florida laurels were not, however, green on his brow; the Seminoles not allowing themselves to be conquered. Jessup did little better. There was some complaint of the want of refreshments, as it had been usual to have them in the administration of Mr. Madison and Mr. Adams.

Mrs. Adams and Mrs. Madison received company on the same day. Mrs. Madison moved like a queen in her crowded rooms, dressed in black, with a turban she had been accustomed to wear at the White House. She seemed much pleased to welcome her friends, among whom were Clay, Bell, Preston, and several whig Senators. The stream of visitors was continually ebbing and flowing. Mrs. Madison, though some seventy years of age, did not look more than fifty. At Mrs. Adams' house, too, the company consisted of the élite of the city. It was singular to be able to visit in one day a President, an ex-President, and the widow of an ex-President.

It was said there was but little musical taste in the capital at that period. The theatre was well patronized, and there was no lack of excellent actors.

Mr. Legaré had the character of being a good speaker, and when he was to address the House on the Mississippi election, the galleries were crowded by auditors. To give an idea of the jam, a single incident may be mentioned. A shabby-genteel dandy, with a rusty cloak fastened round his neck by a gilt clasp, had been pinioned against the wall, and made vain efforts to escape. The wave of the crowd pushed him one way, while his cloak, pressed by those behind him, held him fast. One arm was thrown forward, and the other, in the hand of which he held a shabby old cap, was fastened to his body by the outside pressure. In this position he remained, in imminent danger of suffocation from the stricture around his throat. "Gintlemen!" exclaimed an Irishman, "if ye don't want to sthrangle the man inthirely, let him 'ave the tail of his cloak: for by the powers the balls are shootin' from his head, and he'll have no tongue to his mouth in a second." The man made a sort of gurgle in his throat to confirm Paddy's assertion. When he was released by unclasping his cloak, he made a desperate plunge and disappeared.

Mrs. Kendall's party was numerously attended, being the first soirée ever given by the head of the General Post Office Department. Parties, of course, it will be understood, were always given in the name of the lady. Mrs. Kendall was a simple woman, more inclined to be domestic than fashionable. She had a daughter to introduce. Some of Mr. Kendall's political opponents said that an English attendant had been engaged as master of ceremonies, and everything was given into his management. The names of visitors were demanded at the door, and called out by the servant at the top of his voice. Some one remarking that Mr. Kendall looked pale, an elderly belle said he had never recovered his complexion since the defeat of the Locofocos in New York; and thereupon she darted her hand into a plate and grasped a handful of gingernuts and macaronies. The escort of another lady cut away with a spoon at a pyramid of cake which he took for one of ice-cream, and overthrew the whole structure. A young lady cried out that he must have taken it for an Indian.

Mrs. Madison was seen at the dinner and evening parties, and was the observed of all observers. She was at a dinner at the President's, where Mr. and Mrs. Webster were also present with their daughter; the ladies superbly dressed. The banquet was in the Parisian style.

Mr. Van Buren made Mr. Paulding Secretary of the Navy. His wife was the sister of Gouverneur Kemble. The word "lady" hardly defined her; she was a perfect gentlewoman. Scott called Mr. Paulding "the most thorough gentleman in the United States." He belonged to a distinguished English family on the father's side, and was the nephew of Lady Gage. His house was the favorite resort among all the secretaries. At the age of eighty, he still entertained visitors at his residence at Cold Spring, opposite West Point; inviting the professors and distinguished strangers every Saturday to visit him and his superb gallery of paintings.

Justice has never been quite done to the splendid qualities of Mrs. Winfield Scott. She was highly educated, and possessed remarkable powers of conversation. Her witty sayings were often sarcastic and always ready. When she heard it said of a diminutive man that he had not much mind, she added "He has neither mind nor body." On one occasion she remarked: "They call the General 'Fuss and Feathers;' Mr. —— is fuss without the feathers." When a young girl—a belle in Richmond—one evening at a party, an old gentleman came up, laid his hand on her neck, and said, smiling: "How do you feel, my dear?" She replied, quickly: "Ugh! I feel as if old age were crawling over me."

Mrs. DeWitt Clinton was a noble woman, of masculine understanding and energies. For years she was a leader in New York society. She was in her autumnal prime and the meridian of her influence during Mr. Van Buren's administration. She was displeased at his political intrigues in regard to her husband, and at Saratoga in 1838, she refused to recognize him. During General Jackson's Presidency, when he and Mr. Van Buren called on her upon one occasion, she sent for the General to join her in another room, and would not meet his companion. There was a power about this lady, acknowledged by all who knew her, and she had a hearty appreciation of humor.

One of the chief leaders of fashion was Mrs. Gales, who was "at home" every Friday evening. Her parties were well attended by members of Congress, residents and strangers. Her nieces, the Misses Walker, were pretty and danced remarkably well. Her house was rather small for brilliant display, but one always met at her not overcrowded soirées, distinguished foreigners and visitors to the capital. Her husband was said to be one of the most generous and charitable of men. Mrs. Seton, his sister, was a very superior woman, given to hospitality, and always employed in doing good to her fellow creatures. She was instrumental in getting up many charitable institutions, and society owed much to her philanthropic exertions. She did not care for the vanities and frivolities of the world. Her charming daughters had similar tastes. Mrs. Dickens was prominent in giving and attending parties. Hers were usually crowded. Her daughters were pretty, and she was hospitable and fond of company. One representative from New York, seen often at her house, was Mr. Hoffman, who had made a brilliant speech in the House. He was a great admirer of beauty, and went to all the parties.

Whenever it was known that Webster, Clay, Preston or Calhoun was to speak, the galleries were crowded; if less favored orators rose to address the Senate, they were cleared in fifteen minutes. When Henry Clay was to address the Senate on the Sub-Treasury bill, the lady spectators got on the floor, and spread themselves on each side of the circle behind the bar. They were forced to retire, to their great vexation, pouting and throwing disdainful glances on poor Haight and Weir, who were obliged to order them away. Clay sustained himself with great ability, speaking for nearly six hours.

In the latter part of February of this year, Washington was thrown into excitement by the fatal termination of a duel between Mr. Cilley, of Maine, and Mr. Graves, of Kentucky, acting for Colonel Webb, of New York. The duel grew out of the imbroglio produced by the letters and acts of M. L. Davis, the "Spy" correspondent of the Courier and Enquirer, and the subsequent criminations and recriminations. Mr. Cilley fell at the third fire.

A party given by the wife of General Towson was very brilliant, the house being well calculated by its size and arrangement for the reception of company.

Mrs. Towson was dressed in exquisite taste, and a young lady stood at her side. The ball-room was up stairs; and amidst the brilliant crowd might be seen Mrs. General Macomb, and Mrs. Schaumburg of Philadelphia, said to be one of the best amateur singers in the country. Mrs. Pleasants of Washington, radiant in beauty, stood leaning on the arm of her escort, proud to have her under his charge. Her head was encircled by a magnificent coronet of pearls; her dress was black velvet; and she looked like the goddess who punished the presumption of Acteon for daring to gaze on her loveliness. The supper was capital. A guest remarked: "I left the great intellectual giant of the Senate, Webster, forking pickled oysters with as much goût as he would read a law case; and Speaker Polk, with his mouth so crammed with chicken, celery and beef's tongue, that even the offer of a foreign embassy could not loosen his jaws. Wise was washing down his tongue with champagne, and ex-Speaker Bell was meditating the demolition of a plate of blanc-mange."

The great national birthnight ball took place in Carusi's saloon. Among the distinguished guests were Clay and Webster, who seemed to participate feelingly in the hilarity of the fête. The Vice-President was also conspicuous, and all parties were mingled in the most agreeable harmony. The floor was marked with the insignia of the different states, and the pillars of the supper-room were decorated with festoons and wreaths of artificial flowers. The President came in about ten with Mr. Clay, to the tune of Hail Columbia.

On the evening of Cilley's burial, a musical party was given by the wife of the Solicitor of the Treasury. Many members attended it after returning from the funeral of their friend and fellow-legislator. Among the groups talking of the unhappy event, one might hear a lady remark: "Poor man! how I pity him! But don't you think Mrs. Schaumburg sings divinely!"

"Exquisitely!" the reply would be: "Dear me, how shocking it was! and his poor wife!"

"Have you been introduced to Captain Marryatt? What a strange creature!"

"Indeed I sympathize deeply with his family."

"It will be so sudden—so unexpected—"

"What a fine voice Mrs. Schaumburg* has!"

"Captain Marryatt don't seem inclined to be introduced to anybody!"

"I do feel for poor Mrs. Cilley. Were you at the House to-day?"

"Oh, yes, I attended the funeral, and heard the chaplains pray and exhort, and saw all the ceremonies. Is Captain Marryatt a married man?"

"Poor thing! how afflicted she will be! These musical soirées are very charming. Nothing affects me so much as music."

"This city don't appear very propitious to matrimony."

"No marriage has taken place among the fashiona-

---

* The Mrs. Schaumburg mentioned was the mother of Miss Emily Schaumburg, in later years celebrated in Philadelphia society for her admirable voice and musical skill, and her powers as an amateur actress. A sketch of her is given in "The Queens of American Society."

bles this winter but that of the Chevalier Tacon. It is surprising, isn't it?"

"Very. Did you say poor Mrs. Cilley had three little children? How melancholy!"

"Did you hear how Captain Marryatt cut that dandy! Served him right!" etc.

Marryatt was looked on as a lion, and attended all the parties, though objecting to be introduced to any one.

On an early Thursday in March, the President opened his drawing-rooms for the first time since his accession. M. Pontois, the French minister, gave a party the night before. The minister was a large man and his secretary a small one; both wore eye-glasses, more, it was said, from affectation than necessity. M. Pontois was not so popular as some of his predecessors. None of the ministers had their wives with them. Fox was a solitaire and very eccentric; he kept himself aloof from the fashionable world, and was studious and retiring. At this time Calhoun, Clay and Webster were called "the three great competitors for the throne." In the intellectual amphitheatre of the Senate, they showed their skill and dexterity in couching the lance and wielding the battle-axe. The massive war mace was wielded by Webster with the force of a giant refreshed by the slumber of ages. Nothing could resist the vigor and tremendous weight of his blows, and the enchanted castle of the Sub-Treasury fell before his resistless energy. The Speaker, Mr. Polk, gave a soirée at his lodgings, on the same evening that Forrest ranted and thundered in Metamora to the delight of the fashionables.

Mrs. Forsythe, the wife of the Secretary, gave the second of her parties. Mrs. Poinsett had given but one, and Mrs. Woodbury had been prevented from exercising her usual hospitality by the death of a relative. The crowd at Mrs. Forsythe's included the belles and beaux of the three cities of the district.

M. Pontois invited Madame Caradori Allen to a dinner, and had a number of guests whom he had invited to hear her sing. But the cantatrice had no idea of being made to amuse the company, and therefore pleaded a bad cold as an excuse for refusing.

The singer gave a concert, which was well attended notwithstanding the lack of musical taste. Some thought the richly dressed Mrs. Schaumburg not inferior in voice to Caradori. The Major-General, Clay, and many distinguished persons were in the background at the concert; the gentry in front affecting to be connoisseurs, and crowded around the singer.

The arrival of Lord Gosford created quite a sensation. Though an Irishman, he was a lord; and invitations to dinner and supper awaited him on every side. The "Geologists of the United States" waited on him. That singular genius, Fox, was roused from his den and made to revisit the glimpses of the sun. The battle between the champion of Nullification—Calhoun, and the champion of the Constitution—Webster, occupied universal attention. A member from Pennsylvania, Mr. Petrikin, wore an old-fashioned pigtail or cue. Another member, making some remarks on what he had said, observed: "The gentleman has thrown out some insinuations that deserve notice, and I will thank him for the cue." "I'll be hanged," said the little old member, "if you or any other man shall have it, I have nursed it till it has grown into a respectable tail, and no man shall *curtail* it."

In April, complaints were made of the dullness of the metropolis; the President having opened his house but twice during the winter. During the preceding administration, it was remembered that the secretaries and other members of the cabinet showed their hospitality by giving parties week after week; the present members had shut themselves up in the recesses of their mansions. "The court of Martin the First" was voted a shabby concern. It had devolved on private individuals to sustain the social character of the government, and show by their elegant hospitality that refinement and civilization existed in the metropolis of the nation. But they seemed to have wearied of leading the fashionable world. All were astonished at the prospect of two May balls, a party at the house of M. Pontois, and a party given by Mr. Fox. The latter was an unexpected novelty; the first given by the minister, and in honor of the birthday of his Queen Victoria. At the French minister's party, a lady carried away the palm for grace and dignity, who had sojourned at the splendid Court of Austria.

The arrival of the steam frigate Fulton created a great sensation. Mr. Van Buren and a portion of his cabinet took a trip down the river on board of her, returning in the evening. A regatta was got up in honor of her arrival; five boats to row a mile and back. The crowd of spectators was immense. The evening was concluded by a ball and collation given by the officers. This was greatly enjoyed by the belles and beaux, who danced to the music of the marine band.

The arrival of the Prince de Joinville with his suite, opened the prospect of more fêtes and parties. This son of Louis Philippe was a strapping youth of eighteen, more desirous of displaying his equestrian skill than of figuring as a lion. On his first ride, the morning after he came, he was thrown, but sustained little injury, and afterwards made his appearance in the Senate Chamber with the French minister. Next day he went to Philadelphia.

The summer heats of this year were excessive, but the ardor of fashionable gayety continued. Mrs. Woodbury gave a soirée in July, and Mr. Kendall a raspberry party at his residence on Jackson Hill. After the adjournment of Congress the city began to look deserted; the office-holders and fashionables flying off to the springs, to spend their money and kill their time. Mr. Van Buren shut himself up in his palace, and was seldom seen.

"Does the President mean to give any drawing-rooms next season!" was asked in the following October.

"Oh, certainly," was the reply. "His son, the private secretary, is to be married in a few weeks, and his wife will receive the company; a fact that has produced a great deal of satisfaction. Mr. Van Buren, too, is so elated at the success of the Locofocos, that he is determined no longer to burrow in one of the solitary nooks of the palace, but to be visible to all his friends of both sexes frequently during the next session."

The second session of the Twenty-fifth Congress was opened early in December, 1839. A brilliant party was announced to be given by M. de Bodisco, the Russian minister, at his residence in Georgetown, where he lived in great splendor. He was at this time a bachelor, and it was his first fête. His reputation as a man of taste, and his familiarity with fashionable life in Europe, rendered most persons curious to go. As they approached his residence through the dark streets, the blaze of light resembled a conflagration. Servants at the door, in livery, took charge of the hats and cloaks, and the names were announced, first below by a servant, at the head of the staircase by another, and at the entrance to the drawing-room by a third. M. de Bodisco, magnificently dressed in the costume of his court, received the company with ease and courtesy. He was a fine-looking man, about forty-two, with brilliant black eyes, dark, thick and curling hair, and a face expressive of benevolence and good humor. His manners had a grace derived from constant intercourse with the most polished courts of Europe. This was his fourth embassy in different countries. He spoke English and several modern languages. Every room in the house, except one, was thrown open, and brilliantly lighted with lamps and candelabras. Most of the splendid furniture was of European make, and not a house in the country contained such a variety of artificial ornaments and curiosities. The china services were very rich, and the plate costly and magnificent. One retired room was called "Flirtation Gallery." All the foreign ministers and their attachés were in their court dresses. The costume of the Austrian, a marshal, consisted of a coat of white cloth, covered with orders, and pantaloons of scarlet, richly trimmed. M. de Bodisco's dress was blue, covered with silver lace to a great depth, and ornamented with precious stones. The buckles of his pumps were set in brilliants. The French minister's dress was also splendid and costly. Among the refreshments were ices of all kinds; iced chocolate, iced crab apple juice, ice-creams, iced punch, lemonade, sangaree, &c., brought on silver waiters and eaten with gold spoons. The music was delightful. The rooms were kept warm partly by Russian stoves. The supper was served about one; a long apartment in the second story being set apart to accommodate the ladies. They were seated the whole length of the table, which was covered with gold and mirror plateaus, splendid candelabras, Grecian temples, castles, &c., made of candied sugar; fruits of all sorts in ornamental dishes; china ornaments, gold forks, &c. The gentlemen were excluded from this room, and the ladies were waited on by the servants. The gentlemen's supper-room was in the third story. Among the members—of whom there were few—were Mr. James K. Polk and Mr. Cambreling. The card-room was near, and in it the Secretary of State and the Secretary of the Navy were deeply engaged at whist. The company retired between two and three. This was said to be the most superb fête ever yet given in the District. It was in honor of the birthday of the Emperor Nicholas, and eight hundred guests were invited.

A party by the Austrian minister was looked for to

rival M. de Bodisco's. Poor Mr. Fox, with an income of thirty thousand, managed only an occasional dinner, very late at night; mutton boiled, roasted and fried. People said the house smelt of sheep. Fox was called the spectre minister, from the unnatural paleness of his face, and the blackness of his bushy eyebrows.

Prentiss, the Mississippi orator, "is a small man, about five feet six inches in height, lame in one of his legs, which he rests on his cane when he walks. His head is large and well cast, and his body well proportioned. He is said to be a native of Maine, and commenced life in poverty. He taught school in Mississippi when he first went out to that State, while quite a lad; studied law afterwards and soon became distinguished at the bar, where he not only acquired fame but wealth. He appears to be about thirty years of age. His countenance becomes lighted up in speaking by the warmth and glow of his feelings. He has all the elements of an orator; he is logical, imaginative, sarcastic and humorous. His early reading seems to have been Scriptural, and from the Scriptures he brings most of his illustrations, which are always happy. His judgment, memory and imagination seem to be equally prominent."

On New Year's day the President again opened his house to visitors. Henry Clay also received in his rooms at Borlanger's, a restaurateur on Pennsylvania avenue. At twelve the President's palace was thrown open, and the immense crowd poured in. Mr. Van Buren stood in the reception-room, with gentlemen on either side. A little behind him stood the youthful bride and bridegroom, Mr. and Mrs. Van Buren.

She received the ladies. She was said to possess great wealth, and to belong to an ultra whig family.

A lady asked: "Why does M. de Bodisco carry that beautiful silver key on the back of his coat?"

"To denote that 'Love laughs at locksmiths,' or that he keeps the key to the secrets of the emperor, and has locked up his own," somebody answered.

"And who is that standing near him so splendidly dressed?"

"The French ambassador, Monsieur Pontois. He has given up housekeeping, and now boards at a restaurateur's, where, of course, he cannot entertain."

"A minister that don't give parties ought to stay at home."

"And what would you do with the British minister?"

"Bury him in the cave of Trephonius, or change him into an owl." "Is not that the Vice-President with some lady under his arm!"

"Yes, and Major-General Pontiac is making up to him, in the path made by the Infant of the House, Mr. Lewis." Benton and "the Previous Question" were cheek by jowl together. Some looking at Van Buren, thought of Henry Clay, erect and tall, and "proudly eminent," receiving the obeisance of a few who came from pure respect, and wondered at the ingratitude of a republic, that a man whose name was identified with the leading measures of the government for the last thirty years, devoting his life to the good of his country, should not have been preferred as a ruler.

Mrs. Madison also received her friends, dressed in

mourning for the death of two near relations. She retained her gracious manners and liberal hospitality.

Parties were announced in honor of the marriage of Major Van Buren, and the city anticipated gayety during the coming season. Mr. Blair gave a party, the cards of invitation to which had long colored ribbons attached to them, streaming through the air as they were borne along. The French minister made preparations for the arrival of Signora Vespucci. The roaring and ranting of Mr. Pickens drew startled attention from the galleries. A party given by the wife of General Macomb was attended by all the officials and distinguished persons disposed to pay respect to the Commander-in-Chief. M. de Bodisco had two young nephews at the college in Georgetown, and issued cards of invitation to a children's ball. The little girls and boys enjoyed themselves, and ate like demi-gods. Suddenly Mr. Clay was seen escorting a lady—Miss Vespucci—recently arrived in Washington. She was saying in French: "I would give half what I ever expect to possess to be able to converse with Mr. Webster in his own language. I saw him in the East, and was struck with his noble head. Before I heard who he was, I felt that he was a great man."

Mr. Clay's meeting with Mrs. Madison at a party given by the French minister, was noticed; the lady rose at his approach, extended her hand, and gave him one of those smiles which no doubt helped to make the dominant party adhesive, in the days of her presidency. Her movements had all the grace, ease, and elasticity of youth. On one occasion a gentleman went up to her and said: "You do not remember me, Mrs. Madison!"

"Yes, I recollect you very well, Mr. ——" she replied. She had not seen him in twenty-six years!

It was this intellectual power, combined with all the graces and elegances of her sex, that made her once almost the center and source of power in the government.

"When are we going to have a grand quarrel in the House?" asked a beautiful woman with an arch smile. "I can't tell," replied her companion; "Mr. Wise is gone to New York; I am afraid we shall be quiet for a fortnight." "I don't like quiet; I don't like peace; I like to see you all quarreling," said the beauty. But in tranquillity the gay world dashes out. At a party given by Mrs. Woodbury, three apartments and the ball-room on the lower floor were full; several up stairs in the same condition, and the stairways strewed with lovely girls. The hostess was dressed with splendor. As the company arrived and were presented, they filed off into another room, leading to the ball-room.

"Every Friday evening Mrs. Gales has reunions during the session, and all who attend them are in raptures with the beauty, order, simplicity and elegance of the arrangements."

Mr. Adams was noticed at the theatre during Hackett's performance, seated in the center of the pit. "During the whole evening he looked neither to the right nor the left. He was surrounded by large numbers of the members of both houses, who came to enjoy the character of Falstaff. Adams became interested—absorbed—and occasionally laughed till his eyes filled with tears. He has an enthusiasm for the old English drama, and its effects on him were as strong and natural as the first play on the nerves of an innocent country girl. His appearance, with his fine bald head and few silvery locks, had a picturesque and pleasing effect."

Mr. Van Buren invited the Vespucci to a cabinet dinner he gave towards the close of January to the judges of the Supreme Court. It was remarked that he seemed much struck with the splendid Tuscan beauty, and had been turning his attention to the Italian language. He placed Vespucci between himself and Mr. Webster. On sitting down, he asked her if she spoke English; she replied "a lit," with a charming smile. But his excellency was prevented from bringing his Italian into play, by Mr. Webster's "Parlez vous Français?" and the lady's "Oh, oui Monsieur." An amusing account was given of the efforts and failures of the two great statesmen, whose French and Italian were soon exhausted. "Never was there seen such a specimen of classical pantomime; Mr. Van Buren and Mr. Webster, sitting on either side of Vespucci, as dumb as if they had lost their tongues. Not a single word could they say that she understood; and not a word she said did they understand. In this crisis of affairs, an interpreter was discovered at table, after which the conversation with the fair Florentine went on with great spirit."

An artist from New York—Mr. Linen—painted an excellent cabinet portrait of Henry Clay, which was shown in Washington. While Clay was dining with

MRS. J. T. THOMAS.

the President at one of his regular cabinet dinners given in rotation every Saturday to the members of both Houses, a servant whispered to Mr. Van Buren, "The house is on fire." Van Buren rose very coolly, apologized to the gentleman next him, and left the room for a few minutes. His whole kitchen department was in flames; but a few pails of water quenched the fire, which had made little progress. When Van Buren returned to his company, and explained the cause of his absence, Mr. Clay turned to him, and with a peculiar look, said: "Mr. President, I am doing all I can to get you out of this house; but, believe me," here he put his hand upon his breast, "I do not want to burn you out." The expression the artist threw into his portrait was the same with which Mr. Clay said these few words. The eyes lighted up, the lips slightly apart, the big, broad mouth apparent, a half smile spread over the face, the whole countenance beaming with the lofty intellect, and blending wit, dignity and good humor.

Mr. Van Buren's carriage was superb; of a dark olive hue, with ornaments as bright as burnished gold. When he entered it, the servant dashed up the steps, banged to the door, jumped up behind, and away it rolled as if the vehicle were conscious of bearing the head of the Republican party.

Henry Clay usually walked from the church to his lodgings, without blue or gold carriage, blood horses, or livery servants.

In politics Mr. Clay was the master spirit of the opposition. Almost every act of general legislation was determined by the influence it was supposed to have on the prospects of the next Presidential election. The venerable John Quincy Adams was at this time about seventy-two, but full of health, activity and vigor both physical and mental. Relieved from political cares and anxieties, his mind had full play, and he was one of the best of companions.

A "splendid locofoco jam" was given in February by the wife of the Attorney-General, Mrs. Gilpin. Her former husband, Senator Johnston, perished in a steamboat explosion on Red River. A musical party given by Madame Calderon, wife of the Spanish minister, was also an event in the beau monde. She was a young Scotch lady, who came to this country with her mother, Mrs. Inglis. She was allied to a noble Scottish family and occupied a high position in Edinburgh. Misfortunes compelled them to emigrate to Boston, where the mother and two accomplished daughters established a female seminary, and one afterwards at New Brighton. Here Mr. Calderon became acquainted with the family.

"It is the fashion of the day to cry up Preston as one of the greatest speakers of Congress. A gentleman who had heard a splendid speech from him, said he had heard every fine figure, every classical allusion, every brilliant thought, several years before, applied to a widely different topic." This remark was hardly just to Mr. Preston; though he had the habit of collecting and saving for use, brilliant figures similes, &c. The writer of this work, while living in South Carolina, once lent him the poems of Lamartine. When he returned the volumes, several sheets of manuscript were found in them, filled with translations of fine points and passages, some of which he afterwards introduced into his speeches. Sometimes he improved on the poets quoted. One passage described an eagle on a dizzy height, pluming himself on his occupancy of a lofty situation, and rebuked and humbled by seeing a worm, which had *crawled* to the same elevation. Mr. Preston, sympathizing with the proud bird, thus improved the thought:

"The worm that had ignobly crept to the height, dared to compare himself to the eagle! The worm had *crawled* up; whereas the eagle had stooped from his companionship with the sun!"

The birthnight ball was given in Carusi's spacious ball-room. The floor was chalked with eagles, stars, banners, and the names of twenty-six States. Nicholas Biddle, then a noted lion, was among the guests. Amos Kendall, in ball-room costume, with white kid gloves and satin vest, jostled against the ladies. Richard Johnson, the Vice-President, presented Mr. Biddle to the President, Mr. Clay, Mr. Woodbury and Mr. Forsythe standing by. "How do you find things in Washington?" asked some one of Mr. Biddle. "In ten years," said he, "I have not found politicians of all parties so amiable and friendly." At supper he was seated next to a lady next the President, at the head of the center-table. At the close of the supper, a rush was made for the roses with which the chandeliers were ornamented. One hung over the head of the President, and so eager were those who contended for the spoils, that they broke the fastenings of the chandelier, and down it came on Mr. Van Buren's head, roses, grease and all, causing him to retreat to his carriage with his whole outward man in disorder. Mr. Biddle and Mr. Clay saved themselves and the ladies under their charge. The eloquent Menifee of Kentucky was there, with light hair floating loosely around his fine head, his large mouth made more capacious by a laugh, his white wristbands turned carelessly over the sleeves of his coat.

General Scott arrived the next day, and departed with full powers to allay the excitement in Maine on the subject of the boundary question. General Scott was probably at this time the most remarkable man in the nation, and the man to whom contending partisans resorted to restore order and protect the national honor. In the Black Hawk war, in the Seminole war, in the Canadian insurrection, he was the hero, negotiator, statesman and military chieftain, who flew to the scene of trouble and calmed the turmoil and confusion. He occupied the same attitude in the Maine troubles, having given ample proofs of the highest order of talent.

A grand fancy ball was given on the 21st February by the wife of the chief financier of the Bank of Washington. Mrs. Weightman appeared in the character of Pocahontas, magnificently attired as an Indian princess, receiving the company in her royal wigwam. Mrs. Haight of New York, who had just returned from a tour through Russia, Turkey and western Europe, sketching descriptions by the way, appeared in a real Turkish dress procured at Constantinople. Mlle. Vespucci as a young Greek girl; a lady of Louisiana as the Maid of Athens. Miss Peters of

Philadelphia, was the Irish basket girl, carrying a basket full of relics and curiosities for sale. "Will yer honor buy anything of me? I have nine small children, six praties, and not a pen'worth of a husband."

The first half century of Congress under the present constitution, closed on the 3d of March, 1839. The grand closing fête was given at Mr. Bodisco's house in Georgetown. In the second suite of rooms, in glass cases, were various curiosities, the presents of emperors, kings, diplomatic and learned bodies in Europe, received by the minister during his diplomatic career. The plate on the supper-table was of pure silver inlaid with gold and steel, and of curious and novel workmanship. Mr. Bodisco opened the ball by a grand promenade round the ball-room to the music of the band, with the wife of Major-General Macomb. Among the ladies, Miss Adêle Granger of Canandaigua, was noticed particularly. Her naïve manners and original, discursive imagination, marked the brilliancy of her intellect. This lady afterwards married Mr. Thayer, a gentleman of Boston, and is now the wife of Robert Winthrop. Mr. Webster was moving through whole phalanxes of ladies, talking and smiling. Mr. Jennifer of Maryland, was equally brilliant among the young ladies.

The entertainments given by the foreign ministers were not all idle, profitless amusement. They formed some of the links that bind distant nations together. His Imperial Majesty of all the Russias had never yet been represented by a minister of half the popularity or tact of M. de Bodisco. The singular retirement in which the British minister lived, created an impression of hostility to England, much deeper than shallow observers imagined. Some of the ladies playfully declared his seclusion sufficient cause of war.

General Scott arrived at Saratoga early in August, many of the magnates of the nation being there already. Scott came unheralded and unattended; yet he created a deep, quiet and uncontrollable sensation. After dinner at the hotel he walked into the grand drawing-room, where he formed the center of a group; the strangers and villagers being collected under the portico in anxious groups, to catch a glimpse of the hero and statesman. "Can you point out General Scott?" asked a countryman, pushing his head through a window. "Very easily; pick out the man a head higher than all the others; that is General Scott!" During the promenade Mr. Van Buren was walking with an old lady on his arm; when he met the General, the latter had to bend down considerably to put himself on a level with the little President; Mr. Poinsett and other distinguished personages promenading the drawing-room at the same time.

The grand entrance of Mr. Clay into Saratoga, his speech under the trees of the United States Hotel, his coronation with the garland of roses and hyacinths as he passed through the grand porches, and the splendid coronation ball, were incidents long remembered. While Mr. Clay spoke, at a front window opposite him, with the piazza intervening, stood the venerable and dignified Mrs. DeWitt Clinton, looking like a queen attended by her maids of honor. Lady Westmoreland stood in the front rank of the crowd, her brow sparkling with diamonds; General Scott was leaning against a beech-tree. As Clay came near the door, the coronet descended from the window of Mrs. Clinton's room, attached to a silken cord, and touched the brow of Henry Clay. He put it aside, and it lighted on the shoulders of a gentleman from Richmond, Virginia.

A lively writer thus described the meeting of Mr. Clay and Mr. Van Buren in the drawing-room:

"Mr. Clay first observed his rival at the distance of seven women and a half, and straightened up two inches; a few flashes of lightning came from his eyes, and a smile extended along his rugged cheek. At a short distance beyond one of the center-tables, stood General Scott, like a lion looking over a prairie of heads towards the fox and the wolf approaching each other; the lion measuring in his mind whether it might be worth his while to eat them both for his supper now, or to wait till they became a little fatter, and then to salt them down for a dinner. Every eye in the grand drawing-room was fixed on the approach of these great men.

"'Mr. President,' said Mr. Clay, as he came within a petticoat and a half of Mr. Van Buren, 'How do you do?'

"'I thank you, Mr. Clay, I am happy to see you. How is your health? I hope I don't obstruct your progress?' perceiving the promenade blocked up by the crowd of ladies.

"'Not at all,' replied Mr. Clay, 'I have found the utmost facility in my progress since I entered your dominions.'

"For an hour the three luminaries, Van Buren, Clay and Scott, continued their promenade; Scott outstripping both in the dignity of his person and manners, the military grace of his movements and his engaging conversation.

"Mr. Clay's conversation is fresh, witty and sometimes eloquent; but his manners and air are coarse, rough-hewn and uncultivated. Mr. Van Buren has little conversation; his nature is too cold for wit, fancy or humor. Mr. Clay has a great deal of wit, humor and fancy, but he wants delicacy, fine taste, and exquisite finish. General Scott seems to possess all these qualities of mind and manners, mixed in such due proportions as peculiarly to fit him to command men and to shine in general society."

Mr. Calhoun's dining with the President the last of December, was the subject of general comment among the political gossips of the metropolis. The visit was understood to have a meaning; and the President's object was supposed to be healing the bad blood between Mr. Calhoun and Colonel Benton, and inducing them to be quiet till after the election.

Forsythe, Paulding, and Poinsett, were the chief companions of Mr. Van Buren. Mr. Poinsett was the master spirit of the literary section of the cabinet. "The amiable disposition of the Secretary of the Treasury, and the fascination of his excellent wife and family, produced, for one night, an entire suspension of political hostilities and bitterness." Thus social life brightened up, though Congress was voted dull.

In January, 1840, the fashionable world was quiet. Mrs. Gales and Mrs. Woodbury were both in mourning. At this time there was said to be wintering in Washington, eight or ten young ladies of large fortunes and great accomplishments. One of the principal topics of conversation was the approaching marriage of M. de Bodisco to Miss Williams of Washington; only seventeen, but tall and splendidly developed. The minister had been struck with her at one of his children's balls the preceding year. He was a devoted lover, while awaiting the arrival of his emperor's permission and the bridal robe. Mr. Fox, it was said, was to be his groomsman.

The fashionable movements were inaugurated in February. A party given by Mrs. Polk went off with great eclät, and the first "Washington assembly" was held in the dancing saloon at Carusi's rooms. The marriage took place on the 9th of April. The attendants of the bridegroom were assembled about four in the afternoon, and proceeded to the residence of Mr. Williams. They were, in regular order: Senator Buchanan, Mr. Fox, General Dunlap, Texan Minister; Mr. Martini, Minister from the Netherlands; M. Seruys, Belgian Minister; Mr. Stockel of the Russian Legation; a son of the President, and a son of the Secretary of the Navy. There were eight bridesmaids; the first, Miss Jessie Benton, who walked with Mr. Buchanan. In the church the attendants made a circle, the bride and bridegroom in the center, the relatives and witnesses around them. The bridal cake was in the form of a pyramid, and encircled with a wreath of white roses.

The bride wore a rich satin brocade, and veil of Honiton lace; her ornaments simply a pearl sprig and pin. The brides-maids wore rich figured satin trimmed with lace, a plain gold bandeau and wreath of orange blossoms. Mr. Clay gave away the bride. M. de Bodisco wore his splendid court dress of silver decorated with several orders; the foreign ministers of his train wearing their uniforms. A magnificent dinner was served at his house for forty persons. The Vice-President, General Scott, Mr. Forsythe, General and Mrs. Macomb, and other distinguished guests were present.

Fanny Ellsler made her first appearance in the capital in July, 1840, before a brilliant house; a sea of moving beauty, fashion and talent. Congress adjourned at an early hour to see the enchantress in the tarantella and the cracovienne. The venerable ex-President Adams appeared delighted with the performance.

At a party at the Spanish minister's in January, the great attraction of the evening was a Chinese mandarin, from Canton. He stood upon the rug in one of the luxurious apartments, and looked upon the scene with great gravity for some hours. He was presented to many of the ladies, and one of them asked him "how he liked the dancing." He replied that it seemed a pretty amusement, but rather troublesome, he thought, for those engaged in it; adding that in his country they always hired the dancers at parties. Being asked if he thought the women pretty, he answered that women were pretty all over the world; and so they were in America, and so they were in China. When asked how he liked the large feet, he replied that "in China it was customary to make the feet small; and in America, he supposed, it was the custom to have them large." Thus he answered every question like a diplomatist.

The following remarks were made on Mr. Crittenden: "Mr. Crittenden is one of the most forcible and impressive speakers in the Senate. For a sudden, unpremeditated effort, he certainly has no superior. His diction is rich almost to superabundance; his style is chaste and energetic, and his manner agreeable. To the discussion of every subject he always brings a store of valuable information; his illustrations are always apposite, and he illuminates every topic with such a flood of light, that none but a blind man can fail to see the whole matter clearly and distinctly. Mr. Buchanan spoke in opposition. Mr. Crittenden followed in reply, and scattered his arguments like dry leaves before a hurricane."

A singular double lecture was given at the Tabernacle in New York, by General Gaines and his wife, on "National Defence" and "The Horrors of War." Mrs. Gaines occupied the third seat from the platform, immediately in front of the General while he was speaking. He wore the full uniform of a general officer, and had a diagram of the embouchure of the Mississippi behind him, to which he pointed with his drawn sword. When he had concluded his address, Dr. Griscom advanced to Mrs. Gaines' seat, and conducted her to the platform amid immense cheering. She was dressed in a black velvet pelisse, and wore ear-rings and diamonds in her hair, with a rich silk hat ornamented with a waving plume of bird of paradise feathers. She held in her hand a small manuscript from which she read her lecture. General Gaines stood behind her during most of it.

Senator Hugh Lawson White of Tennessee, resigned his post in 1840, on account of "instructions" he could not follow. He died in the May following. Senator Preston pronounced a beautiful eulogium on him. Senator Hayne of South Carolina, was in person of the medium size or a little taller, and of a graceful form. He had a fine, manly and expressive face. His manners were easy, cordial and unaffected; his address was winning; and his mental qualities were solid, brilliant and practical. He was always employed in useful objects, pursued from high motives and by fair and open means. With varied talents, he was distinguished as a Senator, and during his ten years of service, worked indefatigably. He bore a name dear to the South, and had the advantages of fortune and family connection. He was twice married, into the Pinckney and Alston families. He was a party in the great debate with Webster, and became Governor of South Carolina to enforce the nullification ordinance.

Philip P. Barbour, Justice of the Supreme Court, was in 1820 a Representative from Virginia, and his duties in one office or another occupied him at Washington during twenty-one winters. He was called "a man worthy of the best days of the Republic; modest, pure, patriotic, full of domestic affections, devoted to Virginia as his mother State, and a friend to the Union. He was for some time Speaker of the House, and was appointed to the bench of the Supreme Court by President Van Buren, in 1837, in place of Justice Duval. He was in turn succeeded by Peter V. Daniel. Barbour was a Virginia country gentleman, after the most perfect model of that class; living on his baronial estate with his family, slaves, flocks and herds. He was a strict votary of that school of politics of which Jefferson, Madison, John Taylor of Caroline, Monroe, Macon, &c., were the great exemplars.

The naval career of Commodore Porter illustrated the benefits of the cruising system in our naval warfare. His personal history was full of incident and adventure, in keeping with his generous and heroic character. He was a lion on the quarter-deck and in battle, "the Paul Jones of the second war of Independence." His death occurred during Tyler's Presidency.

X.

HARRISON'S ADMINISTRATION.

Grand Jubilee in honor of Harrison's Election—The President's Dinner—Crowds to witness the Inauguration—"The Father of the House"—"An unruly Set of Boys"—Major Barney—The three Generals Candidates for the Succession—The Farmer and the President—Heiresses and Beauties—Phases of Society in Washington—The Southern Aristocracy and the Official Circles—Forms and Barriers swept away by the Russian Minister—The Circle professional—Death of the President—The Military Funeral—The Ladies of the Family—Fears for Mrs. Harrison—Third time of Tyler's stepping into Place by the Death of the Incumbent—His Arrival in Washington and taking of the Oath of Office—Character of President Harrison.

THERE was a grand jubilee in Alexandria in November, 1840, in honor of the election of General William Henry Harrison to the Presidency of the United States. The freedom of the city was given to more than two thousand visitors. There was a procession; and a car drawn by four white horses, carried nineteen young girls, each waving the flag of a victorious State. "Welcome" was written on every house, and all the doors were thrown open to strangers and guests; the ladies crying, "Enter, Whigs!" Mr. George Washington Parke Custis, of Arlington House, addressed the crowd in Market Square, commencing with "Friends and fellow-patriots, and most patriotic ladies." The adopted son of Washington, whose hair was white with the snows of many winters, was very enthusiastic over "the glorious second revolution."

General Harrison had already received thousands of applications for office, filed them all and docketed them, with the careful indorsement, "To be last considered." He wrote to a friend: "I shall make no promises of office to any one, nor shall I give any intimation of my purposes in regard to the formation of my cabinet. I am determined not to quarrel with any of my friends before the 4th of March."

"The Hero of North Bend" was to arrive in Washington February 11th, the day after the votes were counted in the House of Representatives. Mr. Van Buren intended to break up his household on the 20th February, and to stay for the rest of his term of office with his friend the Attorney General, Henry D. Gilpin.

A splendid reception was given General Harrison in Baltimore. He was received at the railway station by a deputation headed by the Chief Marshal, and escorted to his hotel. The President elect was left on Sunday in peace, but on Monday morning the crowd assembled in front, and the old gentleman came out, was introduced by John P. Kennedy with a neat little speech, and received his visitors. At one o'clock he received the ladies of Baltimore in another part of the hotel. His reception in Washington was on his birthday, and his welcome was enthusiastic. He called on Mr. Van Buren, who invited him to dinner. At this dinner were present the cabinet, Mr. Wright, Mr. Vanderpoel, and Mr. Kemble, besides the

President elect and his suite. Politics were banished from the conversation; and it was said the French cook did his best, hoping to be retained by the new President. General Harrison said to Benton across the table: "Benton, I beg you not to be harpooning me in the Senate; if you dislike anything in my administration, put it into Clay or Webster, but don't harpoon me." Benton, it was said, very good humoredly agreed by a nod, to separate the responsibility of the throne from "the power behind the throne." Harrison visited the capitol the next day but one. The greeting between him and Mr. Benton was courteous and cordial, and he spoke to Mr. Calhoun, as to an old and attached friend. Calhoun left his seat and retired with Harrison to the recess. It was remarked: "General Harrison seems the only man among the whigs who is happy, contented, smiling, satisfied, benevolent, and capable of taking a night's rest. He cracks his jokes, and fights his battles o'er again, and appoints his cabinet with the greatest enjoyment. Mr. Van Buren meets his fate like a philosopher. The President coming in, and the President going out, seem to be the only two quiet and satisfied men in Washington. General Harrison having the most wit and repartee, and Mr. Van Buren the most indifference and carelessness."

The Herald gave the private history of the selection of the cabinet, as a curious series of movements. Soon after the election, General Harrison offered the State department to Mr. Clay, and intended to give the Treasury to Mr. Webster, designing the four remaining departments for four prominent men from the different sections, based on geographical, political and personal considerations. Mr. Clay declined, preferring his position in the Senate, where he could shape and support the measures of the new administration. General Harrison then resolved to offer the State department to Mr. Webster, the Attorney-Generalship to Mr. J. J. Crittenden, and the Post-office to Mr. Ewing. A movement was made in the newspapers to overawe the action of the President, by declaring that neither Webster nor Clay ought to be in the cabinet, because they were the two greatest men of the whig party, and their intellect and talents were of course a disqualification for the cabinet, inasmuch as many would think of them for the succession. Mr. Webster defeated this small intrigue by accepting the offer, as did Mr. Crittenden and Mr. Ewing. The vacancies were filled on sectional principles. Nearly the entire whig delegation of New York selected Mr. Granger, a gentleman of intelligence, education and high character, who had the Post-office given him—Mr. Ewing taking the Treasury department. The War office was given to John Bell; the Navy, which was to be given to the South, was assigned to Mr. Badger by the Southern whigs.

General Harrison was noted as one of the most benevolent men of the age; kind-hearted to a remarkable degree and very patriotic. "The fierce, obstinate, energetic will which characterized General Jackson did not belong to him. His presidency will be the most beneficent of all, if his spirit prevail to any extent. His cabinet will have great sway, as it ought, Daniel Webster being the master spirit, the organizing impulse, the comprehensive soul, the representative of the age and century. The eyes of Europe and America are upon him, and in his present position he may exercise a greater influence upon the age than any man since the days of Washington."

Mr. Clay was the premier of the legislative department, while Mr. Webster was that of the executive. "They will check and counter-check each other, while the old General himself takes things very easy—sits in his arm-chair in the White House, cracks his jokes by the fireside, fights his battles o'er again, compliments the married ladies, rallies the old bachelors, and pats the cheeks of the pretty girls with great glee and pleasure. Yet I think it must be a hard-working, an up-hill administration that will be met with opposition from the jump." The most untiring, unforgiving and relentless opposition was to be encountered.

The weather was very cold, while Washington was filling with crowds to witness the inauguration. Mr. Van Buren took advantage of the cold to fill the Presidential ice-house. He is said to have remarked: "The President elect is the most extraordinary man I ever saw. He does not seem to realize the vast importance of his elevation. He talks and thinks with as much ease and vivacity as if he were a young man. He is tickled with the Presidency as a young woman is with a new bonnet."

Others thought Harrison would succeed the better in his management of public affairs from the very fact that he entered the White House with a joyous joke on his lips. "Let his cabinet be harpooned, but he himself will have a happy time in the White House. General Jackson filled the palace with the vulgar fumes of smoke from an old long pipe. Mr. Van Buren, at an expense of sixty thousand dollars, cleaned the apartments, whitewashed the smoky ceilings, and filled it with preciseness and cold pedantry. General Harrison will change the vulgarity of the one, and the pretension of the other. He will make these gorgeous halls reverberate with merry peals of laughter, refined repartee, excruciating anecdotes and sparkling bonmots."

"Let me introduce Mr. Williams, of North Carolina to you, General," said a member of his new cabinet to him one day. "Mr. Williams is the oldest member of the House of Representatives, and you know is called the Father of the House."

"Mr. Williams," replied Harrison, shaking him by the hand, "I am glad to see the Father of the House, and the more so because you have a very unruly set of boys to deal with, as I know." The General's face was beaming with a benignant smile, and the bystanders broke into a roar of laughter.

Allen, the editor of the Madisonian, a small, slight young man, not much of a lawyer, was introduced to the General. "Happy to see you, Mr. Allen. You are a good-looking chap for these parts of the world, but there is hardly raw material enough in you for the girls beyond the Alleghanies!"

During General Harrison's sojourn in Baltimore, when he received the visits of the ladies, the Hon. John Barney, formerly member of Congress from Maryland, stood beside him to assist at the presentations. Looking at the lovely assemblage, Major Barney waved his hand, and appealed with, "Now, General Harrison, have you ever seen such a blaze of beauty and loveliness!" The old General looked at them, then at the gallant Major, and replied with a half benevolent, half satirical smile, in the words of the old song:

"Oh, Barney, leave the girls alone,
Oh, Barney, leave the girls alone."

the Major exploding like a steamboat on the Mississippi. The anecdote flew over Baltimore, and for once the office seeking lazzaroni and suspending financiers forgot their wretchedness in one good sound, substantial broad laugh, at the joke.

General Harrison had been a guest at the house of Mr. Seaton, Mayor of the city, for a few days before the inauguration. At noon the procession entered the northern gate of the Capitol Square, and the President elect was escorted into the Senate Chamber. He proceeded escorted by that body, the Judges of the Supreme Court, and the Foreign Ministers, to the platform under the grand eastern portico, where the inaugural address was delivered. Over the heads of the august company rose the splendid Corinthian columns, over them the magnificent dome, and over that the bright blue sky. In front were the musical bands; to the right and left military companies; and immense crowds of people filled the square in every direction. They hung around the steps, pedestals and columns; some were seen crawling, small as bees, around the foot of the dome, and leaning over the dizzy heights of the highest porticoes. After the ceremonies, the

President proceeded to the White House, where he received the congratulations of his friends.

General Scott had arrived shortly before the inauguration, accompanied by General Coombes of Kentucky, and Colonel DeKay of New York. "The hero of Lundy's Lane" was well and in good spirits. General Gaines was there too; and "all standing in the position of capital candidates for the succession in 1845."

The pomp, parade and pageantry of the inauguration having passed away;—the session of the Senate succeeding it, with the arrival of the English messengers and the struggles for office, the great business of the administration began. General Harrison won golden opinions from all sorts of people. His frank, plain, unostentatious demeanor became the soldier and one to whom the simplicity of a patriarchal age was natural. At North Bend he had been distinguished for hospitality and benevolence, and he brought to Washington all the habits and feelings which had endeared him to the people of Ohio.

A plain, farmer-like man called to see the President one stormy day while he was at dinner, and was shown by the servant to a room where there was no fire. General Harrison asked, "Why did you not show the man into this room, where it is warm and comfortable?"

The servant said something about soiling the carpet. "Never mind the carpet another time," said the General. "The man is one of the people; and the carpet and the house too, belong to the people."

An extra session was called for, to commence on

the 31st of May. Meanwhile, towards the close of March the President was a sufferer from bilious pleurisy, which confined him to his bed. The bell of the palace was muffled, the physicians directing that the patient should be quiet and undisturbed.

The beautiful weather of this season brought out the fashionables in bevies. New York heiresses and beauties, and beauties and heiresses from the District, Baltimore, Richmond, Maryland and Virginia, all were in Washington; and it was expected that the extra session would bring hundreds from Alabama, Mississippi and the evergreen homes of Louisiana.

"Society in Washington," said an observer, "is very clannish, and there is not a place in America where there is so much sycophancy to station. By this I mean that the resident population make it their business to court the influence of office-holders, of men of public distinction. During the last inauguration, there was in this city, the greatest collection of private gentlemen ever convened in this country. Most of those men were of high character, wealth and learning, and their letters of civility were received and treated like an application for office. There are several divisions in society. Probably the first and most worthy and well mannered is the ancient aristocracy of Virginia and Maryland. This class is not very rich, but is very proud. All the families attached to their circle have pretty and educated daughters; and he who can show the most title-deeds and will bid up, is likely to win the brightest flower in their field of beauty. These families are very envious of the lovely daughters of Kentucky and the remote

South, and without intending it, they are sure to point out a hundred faults in every girl who comes here to dash for an elegant husband. And yet this aristocracy is a most worthy part of society in the District. In its ranks may be found the widows of distinguished soldiers in the army and of gallant captains in the navy; the children of dead senators, lawyers and judges. They are truly proud of their lineage, and not unfrequently call up the achievements and exploits of their ancestry.

"There is always a large circle in Washington formed by the President, Secretaries, auditors and chief clerks. This class embraces a great multitude of visitors from every part of the Union. General Harrison and his cabinet can make any favorite girl a belle, and so can Clay or Preston. This official circle in the more agreeable amusements of society, is from necessity considerably exclusive. They receive and entertain a great many upon the common forms; but none save intimate friends ever reach their fireside sociability and freedom. On public occasions and at great parties the leading officers of government are very complacent and patronize strangers. They are willing to do this much, and then they expect you to make your way through society and bother them no more.

"The foreign ministry have in their train a long list of sycophantic good-for-nothings, who have little modesty and less behavior. The ministry proper, though a little odd in their ways and grotesque in appearance, are all clever fellows; they are treated politely by American citizens, and some of the ladies, who are full of romance and curiosity, grow very frisky at sight of an attaché, and cannot conceal a longing they have to dance and flirt with the interesting foreigners. The ministers live high, and are fond of company and gayety. Bodisco, the Russian minister, by his marriage in the District, has broken down and swept away many of the forms and barriers formerly in the way of a more intimate association with the foreign diplomatic corps. Curiosity, as much as any other consideration, makes these men interesting. To their trailers, every now and then, they give expensive entertainments.

"There is then an extensive circle, made up of lawyers, merchants, and half made people, who by luck have come suddenly into possession of what the miser loves most. These people form their own coteries and have very merry times; in their families there is much beauty and quite a dash of intelligence and accomplishment. Some of them are modest and retired; some religious; some fashionable, and some foolish.

"It takes all these circles to make the society of a court-city like Washington. Out of them may be carved a distinct and extensive army who rally as 'the glass of fashion.' This division of every class is very lazy and for the most part very stupid; the members lead a life of excessive dissipation."

One month from the day of his inauguration, on the 4th April, 1841, William Henry Harrison died at the White House. The Rev. Dr. Hawley was in the room where he lay, with his medical and personal attendants, and in the adjoining room were a number of his friends, anxiously waiting for intelligence. At twenty minutes before one o'clock on Sunday morning, Dr. Hawley announced the dreaded event.

The cabinet, assembled in the adjoining room, immediately drew up an official statement. Mrs. Harrison was still at North Bend.

The last words of the President were: "I wish you to understand and remember, the principles that govern me, and carry them out. I ask no more."

Mrs. William Harrison, the President's widowed daughter-in-law, had been constantly at his side till consciousness departed. Miss Clark of Baltimore was there too, till compelled by her feelings to leave the room. She was the daughter of a lady who, General Harrison had often said, saved his life when he was a member of Congress. He always bore the warmest gratitude and affection to every member of the family. During the last day of his life, he received everything from Miss Clark with more satisfaction than from any other hand. She remained, with Mrs. Findlay, Mrs. Harrison and Mrs. Taylor of Richmond, niece to the President, constantly at his bedside during his illness, and nothing human foresight or unremitting attention could do to alleviate the fatal disease was left undone. The other relatives and connections present in the executive mansion were Mr. D. O. Copeland, the nephew of the President; Henry Harrison of Virginia, his grand-nephew, and Findlay Harrison of Ohio, his grandson. The disease, according to the report of the physicians, was pneumonia, with congestion of the liver and derangement of the stomach and bowels.

On the following day the public were admitted to

view the remains, lying in the large hall just within the entrance to the palace. Mr. Thatcher Webster, chief clerk of the Department of State, had been immediately despatched to bring Mr. Tyler, the Vice-President, to Washington. The military arrangements for the funeral were under the direction of Major-General Macomb, Commander-in-Chief of the army, and Major-General Walter Jones of the militia of the District of Columbia. The civic procession was directed by the Marshal and the Mayors of Washington, Georgetown and Alexandria.

Fears were expressed for Mrs. Harrison, who was then aged and infirm. She had feared the worst, knowing how little the General would spare himself when his public duties demanded his time and action. She had not wished his election; in fact had expressed herself opposed to it, valuing her family comfort before all worldly honors. General Harrison had completed his sixty-eighth year the day he entered Washington in triumph on his way from North Bend to Virginia. He was a pure patriot. His youth had been passed among scenes of the Revolution, and love of liberty, courage, and devotion to his country, had marked his whole career. He was benevolent, sincere and ardent in his attachments, frank and unostentatious in his demeanor and cheerful in his disposition. It was said by one who knew him well, that his suavity of manners, his generosity and kindness of heart, invariably won him the warm affections of those who were placed under his authority; while his moderation, his disinterestedness, his scrupulous attention to the public interests, and the wisdom with which he exercised the extensive powers entrusted to him, commanded respect and confidence.

In person, General Harrison was slender, and rather under the middle height. His features were irregular and rather strongly marked. His eyes were dark and penetrating; his forehead high but narrow; his mouth denoted firmness, and his expression indicated benevolence.

His constitution had never been robust, and the fatigues of his journey from North Bend, with the excitement consequent upon the inauguration and the subsequent scenes, conspired to produce the fatal disease.

It was noticed as remarkable that Mr. Tyler now stepped for the third time into a high public trust by the death of the incumbent. He was made Governor of Virginia by the death of the Executive; he was made a Senator by the death of one before his time expired; and now he became President of the United States.

The greatest anxiety was expressed by all whigs to know if he would carry out General Harrison's plans and wishes; if he would retain the cabinet; or if he would branch off on a new track of Virginia politics.

Mr. John Tyler arrived in Washington on Tuesday, taking the oath of office on the 6th April.

XI.

TYLER'S ADMINISTRATION.

Confidence in John Tyler—A Model of Courtesy and Dignity—The weather-beaten Englishman—Scene at Tyler's Home—Rumors of the British Minister's Marriage—The Ladies of the Executive Mansion—Mrs. Robert Tyler—Extracts from her Letters describing Life at the White House—Receptions, &c.—The First Diplomatic Dinner—The City full of splendid Women—A Lady's Conversation with the President—Summer Assemblages in the Executive Grounds, with Music—The Fourth of July—Fashionable Belles and Statesmen on the Promenade, at the rural Re-unions—Fancy of the Negroes about the Veto—Political Disagreements no Bar to Social Gayety—Incident at Mrs. Crittenden's Party—Mrs. Bell's Party in August—Mrs. Robert Tyler's Description of her New Year's Reception, and of Madame Bodisco's Party, and the Ball in the Theatre—Lord Morpeth at Dinner at the White House—Justices of the Supreme Court—Party at the "Mess" at Kennedy's—The Butcher at the President's—Mrs. Tyler's Reception for Dickens.

All eyes were now turned, with doubt and anxiety, to the organization of the administration under the new President. The whigs were excited and agitated, and the conservatives full of joyous expectations. Yet it was admitted that, so far as the interests of the country were concerned, Mr. Tyler might be relied on with perfect confidence. He was acknowledged to be a man of a very high order of talent and much experience as a statesman. Elevated and patriotic in his views, of a frank, gallant and independent spirit, it was known that he would administer the government with reference to the true interests of the people, without regard to the wishes and schemes of cliques. He belonged to the national and practical class of Virginia politicians. Without running into the extreme of radicalism which distinguished Mr. Jefferson, and avoiding any loose interpretation of the Constitution, Mr. Tyler coincided generally with the views and principles of Mr. Madison. He had always been held in very high estimation by the citizens of his native State, and had occupied important positions. After having served as Governor of Virginia, he had been elected over John Randolph to the Senate of the United States, in 1828.

After it had been determined to nominate General Harrison for the Presidency, Mr. Tyler was selected for Vice-President, to receive the support of the South, and without reference to his political principles, or inquiry as to his sentiments upon the prominent measures of the whig party. Thus everything in his history and character warranted the supposition that he would administer the government on the most elevated and honorable principles.

"Nothing can be more admirable than the bearing and demeanor of President Tyler to the innumerable applicants for his countenance and favor. He is a model of courtesy, urbanity, kindness and dignity. I have never seen a President whose port and manner were so commanding, and at the same time so acceptable to all who approached him. General Jackson was a man of much dignity of manner, and most imposing presence; but he was capricious, fastidious, irritable, and sometimes overbearing. President Tyler is abundantly courteous and graceful in his address, but there is nothing of hauteur or condescension in his manner; it is affable, natural, frank and gentlemanly. He is considerate to the applications of all, but none go away with delusive hopes. No man has a kinder or more benevolent heart, none a more resolute and determined spirit. An old weather-beaten Englishman called on him for assistance to-day. He carried a letter from the English consul at Baltimore. The President read his papers over attentively.

"'Sir,' said he, 'I am not the proper person to apply to. You must go to the British minister.'

"'I have been to Mr. Fox,' said the old man, 'but he declines to do anything for me. The consul at Baltimore sent me to the vice-consul at Alexandria; but I got no relief from him.'

"'Go to the Secretary of State,' said Mr. Tyler, 'and say that I request him to take your case into consideration.'

"'I have been there, and Mr. Webster says he has no jurisdiction in the matter.'

"But the President would not permit the broken-down old man to depart.

"'John! John!' His private secretary had stepped into the next room: 'Go in there, and my son will see what can be done for you.'"

Whether the case was one that admitted of relief from the Executive is not known; but the old man was sensibly touched by the sympathy and interest manifested in his behalf.

A scene was said to have occurred at his private

dwelling in Williamsburg, immediately after receiving the news of his accession to the Presidency. He called his sons and daughters, including Robert's wife, about him, and in the presence of some intimate friends, addressed them, informing them of the deplorable event which had brought about his unexpected elevation; reminded them that the promotion was only temporary, and should be sustained with humility and meekness. "To you, Priscilla and Elizabeth," he continued—"it is, I trust, scarcely necessary to say, that, as upon you will presently devolve the duty of presiding at the White House, you should be equal and untiring in your affabilities to all; and you should remember that nothing betrays a little soul so much as the exhibition of airs or assumptions under any circumstances. My sons, too, must not forget the saying of the ancient hero who desired his family, instead of abandoning themselves to exultation for his triumph, to bear in mind that in the next battle he might be beaten. True nobleness of soul is only evinced in never suffering station to tempt us into a forgetfulness of ourselves, and of what we owe to others. In short, my sons and daughters, whatever you say or do, act with reference to the day which is so close at hand, when I must return to plain John Tyler, and may you never, as the President's family, either in thought, word, or deed, do aught which you will regret to be told of hereafter, when you shall be nothing higher than plain John Tyler's children." Could they be anything higher than the children of a great and good man, with such a soul as is here indicated?

The President once remarked to an acquaintance that it seemed there could not be a thought in the human mind, which might not be found somewhere in Shakspeare.

The other answered that it must be so. "I remember even the substance of Mr. Clay's long argument against you for signing the veto, comprised in two lines of the bard of Avon:

"'Conscience! 'tis our coin! we live by parting with it,
And he thrives best, who has the most to spare.'

Had *you* parted with your conscience by permitting the ten days to elapse, which were required to make the bank bill a law, Mr. Clay is of opinion you would have thriven better."

It was thought that the extra session would obliterate all the old party lines, and that a new organization would be formed.

Washington was always an extraordinary place for rumors. When the Spanish minister sold out his furniture, and Mr. Fox bought many elegant and valuable articles and sent them to his house, the report that he was going to leave the country in a rage, gave place to one that he was about to get married. The ladies talked a deal about this antiquated mummy-like representative of Her Majesty, but none of them could tell what was going to happen.

Summer commenced in May, in all its beauty and brightness. The capitol yard and public grounds were decorated with the richest variety of roses, tulips, hyacinths, and beautiful exotics. One peony bush bent under the weight of nearly a hundred flowers, many of which were six inches in width. Some of the ladies of the President's family arrived the last of April—Mrs. Tyler, Jr., the wife of his son, and Miss Tyler. The wife of the President was in delicate health, and would not leave home till the weather became settled. The younger Mrs. Tyler was described as a very elegant and accomplished woman, and Miss Tyler as beautiful, graceful and lady-like. With such aids to the proverbial urbanity and dignity of the President, it was reasonably expected that the hospitalities of the executive mansion would soon be dispensed in a style of elegance and good taste. John Tyler's first wife was Letitia Christian of Virginia.

Mrs. Robert Tyler possessed great conversational powers, with a playful humor and readiness at repartee, which made her society peculiarly fascinating. She had, too, a tender heart, "open as day to melting charity;" and her devotion to parents, children and friends, had rendered her the idol of a domestic circle. She was the grand-daughter of Major Fairlie, of New York, an officer in the Revolutionary war, and a distinguished citizen. Her mother was a celebrated belle, whom Washington Irving remembered vividly as his friend, and one of the most brilliant women of the day; a fair and witty and most worthy lady. Her father was Mr. Cooper, one of the most eminent tragedians of that time. Educated with great care, her splendid natural qualities of mind were so developed as to dignify and adorn the highest station. She had been accustomed from childhood to the best society, and among her mother's intimate friends were the Hosacks, the Livingstons, the McEvers, the Pauldings, and many of the most distinguished families in New York. The young lady first met Robert Tyler in Richmond, and was married to him less than a year afterwards. He was said to be a young man of brilliant genius, in high-wrought and vivid imagery resembling Shelley, whom he was like in person; and as an orator, he had made a very favorable impression.

The following extract is from a letter to Mrs. Tyler's sister, dated Washington, April 29th, 1841:

"What wonderful changes take place! my dearest M——. Here am I, née Priscilla Cooper ('nez retroussé' you will perhaps think) actually living in—and what is more, presiding at—the White House! I look at myself like the little old woman, and exclaim: 'Can this be I?' I have not had one moment to myself since my arrival, and the most extraordinary thing is that I feel as if I had been used to living here always; and receive the cabinet, ministers, the diplomatique corps, the heads of the army and navy, etc., etc., with a facility which astonishes me? 'Some achieve greatness—some are born to it.' I am plainly born to it. I really do possess a degree of modest assurance that surprises me more than it does any one else. I am complimented on every side; my hidden virtues are coming out. I am considered '*charmante*' by the Frenchmen, '*lovely*' by the Americans, and '*really quite nice, you know*,' by the English." . . . . .

"May —, 1841.— . . . . We have had a cabinet dinner, and I have disgraced myself with father forever:—just in the full tide of successful experiment, at the moment the ices were being put upon the table, everybody in a good humor, and all going 'merry as a marriage bell'—what should I do but grow deathly pale, and, for the first time in my life, fall back in a fainting fit! Mr. Webster, who was sitting next me, picked me up in his arms, and took me away from the table; and Mr. Tyler, with his usual impetuosity, deluged us both with *ice-water*, ruining my lovely new dress, and, I am afraid, producing a decided coolness between himself and the Secretary of State. I had to be taken to my room, and poor Mr. Webster had to be shaken off, dried and brushed, before he could resume his place at the table! What a *contretemps!* . . . .

"May —, 1841. . . . . Besides the cabinet dinner I mentioned in my last letter, we have had two other dinners, and are about having a State diplomatique dinner—at all of which entertainments your 'accomplished' sister presides—sitting opposite the President with the most important man in the company at her right hand! I have had some lovely dresses made which fit me to perfection—one a pearl-colored silk that would set you crazy. Its effect, with pink roses in the hair, and bouquet de corsage of the same flowers, I will leave you to imagine.

"I occupy poor General Harrison's room. I had no superstitious feeling upon the subject, and it is as pleasant as possible. The nice, comfortable bed-room, with its handsome furniture and curtains, its luxurious arm-chairs, and all its belongings, I enjoy, I believe, more than anything else in the establishment.

The pleasantest part of my life is when I can shut myself up here with my precious baby. You ought to see her, she is too lovely! The greatest trouble I anticipate is paying visits. There was a doubt at first whether I must visit in person or send cards; but I asked Mrs. Madison's advice upon the subject, and she says: 'Return all my visits by all means.' Mrs. Bache says so too. So three days in the week I am to spend three hours a day driving from one street to another in this city of magnificent distances. The victim for this sacrifice is to be adorned in a white chip bonnet, trimmed with moss rose-buds, from Lawson's in New York. I could spend my time here charmingly if it were not for 'the duties of my situation.' I do not see nearly so much of Sophy Irwin and Mrs. Bache as I could wish, ... and I see so many great men, and so constantly, that I cannot appreciate the blessing! I know you will think I ought to give you my impressions of these 'intellectual giants,' instead of talking of dresses, bonnets, &c., &c. The fact is, when you meet them in every-day life, you forget they *are* great men at all, and just find them the most charming companions in the world, talking the most delightful nonsense, especially the almost awful-looking Mr. Webster, who entertains me with the most charming gossip. There is one thing particularly gratifying to me: among the many distinguished men I have met, there are but few who do not speak of having known and admired our dear father and mother. Aunt Louisa's wit and beauty, too, are constantly alluded to." . . . .

"WASHINGTON, ——, 1841.

"Well, my first diplomatique dinner is over—oh! such a long one! Our first dinner in the state dining-room. I was the only lady at table. What with the long table, the flowers, and lights, and brilliant dresses and orders of the *Dips* (not dip-candles) the various wines and innumerable courses—I felt dreadfully confused. Mr. Webster says I acquitted myself admirably. I tried to be as cheerful as possible, though I felt miserable all the time, as my baby was crying and I received message after message to come to the nursery. . . . . I think that father is a charming host—he received his guests with so much courtesy and simplicity of manner—and I do not think his powers of conversation surpassed or even equalled by the great men around him. The British minister, Mr. Fox, is frightful to behold. He has the reputation of great ability. I will write you, soon, a description of each legation." . . . .

The death of General Macomb furnished an opportunity to abolish the office of Commander-in-Chief of the army, then little more than a sinecure, and the duties of which could be divided between the Secretary of War and the Adjutant General. It was desired, too, to save the President the difficulty of deciding between Generals Gaines and Scott.

The difficulty of President Tyler's position was made greater by the numberless promises, real and pretended, absolute and conditional, of General Harrison, brought forward by the office-hunters. Instances occurred of men presenting themselves with so-called promises, who never had anything from the good old man but a nod of the head. Others came who were totally unfit for the places sought. A dilapidated, worn-out old man from Cincinnati, claimed the post of first Assistant Postmaster General, insisting upon the promise of General Harrison, and when refused, went away in a rage, and denounced the administration. The course of the President seemed to give general satisfaction. He had done just what was expected from his republican principles and associations. He recognized the right of the people to approach him under all circumstances and on every subject, and gave to their requests the most respectful consideration.

The immense rush for office continued into the summer. The city, too, was full of beautiful women, representatives of every section of country. The east garden of the capitol, on Wednesdays and Saturdays, was a charming spot. It had fine trees, walks and clumps of shrubbery, with a small lakelet; and parties resorted there for conversation and flirtation. There might be seen the Russian ambassador, in something of a hurry, though the flag was still flying over the Hall of Representatives; the noble looking Madame Le Blane, with her young and wealthy relative, Mrs. Hughson, from Kentucky, walking behind her with a large retinue of disinterested admirers; "the immortal Harry," in a straw hat, with a smile on his cheek, and stopping to talk with his acquaintances a minute at a time; Mrs. Calvin, one of the great reformers; the fashionable, literary and scientific Mr. Robertell, and many others.

When a lady of the District was at the President's

house, he praised the prospect from the garden window, observing:

"Madam, I delight in this window; it gives me a view into Virginia."

"Would it not be well to extend your view, sir, farther than Virginia?"

"Madam," replied the President, with a benignant smile, "my view extends over the whole United States."

And "if anything be an earnest of this"—said one, "it is the charmingly republican system upon which he and his family regulate their deportment."

Mrs. La Cloche commanded much attention in the main alley of East Capitol garden, on one of the music nights. She was what Washington Irving called "a fine, manly sort of a woman."

As a gentlemanly-looking person passed, a young officer exclaimed; "Why am I like that man, who is little, while I am large! Why, I am Owen the Tailor!"

At the President's house, in July, the night was beautiful. The wide-spread plain was fringed with carriages and spectators; the elevation before the wall of the White House garden was similarly crested; and upon the garden terrace overlooking it stood well dressed multitudes of either sex. The artillery wheeled about, in fine order, changing form and front as if by magic at the bugle's note; firing first in one direction, then in another, with precision and rapidity.

The President sat in the south portico of the White House; his daughter and daughter-in-law had stationed themselves on an elevation in the garden; Miss Tyler with her bonnet off, blooming as Hebe; and both as truly delighted with the show and the fine sunset and the gentle evening breeze, as the passer-by with their amiable courtesy.

The Fourth of July passed much as usual everywhere; squibs and pop-guns and cracked bells, with vapid orations, stupid toasts, and execrable speeches; hot meats and cold wines; the customary laudation of the nation, and the quantum of headaches that follow unusual indulgence. There was a levee at the White House, and the Sunday school children marched through the walks of the capitol grounds; Mr. Adams watching them with satisfaction and interest. At the Presidential mansion there was a commingling of all the central functionaries with citizens of every class; the marine band in the hall playing appropriate martial airs. The President stood near the entrance of the elliptical saloon, supported by his two sons, and two subordinate officers of the government, who introduced the citizens as they entered. Farther on in the room, the daughter and daughter-in-law of the President received the compliments of the visitors. The deportment of Mr. Tyler was easy and natural, yet sufficiently dignified, placing every one at his ease. And nothing could surpass the quiet, unaffected grace with which the ladies received and acknowledged the courtesies of all who paid their respects. The throng, comprising beautiful women, grave senators, cabinet and foreign ministers, dashing army and navy officers, office seekers, citizens and loungers, was great from twelve to three. Between five and six about forty gentlemen sat down to dinner with the President.

The appointment of General Scott as the new Commander-in-chief, disposed of his claims to the Presidential succession. Placed at the head of a bureau in the war department, secluded from the people, he could hardly fail to subside from public view, even with the interest produced by his recent meritorious services on the frontier.

After the Fourth, it was decided that on Wednesdays the marine band should play at the President's garden; on Saturdays, as before, at Capitol Hill. On the Wednesday, accordingly, the band placed themselves under a clump of trees on the enclosed green, between the President's garden and the war office. The drive up to the porch of the White House was full of carriages. People were congregating under the President's porch. Martin Ranahan, the little Irish porter, was as busy as if he had been at a shillelah frolic in Ireland. When General Harrison came to the White House, it was said that Ranahan addressed him with,

"Plaze yer honor—they say you're goin' to make a clane swape. I'm the last Martin in this nest; must I take wing?"

"No, Ranahan. They say 'tis ill luck to drive the house martins from where they build. Stay where you are."

Hearing one Smith, a schoolmaster, criticising speeches as not classical enough, Ranahan reproved him:—"When was there any good in the name of Smith! 'Twas always an *Orange* name, even in ould Ireland, and by St. Pathrick, it has never gained by exportation. Criticise! I only wish that Cicero and

Demosthenes, and the whole list of them dead ancients had been at the dinner; and if they wouldn't have hid away their heads it would be only because there was no Irish modesty left in 'em."

When the storm threatened, President Tyler came to the door, and invited the people to take shelter in the house; handing in the little children and ladies, and asking in the gentlemen. The sovereign people seemed to put themselves in absolute possession of the sovereign's habitation. Some of the ladies took off their bonnets and were ensconced with their beaux in the window seats. One asked where was Miss Tyler; another where was Mrs. Robert Tyler, and enquiries were made for her baby. This lady was endeared to her native land by many claims; being connected on her mother's side with some of the benefactors of the republic, and on her father's with the most brilliant recollections of our fine arts. "She herself at one time had made a sacrifice to circumstances and to filial piety, equal in loftiness of motive to the far-famed devotedness of the Grecian daughter" by appearing for a short time on the stage.

In her sudden elevation she preserved the simplicity and directness of her character, and went through her hospitalities with cheerful good feeling and impartiality. Her husband, under an unpretending and diffident exterior, showed qualities of no common order.

The weather cleared, and the people departed, and then the storm came back, with thunder, lightning and rain that drenched the metropolis.

On the Saturday the weather was charming; carriages, horsemen and couples steamed up Pennsylvania avenue, and through the various western garden alleys on one side; and from all the four quarters of Capitol Hill on the other. John C. Calhoun came in smiling and happy with Mr. Charbon on his arm. Miss Black came with a General in a carriage and four; John Quincy Adams appeared with alert step and animated countenance, conducting a young lady whose society he seemed to enjoy, and she his; for who could be insensible to the honor and delight of conversing with the venerable and enlightened ex-President, now pleased to be a simple citizen among those of whom a few years since he was more than monarch!

The music meetings at the President's garden seemed to gain the victory in popularity. Georgetown and Alexandria, the following Wednesday, sent their stores of beauty and fashion to swell the crowd that poured into the enclosure between the entrance to the White House and the war office; the green once called "the cow pasture!" Nothing could be seen but moving belles and beaux, and staring and admiring wonderers. A pretty blonde was pointed out as the sister of Madame de Bodisco, Miss Williams, from Georgetown.

Benches were provided for the musicians. A fine looking woman was noticed with the Postmaster General; a widow of Baltimore. In a group on the western terrace, without bonnets, was seen Miss Tyler—"the young princess," as some called her,—a good and gentle girl, with quick perceptions, lively, well-educated and well-bred; full of Virginian warmth of heart, prepossessing in appearance and captivating in manners. Her affectionate devotion to Mrs. Robert Tyler's child was remarked. One lady saw her in a carriage trying to hush the baby while waiting for the mother to come out from some place where she was calling. The child was said to have an extraordinary sensibility to music; her blue eyes would dilate and fill with fire, and her little feet would flutter and dance on hearing it. Another lady, who bore the family name, the wife of a relation, resided in the District.

There was a Senator—one of the lights of the land —walking and talking flat gossip with a young girl; illustrating the remark that wisdom may be wrapped up in trifling. There were also the interesting step-daughters of the Attorney General;—petite damsels, somewhat below the average height, but taller than the sprightly and lovely creatures advancing under the escort of William Cost Johnson and Mr. Rayner. Their name was Bruce. The French ambassador, a fine-looking man, was conspicuous; and Mrs. Bruce, promenading with Mr. Cushing of Massachusetts, while people thought he ought to get a step lower in the alphabet and take a Mrs. C. good-looking and agreeable as he was, and pleasing in social life as in political. Butler King was observed, and the commanding presence of the wife of the Secretary of State was acknowledged.

Mrs. Daniel Webster was Miss Caroline Le Roy. She was a native of New York, and married Webster in 1829. They passed the winters in Washington; their summers at Marshfield—their country-seat on the Massachusetts coast. Mrs. Webster was a helpmeet to her husband, both in domestic and public affairs; reading to and for him, culling and arranging useful facts and ideas, and assisting him in his extensive correspondence. While he was Secretary of State, she was his efficient aid, and made his house the center of a brilliant society, drawing around them the finest spirits of the century, and many of high repute.

After the music ended and the company had dispersed, the President and his family passed on to the theater, where they had promised to attend Miss Monier's benefit. She had selected "Money" for the play, perhaps as a gentle hint to the people that the government wanted some of that commodity! It was the first successful evening she had had. The audience welcomed the entrance of the Chief Magistrate with a burst of applause. Such a reception had not occurred since the fever of Jackson's popularity was at its height. It was spontaneous and hearty, and was acknowledged with grace and dignity.

On the next Saturday the clouds had portended a storm; but the sky cleared as the fashionables began to gather around Capitol Hill. Mrs. Tyler and her husband and infant daughter, and the Boz family were noticed, and a true, warm-hearted major with his gentle lady, "with the well instructed head and the Cinderella foot." There were more carriages than usual; though the promenaders made no show comparable with the hundreds who had filled the President's grounds on Wednesday. The "classical" party of the previous evening at the President's, was freely discussed. Such "droppings" from the candelabras and chandeliers, visited by the breezes from the open windows! "And that gave the assembly such a classical look! All exhibited signs of having been in *Greece!* Webster's coat was covered." "And how did the lady look who got such a shower of it upon her adornments?"

"Look? never lovelier. As Pierre says in Venice Preserved:—

> "'I could have hugged the *greasy* rogue; she pleased me.'"

When one young gentleman looked forlorn, some wag quoted Shakespeare to remind him that

> "The sovereign'st thing on earth
> Was 'parmaceti for an inward bruise."

The puns brought to mind one by the mother of Mrs. Robert Tyler, a lady famed for her wit. A wealthy tallow-chandler prated in her presence of his travels in Greece. After listening long and patiently, she exclaimed, "Indeed, Sir, you must have found yourself very much at home there."

After this discomfiture from flaring candles, it was agreed that the rooms ought to be lighted with gas, on the new plan then under experiment in front of the treasury.

Some one mentioned that the French minister had complained to Wise the preceding night, of the new duties suddenly imposed on French wines and silks, and another spoke of having seen Mrs. Wise there. "Then," said a third, "you met a woman of sterling worth, and manners equally unostentatious and winning." "There was another conversation at the President's party between Wise, Ball, Granger, and others, about the Florida war, ending in a laugh and another glass of champagne all round."

The south garden was the next scene of the musical reunion. The ground was undulating, varied with tree-topped knolls, around which the graveled walks sweep gracefully. In the distance the sun silvered the broad Potomac, and threw it into picturesque contrast with the dark green of the forest-covered amphitheater of hills upon the shores beyond. Glancing sails and steamers performed their part in the view. The marine band was stationed on the top of one knoll, surrounded by listeners; while groups dotted all sides of the hill, and stood gossiping at the base or perambulated all about it. Promenaders were passing through the trees and cresting the knoll opposite. The President stood on the portico with his family some time, enjoying the view.

The talk was of the exhibition at the Georgetown Visitation Nunnery Academy. It was a small but tasteful exhibition-room. There was a piano on a raised platform, and three harps, with music stands. Behind a table sat two nuns, heads of the establishment; at their left Father Matthew. The President of the United States gave all the medals, prizes and honors. Next to Mr. Tyler sat the Bishop of Maryland; behind them Father Ryder and others, and several priests opposite. Miss Tyler assisted in arraying those pupils who received academic honors. Her whole heart seemed absorbed in the scene. When any one from Virginia was to receive an honor, she blushed and appeared in a tremor; and when a prize was announced for some one from Williamsburg, Virginia, she involuntarily half rose from her seat and bent back to catch the first glance of her triumphant town-mate coming from below to mount the platform. President Tyler invested a young lady of Martinsburg, Virginia, with the crown and gold medal for excellence of conduct in the senior circle, and the other recipients were adorned by Miss Tyler, whose hands trembled with delight.

"As I quitted this garden scene," remarked a spectator, "it struck me that two things only could improve it—statues and fountains."

The storm began to threaten, and again the courteous President insisted on the pleasure-seekers making use of his house. He was busier than any of his servants, finding places for the ladies and urging the bashful ones to come in. "Martin, see that refreshments are handed round," was his hospitable order.

It was a grief to all to hear that Mrs. Robert Tyler was to depart the next day; and her little daughter had her voice in the general regret.

Some jokes were passed at one of these meetings, on the accident of Mr. Webster's horse having run away with him, kicked his buggy to pieces and lodged the honorable Secretary in the capitol yard. He was walking down the avenue five minutes afterwards, as unconcerned as if nothing had happened. General Scott and the Boz family were at the reunion, and the fascinating Miss Chase—"the Trojan Helen"—with Mr. Crittenden and an admired lady. A by-stander observed that Mr. Crittenden had filled a larger space in the public eye than any other man in the cabinet except Webster. No man in the Senate had been more conspicuous or more useful. "His position as the first law officer under the government ought to have made him one of the most important men in the cabinet on a question like the action of the cabinet on the bank bill."

Hugh Legaré was pointed out, the accomplished scholar, the elegant gentleman, and the experienced statesman. It was thought he might be offered the place of Secretary of the Treasury in certain contingencies. Mrs. Ashley was remarked as a magnificent creature; but hardly surpassed Mrs. Calvin as she stood on the edge of the green terrace. Two new arrivals among the gentlemen were sons of the celebrated Alexander Hamilton.

On one occasion when the day was too much overcast for an assemblage on the green in front of the portico of the southern garden, and only a few stragglers appeared, one of them observed to the President that the weather had put its *veto* upon the music, and mentioned that when the whirlwind that morning tore away part of the market-house, and flung the fragments into the air, exclamations were heard of "There it comes! stand clear! there comes the veto!" The negroes' comment was curious enough. "You Cesar, what dem niggers waitin' dar for?" cried one to another, as, at the hour for the arrival of the evening cars, a group of darkies were seen looking out attentively. "Dem niggers? Dey be waitin for de weto. Massa Webster, and Massa Bell, and Massa Badger and Ewing, and Massa Granger, and ebber so many massas, all went to 'Noplis dis mornin' right arly, to fetch him from de man-ob-war whar he ben kept chained up."

"Be he alive?"

"Live—yes—dat he be! Live and peert enough, and bigger dan de big alliphant. Why, dey let him out once to try him!"

"My!"

"Dey did, though—and didn't like him; so dey put him up agin and kept him fast ebber since aboard ship; and now—why, nigger, dey be pullin down capitol wall to let him through a hole in de side; cause dere be no place for him big enough and strong enough only de rot-under! so iron gates is makin' to fasten him in: and all de people will have to go into de two houses arter dis by de two end doors, and dey can look at de weto through de new railings as dey go!"

"And notting to pay, Cæsar!"

"Notting. Massa Tyler gibs de people dis show free gratefish for notting, so as to keep friend wid um and get um to make him next Pressumdit."

This confusion in Cæsar's mind of the preparations for the reception of Greenough's statue of Washington, the visit to the man-of-war at Annapolis, the universal talk of the veto—the various anticipations of the President's purposes, and the diverse constructions of his motives in relation to the veto, seemed to afford no unfair specimen of the political speculations of many of the poor black's superiors.

The President's political situation became a singular one. He was surrounded by men whose sympathies were with those who assailed him in the dead of night, pouring out under his windows insults and threats. Even Webster presided at banquets where his political friends drank damnation to Mr. Tyler. The rank and file of the party claiming to support him, burned him in effigy, while their leaders cursed him at festivals. He was surrounded by political enemies. But the tide of social gayety was not interrupted by such disagreements. The prediction that most of the people would keep away from the music at the southern garden, after the awful veto, or would come with fierce looks and brimful of fight, was not verified. The music was elevated on a platform in the center of the lawn; on the river road stood a vast collection of carriages. Two Cherokee damsels were seen walking with Governor Call and Colonel Pendleton, the new chargè to Chili. Mrs. Semple, a daughter of President Tyler, and a most intelligent and accomplished woman, with a noble, intellectual face, was chatting with Mr. Butler King. Another married daughter—Mrs. Jones—was on a visit. Mr. Tyler had all his family about him.

The war on the President for refusing to give his assent to the creation of a great national bank, continued, and effigy burnings and other disgraceful scenes were enacted in various parts of the country. There was a story about the President and Mr. Clay at a party given by Mrs. Crittenden. She was doing the honors with the perfect grace and dignity that ever distinguished her, and about ten o'clock, when it was expected that Mr. Tyler would be rid of his own visitors, Mr. Dawson and six others proceeded to the White House to escort him to the Attorney-General's. On his entrance Mr. Clay came up, and, extending his hand, said, "Whisky, Mr. President, or champagne?"

"Whisky," replied the President, and they went together to the sideboard. The politicians whispered that as "veto" began with V and whisky with a letter beyond it, Mr. Clay had triumphed over the President; all his measures would prevail and there would be no more vetoes. It was even reported that Mr. Clay was heard to quote from Shakespeare, while drinking to the President's health: "Conscience! it mutinies in a man's bosom; it fills one full of obstacles; it beggars any man that keeps it; it is turned out of all towns and cities for a dangerous thing." Of course no one vouched for the truth of that bit of gossip.

Mrs. Bell gave a party in August, at which there were some three hundred persons. The hostess was a woman of fine presence, earnest in character, and possessing great conversational eloquence. Miss Yeatman, her daughter, sparkled in diamonds; even her brilliant adornment setting her off less than her amiable and unaffected manners. Miss Tyler was gentle, guileless and charming as usual; and there was a tiny Miss Bell, an infant a year old, with whom the Secretary of the Navy glided into the room to a merry tune played by the band.

Some gossip said Mr. Clay introduced Mrs. Bell as "the lady of the Secretary of War" to a deaf stranger, who, catching only the phrase "the Secretary of War," opened his eyes in extreme wonderment.

Another said that Bailie Peyton asked the President where was his old friend Wise.

"Oh, he is not invited to the cabinet parties," was the reply. "He is no doubt at home now with his amiable wife—almost as intelligent and effective a politician as Wise himself."

The company broke up by twelve. The marine band was stationed on the balcony terrace outside, and the night was magnificently bright.

The cabinet was broken up in September by voluntary resignations. Mr. Webster and Mr. Granger were expected to remain, and it was thought to be the purpose of Mr. Clay to wage a war of extermination against the President.

The last assemblage of the season took place at the capitol gardens, toward the end of the extra session.

Mrs. Robert Tyler had spent some months at her father's house in Bristol, to which she went in the summer.

The following extract is from a letter dated January 1st, 1842:

"The first of January, eighteen hundred and forty-two, is past, never to return; and I am nearly on the point of going off with it. I never felt so tired in all my life as I am this evening, standing up for three hours, and shaking hands with, I don't know how many thousand people—such big fists as some of the people had, and such hearty shakes as they gave my poor little hand too! One great hearty countryman gave me a clutch and a shake I almost expired under, but I could not help laughing when Fletcher Webster whispered to me; 'when taken to be well shaken!'

"At half-past eleven we ladies took our station at the upper end of the blue room, while father stood in the center (we being the lesser lights) to receive the foreign ministers and the cabinet, who made their appearance half an hour before the crowd. This first half hour was a very pleasant one, and passed rapidly away. The diplomatique corps were all present but Mr. Fox, who sent an apology pleading indisposition. He is a complete *bat*, only making his appearance by candle-light. The costumes of the foreign ministers were very beautiful, and as each entered, surrounded by his *attachés*, the scene was quite imposing. The Baron de Roenné is peculiarly soldier-like and noble in his appearance; and there is a simplicity and quietude in his whole bearing and conversation, that to me is peculiarly agreeable. Mr. Bodisco and his beautiful wife came later than the rest. She is rather on the milk-maid order of beauty. I can imagine her dropping a curtsy like the maid in the song, with 'my face is my fortune, sir, she said,' and her face really has been her fortune as regards a fine house, fine carriage, and fine clothes; and a fine husband, too, for the matter of that, for nothing could be finer than Mr. Bodisco's uniform. It is perfectly dazzling in its magnificence, his whole breast glistening with orders.

"At twelve o'clock the crowd rushed in,—men, women, and children,—a very orderly crowd though, and nicely dressed. A little after the first rush of the 'sovereign people,' came the ladies, and their respective escorts. I cannot say who I thought the prettiest woman—perhaps it was Mrs. Potts, Mr. Rose's sister;

MRS. ROBERT TYLER.

Eng'd by H. B. Hall, N. Y.

she is very lovely-looking. Of course Mr. Calhoun and Mr. Webster were the most distinguished looking men. Mr. Calhoun is more abstracted in ladies' society than Mr. Webster. Although Mr. Webster looks so overwhelmingly sensible, he can talk the most agreeable nonsense possible. I do like him very much. 'In virtue of my office' he always leads me in to dinner—and often informs my ignorance of the nicest entremets to eat, the nicest wines to drink, &c., &c. Then he tells me charming anecdotes about his visits to the great houses in England, just the gossiping things a woman loves to hear." . . . .

In January, 1842, a new practice was adopted in reference to social visits at the executive mansion. Since Mr. Tyler's accession the drawing-room had been open every evening for the reception of acquaintances and persons having the privilege; it was now determined to receive visitors only on Thursday and Saturday evenings. The new year inaugurated a gay season in the court circles. The most brilliant entertainment was given by Madame de Bodisco, and the rank, talent, fashion and beauty of the capital were invited. Rumor announced the approaching marriage of Miss Tyler with Mr. Waller, a young lawyer of Richmond; and engagements and marriages formed the subject of general conversation. The new Attorney-General Mr. Legaré, was said to be on the eve of abandoning his fortress to gentle hands.

Mrs. Tyler wrote in January 1842:—

. . . . "I very seldom go to parties, but, of course, could not refuse Madame Bodisco's invitation. Her ball was expected to be the grand affair of the season. I confess myself disappointed: the crowd was so dense that one could not appreciate either the arrangement of the rooms or the dress of the ladies, although they were all '*en grand toilette*.' The Baron de Bodisco is a very attentive host, almost too much so. He led me in to supper, and asked me how my 'Empress of a baby' was. I suppose he thought of his own little Emperor 'Nicholas,' who, aged eight months, was up at two o'clock at night, carried through the rooms dressed in blue silk and white muslin. The fact is, I suspect the poor little fellow had no bed to go to, for the whole house was thrown open, even to Madame de Bodisco's bed-room. The bed was covered with a magnificent green satin coverlet, pillow-cases to match. Madame de Bodisco looked lovely, and was magnificently attired in pink satin with lace flounces, and such splendid diamonds—stomacher, ear-rings, breast-pin, bracelets! I never saw such beautiful diamonds. . . . ."

"—— 1842.—I went to the Assembly last night, matronizing five young ladies—all dressed in rose-color—all so lovely too! Clementina Pleasantan and Belle Stevenson the prettiest of all. Belle has the most perfect face and figure I ever saw, but Miss Pleasantan has a style and *je ne sais quoi* about her that makes her the more attractive of the two. The ball was a brilliant one, admirably lighted and not crowded; the ladies all well dressed and showing to advantage. I spent a delightful evening. As I declined dancing, I had the pleasure of talking to many grave Senators, and, among the rest, had a long conversation with Mr. Southard. As we stood at the end of the room—which is the old theater transformed into a ball-room—he said: 'On this very spot where we stand, I saw the best acting that I ever witnessed. I came in the theater and took my seat by John Quincy Adams—and there were never two more delighted people. He said he had seen the same play abroad—in France and England—he had seen John Kemble and the great Talma in the part; Kean, Cooke and Macready; but he had never seen it so admirably acted as then. I entirely agreed with him in his admiration, though I was not so capable of judging by comparison as he.' Mr. Southard here paused. Though my heart told me to whom he alluded, I could not help asking him: 'What was the play and who the actor?' 'The play was Macbeth, the performer Mr. Cooper.' I could not restrain the tears which sprung to my eyes as I heard my dear father so enthusiastically spoken of. I looked around too, and thought that not only had papa's footsteps trod those boards. I looked down at the velvet dress of Mrs. Tyler, and thought of the one I wore there, six years before, as Lady Randolph! when we struggled through a miserable engagement of a few rainy nights!!!" . . . .

"January 28, 1842.—I am afraid you poor Alabamian plebeians will expire with envy when I tell you that a real live English Lord was among the guests at the President's house last week; Lord Morpeth now, Earl of Carlyle that is to be, with the blood of all the Howards coursing through his noble veins! Yes, he dined here! and had the honor of handing me in to dinner and sat next me for three hours! I can't tell you what we talked about; I don't think either of us made a remark worth remembering. He attacked our '*Americanisms*' (as most Englishmen do) especially the use of the word 'lovely' when applied to *amiable* women even if they were shockingly ugly. I contended it was not used by well-bred Americans, whereas '*nice person*' in England covered every degree of excellence in mind and body, and was used by every one. He laughed, and could not contradict me. He is not handsome, tout au contraire! not distingué-looking; his face is red, his hair is light, his manner awkward! Indeed, instead of that 'composure of aristocracy' which I anticipated in a scion of one of the noblest English houses, I found even a very fidgety manner. He seemed very amiable and unaffected though, and I felt entirely at my ease talking nonsense to him." . . . .

"January.—Lizzie Tyler was married last night. She looked beautiful in her bridal dress and flowers, blonde veil, &c. The wedding was a very quiet one. The members of the cabinet, Mrs. Madison, Mrs. Bache, Mrs. Wise, and Mrs. Commodore Warrington formed the party, besides all the relations and friends from Virginia. The whole house was thrown open, though, the next night, and a most brilliant reception took place. I was too unwell to be present." . . . .

The daughters of the late Secretary of the Treasury had added to the list of vanquished among beaux; and the witty daughter of Mr. Granger had commenced a severe and dangerous cannonade. A bevy of widows and maidens were assembled nightly at Mrs. Peyton's and Miss Polk's; where also shone the still celebrated Mrs. Florida White, enchanting the crowds allured by her loveliness. Lord Morpeth, it seems, excited but little curiosity. "A nobleman to make a sensation in Washington must be both young and handsome."

The Supreme Court was a popular and instructive place of resort to strangers. The nine judges in their robes of office, presented a very imposing appearance, apart from the associations connected with the most exalted legal tribunal of the land. In the center sat Chief Justice Taney, a tall, spare man, with a strikingly intellectual countenance; a jurist of profound acquirements, large experience, endowments of the highest order, great independence of character, and of integrity unquestioned. On his right was Judge Story of Massachusetts. He was inclined to democracy when young, but association with Judge Marshall and other great men of the court, soon made him federal enough for all the purposes contemplated in the organization of the Supreme Court.

On the left of the Chief Justice might be seen Justice Thompson of New York, thin and spare almost to emaciation, of great acumen, strictly legal in all his tastes and pursuits, of quick apprehension, skillful in weighing the arguments of counsel with unsurpassed powers of discrimination, analysis and generalization. Judge Thompson was a bright ornament of the illustrious tribunal whose decisions contributed so much to give stability to the government by its luminous expositions of the constitution.

Next to Judge Story might be seen Judge McLean of Ohio, once Postmaster-General. He was a stately and fine-looking man, with clear head and strong mind. Judge Baldwin was near Judge Thompson. Probably no man had a more logical mind, understood a subject more thoroughly, or mastered it with greater facility. He had been a distinguished member of Congress.

Judge Wayne of Georgia was the handsomest man on the bench. Near him was Judge McKinley of Alabama, a plain, unpretending, quiet gentleman, whose thoughts were sound and sensible. There remained Judge Catron of Tennessee, and Judge Daniel of Virginia.

The most distinguished legal abilities in the land were daily engaged in this court. Mr. Legaré, the Attorney-General, made his début at this time. He was a lawyer of eminence, as well as a scholar of extensive and varied acquirements. His information seemed to be affluent on every subject; his address was always dignified and gentlemanly. The observation of genius enriched his mind with illustrations. The fruits of the diligent reading of years, the experience of life, office and society, were at his command. His taste was cultivated and his fluency was extraordinary. The day he made his first argument as Attorney-General, there were four Attorney-Generals in the room; Mr. Burien, Judge Taney, Mr. Gilpin and Mr. Crittenden. This highly accomplished and learned gentleman was accustomed to confess himself a vain man; and he insisted that all persons of genius were noted for vanity. He was very fond of ladies' society, and was well fitted to please them, in spite of a slight personal deformity, perceptible when he was standing, that impaired the dignity of his appearance. South

Carolina had reason to be proud of him. He had a sister, distinguished as a painter, who after her marriage went to reside in the West.

Among the lawyers prominent at this period in Washington, were David R. Ogden, Daniel Lord, Jr., Mr. Wood of Newark, Mr. Wilde of Georgia, and General Wall, the late senator from New Jersey.

Some prominent men in society belonged to Philadelphia. Joseph R. Ingersoll, the son of Jared Ingersoll, was esteemed one of the ablest lawyers at the bar. He and his brother, Charles Jared Ingersoll, married sisters, the daughters of John Wilcocks. Nicholas Biddle had married the daughter of John Craig, and received a large fortune with her. Joseph R. Chandler was the publisher and editor of the "United States Gazette." William Bayard Reed was the son of Joseph Reed, and grandson of the distinguished Joseph Reed, who was president of the Supreme Executive Council of Pennsylvania, before its organization as a State. It was he who made the declaration in answer to a royal proposition: "I am not worth purchasing; but, such as I am, the King of Great Britain is not rich enough to do it."

Mr. Webster gave a ball and supper in honor of Lord Morpeth, to which the whole town was invited. A great social party was given by the congressional "mess" boarding at Kennedy's in the avenue, at which the amusing incident was reported of Mr. Buchanan, the grave Senator from Pennsylvania, and Mr. Crittenden, figuring in the same quadrille. To those who had seen them in an argumentative contest on the floor of the Senate, this saltatory one must have been very comical. Members from the various sections of the Union, intending to domesticate with their families for a session, arranged what was styled a "mess." These were generally formed of persons professing the same politics, having an identity of interest, associations, feelings, &c. Sometimes friends not in Congress were admitted into these coteries. Few congressionals having the means or inclination to form permanent establishments of their own, these mess parties were frequently resorted to, to reciprocate the hospitalities of the stationary society. The mess at Mrs. Kennedy's was composed of old and young. Since the opening of the season at M. de Bodisco's, nothing comparable in comfort and elegance had been exhibited, without, however, any parade of illumination or tinsel livery. Mrs. Linn of Missouri, and Mrs. Gaines, the distinguished wife of the General, presided as matrons at the ceremonial. Mr. Buchanan led in a graceful, brilliant woman, bewitching with her arch expression and the turn of her head. Some thought they might be discussing Clay's amendment to the constitution; others, that the best she could propose would be an amendment to the gallant Pennsylvanian's confirmed bachelorship. "The King of Alabama" drew near them. Buchanan and King were called "the Siamese twins;" they ate, drank, voted and visited together. Then came up Tom Allen, late of the Madisonian, with the wealthy lady whom he married afterwards, Miss Russell from Missouri; a neat, plump, pretty little creature, wearing a tiara and necklace of diamonds. The belle of Washington, Miss Dawson of Louisiana, dazzled all around her like a fairy vision. There was no rush of admiration; all paid their homage in silence to her innocent and beaming loveliness. Almost the entire beau monde was present. A celebrated widow was seen leaning on the arm of the Fabrician General. She was pronounced like Josephine in stature, elegance and perfect finish. Her stately pride was blent with winning grace; she had the majesty of Juno with the simple naïveté of childhood. Senators, cabinet and members acknowledged her intellect, wit and genius. Around her stood Tallmadge, White, Evans, Linn, and a host of admirers. Whenever she went to a party, which was seldom, for she wore deep mourning, the talent of the assemblage seemed clustered in a knot which she commanded for the evening. This extraordinary woman was loved and esteemed by all and envied by none; her beauty being praised even by rivals, and her tact and judgment securing her unenvied supremacy. Her life had been one of vicissitude and trial. Not far distant was "the lazy and eloquent Carolinian"—William C. Preston, with his wife, one of the most delicate and polished of women, with a rippling voice, and tender clinging air of dependence on her "liege lord." Mrs. Gaines bore her part with a kind wish to gratify all, and the enthusiasm of a noble and generous heart.

A story was told of the appearance of a new face at the President's table, whom Mr. Tyler asked to take wine with him, but who preferred brandy and water. The stranger was discovered to be a sturdy butcher from Wilmington, Delaware, who had presented a noble sirloin of beef, and the finest mutton in the world, to the Chief Magistrate, and had been honored with an invitation. On his departure he shook the President heartily by the hand, exclaiming, "Sir, I've heard of republican Presidents, but I never saw one till I saw John Tyler. You've made me feel as if I was in my own house; and when I get back to Delaware I shall tell my neighbors that I, a plain man of the people, have been received by the Chief Magistrate in the house provided by the people, with as much hospitality and kindness as if I had been the most distinguished man in the country." This feeling of the butcher was a prevailing one among the middle classes.

The last Presidential levee of the season was crowded and unusually brilliant. "Clay Whigs and Van Buren Locofocos, and Tyler Americans" were whirled together in the throng. A new arrangement was the announcement of each visitor's name on entering; and many a laugh was raised at the mistakes. One gentleman found himself suddenly dignified with the handle of "Honorable;" a foreign minister or two was transferred from his own court to another; and maidens and bachelors found themselves unexpectedly coupled and given to each other. Mrs. Van Ness, with her husband, the late ambassador to Spain, was very much admired. The President gave an unostentatious, but elegant dinner-party on the anniversary of his first official introduction to Washington. The members of the cabinet and their wives were present, with ex-President Adams and the nearest connections of two other ex-Presidents, and one or two foreign ambassadors; also Mrs. Madison and the daughter of Mr. Monroe, Mrs. Gouverneur, and Madame de Bodisco with her husband.

It had been wisely determined to give Mr. Charles Dickens, on his arrival, a plain reception, and commit no remarkable act of folly. Mrs. Tyler wrote in March, 1842:—"I cannot tell you anything about *Boz* that you have not seen in the papers. I was determined I would see him when he came, and I did, in spite of my orders to remain in my room for the next two months. I have seen him twice; once in the morning when I had him "all to myself," and then again at the levee in the evening.* He is not at all romantic looking, rather thick set; his face of course most intelligent and bright—but his dress does not suit me; he wears rather too much jewelry, and is thoroughly English in his appearance, and not the best English. At the levee he was accompanied by

* The correspondent of the "New York Herald" gave the following account:

"It was intended that the levees should close at the accustomed time; but, probably, the nearly simultaneous arrival of the two great literary lions, Washington Irving and Boz, at our national menagerie, may have caused a new arrangement. Tuesday, the 15th, happening to offer the only evening not preoccupied at the White House, it was thought expedient to give the numerous strangers in town another treat, and as a part of it, the opportunity of seeing Irving and Dickens, and of seeing too, that the President is incapable of being behind the people in due honors to genius.

"When it was understood that there would be a levee, and that Irving and Dickens would both be there, the rush was tremendous. It was as much as the police officers could do to keep the passages open. Even the circle usually left open around the Chief Magistrate was narrowed to almost nothing by the pressure. It was computed that the east room alone contained upwards of three thousand persons.

"There was one point of interest. Washington Irving and the lady who presided on this occasion with surpassing courteousness and grace—Mrs. Robert Tyler. Irving, now grown 'more fat than bard beseems,' is yet still distinguished by that glow of genius, and humor in his eye, and smile and utterance which made him the adored of the New York world of fashion. Washington Irving is at the executive mansion, not now as Washington his wife, quite a sweet-looking plump woman, tastefully dressed though, and more English looking than Boz himself. Poor fellow! He seemed horribly bored by the crowd passing round him. What think you? He and Washington Irving were both speaking to me at the same time! I am charmed with Washington Irving. He took me in to the dinner which father gave him, and he talked to me of mamma all the time, telling me a great many anecdotes of grandma's house and surroundings in old times. . . . . The more distinguished well-bred and sensible people are, the more perfectly unembarrassed and at home I feel with them. Query: Does this emanate from *their* good breeding and intellect, or, from my own superior nature finding its affinity in these sort of people? Que pensez vous?"

Irving, but as the Ambassador to Spain. Who is that lady receiving such homage from the new Ambassador? She is a player's daughter—but she is a President's daughter—and she is welcoming, from her elevation, in her mother's friend of by-gone years, the Ambassador newly created by her father.

"I ask—ought there not to be almost as much interest for an American in these associations, as in the presence of Boz? Yet nothing could surpass the curiosity to see the great author from England. 'Where is he? How does he look?' Such were the questions on every side. A few had seen him—and, not a few were seeking to see him, and seeking in vain. 'Why don't they set him on a tray, and carry him over their heads?' cried some. Others, being told he was a short man, and was in a dense throng, grouped at a distance, jumped up and down, hoping, while up, to catch a glimpse, but all to no purpose. Boz retired after an hour's exhibition, bequeathing all the unused literary enthusiasm to be poured on Washington Irving."

XII.

TYLER'S ADMINISTRATION.

Clay's Adieu to the Senate—Lord Ashburton's Arrival—Men prominent in the Court Circle—Mrs. Robert Tyler's Letter after the Death of her Mother-in-Law—Seven Thousand at the New Year's Levee, 1843—Webster's Reception—Receptions of Mr. Adams and Mrs. Tayloe—Mrs. Tyler's amusing Description of her Party and Supper given to Marshal Bertrand—a Juvenile Fancy Ball at the White House—"The Washington Assemblies" organized—Ladies most admired—The new British Minister—Olé Bull—Receptions by the Secretaries—Mrs. Gouverneur's splendid Party—Self-styled Leaders who were Parvenues—Brilliant Entertainments—General McDuffie—Captain Stockton—Madame Pageot's Party, and Disappointment of the Expectations of a Parisian Supper—The Excursion on board "the Princeton"—Terrible Catastrophe—Mrs. Madison's Party in May—The Marriage of President Tyler to Miss Gardiner—Memoir of the Bride—Mr. Pakenham's Entertainment—The new President elect—Grand Ball given by Mrs. John Tyler—Colonel and Mrs. Tuley of Virginia.

THE last day of Mr. Clay's political existence was marked by his adieu to the Senate, after which he was to return to his home in Kentucky. So elevated had been his position, so decided his political course, and so marked the points in his character, that for more than thirty years almost every man in the country had been his devoted friend or his bitter enemy. His place in the Senate was immediately filled by Mr. Crittenden. Mr. Clay's valedictory was listened to by a dense crowd of citizens and ladies. Mr. Calhoun came to him when it was concluded, and bade him an affectionate farewell.

Lord Ashburton, the new British minister, came early in April. He was nearly six feet in height—a stout man, pale, but active in movement, with a mild and pleasing expression of countenance. He immediately proceeded to a house hired and prepared for him on President Square, near Mr. Webster's. Three secretaries and five servants comprised his retinue. A splendid dinner was in waiting for him. The age of his lordship was sixty-five; but he was a finer looking man than Lord Morpeth. According to the etiquette between minister and ambassador, he was to call on the morrow upon Mr. Fox, who would present him to the Secretary of State. It was not supposed that Mr. Fox was to be suspended. The warm spring weather brought on renewed gayeties. The wife of the Secretary of State held her levee on Tuesdays, the visiting-day of the week for the families of the cabinet. A grand dinner and a ball were in prospect, to honor the great retiring orator, Mr. Clay. The fashionables expected some agreeable entertainments from Lord Ashburton. This nobleman came charged with full powers to settle, among other points, the boundary question on a principle of compromise. He brought his own carriage and horses and a great quantity of luggage; it was therefore supposed he intended a long residence.

Horace Everett, of Vermont, a whig, one of the fathers of the House of Representatives, entered Congress in 1829, and for twelve years had been one of the most assiduous members. He was then about fifty, of medium height, retiring in manners, and enjoyed the confidence of all his constituents. Dixon H. Lewis, a democrat, was the largest man in the House of Representatives, and weighed over four hundred pounds. He had first taken his seat in 1829. He was a good speaker, and very popular. At this time he was about forty. Thomas Hart Benton, of Missouri, was democratic. He had been a member of the Senate since 1821, and was the oldest in service in that body after Mr. King. He was characterized as the most indefatigable and persevering of men in any matter he undertook. "Solitary and alone, I put this ball in motion," was the opening of his speech on the famous expunging resolution, which he carried through after a struggle of several sessions. In debate he was clear and forcible, always armed with statistics and dates, but stormy and overbearing; and in a passion he became furious. In figure he was portly and robust, and when wrapped in his Spanish cloak, he stepped with the air of a tribune. Kind and affectionate in the domestic circle, he educated his own children till after a certain age. At this time he was not much over fifty. James G. McKay, of North Carolina, had been a member since 1831. He was plain in appearance, but constant in his attention to duty. George N. Briggs, of Massachusetts, was elected in 1831. He was a whig, and an attentive and efficient member. James Buchanan had been a prominent and distinguished member of the Senate for seven years. He came into Congress in 1821, in the lower house, of which he remained an active and influential member till 1831. In 1833 he was appointed minister to Russia, and on his return two years later was elected to the Senate. He had much weight and influence, and for the preceding twelve years had been identified with the Jackson and Van Buren dynasties, though in Tyler's time he ranked among the opposition. He was strict in his party devotion, but never ultra in his doctrines. In figure and address he was aristocratic-looking, with the blandest and most polished manners; specious in debate and fair-spoken, inclined to be witty, and with much dignity of character. He was "a stricken bachelor," and always wore a white cravat.

An accomplished New York lady wrote from Washington, June 7, 1842:

"This morning paid a visit to Mrs. Tyler and Mrs. Madison. The latter is a delightful old lady, so amiable, with such fine manners. Mrs. Robert Tyler is also very pleasing and amiable. Mr. Roosevelt and I dined with Lord Ashburton to-day. The dinner was very pleasant. Our company consisted of Mr. and Mrs. Berton, Mr. and Mrs. Rhett, Dr. Linn, Mr. Conrad, Mr. White (Speaker of the House), Mr. Fillmore, General Jones, Mr. Finis, General Van Ness and Mr. Poinsett. The entertainment was simple and elegant, and passed off very pleasantly. Lord Ashburton has three secretaries."

June 22d.—"Mrs. Madison sent me this afternoon an album of her niece, Miss Payne, to look at. I found a very pretty piece of poetry written by Mr. Adams: 'To Miss Anna Payne.'

"Last evening I went to the President's grounds with Mr. Roosevelt. Mr. Ingersoll joined us; we met a number of acquaintances there; Mr. and Mrs. Lawrence of Boston, Mr. and Mrs. Webster, Senator Bates, Mrs. Middleton, &c."

After the death of Mrs. John Tyler, Mrs. Robert Tyler wrote in October, 1842:—"As you know, we were summoned from Brooklyn by mother's last illness. We started immediately, but only arrived here after her death, and even after the funeral service had been performed. Nothing can exceed the loneliness of this large and gloomy mansion—hung with black—its walls echoing only sighs and groans; of course their mother's death was a most agonizing blow to the whole family. My poor husband suffered dreadfully when he was told that mother's eyes were constantly turned to the door watching for him. He had left Washington to bring me and the children at her request. She was very fond of me, and I loved her dearly. She had everything about her to awaken love; she was beautiful to the eye even in her ill-health; her complexion was as clear as an infant's, her figure perfect, and her hands and feet were the most delicate I ever saw. She was refined and gentle in everything she said and did; and, above all, a pure and spotless Christian. Indeed she was just my beau ideal of a perfect gentlewoman. The devotion of father and her sons to her was affecting; I do not think I ever saw her enter the room, where they were assembled, that they did not all three spring up, to lead her to a chair, to arrange her footstool, and caress and pet her.". . . .

The return of General Cass from his mission to France, and the important associations connected with his name, excited a great sensation in political circles. His history embraced the record of numerous patriotic deeds during the war of 1812, and he occupied a larger share of public attention as the question of the next Presidency began to be agitated. On the first day of January, 1843, the President's house was thrown open for visitors; Mr. Webster, M. de Bodisco, General Cass, John C. Calhoun, Mr. Adams, Mr Roosevelt and other distinguished citizens receiving the company. General Cass had received the visits and cordial greeting of almost all the members of Congress, and was very happy with his charming family. Seven thousand were guessed to be present. Among them were seen Senators Tallmadge, Choate, Rives, Evans, Merrick, Bates, Carr, Calhoun, Sevier, King, Allen, Linn, Conrad, Woodbridge, Porter, Young, &c. Of the House of Representatives the most conspicuous were Messrs. Pickens and Morgan, General Dawson, General Ward, Colonel Sumter of South Carolina, Frank Granger, Mr. Roosevelt, John McKeon, Governor Pope, Albert Smith, Allen of Maine, John C. Clark, Judge Edwards, Gwinn and Thompson of Mississippi, &c. Among the charming women present were Mrs. Bodisco, Mrs. Fletcher Webster, Mrs. J. J. Roosevelt, Mrs. Wickliffe, Mrs. Greenough, the Misses Dawson, Gales, Granger, Wickliffe, Elizabeth Blair, Miss Woodbury, Bayard, Mason of Alexandria, the accomplished daughters of Thomas L. Smith, &c. The arrangements were admirable. Robert Tyler and his lovely and accomplished wife stood by the President to receive their friends, and Mrs. William Tyler was the object of universal admiration. John C. Calhoun stood in the center of the east room, with many lovely women around him. General Cass held a levee of intellectual men and beautiful women. Mr. Webster's house was also opened to a brilliant crowd. Here were Daniel "the godlike man," General Cass and General Scott, and other congenial spirits. Mrs. Webster did the honors; and the star of attraction was Mrs. Fletcher Webster, who was a woman of surpassing loveliness, as was her sister Mrs. Page. Mr. Roosevelt, who resided in Mrs. Madison's house, received visitors, to whom the beautiful and accomplished Mrs. Roosevelt did the honors "in the true old Knickerbocker style, like a worthy descendant of the honored family of Van Ness." Her guests were numerous and distinguished, and her table was said to be the best of the day.

A most intellectual treat was met with at the house of John Quincy Adams. The "old man eloquent" fired up with the vigor of youth. Leading men of all parties, and every man of distinction in the city, called to pay their respects. Mrs. John Adams, and his lovely grand-daughter, assisted in the reception of guests. Mrs. Tayloe also threw open her splendid mansion, Miss Custis assisting Mrs. Tayloe to preside. Hon. Aspbury Dickens gave an entertainment; also Major Thomas L. Smith, and Mr. Larned of the Treasury department. Senator Tallmadge is said to have declared, on his honor as a gentleman, that "the eggnog at this house was superior to any he had ever tasted."

Afterwards Mrs. Tyler wrote to her sister in 1843: "You say you hear Bertrand is to come to this country! My dear, he *has* come! come, seen and conquered—he has come, seen *me*, and *been conquered!* The Marshal arrived during the President's absence in Virginia, and the whole duty of entertaining him devolved upon me! To be sure, Mr. Tyler is here; but he is only the Prince Consort, you know. He arrived on Saturday, and sent the same evening to ask if I would receive him, and at what hour he should call. I appointed eight o'clock, it being then past seven. I immediately sent for the officers of the cabinet, and was surrounded by them when the old hero arrived, accompanied by his suite. He bowed to the very ground, and I curtsied quite as low. I cannot convey to you an idea of how charmingly I received him. The hour he remained he spent in complimenting me in French and English, rather jumbled together, while I returned his compliments in the same eccentric mixture of languages. At last, after a flourishing speech, squeezing my hand, with a second low bow over it, he departed, followed by his suite, each first making a profound obeisance. I could not resist the impulse, and, as the last mustachioed Frenchman left the room, I turned a pirouette upon one foot on the rug, and then, dropping a low curtsey, said: 'I beg the cabinet's pardon.' Whereat Mr. Tyler was exceeding wrathy, though every one else said it was the 'sweetest thing' I had done the whole evening. The Marshal was to leave the next morning (Sunday), but I sent him an invitation for Monday evening. You should see the note of acceptance he wrote (I have it in my book of autographs): he 'had intended leaving;' 'my gracieuse invitation was not to be resisted. I had but a short time in which to effect a great deal, but my usual administrative powers were called into action, and I succeeded in doing all I wished to do. I sent out two hundred invitations to the '*crême de la crême*' of Washington society.

"At eight o'clock my party was assembled, formed of the very prettiest girls, and nicest people I could collect. All the officers of the army and navy appeared in their uniforms. The diplomatique corps in full court costume. I stood at the head of the blue center room under the window. As the Marshal arrived and walked through the hall, the band struck up the 'Marseilles Hymn.' The guests fell back on either side as he entered the room, leaving a broad path for Bertrand to advance to where Josephine—I mean, to where *I* stood surrounded by the cabinet. To describe the reverences he made, followed by his son and each of his suite in turn, would be vain! I returned them with grandma's old-fashioned curtsies, such as must have existed in the days of the Empire. Soon after his arrival the quadrilles commenced. I only danced twice. Once, to open the ball, with Count Bertrand, the Marshal's son, and again, at his request, with his aid-de-camp: two young Frenchmen composed of full pantaloons and mustachios. For the rest of the evening my guests demanded my attention. No party ever went off better.

"Father, with his usual kindness, had given me a carte-blanche before he left, and my supper was *splendid*, (it is so easy to entertain at other people's expense.) The prettiest things on the table were two pyramids composed of pomegranates with the skins peeled off, and Malaga grapes. They looked like rubies and emeralds. I had quantities of vases of natural flowers down the table, and festoons of grapes going from vase to vase the whole length of the table, which, of course, was covered with everything possible in the way of jellies, ices, creams, &c., &c., and quantities of the most beautiful French bonbons. Nothing was on the long principal table but things of the most aerial, glittering description. Meats were all banished to the side table. . . . . Altogether every thing was as plentiful and brilliant as I could make it, and I personally directed everything myself. As the Marshal led me in to supper, he seemed completely overcome, and putting his hand upon his heart, said: *'Oh, Madame, all zis for me?'* The only contretemps that occurred was, that I gave him with a smile, a most splendid looking French sugar plum without observing the picture on it, which I afterward discovered, to my horror, to be that of an ass!—I hope the Marshal did not think it personal! The old gentleman did not leave until all the guests had departed, and then made me a long speech of adieu, saying at the end: *'I sink vous êtes charmante, Madame; I sink you are very good woman, and all your people must lof you. Adieu, Madame, I shall nevare forget you!'* Then saluting my hand in the most chivalrous, French, respectful, delicious manner, he departed, and left me alone in my glory. I looked very well—for *me!* I was dressed in a rose-colored satin, trimmed with blonde lace and flowers, a charming little head-dress of white bugles. By the way bugles are all the rage! Are you not tired of all this egotism?"

A juvenile fancy ball was given by Mrs. Robert Tyler on the third birthday of her daughter. The child was dressed as a fairy with silver wand, gossamer wings, and a diamond star upon her forehead, holding the hand of her young mother while she received her guests. The daughter of the Mexican Minister, a very little girl, represented a princess of her own country in embroidered satin and one blaze of magnificent diamonds. A son of the Schemerhorn family of New York, appeared as a Greek boy—with the most elaborate and perfect costume in the room. Little Miss Cutts, afterwards Mrs. Senator Douglas, also graced the occasion, giving promise of the intelligence and beauty which in later years led captive the great statesman of the West. The boys and girls of the famous Henry A. Wise moved upon the scene, the youngest in the arms of its sweet mother, formerly Miss Sergeant, of Philadelphia. Also some younger scions of Mr. Wickliffe's family, the then Postmaster-General; the beautiful children of Mrs. D'Arguiz and the Spanish Minister, &c. In fact the diplomatique corps, the Cabinet, Senate, Supreme Court, House of Representatives and the principal cities of the Union, were represented by the lovely little ones assembled. But the most noticeable feature of the evening was the supper table, where, opposite the little hostess of three years, sat the venerable Mrs. Madison, the only invited guest of adult years admitted to the table, while the ladies of the family attended to the children's wants and distributed the gifts from branches of the brilliant Christmas tree which adorned the center of the well laden board.

Mr. and Mrs. Robert Tyler suffered greatly in the late war, and the lady described her painful experiences in eloquent letters to her relatives. If published, they would form a most interesting addition to the literature of that period. They now reside in Alabama.

Besides the numerous private entertainments, a club of resident gentlemen, composed of the first class, arranged an annual set of parties, under the title of "The Washington Assemblies," to which all were invited who had the entrée to fashionable circles. The opening one took place in January. There was the inevitable M. de Bodisco, with his dignified air; and near him, with petitmaitre manners, might be seen the Spanish envoy extraordinary. A squatty figure, with high cheek bones, long black hair and well-spread forehead, was Mr. Almonte, the new Mexican Ambassador. There were Bayard and Huntington, fresh from a warm debate, and there was the Colossus in mind—Daniel Webster—among the thoughtless; and there was a well-dressed elegant person, talking with the last American minister to Spain; the first delegate from East Florida, and a distinguished officer in its Indian wars—General Hernandez. A tall young man, in brown and black, with simple white vesting, was young Harvey from South Carolina; he had an elastic step and a haughty mien, and conversed well. A noble beauty was Mrs. Van Ness of Spanish birth; her speaking and eloquent eyes caused her to share the admiration with the majestic and queenly Mrs. Webster. Leaning on the arm of the Mexican minister was "the far and wide celebrated widow," Mrs. White of New York. Not only peerlessly beautiful, she had a warm and feeling heart. Her life had been checkered for one so young; but she wore no mark of sorrow, nor was there a line of grief in that face of sunshine. With thousands at her feet, she had not the bearing of a conqueror. The stately girl opposite Mr. Waldron of the navy, was the celebrated Miss Gardiner of New York. Sparkling and attractive without affectation, she had a high and daring spirit, and had been much admired in Parisian circles. Next to her, prattling with innocent naïveté, was her younger sister, and close to her a Southern belle, Miss Lawson of Louisiana, all vivacity and life, with wit that gathered a crowd about her. Alexandria's most beautiful flower, Miss Bryant, was conspicuous and Mrs. Stanley, a whole-souled and fearless woman.

As March approached, squalls were anticipated in the political horizon which would stir the social atmosphere. The continuance of Mr. Webster in the cabinet, in spite of the opposition of the whigs or the democrats, caused a disturbed state of things. Tyler, with his veto in one hand and his spoils in the other, had demolished and destroyed the expectations of the whigs during the last two years. The Calhoun men were in high spirits, feeling sure that Mr. Calhoun would get the nomination at the Convention in 1844. He was in capital health and spirits, while McDuffie's health had greatly improved. The winter, so far, had been rather dull. The only parties worth mentioning had been given by Mr. Webster, Mr. Wickliffe and Lieutenant Kearney. The gossip of society announced that Hon. Caleb Cushing would shortly lead to the altar a beautiful, intellectual and wealthy lady—a Roman Catholic—from Baltimore. Another rumor was faintly heard—of the President's marriage being anticipated. A little later in March, ex-President Van Buren was at Albany, preparing the machinery for the next election, John Van Buren with him. Henry Clay was in Ashland, after a visit to New Orleans. General Cass was in his home at Detroit, where he had been received with great eclat. John C. Calhoun was in Charleston, South Carolina, said to be also preparing for the next Presidency. Daniel Webster had not yet left the cabinet, but it was supposed he would soon go to England as minister in place of Edward Everett, who was destined to go to China. In December, Pakenham was the newly appointed minister from the court of St. James, in place of Mr. Fox. His special mission was to settle the Oregon question.

At the close of this year, Olé Bull, the simple-minded, the warm-hearted, the enthusiastic child of nature, was the lion of Washington. He was said at the time to be about thirty-three. He was broad-shouldered, with a remarkably full, prominent and expansive chest. In conversation he exhibited occasional outbreaks of good humored, nervous excitability; and he often tapped his head with his fingers, as though he felt a consuming fire within. "No man," he said, "can do any ting in dis world widout entusiasm; he must 'ave de mania; people vill tink he ish mad; he must trow his whole soul into his business, or else he can't excel."

At the next New Year's day it was declared that Pennsylvania avenue never before witnessed so much joy, so much dress, so much beauty, so much gallantry, so much fashion, so much intelligence. The grand feature of the day was the President's levee. Higher than all the rest could be seen the waving plume of General Scott, rivalled only by the towering height of long John Wentworth, member from Illinois. Dixon H. Lewis ploughed through the mass like a seventy-four well rigged; diminutives following in his wake. All the secretaries of departments were "at home," and Mrs. Madison, too, with a pretty bouquet in her hand. John Quincy Adams also threw open his house. The privilege of the floor of the House was granted by vote of Congress to Mrs. Madison.

The exciting scenes in Congress, and the struggle of political parties, occupied public attention to the overshadowing of social matters. The fashionable season opened about the middle of January with the President's levee. A wholly new feature was introduced to the delight of the guests—dancing. A noted event in the fashionable world was the ball and supper given by Mr. Gouverneur, late postmaster of New York. Mrs. Robert Tyler had gone to Virginia; but the White House had a fair representative in the President's niece. In the little world of Washington, the New York variety of equipage was equalled. Now would dash by the beautiful low Parisian carriage of the French minister; the servants in drab and silver, followed by the carriage of some patrician

Virginian, driven by an old negro in battered hat and torn coat, the harness mended with ropes, the leather curtains shrunk and flying in the wind. Anon came along a provincial dandy on a prancing big-headed horse whose sides the rider lacerated with his long spurs, and by checking him with the curb forced him to go sideways, so that the most prominent objects were the horse's long tail and the rider's large nose, his military saddle denoting that some of his ancestors were in the army. Then came the handsome carriage and blood horses of a member from New Jersey; the two colored servants in neat plain clothes, respectable and grave in their appearance. Now, walking briskly along, came the President's private secretary, John Tyler, Jr.; the handsomest man in Washington. He was accustomed to carry the President's messages to the Senate and the House.

Yet even in this kingdom of fashion there were fine ladies, self-styled leaders of the *ton*, who considered themselves too exclusive to visit the family of "that honest, courteous gentleman, the President," and who boasted that they had never been inside the White House since the death of General Harrison. One of these high dames, the moment it was announced that the President would hold his first levee, issued invitations for a supper-party the same evening, inviting those she regarded as belonging to the first set, and intimating that their non-attendance would be followed by expulsion from the coterie. This lady who tried to put a slight on the family of the Chief Magistrate was no scion of "the first families in Virginia, born on the banks of the Potomac before the Revolution, in a gubernatorial mansion of the days of George the Second, situated in the center of an estate of a thousand acres, with five hundred slaves to tremble at her nod." Her husband was a printer, and for some thirty years his family had lived on the patronage of the government. "It was but the other day that the Calvert family, the lineal descendants of one of the lord proprietors of Maryland, in their old-fashioned chariot and four roan horses, drove ten miles over a very bad road, to pay their respects on New Year's day to the Chief Magistrate." Three of the most respected navy officers—Commodores Stewart, Shubrick and Bolton—were at this time mingling in the social circles of the capital. Mrs. Wickliffe, the wife of the Postmaster-General, gave her first party for the season in January. Misses Mary, Margaret and Nancy Wickliffe assisted in the reception of the company in the most charming manner. The wife of the Mayor, Mrs. Seaton, followed with a brilliant ball and supper; and Senator Rives gave a select dinner party on Saturday. The ladies of Washington were devotedly attentive to Mrs. Rives.

After the first "Washington assembly," Mrs. Richard S. Coxe gave a splendid party. She was the wife of an eloquent and learned lawyer, and the daughter of the eminent merchant and worthy man, John G. Warren of New York. A new topic of curiosity and excitement were the movements of Captain Stockton, who was to make some grand exhibitions of his corvette sloop of war "Princeton." Mr. McDuffie at this time made his second speech on the tariff. He was regarded as "a second Calhoun, and in his particular way the greatest, ablest, most eloquent, most comprehensive statesman in either house of Congress. All the rest are pigmies to this intellectual giant." He was the boast and pride of South Carolina.

Captain Stockton made his first appearance at the President's levee, and was attended by a crowd wherever he moved; being obliged again and again to recount the exploits of the "Princeton" in coming up through the ice of the Potomac. The astonishment she created among the inhabitants on the banks of the river, is not easily conceived; as they beheld a fairy phantom ship, without a patch of sail spread upon her spars, or a living soul upon her decks, without the slightest evidence of steam, fire, light, or life on board, still ploughing her onward way through the immense thickness of ice; ripping, tearing, breaking, crushing, with irresistible power! The President and suite—a private party—were to visit her the next day.

On the 8th February Madame Pageot, the wife of the French minister, entertained her friends. Lemonade and sponge cake were handed about, but sparingly tasted; for whispers of a "Parisian supper," "patés perigord," &c., were heard faintly; and the thermometer was below freezing point. About twelve, one of the elder ladies took the arm of the hostess, for the purpose of going to the dressing-room for a moment. It was understood that supper was ready; and two by two, with stately step, the company followed —— to the dressing-room. Supper there was none; and to return to the drawing-room would have been ungraceful; so everybody went home.

It was on the 28th of February that the dreadful and heart-rending catastrophe occurred which was to fill Washington and the land with mourning. The fête was given by Captain Stockton on board the Princeton. The ship proceeded down the river below Mount Vernon, and on her return, when within some twenty minutes' run of Alexandria, the large gun on the bow was fired. It exploded at the breech, and spread death and destruction over the deck! The Secretary of State, Mr. Upshur, the Secretary of the Navy, Governor Gilmer, Commodore Kennon, Chief of the Bureau of Construction of the Navy, Virgil Maxcy, and Mr. Gardiner of New York, were instantly killed. Colonel Benton and Captain Stockton were slightly injured. Several others suffered severely. A steamboat from Alexandria, which was passing, was sent back to town, and returned with several surgeons. The President, Colonel and Mrs. Tuley of Virginia, and many ladies who were on board, escaped without injury. Judge Wilkins was "saved by a witticism." He had been standing beside Governor Gilmer, and perceiving the gun was about to be fired, exclaimed: "Though Secretary of War, I do not like this firing, and believe I shall run." So saying, he retreated. The two daughters of Mr. Gardiner were on board, and were overwhelmed at the death of their father; while Mrs. Gilmer sat on deck with hair dishevelled, pale as death, striving to control her feelings; her lips quivering, her eyes fixed and upturned, without a tear. Five hundred guests were on board; the ladies and gentlemen had just dined, and the toasts were being drunk. Shortly before the catastrophe, Judge Upshur had been called on for his toast. He accidentally took up an empty bottle, and pleasantly remarked that "the dead bodies" (the empty bottles) must be cleared away before he could give his toast. By chance another empty bottle was pushed towards him; he repeated his joke, which drew from Captain Stockton the reply that there were plenty of living (bottles) to supply the places of the dead. The President then gave the toast: "The Princeton and her three guns, &c." The leading gentlemen then withdrew from the table to make room for others; and within ten minutes Judge Upshur himself was a dead body! Six hearses were escorted by Mr. Wickliffe to the President's house, where the body of Colonel Gardiner remained till the funeral.

At this time the two great questions of the annexation of Texas, and the negotiations concerning Oregon, were before the country. Mr. Webster took ground against the annexation. Calhoun, who had accepted the office of Secretary of State, was decidedly in favor of it, and not disposed to yield an inch in Oregon. Mr. John Y. Mason was the new Secretary of the Navy. Mr. Choate's great speech in the Senate on the Oregon question, was esteemed a masterpiece, highly finished, elaborate and classical. Mr. Tyler was reported to have said: "I'll tell you, gentlemen, this Texas question will ride over and ride down every other; and the politicians will fall before it as the soldiers fell at New Orleans. It will kill all the men and parties that are opposed to it; and the voice of the people will come back in favor of the annexation, like a mighty avalanche, sweeping both factions into ruin before it. I at least shall have the consolation of knowing that I have done my duty. I have no desire that war should come during my administration: but, gentlemen, if it does come, I shall push it through. I shall not give way one inch; nor shall I yield one foot of our territory of Oregon." Mr. Webster was now considered opposed to the administration. General Henderson, the Texan minister, shortly after arrived with full powers to negotiate the annexation. The other minister, Mr. Van Zandt, had awaited him in Washington. Henderson had been appointed by President Houston, in obedience to the secret instructions of the Texan Congress. In case the American government should refuse to accept the proposition of annexation, Henderson was authorized to proceed immediately to England, and to propose an alliance of some kind with that power, either as a colony, or in some other independent shape. Mr. Calhoun thus entered upon his duties at a most momentous era. He had on one hand the negotiation with Mr. Pakenham, which was to settle the fate of Oregon, the fortunes of the West, and one might say of the great Pacific empire; on the other, the negotiation with Henderson, to settle the fate of Texas and the fortunes of the Southern and South-western States.

Mr. Calhoun now became the master spirit of the American government, and his energy, decision, and courage found a field of action. The impending measure of annexation plunged Washington and the country into a state of ferment and excitement. Mr.

Clay's letter, Mr. Van Buren's letter, Mr. Tyler's letter, went with the Virginia election to add fuel to the flame. The atmosphere of Washington was political rather than legislative. Probably never in the history of the government, had there been so much manœuvring, intriguing and management. The master key to the intrigues was found in the fact that a desperate game of chess was being played for the Presidency.

Mrs. Madison gave a large party on the 21st May. It was attended by the Secretaries of State and of the Navy, the Postmaster-General and Attorney-General, Mr. Spencer, late Secretary of the Treasury, many of the diplomatic corps, members of Congress, &c. Mr. and Mrs. Barrow had lately returned from the mission to Portugal. Mrs. Barrow was a splendid-looking woman. A gentleman who had been American Secretary of Legation at Mexico, was describing to Mr. Pakenham the beauty of a New York lady, who, he said reminded him of what a queen ought to be, "such a magnificent queen as Zenobia." "But," asked Mr. Charles J. Ingersoll, "What was the color of Queen Zenobia? Might it not have been the subject of animated correspondence between Mr. Pakenham and Mr. Calhoun?" "Yes," rejoined Pakenham, addressing Mr. Ingersoll; "and you, perhaps, would have written a report about it!"

A delegate to the Baltimore Convention arrived in Washington, who had come by way of Nashville, and called on General Jackson. In conversation with the old hero, he expressed his embarrassment as to the vote he should give at the convention, in consequence of Van Buren's opposition to annexation. General Jackson, lifting his long skinny finger, said, emphatically, "You must forsake your friend, and cling to your country." Delegates now thronged every corner and quarter of the city. The musical sylvan levee at the capitol the 23d May, in the afternoon, was fashionably attended; but the prospects of the nomination to the next Presidency occupied all conversation.

As the marriage of the President took place this year, a brief mention of his bride is appropriate. All who knew Miss Julia Gardiner remember the charm of her conversation, her wit, her piquancy, and her radiant countenance, bewitching grave and gay, old and young. She was one of those born to shine, to carry hearts by storm. The daughter of the Hon. David Gardiner of Gardiner's Island, she was educated in refinement and luxury, and early showed her possession of a mind of rare powers. When she entered society, at a very youthful age, many were the poetic tributes that proved her attractions — and grave Senators, Judges, and State Governors were among the suitors for her hand; yet she remained heart-whole and fancy-free. Her parents took their two daughters, Julia and Margaret, abroad, and their beauty and grace everywhere met with distinguishing attention. The recipients of homage from men of princely rank and fortune, had they been less true to their American instincts their destinies would have been cast in a foreign land. Miss Gardiner was unmoved by rank and wealth and refused to exchange her republican home for one under a monarchical government. Mrs. Sigourney wrote from London that "English beaux, on meeting her, seemed suddenly to become aware of the value of their lost colonies."

By this time Harrison had been elected President, and his sudden death had called Vice-President Tyler to take his place. When Miss Gardiner, on her return from Europe, attended the reception of the President, he could not but feel the happy influence of her presence, and he lost no time in expressing his sentiments. This suit was successful after the death of her devoted father, who was one of the five victims of the disaster on board the ship of war "Princeton." On the 25th of June following, the unexpected arrival of the President in New York created a great sensation. What could be the cause of his sudden visit! Numerous and contradictory were the rumors concerning it; the annexation of Texas; trouble with England; and every cause but the true one was assigned. It had been understood that he was to spend a few days at the Rip Raps of Virginia; and this unannounced change of plan was unaccountable. The next day at one o'clock the mystery was solved! Bishop Onderdonk performed the ceremony; and Miss Gardiner and President Tyler were joined in marriage in the presence of a few friends at the Church of the Ascension in Fifth Avenue, New York.

The wedded pair embarked at four o'clock on board the steamer Essex, amidst a shower of salutes. During the firing from one of the Mexican vessels in the harbor, a perfect aerial ring appeared, soared upward for some time, then gracefully sank till its rim touched the water, when it broke and vanished. It was an incident which seemed to betoken the rare and perfect happiness that ever followed this union of youth and age until the death of Mr. Tyler in 1862.

Mrs. Tyler's receptions at the White House were noted for their simplicity as well as elegance and refinement. Mrs. Madison was an always included, and an always present guest at the State dinners, and the large or small reunions. Though so young in years when it became her lot to do the honors of the executive mansion as "the President's Bride," it is an admitted fact that she never lost sight of the claims of age and position.

In 1853, the Duchesses of Sutherland, Argyle and Bedford, Viscountess Palmerston, and a host of other ladies of the English nobility, addressed a letter to the ladies of the United States, urging them to effect the abolition of slavery. Mrs. Tyler, then living in retirement at "Sherwood Forest," her country-seat on the James River, Virginia, wrote a spirited reply, which met with universal commendation.

During the civil war Mrs. Tyler resided at the South until her husband's death in 1862, when, ill and heart-stricken, she repaired with her children to Staten Island, in reduced circumstances, to receive the protection of her mother's roof. After a deep share of sadness and trouble, fortune has again smiled upon her; yet she continues to reside on Staten Island.

The approaching contest was one of unusual importance. The two great parties were the democrats and whigs; of the latter, Mr. Clay being the universally acknowledged and favorite candidate. The nomination of James K. Polk for President, George

M. Dallas for Vice-President, completing the defeat of Van Buren and Cass, was received by every faction and portion of the democracy with the strongest marks of enthusiasm.

The election of Mr. Polk was viewed as a complete vindication of the administration; and the President, cabinet, and subordinates, were in exultation. The fashionable world expected to reap the natural fruit of this unbounded joy, and preparations were in progress to make this the most brilliant season ever yet known in Washington. At stated periods the executive mansion was to be thrown open under the auspices of the President's youthful bride—called "the most splendid and accomplished woman of the time." "Possessed of the highest order of beauty and intellect, with manners the most elegant and popular, she will draw about her a court circle rivalling that of Louis le Grand." Other magnificent entertainments were in progress. John Quincy Adams delivered a lecture in one of the Baptist churches. Some concerts were given at the President's mansion.

Colonel Polk, the brother of the President elect, came to Washington accompanied by Dr. Gwynn of Tennessee, and created a great sensation among the political circles in that capital. He was a State Senator in Tennessee, frank and manly in his general intercourse, shrewd and wary in politics. The capital began to be crowded—the men looking after offices: the women flocking to parties. Mr. Pakenham, who had become extremely popular, gave the most select and elegant entertainment given since the days of Sir Charles Vaughan. At the birthnight ball, besides the President and President elect, officers and ministers in costume, heads of departments, &c., the occasion was honored by the presence of Mrs. Madison, and Mrs. Alexander Hamilton, then nearly ninety years of age.

Mr. Choate was called "the nosegay orator." His speeches against the annexation filled the galleries with the fashion and beauty of the day. "He could fill their minds with fancied ambrosial vales, strewn with flowers of richest hues, sending forth perpetual sweet scents. He could paint the colors of the rainbow; send up a thousand jets of the crystal fluid, set over the whole a thousand bright diadems, darting rays of brilliancy athwart the wide-spread paradise, &c."

The President elect, Mr. Polk, was obliged to close his levee at two o'clock, holding a short one every day. A "parting invitation ball" was given by Mr. and Mrs. Tyler late in February, and was crowded as usual. The President elect was invited, but the illness of Mrs. Polk prevented his attendance. Mrs. Tyler was gay and cheerful, and the radiance of her smiles was reflected on all except a few anxious applicants for office. Madame de Bodisco attracted all eyes by her graceful movements in a cotillion with Mrs. Tyler and the representatives of Austria, Prussia, France and Russia. Supper was announced at about ten, and such a rush and crush to obtain entrance was never seen at a Presidential entertainment; not one-twentieth of the crowd obtaining admission at one time. Among the distinguished gentlemen were General Scott, Commodore Stewart, General Lamar and Commodore Moore of Texas. Mr. Dallas was there, carrying his white head about the room at least half a head higher than the average of the crowd, except Colonel William O. Butler of Kentucky and "long John Wentworth." The beautiful young wife of President Tyler opened the ball with Mr. Wilkins, after which the gayeties of the evening fairly set in. The sons of President Tyler and their wives graced this last grand party of their father's retiring administration. Among other belles, besides Miss Tyler, were Miss Wilkins, Miss Wickliffe, Miss Edwards, &c. New York, Philadelphia and Boston were represented by the presence of their fashion and beauty. New York, it was said, could safely rest its claims upon Mrs. John Tyler as head of the list.

At this ball Mrs. Tuley of Virginia was conspicuous and admired. Her dress was elegant, and her ornaments superb and in good taste. Her stately grace and elegance of manner marked her as an appropriate representative of the proud and luxurious "Old Dominion." She has for years past been extensively known in the Northern as well as Southern cities; but most of her winters were spent in Washington, where she was the center of a distinguished circle. Mrs. Tuley is descended from a noted Roman Catholic family, who, in company with Lord Baltimore, came from England, settling the colony of Maryland under the grant issued by Charles I. in 1632. She was twice married. Her first husband was Dr. Jackson of the United States army. She afterwards married Colonel Tuley of Virginia. Their magnificent estate, known as "Tuleyries," in the valley of the Shenandoah, was one of the finest and most valuable in the State. The

THE PRESIDENT'S BRIDE.

(MRS. J. TYLER.)

Eng'd by [illegible] N.Y.

mansion was large and elegant, the park very extensive, and stocked with elk, deer and smaller game; extensive fields stretched beyond, forming one of the model plantations of the Southern country. The traditions of Virginia hospitality were well observed by Colonel and Mrs. Tuley, and their generous and elegant style of living made their house a delightful resort to a large circle of friends, among whom were numbered the most prominent statesmen of the day and distinguished foreigners, among them many of high rank.

This ball formed an era in Washington society. It was succeeded by a party at the house of Mr. Wilkins, the Secretary of War.

XIII.

POLK'S ADMINISTRATION.

Progress of the President elect to Washington—Mrs. Polk and Mrs. Knox Walker—Visit to President Tyler—The Inauguration—Mrs. Tyler's last Reception—Inauguration Balls—Grace and Dignity of Mrs. Polk in receiving at the White House—Mr. Dallas—An "April Fool" Joke—Curious Habits of Mr. Fox—Spring Evenings at the President's—Mrs. Abraham Van Buren—The May Balls—Madame Pageot's Graduation of Aristocracy—Prominent Statesmen—The Wisconsin Office-seeker—Louis McLane—Mrs. Polk's Elegance of Dress and Manner—George Bancroft—Jimmy Maher's Opinion of Mr. Polk and the Ladies—The Pottawattamies—Mrs. Maury's Introduction at the Court—Descriptions of Mr. Polk and the prominent Statesmen of the Period—Conversation with Calhoun about the Union—Visit to Mr. Clay—A populous New Year's Procession—General Cass and other Orators—The Misses Sloman—The Hero of Chippewa—Death of John Quincy Adams and Dixon H. Lewis.

The progress of the President elect up the Ohio on his way to Washington, was a triumphal one. At Louisville he took passage for Cincinnati, escorted to the boat by military companies. He appeared in good health and spirits, dressed in a suit of black broadcloth, and wearing a black cloth cloak with velvet collar. He took off his hat in receiving the cheers and congratulations of the people, though the day was piercingly cold. Mrs. Polk stood in the center of the ladies' saloon, wearing a purple silk velvet hat trimmed with satin ribbon, striped with broad reddish purple stripes, with a large black silk velvet cloak with cape bordered with fringe and tassels. She held in her hand a rich bouquet of flowers, and conversed with easy, animated manner with a circle of gentlemen gathered round her.

Previously to commencing the journey, it was said that Mr. Polk had visited the Hermitage, to have a private and confidential conversation with General Jackson, and to receive the old patriot's parting benediction. The General at that time was a prisoner in his room from bad health. His last vote had been given for Mr. Polk. The family of Mr. Polk consisted, besides his wife, of his nephew and adopted son, and another nephew who was his private secretary—Mr. Walker. An ovation awaited the President at all the towns and villages on his route, and at Cincinnati he was received with unbounded enthusiasm. At Wheeling "Young Hickory"—as he was called,—had similar demonstrations of welcome. Among the fashionable ladies there presented to him was Mrs. Shannon, the beautiful and accomplished wife of Wilson Shannon, American Minister to the city of Mexico. She was tastefully dressed, and her dark hair hung in rich curls about her snowy neck. Mrs. Johnson accompanied Mrs. Shannon. When the reception was over, dinner was served, and the President's carriage was brought out, of polished dark olive, with gilt borders around the panel work; four splendid horses being harnessed to it. The cushions inside were covered with richly figured crimson cloth, ornamented with lace trimmings; with blue and red figured heavy curtains. The President entered with Mr. Stevenson; Mrs.

Polk following, escorted by Colonel J. Knox Walker. The second carriage contained the Kentucky delegation; the third that of Louisiana; the fourth, Tennessee gentlemen. A band of music played, and the carriages moved off to cross the Alleghanies. Near a town in Pennsylvania they were met by a deputation in two carriages, which fell into the train, while a large company of mounted men brought up the rear. As they wheeled in front of a large seminary for ladies, a hundred young girls rushed to the doors and windows, waving their handkerchiefs to greet the new Chief Magistrate. At Harper's Ferry there was a scene of crowding and cheering that beggared description. At a hurried dinner, while Mrs. Polk's servant woman was seated at a side table, several inquisitive young ladies asked her how many servants Mrs. Polk brought with her; and being told "only one," expressed their shallow surprise. "I thought she would have had half a dozen."

The ladies pressed around for introductions to Mrs. Polk, who received them with ease, grace, and unaffected simplicity. At the Relay House, after leaving Frederick City, a thousand persons had come up in a chartered train to meet the President; and he was received with shouts "loud enough to have prostrated the walls of a cathedral; a cannon joining its roar to the general clatter." A lawyer made an address in a perfectly inaudible voice, and the President's reply was given in concert with the squealing of two or three steam-whistles, and a Babel uproar of human voices. When the cars came in sight of Washington, a cannon was seen to blaze away in the darkness from

Capitol Hill. Fireworks were displayed, and a torch-light procession moved along in awful pomp. Before the hotel the crowd was so tremendous, Governor Polk had to be lifted or passed in through a window. The President elect and Mrs. Polk, accompanied by Vice-President Dallas, ex-President Lamar of Texas, General Ward, Judge Woodward, and others, visited the White House, to pay their respects to President Tyler and Mrs. Tyler. Mrs. and Miss Gardiner, Miss Tyler, and Robert and John Tyler, were present, and the courtesy and good-feeling evinced on both sides rendered the interview most agreeable.

On the first day of March, 1845, President Tyler signed the resolutions concerning the admission of Texas. In the same week Iowa and Florida were admitted as States, increasing the number to twenty-nine. The same evening Mr. Tyler gave a grand cabinet supper at which Colonel Polk was a guest. For the inauguration a grand semi-circular platform was erected in front of and fitting on to the portico. The semi-circular projection had a raised platform at its extreme point, on which the President was to stand, with Chief Justice Taney to receive the oath of office, visible to the vast multitude in front and on the right and left.

The retiring President appointed the afternoon of the 3d of March to receive his friends at the White House for the last time.

Mrs. Tyler looked beautiful in a neat dress of black, with light black bonnet and veil. Several, as they took Mr. Tyler by the hand in farewell, shed tears; while he stood calm and collected, receiving all who approached him with cordiality and politeness. About five o'clock, General Van Ness delivered an address expressive of the regret felt by his fellow-citizens at the parting. The President made a brief, happy and grateful reply.

The largest crowd ever assembled in Washington to witness an inauguration, thronged the grounds and capitol, at the delivery of Mr. Polk's address. Chief Justice Taney officiated. The number was estimated at thirty thousand. President Polk immediately sent in to the Senate the names of his official advisers as selected by him; Senator Buchanan as Secretary of State; Senator Walker, Secretary of the Treasury; George Bancroft, of the Navy; Governor Marcy, of War; John Y. Mason as Attorney-General, and Cave Johnson as Postmaster-General. All were confirmed but that of Mr. Bancroft.

The President and his wife received visitors at the White House the day following the inauguration. Mrs. Polk's ease, grace and simple dignity, combined with the evidence of an amiable and cheerful disposition, won universal admiration.

The inauguration day was a wet one. No carriages were allowed to enter the grounds or square of the capitol. This of course excluded all the carriages of the foreign ministers; they had to alight at the entrance, and having no umbrellas, had to walk nearly a hundred yards through the rain in gold lace and cocked hats.

Among the ladies observed of all bachelors at the ball, were Miss Ward and Miss Ritchie. "The Don Giovanni of the age, the hero of the sea and the western waters, the ruling spirit of the stormy democratic elements of the redoubtable Empire Club—Captain Isaiah Rynders"—was also there. When the new President and Mrs. Polk, appeared accompanied by Senator Woodbury, the dancing was discontinued, while they walked up between the divided crowd, and the ladies craned their necks to get a view of the wife of the President. They were conducted to a raised divan, and the dancing was resumed.

"Mr. Dallas," said a letter writer, "is tall, straight and dignified, with hair almost as white as snow, hanging over his coat-collar. He is beyond the meridian of life, yet is active and buoyant as one of forty-five. In his intercourse with his fellow-citizens, nothing can be more kind, conciliating and gentlemanly. There is nothing of that hauteur about him frequently seen in the conduct of men elected to offices of importance and responsibility; all who approach him receive at his hands that attention which the man of breeding alone knows how to give. Mr. Dallas is one of the most popular of men; popular because of his winning and attractive manner. No one who has had a single interview with him, can efface the strong impression of regard for the man which it leaves behind."

Before this time "female influence" had begun to be developed, on behalf of the occupants of and the seekers after office. Application was made for the widow of Senator Linn, to be created postmistress at St. Louis. It was said that Senator Benton was opposed to her claim; though the idea of placing ladies in clerkships and offices of trust was daily gaining ground. General Jackson's intercession in favor of Mrs. Linn with "Young Hickory," decided the question of the post-office in her favor.

In April Mr. Buchanan left Washington; it was said to escort his nieces and housekeeper to the capital, to take charge of his newly formed domestic establishment. A cruel April fool joke was played upon a number of the department clerks, several of whom in the morning found lying on their desks neatly folded notes intimating that their services were no longer required. Seized with consternation, they repaired to their chief's room with pale and anxious faces, to learn that it was "all fool's day." The office-seekers were served with notes signed by the Secretary of the Treasury, requesting each to call at the Treasury department on the following morning. Such a gathering as there was! each armed with his note, with roused expectation and smiling face, wondering if the office to be tendered would be worth his acceptance. What frowns and scowls, clenched hands and compressed lips, followed the discovery that they had been befooled!

One of the notable social incidents was a wedding at the house of the Secretary of the Treasury, when his sister-in-law, Miss Bache, was married to a son of Colonel Abert's the head of one of the bureaus. Charles James Fox, the late British minister, was still in Washington. He seemed to keep up the custom of turning day into night; being only seen in the streets about sunset. It was said he once wrote from Italy to Lord Byron that he was "so changed by sickness, his oldest creditor would not know him." His appearance at this period was singular enough to prevent the possibility of his being forgotten. At this time cabinet councils were held at the White House at eleven on Tuesdays, Thursdays and Saturdays. On Mondays, Wednesdays and Fridays the President was accessible to the public from twelve to three in the afternoon. The mansion was open to the public on Tuesday, Thursday and Saturday evenings at eight; the President and Mrs. Polk, heads of departments, &c., being usually present.

Mrs. Polk was assisted in her social duties by Mrs. Walker, the wife of the private secretary of the President. She was a strikingly beautiful woman; lively, pleasant and captivating. At these receptions the old stagers in politics and office-seeking walked boldly in, familiarly seized and shook the President's hand, and immediately whispered some profound secret into his ear; which meant that an office was wanted. Then came the officials and gentlemen, who paid their respects and moved aside to allow the President to converse with strangers. There were a number of the substantial yeomen of the country, who came to see and shake hands with the man they had helped to place in his position. Some were bashful, and to them Mr. Polk kindly advanced. The Secretary of State, Mr. Buchanan, was stationed in the center of the room, where he was continually surrounded by ladies and gentlemen. Among those to whom he was most attentive, was Mrs. Abraham Van Buren, formerly Miss Singleton, of South Carolina, an accomplished and charming woman. There was the sagacious looking Postmaster-General, Cave Johnson, with his wife and daughter; and there was Amos Kendall, the white-headed seer, with his keen eye and aquiline nose. There, too, was Major Hobbie, the first Assistant Postmaster-General, with his daughter, who clung to his arm like a frightened fawn. There was the Spanish minister and his wife and sister-in-law, a tall dark-haired and dark-eyed lady. Mr. Pakenham was there; "he has a thoroughly English look, though he is far from looking the wily diplomat, which character is generally attributed to the statesmen of the mother country. He has far more of the frank John Bullism which is characteristic of the people of England, and is more like a republican and democrat than a royalist and an aristocrat." There were also Mr. Bancroft, the Secretary of the Navy, and his wife; and Mr. Haight, formerly consul to Antwerp; Mr. Markoe, the able Secretary of the American Institute; General Gibbs McNiel, the celebrated engineer; Governor Gibbs of Rhode Island, and a host of others. Mr. Ritchie was then sixty-nine, tall, thin, of a spare and rather bent form, an attenuated face like Amos Kendall's, but better looking. His manner was affable and frank. As the head of "The Enquirer," he had been accustomed to dictate to his party in Virginia.

"The redoubtable Chevalier Wikoff" was at this time in Washington, in the goodly keeping of the equally celebrated Beau Hickman. This latter individual usually wore a fine mustache, a hat of the latest Parisian style; a black frock-coat, venerable and respectable, sometimes buttoned up to the chin when the thermometer ranged between 90° and 95°.

A May ball was given on the 6th at the assembly

rooms by Mr. Labbé, whose pupils were the children of the aristocracy of the capital. The queen was Miss Violetta Carroll, a descendant or relative of Charles Carroll of Carrollton. Her maids of honor were Miss Randall and Miss Keyworth.

Madame Pageot professed to be one of the leaders of the *ton*, and was said to have been the first to graduate the aristocracy of the capital according to the salaries received from government. Cave Johnson, with his wife and daughters, were at the party, he appearing heartily delighted to witness the pranks of the juveniles, and smiling and laughing till his face shone and glistened. Mr. Bancroft averred solemnly that his wife would despise him if he did not or would not admire the beautiful women present. Mrs. Walker, the wife of the Secretary of the Treasury, was conspicuous; and so was Mrs. Knox Walker, with her husband and little daughter. The company was brilliant indeed, notwithstanding a degree of stiffness and restraint growing out of division into cliques.

Another marriage was that of Dr. Clymer of the navy, to the daughter of the gallant Captain Shubrick. It took place at the residence of the Commodore, near the President's. Fennimore Cooper and his two daughters were present. The novelist had dedicated several of his works to Captain Shubrick, on account of a long existing friendship. Hon. Joseph R. Ingersoll officiated as the friend of the bridegroom.

On the 9th of May, the concourse at the President's gardens was large. Fanciful flower-beds, gravel walks, groups of trees and artificial knolls presented varied beauty, and the company was lively; but the absence of the President was noticed. People talked of how General Harrison had won the affection of friends and foes by the simplicity and republican familiarity of his manners, and how one morning he bought in market a milch cow of a countryman. The man thought "Old Tip" merely a plain citizen, and chattered away without reserve. "Old Tip" invited him to go home with him to breakfast; the stranger assented, and walked side by side with his companion till they came to the White House. When they turned in at the gate of the mansion, the countryman was struck dumb, and fell back in consternation. Then he began to apologize to the President for his familiarity. "Never mind," cried Harrison; "you are a man, and so am I. You are one of the people, and I am their servant, and their tenant in this house. I shall therefore regard it as an honor to have one of my landlords as my guest." The countryman went inside the gate a strong Van Buren man; he came out with the strongest conviction that "Old Tip" was a democrat.

Alexander Porter, the Senator from Louisiana, was an emigrant from Ireland, but loved his adopted country. He died in 1844, after his second election. John Forsyth, like Crawford, was a Virginian by birth, Georgian by citizenship, and eminent in his day. He was minister to Spain and Secretary of State under the administration of Jackson and Van Buren. He had all the requisites for keen debate; ready elocution, argument and wit; quick and clear perception, perfect self-possession, great power to point a sarcasm and to sting courteously. In social life his manners were refined and polite, affable and dignified. He died about 1845.

The history of Reuben M. Whitney, who died in May, 1845, was known as one of singular transition from princely power to hopeless helplessness. During the administration of Van Buren, he was the great comptroller of the pet bank system, with immeasurable power and influence; a name more potent than that of any other man in the country. When the pet banks went down, his power was extinguished, and he became suddenly an obscure politician. Taken up by President Tyler and provided with a secondary post in the Treasury department, he was necessarily expelled on the advent of Polk's administration. He was turned out a poor man, afflicted with a mortal disease; and from the day of his expulsion he lay down never to rise again. His native energy deserted him; destitution stared him in the face, and death may have been a welcome relief to him. His wife, at one time courted as the cynosure of fashion, elegance and refinement, was left alone with her family.

The leafy month of June opened with excursions and sailing parties. The President and Mrs. Polk, accompanied by Mrs. Madison, Mr. and Mrs. Bancroft, Mr. and Mrs. Mason, Mr. and Mrs. Marcy, and the Marshal of the District, General Hunter, went on a picnic to Mount Vernon, Mrs. Polk having never before visited the tomb of Washington. Picnics to Arlington House, the hospitable residence of George Washington Parke Custis, on the other side of the Potomac, were now all the rage among the fashionables. The hot weather furnished no other amusement.

A gentleman from Wisconsin, an important office-seeker, called at the Treasury department to see Mr. Walker; and found a large number already waiting in the anteroom. After waiting half an hour, he exclaimed: "Look here, door-keeper, ain't you gwine to let me in to my friend Bob Walker, without any more fuss?" "Can't do it, sir, till your turn comes." "Turn!" (walking up and down the hall). "Here I come all the way from Wisconsin territory, (taking from his coat pocket a parcel of letters) recommended by General Dodge—there's his letter; and the young governor—there's hizzen; and by"—repeating a number of names. "Well, I can't stand this, waiter. Look here, stranger! Jest tell the Secretary, before I'll wait here all day to get into that door when my turn comes, I'll see him —— ——." And the young giant from Wisconsin departed in a rage.

The news of General Jackson's death draped the capital in mourning. The departments were all closed, and their doors were hung with crape. The capitol was shut up and the courts adjourned. Due funeral rites were prepared in honor of the memory of the old Hero of the Hermitage.

Hon. Louis McLane of Maryland, went as minister to England. His history as a politician showed his ability to fill the office; and it was thought the State of Maryland would feel the honor of the appointment. Mr. McLane was a native of Delaware, and came into Congress in 1817, remaining ten years in the lower House, and two in the Senate, till appointed by General Jackson, in 1829, minister to England. On the breaking up of the first cabinet he was recalled from London and appointed Secretary of the Treasury. Afterwards succeeding Mr. Livingston as Secretary of State, he resigned that office in 1834, on account of a difference of opinion with the Executive. For eight years he was the President of the Baltimore and Ohio Railroad Company. At this time he was about sixty, and conservative in politics. It was understood that Mr. Everett would await his arrival in London.

"Mrs. Polk," said a letter writer, "dresses in a style rich yet chaste, and becoming her person, character and position. Her husband is so spare that, if his clothes were made to fit, he would be but the merest tangible fraction of a President. He has them, therefore, especially his coat, some two or three sizes large. We think a visit to the salt water, Piney Point, Old Point, or any other point convenient for sea-bathing, salt crabs and oysters, would be a great help to him. We want him to live out his term, and go home to Tennessee, at the expiration of a successful administration, in health of body and mind."

The insufferable heat of the weather as July advanced, the threatening aspect of affairs—a war with Mexico assuming the shape of an unavoidable contingency—and the necessity of an extra session of Congress, were indeed exhausting to mental and physical nature. The White House at this time was undergoing repairs, and its first floor redolent of villanous smells of white lead and oil-cloths. Mrs. Bache, mother-in-law of Mr. Irwin, Chargé at Copenhagen, was about sailing for Europe.

At the White House evening reception the 14th November, there were only seventy-three persons, while as usual, Mrs. Polk, elegantly dressed, kind, familiar, and simple in her manners, gained the good will of every one. Mr. Polk, tired and teased half to death, preserved his equanimity, courtesy, and patience, in a wonderful manner. It was known that he was in the habit of cutting off from his sleep the hours lost, to make up the amount of time which he felt belonged to the nation. He rose at daylight and took an early walk, followed by an early breakfast. Then he worked till twelve; gave audiences till two; took dinner early, and worked afterwards till late at night. He was known frequently to pass most of the night in reading papers of no importance except to some applicant for an insignificant office; for he would not make an appointment without being informed of all the facts in the case. He was said to be the first President except Washington, who observed this rule. "Society in Washington," said a satirist, "is much indebted to the President for bringing on with him a number of young fellows from Tennessee, giving them a chance to see something of the world with offices to support them." To his nephew who wanted an office, he replied that he liked him too well to gratify his wishes and see him destroyed; he must go back to Tennessee and work in his profession. If Mr. Polk had any ambition, it was to be loved and esteemed in Tennessee. He loved that State as his mother; and the wish near to his heart was to see Tennessee come out strongly democratic under his administration. Under no circumstances would he again be a candidate for the Presidency, anxious as he was to perform the duties of his station faithfully and conscientiously.

Mr. Bancroft was described as "of the ordinary height, lightly made, with a high-toned, intellectual air. He can be easily bland and kindly in his address, or as freezing as Greenland." The appointment of this distinguished scholar and historian, was hailed as an honor paid to genius and capacity; but he hardly came up to the standard of the democrats. He made few changes in the fifty clerks under his control, though they were all politically opposed to him. Mrs. Bancroft was an elegant woman, with great personal attractions, and a very graceful address. Her manner produced the impression of a want of warmth, though that may have been due to her New England habits. She was not demonstrative in feeling, though ready and fluent, and even impulsive in speech. No one could possibly be better fitted for the wife of a minister abroad.

Drawing-rooms were still held at the executive mansion, notwithstanding the heat of the weather, during the summer; but they were thinly attended, and the conversation was formal and affected. "The President looks remarkably well this evening," and "I never saw Mrs. Polk look better, more engaging and youthful"—were the stereotyped phrases. A stranger in striped breeches, who gave his name as Colonel Parenthesis of Texas, called one day on the President, who, doubtless expecting news from Colonel Twiggs and General Taylor of the army, ordered his admission. The man, however, only came to say he had voted for Colonel Polk at the last election; that he only wanted to see who was James K. Polk, and being satisfied that he was "nothing extra," bade him good morning. Jimmy Maher's opinion of the President was—"Polk is a nice man; an agreeable man, and a rale republican." Of Mrs. Polk and Mrs. Walker he said: "They are Christian ladies, neither vain nor proud, though they well might be; they are the ladies that do honor to the nation, sir, and ye can't help but like them." Mrs. Walker—the wife of the secretary—was a regular attendant of the Foundry Methodist Church. If by accident she came late, she would quietly walk up stairs and take her seat among the ladies of the choir, that she might not disturb the services. Modest and simple in manner, unaffected and unobtrusive, without vanity and without parade, and one of the most agreeable of women in conversation, she was justly esteemed a pattern to her sex. Mrs. Thomas,—Miss McDowell, the niece of Colonel Benton and William C. Preston,—had been known in Washington some years before as a brilliant and accomplished young lady, and was still popular. She afterwards went to reside among her friends near Lexington, Virginia.

Among the lady visitors to the White House was a fat country-woman, who said she had heard of a woman in Washington who had a good kind of eye-water, and thought the President, knowing everything, might tell her where the woman was to be found; and as he had all the Treasury under him, might give her a little money to get the eye-water, as she, the applicant, did "want some dreadful bad, and no mistake."

The Secretary of the Navy, Mr. Bancroft, it was said, had a way of his own for the reception of visitors, and the selection of his company. The following letter embodied a rather extensive prejudice:

> "Any of the epauletted and gold-laced gentry of the army or navy are promptly attended to, and are not long kept dancing 'attendance'—but an honest jack tar must quietly wait the pleasure of the high functionary, although two minutes would suffice to transact all he would wish. A sailor recently discharged from the frigate St. Louis has been for three days at the door of the Secretary, knocking for admittance, with a check for five years' pay in his hand on the Exchange Bank of Virginia, which was refused to be cashed in specie at the bank. He had called for the purpose of laying his complaint before the Secretary, from day to day for nearly a week, and could not get to see him. Another sailor required the signature of the Secretary to a letter, which the duties of his office required him to sign; yet the poor fellow is kept waiting hour after hour. Such conduct is not altogether democratic, it must be acknowledged!"

Mr. Clay, on one occasion, remarked to Mrs. Polk, that, although some had expressed dissatisfaction with the administration of her husband, not one seemed to have found the least fault with hers. Mr. Clay was always ready with a polite repartee. Walking with the writer of this work, who was leaning on his left arm, at a party at Senator Preston's in South Carolina, Mr. Preston said to him: "You ought to give the lady your right arm." "No!" was Mr. Clay's reply: "a lady should always have a gentleman's left arm; his right should be free to defend her," adding to his companion in his most gallant manner: "I shall always be happy to use this right arm in your service."

The last of October, the delegation of Pottawatamie Indians paid their respects to President Polk in the presence of the Secretary of War, the commissioner of Indian affairs, and a number of ladies and gentlemen. The Indians were presented by Col. Elliott, an agent of their tribe for some years past; and after they had taken seats, "Half Day" arose and thanked their "Great Father" on behalf of his red children. A half breed interpreter officiated. While waiting for the interview with the President, the Indians had reconnoitered the White House, and were delighted with the great pier glasses of the east room, in which they were reflected as large as life, feathers, paint, beads, medals and all, and with the glittering chandeliers, etc.; but more than all with the fine picture of Washington—their first Great Father—in the evening reception room. The delegation afterwards paid their respects to Col. Benton, to whom the stalwart Indian orator, in his speaker's costume, made an eloquent address. The conversation was joined in by the ladies of the family, particularly Mrs. Fremont, who had been much among the Indians of the far West. Her little daughter was rather shy of the chief's caresses; but Mrs. Fremont was a special object of interest.

Mrs. Maury, an English lady, visited the White House on the first day of January, 1846, and praised the good conduct of the immense crowd. "The democracy behaved like a lady." The visitor had had no time to deliver any letters of introduction, but accompanied by her son, "simply introduced myself as an English lady, without even mentioning my name. 'I am delighted, madam, to see you here,' said the President, shaking me cordially by the hand.

I then introduced my son, saying I should hope to see the President again. 'At all times, madam, you will be most welcome.'"

She thus described Mr. Polk: "The President is of low stature; his address is mild and perfectly unassuming; the tones of his voice are gentle and agreeable; his forehead is broad and high; his eyes are well set, dark gray, and his mouth is expressive of much firmness. I should think him habitually grave and thoughtful; for, though I have often seen him smile, I have never seen him indulge in laughter. The President refuses a favor more kindly than any one I have ever heard perform that most ungracious duty of one in power. The art of conferring a favor is as difficult as that of refusing it; but the sagacity and good-feeling which called into active service Slidell M'Kenzie and the veteran Major-General Gaines, are proofs that the President understands the one as well as the other."

At the annual ball at Washington in commemoration of the battle of New Orleans, Mrs. Maury was presented to Mr. Buchanan, then Secretary of State, and said of him: "He looks like an English nobleman of thirty or forty years ago, when the grave and dignified bearing of men in power was regarded as an essential attribute of their office. This aristocratic address and manner, however, are natural, not acquired, in Mr. Buchanan; the result of an elevated character and urbanity of disposition, united with the long practice of office and the habit of command. I have never for one instant seen the least departure from that perfect self-possession which bestows so peculiar a grace on him who can practise it, and which has ever so singular an influence on him who witnesses it. The fair and delicate, though fresh complexion of Mr. Buchanan, his eye of light blue and full-blooded system, attest unequivocally his Anglo-Saxon descent. In social life the Secretary of State is easy and hospitable. In conversation he is rather a listener than a speaker, but he is always in advance of the subject as it proceeds.

"Governor William H. Seward is a remarkable personage, and deserves peculiar notice. His address and manners are very agreeable, though his voice is guttural and uncultivated, which possibly arises from an absence of all pleasure in music; confessedly he cannot distinguish a chant from a jig. His appearance is very youthful for forty-four; he is of fair complexion, and has one peculiarity of feature which is to me of singular interest. In speaking or smiling, the upper lip has a slight nervous and tremulous motion independent of its action in articulation. This is of course involuntary, is observed only in men, and is always accompanied by the most acute sensibilities. Seward's is an eloquent nature, and invokes an eloquent interpreter; his words are flung forth, simple, impassioned and searching, fresh and free as the impulses of his breast."

Of the Hon. William H. Haywood, late Senator from North Carolina, she said: "Mr. Haywood is a man of great elegance. His deportment and address are very distinguished, and he is perfect in all the recognized conventionalisms of polished life. No one understands better how to render social intercourse agreeable; he encourages amusement, enjoys conversation both grave and gay, and his compliments are always gratifying, for they are in good taste. I should imagine Mr. Haywood to be descended from the blood of the cavaliers; his handsome features, his scrupulous attention to dress, and the natural and graceful ease of his manners, combined with his chivalrous devotion to the fair sex and success in the drawing-room, all remind me of the descriptions we have read of those high-bred spirits. I quote him as an admirable specimen of that Chesterfield refinement and tact, which are so frequently supposed by Europeans to have as yet no existence in America. His speech on the Oregon question produced an immense sensation, for he was regarded as the intimate personal friend of the President."

Mr. Hugh White, a member from New York, was wont to relate an incident which contributed to the formation of his character. He had followed the plough till the age of nineteen, and soon afterwards went on foot, with his knapsack, to visit the Falls of Niagara. While he sat at dinner at the hotel, an English gentleman called out the landlord, and said he would not sit at table with one so rough-looking. The host declined interference, and the gentleman dispatched his servant to send off the rustic intruder. Mr. White rose to defend himself, and said to the insolent stranger: "I know not, sir, whom I address; but the moment your servant approaches me, I shall knock down his master, who is responsible for the gross insult to an honest man." The sturdy frame and determination of the rustic warned the "gentleman" to be prudent; he retired from the contest, and the next morning apologized for his rudeness. The young man, on his return home, applied himself with diligence to the improvement of his mind and his fortune, and met with success.

The English lady who dealt in couleur-de-rose sketches, described Abbott Lawrence as "of graceful address; the expression of his face highly intelligent and amiable, and his features very handsome. His language is well chosen, and his ideas are always expressed with clearness. It may be said he has more repose of character than is usual in the men of America, for they are the most excitable of all nations. This peculiarity may perhaps be traced to his early success in life, and his comprehensive knowledge of the world. Ere he had yet attained the meridian of life, wealth, honor, love, obedience, troops of friends, had waited on him." The impression Mr. Benton produced was always decided and abiding. "His action and gesture are expressive; his speech slow. In personal appearance he has much of the Englishman; is of a robust and muscular frame, somewhat inclined to corpulency; his features have also more of the English than of the American character The habitual expression of his countenance is calm and elevated. The forehead is very massive. He has that gentle self-possession of manner usual among those who are conscious of superior strength. He possesses great acquirements." Mr. Samuel D. Hubbard, a member from Connecticut, was a man "who has compelled me, against all my prejudices, against all my sympathies, to love, esteem and respect him. He is a Puritan, a Whig, a Protectionist, and abhors slavery; he condemns dancing; I hop about like a French grandmother; he despises the pomps and vanities; while I, alas! am their loving, faithful votary. Surely no man was ever so maliciously good as this representative of stern old Connecticut."

Mrs. Maury paid a visit to Mr. Van Buren in July, 1846. On arriving at Kinderhook, she took a carriage for Lindenwood, his residence, at a distance from the road, and then shaded by the limes in the luxuriance of summer foliage. "On ringing the bell, a gentleman stepped from the parlor and advanced to receive us. From the resemblance to his portraits, I immediately recognized the ex-President. I had received my husband's command to pay my respects to Mr. Van Buren, but I had no letter of introduction except one from Lord Aberdeen to the British minister in Washington; so I presented it to Mr. Van Buren, observing that it would certify that I was not an impostor. The ex-President took me by the hand, laughed heartily at my mode of self-introduction, himself lifted from the carriage my traveling band-box, ordered the driver home, and then said: 'The name you bear, madam, is of itself a sufficient introduction. Of course you will stay here, for it will give us the greatest pleasure.' We sat down in a cool and pleasant parlor; iced water, lemonade, and wine, were immediately presented; we were introduced to the family, and after tea rambled through the garden and the farm. The ex-President gathered flowers for me, led us to look at his potatoes, presented me with a branch of delicious red currants, and delighted me by calling my boy 'Doctor,' and walking along the fields with his arm around the little fellow's neck. I could not define the charm this magician flings upon his words. His conversation is like a strain of varied music, now grave, now gay; now learned, now simple. He praises the deserving of all parties and all countries with generous candor and with discerning justice; and speaks of himself with that unreserved confidence which is so attractive in a distinguished man."

"Graceful, gallant, and accomplished, Robert C. Winthrop, is the rising glory of the whigs. Possessing the prestige that naturally arises from gentle birth and ample fortune, this promising member from Boston has no interest to serve, no favor to seek." He was the descendant of John Winthrop, the first governor of Massachusetts, and the founder of Boston. "His bearing is highly aristocratic. In conversation the natural and cultivated resources of his mind give him great advantages."

"If you whigs make a President in 1848," said an accomplished visitor, "let it be Judge M'Lean." "Do not wish that," was the reply; "if he were taken away from the Supreme Court, where is the guardian of the constitution!" M'Lean was Postmaster-General in the opening administration of Jackson, who appointed him to the bench of the Supreme Court in 1829. "Judge M'Lean" said Mrs. Maury, "is remarkably handsome. He is fifty-seven; of fair complexion, light blue eyes, somewhat bald, with a fine profile; his expression is of the noblest moral character, with something of playfulness. He has a very melodious voice. He was a member of the Methodist Church. The admirable head and powerful form of

Mr. Webster make him everywhere conspicuous. The brow is ample; the eyes deep sunk, dark, and seated immediately below the strongly marked and shaggy eyebrows. The features and contour denote expressively the strength of every mental faculty. In repose the countenance is absent and thoughtful; as if the reasoning powers were employed inwardly, independent of all external objects; and then as if the mental exercise had resulted in undoubted conviction, the whole face becomes radiant with intelligence and animation. The contrast and transition of expression are very fine. He is always prepared; his mind is full charged with knowledge, and his information is always at hand. On one occasion, I was struck with the admiration he evinced for a brother advocate. Rufus Choate, of Boston, was pleading in the Supreme Court against a sister State for Massachusetts. I have no words to describe the extraordinary effort of this remarkable man. The fluency, rapidity, and beauty of his language, his earnest manners, his excited action, his whole being conflicting with the most intense emotion. He was all nerve; each sense, each faculty was absorbed in the great duty of the day. Sometimes it seemed that tears alone could relieve the uncontrollable agitation which thrilled through his frame, quivered on his lip, and trembled in his voice. For an instant he paused; then again gushed forth his words clothed in each form of argument and persuasion that the reach of mind and knowledge can suggest. His memory supplied quotations learned and to the point; his imagination called each poetic fancy quick to his aid; his voice of music attuned itself to all the varied tones of his discourse, awakening in every breast the sentiments and impressions of his own. He is the Proteus of eloquence. His study of the Massachusetts and Rhode Island case must have been most laborious and profound. He spoke four hours on two successive days. The subject was magnificent; the boundary line of rival States. The Supreme Court was crowded. Judge M'Lean presided on the bench, listening with profound attention and graceful benignity. Mr. Webster sat near Mr. Choate, his eyes riveted on the speaker, and his fine countenance expressing the most eager interest and the highest admiration. I was in my favorite seat on the left hand of the judges, and close to the desk at which Mr. Webster was seated. The important subject, its learned and enthusiastic advocate, the benignant judge, the generous Webster, hanging with delighted ear upon the accents of his gifted friend—I shall never forget the impression left by those three wondrous men. Mr. Webster is sixty-four or five, but looks seven years younger. In society he is convivial. He can work with the severest application, and prepare for any occasion with wonderful precision and rapidity. Many traits of his profound mind remind me of what I have heard and read of Charles James Fox of England."

Edward Hannegan, Senator from Indiana, "is a genuine son of the West; ardent, impulsive and undaunted; thinking, acting and daring with the most perfect freedom. His spirit is youthful and buoyant, and he is ever sanguine of success. When Mr. Hannegan made his speech on the Oregon question, he alluded to Mr. Calhoun in terms of graceful approval; and, after differing from the policy of that Senator, spoke of his genius and virtues in terms of manly and generous eulogy. I was in the gallery with a large party of ladies. All were gratified with the words of praise; and in the excitement of the moment I threw down my glove to the speaker. The chivalrous Hannegan instantly picked it up, pressed it to his lips, looked gratefully up to the gallery, bowed, and placed it in his bosom. Next day the glove was sent by post, to the wife of the Senator, then in Indiana. I preserve the less happy fellow to it. When the speech was ended and the Senate adjourned, the ladies went down to the floor. I had a careless trick of leaving my purse upon the table in my parlor. Mr. Hannegan, and almost all Americans, have a frank and ingenuous habit of imparting advice gratuitously to those with whom they are on terms of intimacy. Having often found the purse thus left, the Senator several times in vain reminded me of the indiscretion. At length, during an illness in Baltimore, he came to see me. On entering my parlor, he saw on the table, as usual, the old green purse, full of fivedollar gold pieces. Upon my appearance, he held it up; and after wishing me good day, admonished me for the last time. 'You pray that you may not be led into temptation; do unto others as you would they should do unto you.' I never received a more efficient moral lesson. One of the most agreeable evenings I spent in Washington, was at an ice-cream party given by Mr. Hannegan. This Senator was born in Lexington,

Kentucky, in the atmosphere of Henry Clay. He seems scarcely forty, has brown hair; wears neither beard nor whiskers; is of the medium height and broad-shouldered. His address is very pleasant."

John Quincy Adams "is the representative of the opinions and the recorder of the events of earlier days. Sometimes the venerable statesman is attacked by a member of the opposition, and then he rises in self-defence with all the indignant warmth of youth and the consciousness of an integrity none can gainsay. When Mr. Rhett of South Carolina made some remarks on the policy pursued by Mr. Adams in 1812, I observed the emotion which gradually became evident in the countenance of the patriotic New Englander. His cheek flushed, his veins swelled, and the fervent blood of twenty summers rushed to his temples. At length he rose, and spoke just at the moment when he ought. Governor Seward had frequently excited my anxious desire to have an opportunity of seeing Mr. Adams when, the cares of the day being ended, he received the visits of his friends, and unbent his mind in social intercourse. I was much gratified when admitted to these 'attic nights,' and listened with delight to those instructive and fascinating lectures, in which learning and taste were so eloquently combined. Poetry, painting, music, history, criticism, all in turn were the themes of his discourse. I was amazed at the range of knowledge displayed by Mr. Adams, and the perfect system with which it was hived and stored for seasonable use. I remember that Mr. Adams, with singular frankness, declared that he had never admired the Venus de

Medici. He gave the preference to painting over sculpture, as being a higher art.

"Mr. Buchanan and Mr. Adams are next door neighbors to each other in Washington, and are excellent friends. At a ball given by Mr. Adams, Mr. Buchanan conducted me to pay my respects to the venerable host. The Secretary added that he had given directions to be summoned to the House of Representatives the moment Mr. Adams should begin his promised speech on Oregon. Mrs. Gouverneur reproached me playfully for not having called upon her. I replied that I spent all day and every day at the capitol, hearing and seeing the distinguished men assembled there. 'And then,' said she, laughing, 'you will go home to England and write a book, and abuse them and all the rest of the Americans.' 'Never,' said Buchanan, on whose arm I leaned; 'never; I answer for her. If she puts pen to paper, it will be to do us justice.'"

"Mr. Albert Gallatin is eighty-seven; and in the winter of 1845–6, when I saw him in New York, was in the full enjoyment of excellent bodily health and mental vigor. In June I had been gratified by a long interview with this enlightened and sagacious statesman. His piercing and original remarks, his shrewd criticisms on men and things, his erudition, his charming raillery, and above all his perfect kindness, made this visit delightful. Mr. Gallatin is by birth a native of Switzerland, and fled from his country in early life on account of his attachment to liberal principles. He was held in the highest estimation by both Jefferson and Madison. His appearance at this time was that of a European; his figure tall and thin, his manner full of vivacity. His son and grandson were present; two gentlemen waited upon him on business, and his amanuensis sat at his side. Finding him occupied, I would have retired, but he would on no account permit this; and he proceeded to converse with us all in turn on affairs of amusement or business, occasionally dictating to the amanuensis."

"Amiable, sensible, brilliant and witty, Charles J. Ingersoll is charming at sixty-three. That gentleman on the Speaker's left, dressed in the old revolutionary costume of buff and blue, is the chairman of Foreign Relations; by reason of which office he assumed the responsibilities of my guardian, and became my almost constant companion during my residence in Washington. His character exhibits all the warm uncalculating sensibilities of youth. Headlong and rash, three-score years and three have failed to cool that hot impetuous blood which dances, rather than flows in his veins; but again a silken cord can lead him; can check his haste and curb his anger. Ingersoll is the wittiest man with whom I conversed in America. After keeping him an hour at a ball, during which time nobody asked me to dance, I observed that for his sake I was sorry I had no offers. 'Madam,' he rejoined, 'I should instantly have *repudiated them.*' It must be remarked that he is the representative of Pennsylvania. I was accompanied by him to Mr. Buchanan's state ball, about a week after my arrival. We had been in the room half an hour, when Mr. Pakenham, the British minister, came up and addressed to me the courtesies usual on such occasions.

He remained near me some minutes, speaking of the ladies, their dress, beauty, &c.; during this time he never once looked at Mr. Ingersoll, who never looked at him. I was somewhat embarrassed at being addressed by two gentlemen at the same moment who did not appear to recognize each other. My position at last became so awkward, that I proceeded formally to present them to each other. They bowed, exchanged a few passing words, and Mr. Pakenham shortly after left us. Next day, when I asked my guardian if he was upon terms with Mr. Pakenham, he replied 'We have not spoken for two years before last night, when, a lady being the mediator, we could do no less.' "

Of General Gaines she said: "This gallant officer is eighty-three; he is pale and white-haired, tall and emaciated; but his habits are punctual and early, and so strict is his adherence to discipline, that a gentleman told me, that having heard General Gaines was indisposed, he went to see him, and found him lying in bed with his military collar on, and his sword by his side. He is the mirror of courtesy to the fair sex, and no gentleman handles a lady's fan with greater dexterity; either sitting or standing he never forgets to relieve her from the task of fanning herself."

In Mr. Tyler's administration, Calhoun, the Secretary of State, was afterwards removed from the cabinet. "On the occasion of his removal," said Charles Ingersoll, "Mr. Calhoun behaved like an angel. His gracious, princely nature, accustomed to give command without appeal, is equally accustomed to receive submission without reserve; hence his gentleness and indulgence, and his compassion; no vulgar upstart display of authority is traced; he is served with the perfect love that casteth out fear. At this advanced age his appearance is unlike that of other men. His action is quick, and both in society and in the Senate very expressive. He speaks with the utmost rapidity, as if no words could convey his speed of thought; his face is all intellect, with eyes so dazzling, black and piercing, that few can stand their gaze. Sixty-four years have left their dark center yet undimmed, and the surrounding blue liquid and pure as the eye of childhood. Sometimes their intense look is reading each thought of your bosom; sometimes they are beaming with the inspirations of his own. I have seen them suffused with emotion, when the feelings of that ingenuous breast have been excited by honest praise, or moved by sympathy. Mr. Calhoun's general expression is that of unceasing mental activity and great decision. His forehead is broad and full; a deep furrow extends quite across, and above the eyebrows there is considerable fullness. His hair is thick, long, straight and gray, and thrown back from his face; the eyebrows are very near the eye, and the cheek is gaunt. The mouth is thin, and somewhat inclined downwards at the corners; it is the proud and melancholy lip of Dante. His complexion is bronzed by the sun of the south. Speaking of America, I once said: 'Mr. Calhoun, you are a great experiment.' 'We are more,' he replied, 'we are a great hit.' 'Will the Atlantic and the Pacific States be divided into separate republics?' 'They cannot be;

the Mississippi, a great inland sea, will keep them united. The Union is indissoluble.'

"In February, I asked: 'Mr. Calhoun, what is in the future?' 'Peace and Free Trade,' said he. 'I have eight sons in England.' 'Bring them all here. We are an exulting nation; let them grow up with the country. Here they do not want wealth. I would not be rich in America, for the care of money would distract my mind from more important concerns.' Mr. Calhoun thought ladies should always be dressed in white, and wear a girdle. He had great respect for such external forms as tend to promote order and dignity, and I believe it was he who established the rule, during his Vice-Presidency, that members of the Senate should be addressed as 'Senators.'"

"On the morning after the free trade measures were carried in the House, I saw Mr. Calhoun for the last time. After a struggle of twenty-two years, truth and he had been successful; but no personal exultation sparkled in his eye, or triumphed in his words. The measure and its great consequences alone occupied his thoughts. I remarked: 'Mr. Calhoun, you are very dear to England, for the sake of this peace, and this free trade.' Twice he has turned his footsteps aside from the Presidency; once for friendship's, once for duty's sake (upon the tariff of 1828.) Never was a man so adored by his State as Calhoun. 'South Carolina,' were his words, 'alone stood by me, mine she faithfully has ever been.' As he hung upon her memory and her devotion, her statesman evinced the tenderness and pride with which a lover dwells upon the constancy of his mistress. His breath came quick and short; his proud head was flung back, and his voice was subdued by emotion."

In later years visitors to Mr. Clay at his home, could attest the truth of the following: "Such as was George Washington at Mount Vernon, retired from the scenes of public excitement and service, such is Henry Clay at Ashland. I saw Calhoun at Washington in the early spring of 1846, calm amidst the strife and hurry of political warfare. I saw Henry Clay in the May following in Kentucky, serene in 'the mild majesty of private life.' Clay and Calhoun are the master spirits of America. Clay's very name is a spell, and no sooner is it heard, than all mankind rise up to praise it.

"We knocked at the door at Ashland, and were saluted as old friends by the faithful negro who opened it. In a moment Mr. Clay appeared, and with that voice of surprising and surpassing melody, with winning smile and open hands, tendered the courtesies of welcome. Assisting me to alight, he accompanied us to the sitting-room, and read the introductory letters I had brought him. Into the garden we went, and Mr. Clay pointed out the trees his own hands had planted, cut for me every flower I looked on, conducted me to see his stock of cattle, and pointed out his pets." He invited the lady and her son to accompany him and his family the next morning to the Episcopal church. "During the service, Mr. Clay leaned his face down on his hands, which rested on his stick, in the attitude in which he has been painted. He almost constantly carried in his hand a full blown rose, with a short stem, and frequently addressed himself to its perfumed cup."

Clay was called, when a stripling, "The mill boy of the Slashes," (a swamp), because he was often seen on the road between his mother's house and Mrs. Darricott's mill on the Pamunkey River, mounted on a bag thrown across a pony that was guided by a rope bridle.

The Right Rev. John Hughes, Catholic Bishop of New York, was called by this lady "the historical man of his day. He assumes his position among the statesmen of America as the representative, priest, controller and guardian, of a powerful body now incorporated in the democracy of the republic; the Roman Catholics. He is the greatest temporal prince in America, and the greatest spiritual prince in the world." Though a stranger to the faith of the Bishop, Mrs. Maury formed an enduring friendship with him; and he pledged his word, at their parting hour, to be near her on her death-bed, if he still lived, and if time and distance could be overcome. "And the Bishop bade me kneel, and I knelt beside him; he laid his hand upon my head, and then from his lips gushed forth, in mingled power and beauty, the full strong tide of human affection; in accents strange and new; for I had dreamed not of the love I had won from that exalted nature; and with faltering voice he blessed me and my way, and those I held dear, to him unknown; and for many minutes he was silent; but the vows, unheard by me, were accepted at the throne of Him who rideth on the whirlwind, and who saith unto the waters 'Peace,—be still.'"

Mrs. Maury had brought letters of introduction from Lord Aberdeen, then Secretary of State for foreign affairs in London, to Mr. Pakenham. Those letters were procured at the personal request of Lord Sandon, and were in the most favorable terms. Mr. Pakenham was civil to his country-woman; but as she remarked, she required not his services. "The President himself, the Secretary of State, and every American took care of me." The only ambassador with whom she became acquainted was M. Serruys, the Belgian minister, whom she met at the house of General Van Ness. And her conclusion was that the time had arrived when the courts of Europe would find it imperative upon them to send to Washington their most gifted, influential and popular statesmen as their representatives.

Lieutenant Matthew Fontaine Maury was the principal navy officer at the observatory at Georgetown. He was a man of science, an accomplished mariner, an admirable astronomer and mathematician, and wrote well.

Of Calhoun a gifted authoress wrote: "The champion of free trade; a slaveholder and a cotton planter; the vindicator of State rights and yet a firm believer in the indestructibility of the Federal Union; now claimed as a whig, now revered as a democrat; now branded as a traitor, now worshiped as a patriot; now assailed as a demon, now invoked as a demigod; now withstanding power and now the people; now proudly accepting office, now as proudly spurning it; now goading the administration, now resisting it; now counselling, now defying the executive; but in all changes of circumstances, all trials of patience, in smiling or in adverse fortune, ever forgetful of self, and faithful only to the inspirations of the genius and the virtue of which his name is the symbol. No vice, no folly, no frailty, has soiled his nature, consumed his life, or extorted his remorse; his country has been his sole engrossing passion, loved with the devotion of a Brutus, and served with the fidelity of a Regulus. Politics may be considered to have almost exclusively occupied the life of this great statesman; not the sordid intrigue of partisanship, not the venal craving of place and pay; not the debasing sacrifice of honesty to popularity; his soul disdains such base employment of her faculties; nay, I question if, with all its keenness, his mind could comprehend such schemes of politics. His are not even the tactics of a State or section, nor alone those of the United States; but they comprise those exalted views which, deduced from philosophy and history, and proved by practical experience, are found to constitute the true policy of all nations, and to be the universal principles of all righteous governments. They are the decalogue of republics. The impression produced by the single mind of this man, by the principles he has advocated, will exercise an influence more deeply based and more abiding upon the institutions of the United States, than any system or movements yet enunciated from the constitution and predicated upon its laws. He once said to me: 'I cannot express the indifference with which I regard the Presidential chair, compared to the honor and usefulness of establishing this great measure of free trade.' "

New Year's day, 1847, was a bright and beautiful one. The executive mansion was crowded with a populous procession for several hours. The absence of the Major-General of the army and his staff, told an eloquent story, as did the absence of many officers of the army and navy. They were in the South fighting the Mexicans. A welcome and inviting refreshments were offered at Mr. Mason's and Mr. Marcy's; at the Vice-President's, at Mr. Walker's, at Mr. Cave Johnson's, at the Mayor's, and at other houses. The estimable widow of Major-General Macomb received her visitors with several young ladies at her side, dispensing cake, wine and cordials, and the best wishes of the season. Her quiet and winning manners caused even the stranger to feel the genial atmosphere of home. Mrs. Madison also received calls, surrounded by a host of young lady relatives and friends. She wore a beautiful white turban, and looked regal as one of the last among the representatives of the glory, chivalry and beauty of the Old Dominion. In the evening there was a ball, with various other entertainments and social reunions.

On the 16th January, 1848, Miss Sarah Benton was married to Mr. Jacob, of Louisville, Kentucky. Miss Jacob had married a son of Mr. Clay, and the family was related to Colonel Taylor, brother of the General. Mrs. Clay was a Hart, and Benton's Christian name, Thomas Hart, was after the family, to which he was related. Henry Clay himself led the bride to the supper-room, and among other guests were present Mr. Buchanan, Mr. Crittenden, Mr. Johnson of Louisiana, and Mr. Vinton. There had been a coldness between Benton and Clay; but this new amnesty made a lasting bond. Mr. Clay had his quarters at the United States hotel, and was waited on every day by large detachments of ladies. Every evening he dined out, and every day at twelve dismissed his visitors to go out.

In a debate in the Senate, General Cass's oratory was described as "an explosion of the fire of a soldier and the fervor of a patriot. He glanced at Great Britain, and with a few strokes painted the vastness of her empire, the graspings of her ambition, and the subtlety of her intrigues." Not a Senator heard the appeal "without a feeling either of exultation or anger, which could not be repressed, and the galleries showed many a fair face flushed with excitement." Mr. Mangum, Senator from North Carolina, rose in reply, and a brief notice of his oratory will be interesting. "From the moment he first took the floor, he trembled with excitement, and his eyes flashed with indignation. He gathered images of power and occasional beauty, and his earnestness made the chamber feel what he himself evidently felt so deeply. His violation of the rules of courtesy towards his gallant and generous antagonist nearly lost for him the sympathy of the House, and this bad move tipped his dish over. Senator Allen rose on his heels like a thunderbolt. His lean cheek was hot with fire. It was a masterly effort, and he carried the House with him. Mr. Mangum writhed under every thrust. Twice he rose to explain, and twice the Buckeye came on again, hurling a deadlier blow than before. If Mr. Allen had more of the stern iron self-control of the great orator, he would be one of the best speakers in the country. Allen's was a stirring, powerful, convincing, logical appeal."

The grand fashionable season opened the last week in December with the first assembly at Carusi's saloon. Four of these parties were announced for the session. The music, dancing, assemblage and suppers were superb and satisfactory. A concert given by Mr. Sloman and his two accomplished daughters was the delight of a full audience of the *élite*. Those young ladies also played the harp and piano and sang at a private party given at the President's mansion. The new chaplain of the House, Mr. Milburn, was nearly blind and very poor. His manner and voice were agreeable, his emphasis and modulations pleasing, and he did credit to his position. It was said Mrs. Linn, the widow of the Senator from Missouri, had induced him to try his chance for the chaplaincy, and her recommendation had acted like a charm in his favor. The President continued a faithful attendant at Mr. Sprole's Presbyterian church, where, in all weathers, his carriage might be seen at eleven. Mrs. Polk would not permit dancing in the White House.

A bill passed the Senate toward the close of December, for the payment to the widow of Alexander Hamilton, of twenty thousand dollars, on the delivery by her to the librarian of Congress, of the manuscripts of her deceased husband, and five hundred printed copies of the same bound in leather. There were five volumes, each to consist of five hundred pages. The arrival of General Sam. Houston from Texas, created a great sensation. "He stands erect as a Norway pine; but is sadly changed from the splendid man of fifteen years ago. He was dressed in a suit of gray, frock coat with metal buttons, and appeared remarkably fresh and vigorous after his long journey. His partial baldness added to the commanding impressiveness of his remarkable countenance." Since the last inauguration General Scott had been a prominent aspirant of the whigs for the campaign of 1848. He had been endorsed by Henry Clay, his friends had multiplied, his competitors had yielded, and he seemed to be regarded generally as the successor to the fortunes of the great Harry. Thus he was courted, flattered, and caressed by the politicians, and needed only to remain in Washington. When the war opened with Mexico, the hero of Chippewa was appointed to head the army of occupation in the South. But his letter to the Secretary of War protested against assuming the command of the Southern army, for various reasons given. The Secretary of War, in the name of the President, reprimanded the Commanding General for his undignified letter of complaints and insinuations.

"The fact of Mr. Clay and Mr. Polk dining together at the White House, was significant and astonishing. Mr. Polk laid aside his usual reserve and entertained his distinguished guest as a friend long absent. Washington was gay with parties and balls this season, till the death and funeral of the great and good ex-President, John Quincy Adams, occupied all minds towards the last of February. Public business was suspended, colors were flying everywhere at half-mast, and a general gloom pervaded the city. Thousands of eager spectators thronged the capitol on the 25th, where the body of the illustrious deceased reposed in a splendid coffin. The President gave orders that all the executive offices should be placed in mourning, and all business suspended for two days. In announcing to the Senate the death of Mr. Adams, Mr. Benton said: "Mr. Adams has just sunk down in his chair, and has been carried into an adjoining room, and may be at this moment passing from the earth, under the roof that covers us, and almost in our presence." The Senate immediately adjourned, and all inquiries were directed to the condition of the stricken statesman. He had been removed to the Speaker's room, where he slightly recovered the use of his speech, and uttered in faltering accents: "This is the last of earth;" and soon after, "I am composed." He lingered two days; passing away at octogenarian age, hung over in his last moments by her who had been for more than fifty years the worthy partner of his life. Mr. Webster was suffering from domestic affliction, the death of a son and daughter, and could not speak at the funeral.

Alexander Barrow, Senator from Louisiana, died about 1848. He had a noble heart, with honor, courage and patriotism; and a quick, clear and strong judgment. He was in the hope and prime of manhood, and time was ripening and maturing his faculties. The death of Dixon H. Lewis, Senator from Alabama, had occurred in October. He was one of the most able and accomplished members of the Senate, and in Alabama he attained a popularity such as no other man in the State enjoyed.

XIV.

TAYLOR'S ADMINISTRATION.

Character of General Taylor—Mrs. Taylor—Their Children—Residence at Baton Rouge—Meeting of Taylor and Clay—The Rush of Office-Seekers to the New Orleans Tailor to put their Petitions in "Old Zach's" Pockets—Setting out of the Ladies for Washington—Progress of the President Elect—Afoul of a Snag—Landing and Rustic Reception—Accident on board a Steamboat—President Polk's last Levee—Amusing Visit of General Cass to President Taylor—His personal Appearance—Ladies of his Party—Inauguration Ceremonies—Comical Description of the Ball—The Cabinet—Death of General Gaines—Return of Henry Clay—The Osage Indians at the White House and at their Hotel—Senator Fremont—Amusing Scene in the Senate—Sir Henry Lytton Bulwer—Death of Mr. Calhoun—Death of President Taylor—His Obsequies—His Career.

ZACHARY TAYLOR, in 1810, married Margaret Smith of Maryland. He was an unexceptionable father and husband. His temper was calm, firm and cool, yet amiable and gentle. Mrs. Taylor was an exemplary woman. Simple and unassuming in her manners, she was courteous and kind to her dependents, and affectionate and confiding to her friends and relatives. Two daughters, and a son of this worthy couple were living. One daughter had married Colonel Jefferson Davis, against the wishes of her father, who for years did not exchange a word with her husband. At the siege of Monterey however, chance placed the two men close together and the opportunity was seized by

Colonel Davis to restore good-feeling by satisfactory explanations. Mrs. Davis had been dead for some years at this time. The other daughter, familiarly called "Miss Betty," was a beautiful girl, and well fitted to grace the White House by her presidency. She was soon after married to Colonel Bliss, who was almost a regular inmate of General Taylor's house. Another living daughter was married to Dr. Wood and resided in Baltimore. When the subject of General Taylor's call to the Presidency was first agitated, Mrs. Taylor was very much opposed to it. A short time after his nomination by the whig convention in Philadelphia, his political friends wrote to urge him to visit the North; but he refused, saying he would not "go across yon ferry, to influence the public choice, or to secure my election. I have never aspired to the Presidency; if the people elect me of their own free choice, my humble services will be at their disposal. If they elect some other candidate, I shall not be in the slightest degree mortified."

Baton Rouge, his place of residence, was said to be intensely dull. The only thing of moment that had taken place for a long time, was the appearance of cholera; its ravages and disappearance causing some excitement, which saved many from dying of ennui. The General was accustomed to walk about like a respectable farmer, and was anything but a "lion." His unassuming manners and singular simplicity of habits, were marked traits in his character; and in the town his name was never mentioned in connection with politics, nor even at the garrison unless in reference to military affairs. He could not have been more unnoticed were he the defeated instead of the victorious candidate for the Presidency. Mr. Clay on his way to New Orleans from Natchez, touched at Baton Rouge and an interview took place on the evening of the 11th January, 1849. General Taylor happened to be on the wharf boat at the time the vessel approached in which Mr. Clay was a passenger. Their greeting was cordial. Clay did not remain at Baton Rouge, nor was he invited to do so. At the meeting: "Why, General," pleasantly remarked Mr. Clay, "you have grown out of my recollection." "You can never grow out of mine," was the ready response of the General, whose face beamed with pleasure and who was unaffectedly delighted to see the great statesman. "I congratulate you, General, upon your election to the Presidency, and I hope your administration may be as successful and glorious as your military career," said Mr. Clay. "I thank you, Mr. Clay; but I am not President yet; and——" As General Taylor modestly hesitated, Mr. Clay broke in with some playful remark, which led to an agreeable conversation. The captain of the "Princess," not wishing to interrupt so pleasant a reunion, detained the steamboat some time. The General and Mr. Clay parted with expressions of mutual esteem, and a hope that they might soon meet again. The great orator at this time had grown thinner, but did not look older than when, a year before, he had participated in New Orleans with the citizens in celebrating the victories in Mexico.

Colonel Bliss, the General's son-in-law, was to go to the North by the Atlantic route at the same time the President elect went by land, stopping a few days in New York. He was a quiet, modest and unpretending man; endowed with a high order of intellect, and a fine literary taste. Mrs. Bliss was amiable and dignified; an excellent young matron; not dashing, nor dazzling in beauty, but gifted with the more estimable qualities of good sense, intellect and feeling.

It was arranged that the New Orleans steamer should call at General Taylor's plantation, and take him to Vicksburg. Several citizens of New Orleans were invited to accompany him to Washington. It was said that a fashionable tailor of the Crescent City, having an order to make two suits of clothes for the General, there was a rush of well dressed gentlemen to the shop, all earnestly requesting to be allowed to look at the clothes, and particularly to examine the insides of the pockets. The shrewd tailor, suspecting their object to be office-seeking, told them they might put their letters into the pockets of the suits, but he should require fifty dollars each for the letters in the pantaloons pocket, thirty for those in the coat pocket, and twenty for those in the vest pockets. Mrs. Taylor, with Colonel Bliss and Mrs. Bliss, Major Hunter and Mrs. Hunter, went from New Orleans to Mobile, and there took passage for Montgomery, on their way to Washington. The family was to spend a month or six weeks in Baltimore with Colonel Taylor, a brother of the General, and Mrs. Wood, the daughter. The suite of the President elect was very limited. At Baton Rouge his personal friends assembled for the purpose of bidding him adieu, and went in procession to his residence, when addresses were interchanged. His subsequent movements were telegraphed to the people: how he reached Cincinnati; how he ascended the crests of the Alleghanies and descended them, etc. Crowds followed him wherever he appeared, and on every public occasion he took care to assume the position he had taken in his letters before the election,—that he did not expect to be the President of a party. At Louisville the streets were thronged; the doors and windows were filled with spectators, and the American flag and white handkerchiefs were waved by fair hands in enthusiastic welcome.

Going up the Mississippi, the steamer on which General Taylor was a passenger, ran foul of a snag, and sustained so much damage the passengers thought it best to go ashore for awhile. General Taylor and others got into a small skiff, to land; a drunken fellow jumped in after him, and stood up in the frail craft so as to endanger it. "Sit down, my good man," said the General, "sit down," but the fellow, instead of obeying, began backing the skiff under the guards of the steamer and across her lines. The General lost patience, and exclaimed: "Sit down, you drunken rascal, or I'll throw you overboard!" This threat brought the fellow to anchor in quick time. Men, women and children were collected on the shore, and the General had to go through the kissing process with the feminines, which he did with a good grace. The "reception-room" was illuminated by one "tallow dip," just enough to make darkness visible. A countryman came up to enquire of one of General Taylor's suite if he ever drank brandy; the whispered reply was: "He never does, but his friends do;" and the black bottle was forthcoming. Among other curiosities produced, was a young Arkansas "sucker," eight or ten months old, presented by his mother. The General took his dimpled hand, and hoped he would one day become a General too; whereupon the child was at once dubbed "the young General." When they embarked again, the cheers of the company were given; the voice of the young General sounding a full octave above the rest.

At Nashville his reception was enthusiastic. The whole city hailed his landing with shouts and discharges of cannon. At the door of the hotel, as he was going out to ride, a crowd of boatmen came about him, and so blocked up the way in trying to get "a look at old Zach," that he stopped, and began to address them in a humorous, off-hand way. "Ain't he a hoss!" "He's one of 'em?" "Kentuck to the back bone!" "He'll do!" "Three cheers for Old Zach!" were the exclamations from the rough honest men, who had voted for him and came to look at him. Through all his jovial manner, he never parted with the air of military command that always distinguished him.

An old farmer and soldier, who had come forty miles to meet him, made his way through the crowd, and seized his hand, saying: "General, I have voted nine times for President, but never gave any vote with as hearty good will as the vote I gave you. I felt that I was voting for an honest man, who would restore the ancient order of things." "I belong to the old school," responded the General, "and I will do my best." A toast given at the Louisville dinner was as follows: "General Zachary Taylor—in his birth, a Virginian; in his boyhood and early manhood, a Kentuckian; his glorious achievements upon his country's battle-fields have made him the common property of the nation, and his wisdom and virtue will render him, as Chief Magistrate of a great republic, the benefactor of the world."

At Frankfort General Taylor was received by his gifted friend Governor Crittenden, with a welcome in the State House. At supper in Madison, he proposed as a toast, "The fair daughters of Indiana." On board the boat, while he was going through a passage, some impediment tripped him and he fell on his side across a trunk, receiving a severe bruise. In Cincinnati he visited the ball given in honor of his arrival, received by the Cincinnati Life Guards in military order. As he entered the room, the company presented arms; and the ladies, abandoning the dance, ran and clasped him around the neck, giving and receiving kisses in compliment to the hero of many victorious battles. He arrived in Washington February 23d. The mayor of the city received him. The Vice-President, Millard Fillmore, arrived the next day, and was acknowledged to be "one of the finest-looking men in the United States." The President elect talked freely and fluently about everything but the offices. On the railway as he came along, he had been escorted by a young whig, who put in a petition for himself for an office. "I have only one office," replied the General, "and you are welcome to it if the people are agreed. Very cold weather for the season, I think, sir." "Yes, but, General, I have lost money during the campaign."

"Very sorry, sir; but do you think it will rain to-night?" "Looks very much like it, General; but really, if I have been too fast, I beg your pardon." "Thank you, sir, let us all do what we can for the country, and we shall have no cause of regret. Thrifty-looking country in this neighborhood!"

Mr. Polk gave his last levee in the closing week of February. There was no one in Washington who did not regret his and Mrs. Polk's departure. Meanwhile, in every bar-room, oyster-cellar, and billiard-room, where speculators in offices abound, and at every dinner-table, General Taylor's cabinet was the standing dish. General Taylor received his visitors from twelve to one. He won every one, whig or democrat, by his unostentatious bearing and kind benevolent manner. A stranger would hardly believe that the plainly dressed old gentleman, with hat stuck on the back of his head, and spectacles shoved up on his forehead, was the President elect of the United States. Mrs. Bliss received the ladies who came to pay their respects, every morning. General Cass arrived, unheralded and scarcely noticed. On the first day of March, accompanied by Senator Fitzgerald, he came to the hotel, and went up to General Taylor's rooms. Taylor at once recognized him, and coming forward, grasped his hand in both his own and shook it most cordially. General Cass, who had not at first recognized him, observed with a drollery that caused every one present to laugh heartily—"By the way, General, you had the advantage of me! That is twice you've had the advantage of me!" "That is true," remarked Taylor,

MRS. JOHN JAY.

"but you know the battle is not always to the strong, eh!" "That is a fact," replied Cass, with an emphasis that renewed the laughter. "How do you feel, sir!" "Pretty well, thank you, except that I have two or three ribs stove in, that's all. I got on board a small boat at Madison to go to Frankfort, and just as she was about to start, stepped out of the saloon, and stumbled over a large black trunk in the dark passage. I thought both my legs, my arms, and all my ribs were stove in."

As General Cass was retiring, a gentleman met him, and said: "Well, General, in all the States where I stumped it, you got the vote." "Indeed," replied Cass, laughing, "I am very much obliged to you, my friend, but—I wish you had stumped it in two or three more."

General Taylor usually dressed in black, and neatly, though without much regard to taste. He was thought by many more portly than they expected to see him, and approaching more nearly what was deemed the beau ideal of a well fed alderman. His hair, white, and but thinly covering his well formed head, was allowed to straggle in all directions without attention to military precision. He had a uniform reply when the multitude cheered him. "Heaven bless you, gentlemen; peace be with you;" and to the ladies who waved their hands or handkerchiefs, his stereotyped phrase was: "your humble servant, ladies." An observer said: "The personal appearance of General Taylor is dignified and noble. He is exceedingly affable in his manners and deportment. His dress yesterday consisted of a plain suit of blue, with a pair of large woolen socks drawn over his boots, denoting that he thinks more of solid comfort than display. His eyes are mild, beautiful and brilliant; he has a stoop in his gait, and his hair is light gray. His voice is soft and agreeable. While speaking of his election to the Presidency, he said his wife had made a nightly prayer for several months, that Henry Clay might be elected President in his place." A gentleman who had accompanied General Taylor up the Ohio, said that one day, while they were noticing a remarkably located log cabin, the General remarked that if he were to follow the dictates of his heart, he would prefer to spend the remainder of his days in that cabin, to living four years in the White House. His leading idea was that he was really the servant of the American people.

Among the ladies and gentlemen who had come from Kentucky with the President elect were Colonel James Taylor and Miss Taylor of Kentucky, Miss Peyton of Louisiana, Mr. Christy, Mrs. Christy, Miss Wickliffe and Miss Johnson, all of Kentucky. The inauguration ceremonies took place in the usual order, as often before described. About half-past one the new President was duly installed in the executive palace, with such a mass meeting gathered in front waiting for admission, as is only to be seen on inaugural occasions. The evening closed with three balls; a grand one on Judiciary Square, a military one at Carusi's, and one at the National. The first presented a magnificent scene, two-thirds of the dense crowd being ladies. The wax lights displayed the sparkling of thousands of diamonds. All the foreign legations were present, some covered with orders and glittering with jewels. Madame de Bodisco was magnificent in white satin embroidered with gold; over it a crimson velvet tunic, with train, also embroidered with gold and studded with diamonds. Her head-dress of crimson velvet blazed with jewels. This dress was said to be the one worn by her when presented to the Czar. She was the only lady in the room who wore a court dress; the others appearing in ball costume. The Russian minister's uniform was also elaborately splendid. A wag described the scene: "Suddenly there was a crash. 'What's the matter?' Only the contact of a lady, whirled with all the enthusiasm which the merry waltz and Gung'l's music combined inspire, against an unfortunate wight in the way. 'Oh, my poor fan! it's smashed to pieces!' 'Dear me! there goes half my skirt!' 'Stop, sir! stop a moment! You're pulling that lady's head off!' 'Where's my bracelet?' 'There goes my bouquet!' etc. 'Ain't it delightful?' 'What! do you think it too crowded?' etc." At half-past ten General Taylor entered leaning on the arm of the Mayor, and bowed on each side till he reached the platform at the end of the room. When Mr. Buchanan presented a number of ladies, the President remarked, "Ah, Mr. Buchanan, you always pick out the prettiest ladies." "Why, the truth is," was the reply, "I know that your taste and mine agree in that respect." Then the veteran said: "I have been so long among Indians and Mexicans, I hardly know how to behave myself, surrounded by so many lovely women!" Colonel and Mrs. Bliss also visited the ballroom. The crowd and heat were intolerable, and some of the men seemed trying to take a wax cast o. their coats, under the perpetual stream from the candles.

General Taylor had counted on Mr. Crittenden as a member of his cabinet, having the utmost confidence in his counsel; but Mr. Crittenden declined office. Of Mr. Crawford, the Secretary of War, no mention had been made before his elevation to that office. Mr. Clayton, the Secretary of State, had been identified closely within the last two years, with the most ultra policy of the whig party. It was said that he entertained the design of building up a republican party to supersede the present organization, based on principles more in consonance with the advancing spirit of the age. He was an able man, of popular manners, with great political experience. Mr. Meredith possessed great talent, and there was every reason to believe he would be the ruling spirit of the cabinet. His was a ripe, clear and vigorous intellect; with a fascinating address, and a freshness of character preserved by few who are long connected with party politics. He had all the attributes of mind and manner calculated to give him ascendency in the cabinet. Mr. Preston, the Secretary of the Navy, had been a respectable member of the House of Representatives. Mr. Ewing was a man of the strongest party ties, very intolerant, and a decided advocate of proscription. Mr. Johnson, Attorney-General, was a very sharp, shrewd lawyer, better suited to his office than the Senate. The main strength of the administration, amid these discordant members, was in General Taylor himself; while he avowedly knew little of public affairs.

A change was announced, to be made in the public agents abroad; ministers, chargés, attachés, commissioners and consuls. A primary consideration with the cabinet was the appointment of men competent to maintain the honor and dignity of the United States among European nations, without involving the country in the war which then menaced the continent. William C. Rives, who had been American Plenipotentiary at Paris under General Jackson, was spoken of for the same mission. He was one of the ablest statesmen in the country, and well fitted from his experience, high talent, and extensive information, to sustain the character of the government in any appointment. Not the least of his recommendations to the French government, was found in his attractive appearance, address, and manners; he being admitted, even in the Old Dominion, to be as perfect a gentleman as one of the ancient cavaliers. Mr. Abbott Lawrence had been mentioned with reference to a mission to England. The news of the death of Major-General Gaines brought sadness to many hearts. Soon followed the official announcement of the death of James K. Polk. The President ordered the departments placed in mourning, and appropriate honors were paid to the memory of the ex-President.

In the absence of Congress and in the heats of summer Washington presented a curious aspect, dried up like a river dependent on the spring rains. In utter stagnation it awaited the return of Congress, and the strangers which December brought back to the hotels and boarding-houses. The gossip was freshened by a strange rumor that M. de Bodisco had been exiled to Siberia by the Emperor of Russia. It brought his beautiful and magnificent wife on the avenue to contradict the report. The arrival of Henry Clay, in November, was an agreeable piece of intelligence. It was said that a wedding in Philadelphia in part accounted for the presence of the sage of Ashland. The parties were Mr. Becket and Miss Bayard. After having recovered from the cholera, and being bruised by the upsetting of a stage near Cumberland, the immortal Harry came again, not as an old man of seventy-two, bent, decrepit and trembling, but with form erect, in the vigor of middle age, with the bewitching smile still playing about the corners of his capacious mouth; the hat still slightly cocked, the shirt-collar still erect; in short, the Harry Clay of 1826. Many thought he would grow fresher and stronger till nominated for the Presidency in 1852.

When the President's house was again thrown open to the public, late in November, it was found that the east room was newly carpeted and re-decorated, and illumined by gas jets from splendid chandeliers. Before ten, the delegation of six Osage Indians, who had been several weeks in Washington, came in to bid farewell to their Great Father. They had been quartered at the Western Hotel, where their King lay part of the time covered in a bed on the floor, his legs stuck against the mantel-piece, and a pipe in his mouth, while the others sang and accompanied themselves with hollow gourds having gravel inside, or squatted before the fire unincumbered with clothing except the breech-cloth. The commissioner of Indian affairs had them dressed like white men, but getting tired of the harness, they took it off before night, and caught cold. At the President's levee they had their broadcloth dress trimmed at the seams with lace, and wore cocked hats.

Senator John C. Fremont was much talked of as one of the most remarkable men of the day, his life having been a highly romantic piece of personal history. A few years before, he had come to Washington from South Carolina, having received an appointment in the topographical bureau. He became attached to one of Colonel Benton's daughters, the celebrated and brilliant Jessie. The young lady saw in him the youthful hero, the enterprising engineer, and the man of distinction and world-wide fame. After their marriage the father took them to reside in his house. At the close of this winter Mr. Fremont was coming to the capital as Senator from the new State of California, and was said to be the most popular man in all that country. In appearance he was slender and very youthful; his face was marked by intelligence, and bore the lines of hardships sustained with energy and perseverance.

There was an amusing scene in the Senate the day Mr. Hunter made a speech against General Cass's Austrian resolution. Though an eloquent and powerful speaker, Mr. Hunter seldom engaged in debate. On this occasion he bore down on Generals Cass and Foote, like an avalanche of rocks. They looked up astounded, and finding they were really the persons meant in the pouring out of the orator's sarcasms, General Cass clutched his pen, and filled half a sheet of paper with notes, which he held in his left hand, while with his right—his eyes resting earnestly on the speaker—he reached out for the sandstand. Instead of it, he caught hold of an inkstand full of ink, which he poured all over his notes, his left hand, coat-sleeve, vest, and pantaloons. The uniformly neat and well dressed gentleman was a sight to behold! Foote of course laughed at him; but Cass had his revenge at the time Hale satirized General Foote. The Senate was in a roar at his witticisms, but Foote pretended not to have heard what had been said. General Cass obligingly repeated all to him, shaking with laughter as he did so.

"The new British minister was Sir Henry Lytton Bulwer. A satirist asked: Where are the pigmies, the ephemerals, the corrupt politicians of the present day, contrasted with the illustrious trio of aged and venerable statesmen, Clay, Calhoun and Webster! Calhoun's speech in the Senate in March, 1850, created an excitement unprecedented. The galleries were jammed. General Hamilton accompanied Calhoun to his seat; Mr. Webster and others warmly grasped his hand. A letter dated March 21st, said: 'John C. Calhoun is dying; a great intellectual light is going out. With the exit of the great Carolinian the sting of rivalry, which rankled against him in the bosoms of Clay, Webster and Benton, dies forever.'"

Franklin H. Elmore, successor of Calhoun in the Senate, died in May at Washington. For years he had been one of the most prominent politicians of South Carolina; he possessed a splendid intellect, and all the elements of a great statesman. He was twice elected to Congress from Charleston district, but retired in 1842, and took the presidency of the bank of South Carolina. On the election of Mr. Van Buren, he was offered and declined, the appointment of minister to England. After Mr. Calhoun's death, he was called on by the governor of his native State to supply the vacancy, and accepted on condition he should not be expected to serve another term. His wife was a sister of Dixon H. Lewis of Alabama. Mr. Elmore was about sixty when he died. He was perhaps the next greatest man in South Carolina to Mr. Calhoun, the last so great that he was like the majestic oak in the open field, which overshadowed and absorbed every other shrub or tree, and prevented their growth. For twenty years it had been political death for any man in South Carolina to differ from Mr. Calhoun. Preston and Legaré had raised an opposition, and in a year their opposition was crushed. The eloquent McDuffie differed from him, and had not illness shelved him the people would have done it. The accomplished Pickens took opposition ground in one measure, and he was heard of no more in political life. J. H. Hammond, who had been Governor of South Carolina, and for some time an able and distinguished member of Congress, was thought to resemble Calhoun. He was a man of splendid talents and acquirements, a planter, and devoted to the pursuit of agriculture.

On the 4th July, President Taylor and his cabinet attended the celebration at the Washington Monument. The General, on his return home, ate dinner with a keen appetite. The next evening he was ill, and on the fourth day an attack of cholera morbus was blended with a remittent fever which assumed a typhoid form. A few hours brought on alarming symptoms; and with a breaking up and collapse of the whole system, the President sank till death closed the scene. His corpse was laid out in the east room on a magnificent catafalque of black velvet, trimmed with white satin and silver lace. The body was in a lead coffin enclosed in one of mahogany with silver decorations.

All the departments and public buildings, with many private houses, were hung in black.

The new President took the oath of the constitution in the House. General Scott arrived to superintend the military arrangements for the funeral.

Zachary Taylor was said to be in his sixty-fifth year at the period of his death. He was born in Orange County, Virginia, November, 1784. His father, Colonel Richard Taylor, was a descendant of one of the earliest settlers of the Old Dominion, and remarkable for hardy and impetuous courage. He was one of the original settlers of Kentucky, and lived on his estate near Lexington till his death. Famous for his desperate encounters with the Indians, he was a prominent man in civil life. At the fireside of such a father, with an elder brother in the profession of arms, Zachary was early disposed towards a military life. He entered the United States army as a lieutenant, when only eighteen, and remained in the service nearly forty years. In the war with Great Britain of 1812, he rose to the rank of Captain. It 1832 he was raised to the rank of Colonel, and the next scene of his active service was in Florida. His engagements had an important result in finishing the Florida war. The appreciation of his services was marked by the appointment of Brigadier-General. He was then ordered to the Southern Department. Placed in command of the "army of occupation," he entered on the duties which led to his subsequent series of remarkable military exploits. His services in the Mexican war are matters of history that need not be recapitulated. At its close he retired to his plantation at Baton Rouge.

President Taylor was acknowledged by the whole country to be in the loftiest sense, patriotic, honest, sincere, virtuous, and free from personal ambition. His military glory no words could dignify or exalt. He went to the grave with an enviable fame, leaving a memory that will live in the hearts of his countrymen.

It was not till 1853 that Mrs. John Tyler's eloquent reply to the appeal of the Duchess of Sutherland and the ladies of England to the women of America, against domestic slavery, was published. The lady drew a sad picture of the condition of the poor and suffering class in England.

XV.

FILLMORE'S ADMINISTRATION.

Mr. Fillmore's Mother a Woman of superior Intellect—Hereditary Virtue a Patent of Nobility—Appearance of Mr. Fillmore—His Public Services and prominent Position in Congress—His noble Character—His Dignity and Urbanity as Vice-President—Accession to the Presidency—His Plan for the Extension of the Capitol—Various Exploring Expeditions sent out—Eminently combines the Requisites for a great and able Chief Magistrate—Mrs. Henry L. Scott—Visit of Kossuth to Washington—Dinner given him by the President—Thirty-six Guests—Seward's Entertainment for him—Dancing of Lola Montez at the Theater appreciated by Fashionable Ladies—Death of Henry Clay—Memoir of Mrs. Fillmore—Personal Appearance—Official Dinners every Week, and Morning Receptions—Mrs. Fillmore's early Life—Romantic first Acquaintance with young Fillmore—Domestic Tastes of the lovely young Wife—Her Presidency at the White House—Her Death in Washington.

Mr. Fillmore was no exception to the rule that distinguished men have generally had superior mothers. His was a woman of high intellect, and refined culture, possessing the graces that adorn social life. She was Miss Phebe Millard of Pittsfield, Mass. Married at a very early age, and taken to a pioneer's home, she showed the judgment of an experienced matron in aiding her husband and managing her domestic affairs. Her son Millard was born in Locke, Cayuga County, in 1800. Descended from a long line of virtuous and patriotic American ancestors, his character was formed by the purest and best influences. "Hereditary virtue," says Irving, "gives a patent of innate nobleness beyond all the blazonry of the Herald's College."

In 1830 Mr. Fillmore was described as of the medium stature, of light complexion and regular features, and of a mild and benign countenance. His disposition was retiring and unassuming. Though young, he had all the prudence, discretion and judgment of an experienced man. His mildness and benignity of temper were blended with immovable firmness, and he was distinguished for rare and admirable mental qualities.

As a debater in the Legislature, it was said of him: "He never rises without attracting the attention of all who are within the sound of his voice. His manner is good, his voice agreeable; he is mild and persuasive; his speeches are pithy and sententious, always free from idle and vapid declamation." He was elected to Congress in the autumn of 1832.

The twenty-seventh Congress was a very memorable one. No presidential election had ever excited a deeper interest than that of 1840. Wide spread financial distress had pervaded the country for the two or three preceding years; business was in a state of stagnation, and the public mind had become impressed with the idea that the general embarrassment was due to political causes. Whether justly or unjustly, the party in power was held in some measure responsible for the condition of the country. The mighty uprising of the masses by which the administration of Mr. Van Buren was overthrown, not only elected a new President but brought together a Congress entertaining political principles the reverse of those which had prevailed during the last twelve years. The prominent position assigned to Mr. Fillmore in this Congress, was a proof of the confidence inspired by his previous career. As financial difficulties had brought the new administration into power, it was its chief duty to devise financial remedies. The highest mark of confidence the whig party could bestow on any member of Congress, was to make him chairman of the Committee of Ways and Means. Millard Fillmore was placed in this responsible position, and acquitted himself in a manner that won for him laurels which any statesman might be proud to wear. In 1842, Mr. Fillmore was spoken of as standing in the same relation to the government in the House of Representatives, that the Chancellor of the Exchequer does to the government of Great Britain in the House of Parliament. He was the financial organ of the legislature; all bills affecting the revenue originating in the House. Capacities of a high order were required to discharge the duties of the post.

Mr. Fillmore was now described as "five feet ten inches tall, stout and finely formed. His complexion is light; his eyes are blue and lively; his forehead is broad, and he has a handsome Grecian mouth. His appearance would attract attention anywhere, as his abilities qualify him for any station. He is always composed, and all his acts are controlled by the dictates of his judgment. He is the incarnation of truth and integrity. He would never raise hopes and then blast them. He is frank, open, and manly. In public life and in private he is without guile; pure and untarnished. His talents are of a high grade; he is a sound thinker, and very sagacious; his judgment is clear, and his emotions never override it; he is always to be relied on, and whatever he undertakes he will master. He belongs to that rare class whose merits are developed with every day's use; in whose minds new beauties and new riches are discovered as they are examined into. He has a high legal reputation, possesses great industry; is agreeable in conversation, and his information upon general subjects is varied and extensive. The queen city of the lakes may be justly proud of so able a representative, so eminent a citizen; of a statesman whose public career is so bright and so full of promise."

In February, 1849, Mr. Fillmore resigned his office as Comptroller of New York, and proceeded to Washington to assume the duties of the Vice-President. Mr. Dallas, the late Vice-President, had been for some time in the chamber, his snow-white hair and noble figure attracting much attention. He occupied a seat in front of the Secretary's table facing the Senators. Presently he was observed to retire, and in a few minutes was seen re-entering in company with Mr. Fillmore, whom he conducted to the chair of the Senate. The oath of office was administered to him by the president *pro tem.* and then he delivered his brief address in the calm and dignified manner for which he was distinguished. While acting as Vice-President, Mr. Fillmore presided over the Senate with a dignity and urbanity never surpassed. Calhoun, in 1826, had announced to the Senate his opinion that the Vice-President had no authority to call Senators to order for any violation of courtesy or transgression of the rules of debate. Mr. Fillmore made a speech in which he explained the reasons why he thought it his duty to preserve decorum, and, if occasion should render it necessary, reverse the usage of his predecessors. This determination met with the warm approval of the Senate, who ordered Mr. Fillmore's speech to be entered at length on their journal.

On the 10th July, 1850, Mr. Fillmore was called to take the oath as President. After the appearance of the Senate in the hall of the House of Representatives, the President entered accompanied by the cabinet, the members remaining standing as a mark of respect. The oath was administered by Judge Cranch. The President, Cabinet and Senate then retired; and the Speaker announced that he had received a message, which related to the funeral obsequies of Zachary Taylor. Mr. Fillmore's first annual message at the opening of the next session of Congress, promulgated the general principles by which he would be governed in his administration. This message was admirable in style, national in its spirit, statesmanlike, and a model of brevity and directness.

In 1851 it was necessary for the President to give Congress a plan for the extension of the capitol. By Mr. Fillmore's plan, two wings were to be added to the previous edifice, connected with it by corridors. Excavations for the foundation were immediately commenced, and the work was in sufficient forwardness to allow the corner-stone to be laid on the 4th July. This was done by the President's own hand, with imposing ceremonies, and amid a great concourse of people, who were eloquently addressed by Mr. Webster, the Secretary of State. The President was assisted in laying the corner-stone by the Grand Master of the Masonic Grand Lodge, who wore the same regalia and used the identical gavel which Washington had used fifty-eight years before, in laying the corner-stone of the original edifice.

The various exploring expeditions to the Chinese seas, the valley of the Amazon, the rivers of Africa, etc., sent out under Mr. Fillmore's administration, showed it to be characterized by enterprise and by a salutary caution. He fully sympathized with the progressive spirit of the age, and his management evinced his high qualities as a practical statesman. Firm when right was involved, bold when occasion demanded, far-sighted respecting the consequences of measures, quick to perceive where advantage could be gained for the country, cool, sagacious, deliberate and inflexibly just, he combined more of the requisites for a great and able Chief Magistrate than any other man known.

During Mr. Fillmore's administration the handsomest woman in Washington was Mrs. Henry L. Scott, who presided over the General's house. She was a blonde, with a clear, bright complexion, and a tall form with a certain grandeur of presence that impressed all who saw her. She possessed uncommon intellect with great sprightliness and noble qualities of heart. In 1847 she was Mrs. Hamilton Holley, and gave agreeable entertainments. She often presided at Mrs. Hamilton's receptions. She was pious and charitable. She died in 1859.

The federal city was rather scant of amusements

at the beginning of 1851. There was a small theater, and parties were given by members of the cabinet, some of the foreign ministers, and an occasional member of Congress; and Jenny Lind's wildwood notes had been heard. Complaints were made that the assemblies were costly, and made up of "the same set of elderly ladies" in all "the glaring importance of dress." The President's levees were voted monotonous and dull by those who had not novelty to enliven them in the round of the east room. The proprietors of one of the hotels organized a weekly hop in the new ball-room, under the supervision of twenty gentlemen managers and twelve lady patronesses. All visitors had to be endorsed by one of those committees. The President and cabinet attended the first, and the diplomatic corps, the Supreme Court, and Congress, were largely represented. At the one given on the anniversary of the battle of New Orleans, Mr. Clay was the reigning favorite; more fascinating than beauty arrayed for conquest, more charming to beauty than the most dashing military dandy. The cabinet and the Supreme Court were represented by Mr. Corwin and Judge Woodbury. New York and Pennsylvania were sustained in the department of belles, and the Carolinas and the far West came up to the maintenance of their respective sections. At eleven the company discussed a bounteous supper.

At the close of 1851, Louis Kossuth visited Washington. His party was received by a deputation and conducted by two Senators to Brown's hotel; shortly afterwards, the hero came out on the balcony and bowed to the assembled crowd. The next day he was presented to President Fillmore, at the White House, and had a strictly private interview. The President gave him a dinner, for which thirty-six covers were ordered. The Secretaries and the ladies —twelve in all—three of the ladies belonging to the President's family—the committees of the Senate and House, the President of the Senate and Speaker of the House, with Kossuth and his suite and a few others, made up the number. The President had a pleasure in showing attention to the Hungarian guest; but officially he had to be governed by the proceedings of Congress. Crowds of visitors waited on Kossuth upon New Year's day. Kossuth asked Judge Beale what State he represented. "Virginia," was the answer. "The mother of States and of statesmen," said the Magyar. The members of Congress then offered the hospitalities of their respective States.

There had been a fire in the beautiful room appropriated to the library of Congress, and a mass of blackened rubbish lay under the west front of the capitol—the ashes and cinders of some forty thousand volumes, piled from five to eight feet high; the leaves of the burnt books, in all languages, strewn about the terrace "thick as autumnal leaves in Vallambrosa." Among the valuable works lost were the records of the British Parliament from the time of William the Conqueror.

Mr. Seward gave an evening entertainment to Kossuth and his suite; and a Congressional banquet was given to him at the National Hotel, three hundred guests being present, including Hon. W. R. King,

President of the Senate, Hon. Daniel Webster, Secretaries Corwin and Stuart, Judge Wayne of the supreme Court, General Houston, Mr. Seward, and other distinguished men. General Scott was not there, being absent in Virginia. He was understood to be dead set against intervention, and all foreign emissaries whose business it was to involve the people in filibustering expeditions. The General was a whig conservative of the old school. General Sam. Houston dined in company with Kossuth, but escaped in time to avoid the responsibility of a speech. A different kind of success was that of Lola Montez, the theater being crowded on the first night of her appearance in Washington. The grace and elegance of her dancing were appreciated by the fashionable ladies. It was said that numerous calls were made upon her by leading persons, but that she declined receiving any one. The President, cabinet, diplomatic corps, members of Congress, and other distinguished persons were present at the entertainment on board the Baltic. Over two thousand persons were on board. In the splendid saloons of the ship a luxurious banquet was set out. Scores of elegantly dressed ladies clambered through and admired the ponderous machinery, bright as a mirror, and too clean to soil the most delicate cambric.

Henry Clay breathed his last on the 29th of June, 1852, at his rooms in the National Hotel in Washington. He had been rapidly sinking for some days, but his mind retained its clearness to the last.

Mrs. Fillmore in stature was above the medium height; her form was symmetrical and remarkably erect and graceful. Her eyes were of a light soft blue: her hair was bright auburn, fine and silky, rippling from her forehead and hanging in natural ringlets. Her complexion was delicately fair and fresh. Her face lighted up with a pleasant smile when she was engaged in conversation, and her manner was winning, though marked by a retiring modesty bordering on reserve.

It was a sad event to Mrs. Fillmore, as well as to the nation, which so unexpectedly called her husband to enter on the duties of the Presidency. She was not able to close her house in Buffalo and join the President till the October following the death of General Taylor. When the winter season opened, and through succeeding ones, Mrs. Fillmore's health was too fragile to allow her to enjoy the elevation to which she had been so unexpectedly raised. The fatiguing ceremonies in which she was obliged to take part often exhausted her strength, and marred the pleasure she would have derived from social intercourse. During the sessions of Congress, the President usually gave an official dinner every week, to which members of Congress and other dignitaries, with their wives, were invited, without distinction of party. In the short session these official dinners were given twice a week. Weekly morning receptions were held from ten to twelve, and evening levees from eight to ten; and at these Mrs. Fillmore was always present when her health would possibly permit. At the evening receptions a band of music played for the entertainment of the company, but no refreshments were offered. In warm weather musical entertainments were given in the public grounds. During the recess of Congress the morning receptions were kept up, though not the levees; and the Presidential dinners were less frequent, fewer guests being invited. It was customary for the President to receive visitors, but never to pay calls; and although Mr. Fillmore gave dinners, he never accepted invitations to any beyond one occasionally at the house of a cabinet minister. Mrs. Fillmore was debarred from making or returning calls by the delicacy of her health, and that laborious duty devolved upon her daughter. At all the public receptions and official dinner parties, however, she presided with great dignity and the demeanor of a high-bred lady, whose intelligence and good sense were as apparent as her unobtrusive moral excellence and earnest piety.

Mrs. Fillmore's maiden name was Abigail Powers; and she was born near the battle-ground of Bemis' Heights, in Saratoga County, N. Y., in March, 1798. Her father, Rev. Lemuel Powers, was a Baptist clergyman. His death in 1800 left his widow with limited means and a large family, of which Abigail was the youngest. When the little girl was but nine years of age, her mother removed to Sempronius, Cayuga County, where the child, being exceedingly bright and fond of reading, early acquired an education. It was her design, which she carried out, to devote herself to teaching; and by this she not only maintained herself, but contributed to the support of her mother. In this retired place she attended the same school with a noble-hearted lad—young Millard Fillmore—with whom she soon formed a friendship founded on

MRS. ABIGAIL FILLMORE.

Engd by [illegible] Hall. N.Y.

a similarity of tastes. He was then an apprentice to the carding and cloth-dressing business. The mutual regard between these young people grew and strengthened, and finally ripened into a love that lasted during their united life. At the age of nineteen young Fillmore gave up this apprenticeship, and began the study of law. He finished his legal course, and commenced practice in Buffalo. In February, 1826, he married Miss Powers at Moravia in Cayuga County, and took her to reside at Aurora in the County of Erie. Four years later they removed to Buffalo, which continued to be their permanent home.

While it was the fortune of Mr. Fillmore to become early involved in political life, his wife's retiring disposition and love of domestic life, caused her to shrink from any share in his celebrity. The peace and quiet seclusion of her own home were far dearer to her than all the glitter, show and admiration that waited upon the rising statesman, and might have made her an object of attention. Her leisure hours were devoted to books and to the cultivation of flowers, of which she was passionately fond. She was tenderly devoted to her children, and frequently joined them in their lessons; French being a favorite study. She was a lover of music, and was never more happy than when listening to her daughter's playing the piano, while her son sang. It was a delight and a pride to her to witness the improvement of those on whom she lavished such affectionate solicitude. Her son was born in 1828; her daughter in 1832; but she survived her mother little more than a year.

As a wife also this lovely lady was tender and exemplary. She never accompanied her husband to Albany during the three years that he was a member of the Assembly; and in the eight years between 1833 and 1843, that he was in Congress, she went but seldom to Washington. While in the capital she entered moderately into the gayeties of the season; but always returned with pleasure to her beloved home and the quiet cares claimed by her young children. Hitherto her health had been good; but in 1842 the accidental sprain of her ankle, for want of rest and care, caused her months of suffering and confinement to her room, which seriously impaired her general health. While her husband held the office of comptroller of his State, her children being absent at school, she accompanied him to Albany; remaining till he resigned his office and went to Washington as Vice-President of the United States. Then she returned to her home in Buffalo. Here she was startled, in July, 1850, by news of the death of President Taylor.

Probably the happiest day of her residence in Washington, was the 3d of March, 1853, when the official term of President Fillmore expired. A journey through the Southern States had been planned for the renovation of Mrs. Fillmore's health; but she was destined never to leave Washington alive. A severe cold taken the day of Mr. Pierce's inauguration, settled on her lungs, and after great suffering borne with Christian fortitude, terminated her life. She died at Willard's hotel on the 30th of March, and was taken home and buried in Forest Lawn cemetery at Buffalo.

XVI.

PIERCE'S ADMINISTRATION.

Excitement at Pierce's Nomination—Delicate Health of Mrs. Pierce—Habits of the President Elect—Early Life and beautiful Character of Mrs. Pierce—Her Devotion to the Duties of her Station—The Accident that made her childless—Departure of Pierce for Washington—Webster, the private Secretary—General Pierce in New York, and Evasion of his Pursuers—A thousand Visitors in Philadelphia—His Cabinet—The last Night in Congress—Scene of the Inauguration—Sketch of General Pierce and the Vice-President—Secretary Marcy—The other Secretaries—Entertainment given by the Brazilian Minister—Array of Beauty—Presidential and Cabinet Doings anatomized at the Tea-tables—Judge Douglas and Beverly Tucker—Diplomatic Dinner—Splendid Parties in Washington—Mrs. Jefferson Davis—The Belles and their Toilets—Grouping of the fair Representatives of the different Sections—Governor Aiken's grand Party—Amusing Story of the British Minister—Marriage of Senator Douglas—Mrs. Douglas—Stirring Scene on Thanksgiving Morning—General Houston—Reception at Secretary McClelland's—Senator Butler, of South Carolina—Mrs. Guthrie's Party—Anecdotes.

THE nomination of Franklin Pierce, the democratic candidate for the Presidency, created great excitement in New Hampshire and elsewhere. The health of Mrs. Pierce was delicate, and he was busy in closing up his professional business. His family consisted of himself, wife, and son twelve years old. His brother, Henry D. Pierce, and his sister, the widow of General John McNeil, were his nearest relations, and resided at Hillsborough. Major Benjamin K. Pierce, of the army, was the oldest brother, but had been dead several years. Mrs. Pierce was the daughter of Rev. Jesse Appleton, D. D., President of Bowdoin College. She was born in Hampton, N. H., in 1806, and was married to Franklin Pierce in 1834.

For years her health had been delicate and she had secluded herself from general society. Her fine natural endowments were developed by careful and liberal culture, and the influences of her home associations were refining and elevating. Her tastes were of exceeding delicacy and purity; and she appreciated the beautiful in nature and art. She shrank with extreme sensitiveness from public observation. Those who noted her in the midst of the undesired duties and responsibilities of her public station, claimed for her an unsurpassed dignity and grace, delicacy and purity. A Christian home was quietly maintained, in the midst of public life.

The private Secretary said of Mrs. Pierce: "She was a very remarkable woman. To a careful, early formal education were added accomplishments of an extremely rare order. Her taste was faultless. If I were to say in what she was most striking, it would be that no one, observing her, could fail to see that she was a *lady* by birth, education and habit of life." She died in December, 1863, at Andover, Massachusetts.

General Pierce himself bore with perfect equanimity the news of his elevation to the highest office in the people's gift. He was the only calm and self-possessed man in Concord the night of its arrival; but, after receiving the victorious bulletins with scarcely a change of countenance, he quietly retired. A letter said, "His habits are plain and unostentatious. His practice yields him a large income, and he is generous to a fault. It is said in Concord that he will spend his Presidential twenty-five thousand every year."

A deplorable accident that occurred on the Boston and Maine Railroad rendered childless the Chief Magistrate elect in the hour of his triumph. The car in which General Pierce, Mrs. Pierce and their son happened to be passengers, was thrown off the track and precipitated down a steep embankment, making a complete turn-over in its descent. General and Mrs. Pierce and ten or twelve others were severely but not dangerously injured. But when the father found his child, the boy was dead. This dreadful affliction overtook him suddenly, when the sky was brightest, and when the hopes and aspirations of a great nation had centred in him. The child had been called Benjamin, in honor of his brave grandfather.

On the 14th of February General Pierce left his residence in Concord for the national capital. He had been a public man for nearly twenty-five years, and for much of that time the most influential man in New Hampshire. Possessing all those generous and noble attributes which never fail to win the regard and lasting confidence of an intelligent people, he early received and always retained a popularity based on so solid a foundation that nothing could impair it. Just in all his conduct, generous to a fault, the soul of honor, liberal in his views, possessing as kind and noble a heart as ever warmed a true man's breast or prompted to chivalrous deeds, and in his constant intercourse with the people ever exhibiting those traits of character, it was not strange that he had won and retained the highest respect of all classes. He selected Mr. Sidney Webster as his private secretary. This relation to a President, being strictly confidential, could be properly filled only by a gentleman of education, discretion, honor and personal accomplishments. Mr. Webster was a native of New Hampshire, the son of Caleb Webster, and the nephew of General Peaslee; he had been thoroughly educated, and was a lawyer of experience, with brilliant prospects. They came quietly from Boston to New York, and took lodgings at the Astor House.

Before the public knew of the arrival, General Pierce had taken breakfast, his companions being Governor Seymour of Connecticut, and Major Kimball, both of whom had fought by his side in the Mexican war. Meanwhile, politicians, office-hunters, and curious people crowded the halls and corridors of the hotel. One or two only had noticed the commanding figure and intelligent countenance of the gentleman in mourning, accompanied by his secretary and a single servant, who had driven to the hotel from the New Haven cars. His luggage had an appearance of severe republican simplicity, "a couple of old hair trunks which might have been the property of a veteran of 1812, and two portmanteaus scarcely less venerable in appearance." The whole army of waiters hardly sufficed to carry up the cards and notes presented by persons who "had done signal service for General Pierce and the democratic party in the late Presidential election." But instead of holding parley with the crowd, the General privately made his exit, accompanied by Sergeant O'Neil, for the purpose of visiting the widow of the late General Worth, then staying on Governor's Island. Fortunately the General's person was not known, and he arrived unmolested at the Battery. There he took a boat for the island; but the small craft was nearly upset by the swell of the sea, and the party narrowly escaped being drowned. The sentry refused to allow the strange visitor to land at the island, unprovided with an order, and presented his bayonet in a menacing manner. When informed that his visitor was the President elect, he was astonished beyond measure, never imagining that a person of so much importance would come in a manner so unostentatious.

After a somewhat lengthened visit to Mrs. Worth, the President returned in a small boat, and found a formidable and increasing crowd of office-seekers collected at Whitehall to await the landing. Sergeant O'Neil espied the harpies, and it was immediately determined to outmanœuvre them; so the boat was pulled to the north side of the Battery. The crowd ran up Broadway to intercept their victim, supposing he would take that route; but on landing, the pursued stepped into a carriage, directing it driven rapidly through West, Washington, and other obscure streets, to the Astor House. A tremendous multitude was now assembled, and a deputation from a committee came to enquire if the General could receive that body. He declined, as he was traveling privately, and had made up his mind to receive no committees; though he was willing to receive gentlemen who called as individuals. A number visited him, among them Governor Seymour of New York, and John Van Buren. At three o'clock, wearied and worried, the General retired, and got away secretly in the afternoon train for Philadelphia; the brakeman raising two flags at the back of the rear car, the one set apart for the General and his friends.

It was determined by Mrs. Pierce to remain in Boston till after the inauguration. The President's party stopped at the Merchant's Hotel in Philadelphia, and the next morning General Pierce received about a thousand visitors. It had been suggested that James Guthrie of Louisville, Ky., would probably receive a cabinet appointment from President Pierce. He was a man of strong mind, great energy of character, and untiring industry; a leader of the democracy of the State. In feeling and interest he was identified with the growth and prosperity of the Mississippi Valley. To commanding talents and an intimate acquaintance with the wants and resources of the whole country, he united urbane and prepossessing manners. James Campbell of Pennsylvania, was also spoken of as one of the cabinet. He was Attorney-General of the State; had been a judge of one of the Philadelphia courts, and was universally admitted to be an honest, upright, able, learned and popular man. At this time he was young, and seemed destined to become one of the most distinguished men of the age. His was an active spirit, cool, calm, and clear, and his warmth of heart was equal to his energy, balanced, too, by discretion and sagacity. He had a happy facility in adapting himself to others. He was a bold uncompromising democrat and proved himself by pen and voice a true champion of popular rights; a friend to civil and religious freedom.

On the 24th February President Fillmore and General Pierce, with two or three of the Secretaries, and many officers, visited the caloric ship Ericson at Alexandria. The invention was exhibited and explained to them, and the naval gentlemen expressed great admiration of the wonderful machinery. A splendid carriage made in the French caléche style, and light bay horses, were presented by the Boston people to General Pierce.

The last night in Congress this year—that of the 3d March—saw a rush and crush and confusion within and without the capitol till the small hours of morning. When the votes were called, the sleepers on the sofas and in the side-rooms were drummed up. President Fillmore was signing bills till after midnight. The city was in an uproar with bands of music, rockets and artillery, and wandering strangers with carpet bags were to be seen at every turn. On the morning of March 4th, the capitol swarmed to overflowing. Hundreds had slept in its warm passages and in the rotunda, lying down in their cloaks, while thousands had walked the streets all night. On the way to the capitol, General Pierce stood erect in the carriage, with President Fillmore by his side, surrounded by marshals and bowing to cheers and the waving of handkerchiefs. The foreign ministers, in splendid carriages, with full court dresses, added to the pageant. An immense staging was erected in the eastern front of the capitol, where the oath of office was administered and the address delivered. In taking the oath, General Pierce said, "I solemnly affirm," raising his right hand and holding it aloft. As he stood with head uncovered and lifted hand, the spectators also uncovered, even in the snow that was falling. Pierce was undoubtedly an effective and graceful speaker. The ladies were in ecstasies, and some climbed upon the pediments of the columns of the capitol, to their no small danger. On the completion of the address, the procession again formed, and proceeded along the avenue, escorting the new President to the White House. Great numbers waited on President Pierce, and the evening closed with balls and other entertainments.

At a crowded reception given by President Pierce, some amusing scenes occurred with the office-seekers. One ambitious fellow stepped up with the preparatory remark: "I'm an applicant for office." "Glad to see you, sir," was the reply: "good morning," and off glided the President. Some had their papers in their hands ready for presentation; but Sergeant O'Niel managed to get possession of them before they could reach their destination. One applicant made out to thrust his memorial into the President's hands, but it was dropped like a hot coal. When the Mayor of Baltimore and a deputation came up, and the worthy civic functionary had just cleared his throat for a formal address, General Pierce, too quick for him, begged the pleasure of shaking hands with all the delegation, and thus escaped the infliction of the oration.

Franklin Pierce was born at Hillsborough, New

Hampshire, in 1804. He was the youngest man who had been yet elected to the Presidency. In 1833 he took his seat as a member of Congress. In 1837 he was elected a Senator, but resigned his seat in 1842. He was esteemed one of the most eminent lawyers in New Hampshire. In the war with Mexico he enrolled himself as a private soldier; but the President sent him a colonel's commission, and in 1847 he was advanced to the rank of brigadier-general. He wished to decline the nomination to the Presidency in 1852. The office he would not seek was conferred upon him by the voice of the people.

William Rufus King, the Vice-President, was born in North Carolina in 1786. At this time he was sixty-seven, and in precarious health. He removed to Alabama in 1818; was chosen one of the first United States Senators, and continued a member of that body for over twenty-four consecutive years. He accepted the mission to France offered him by President Tyler. In 1848 he was again Senator from Alabama, in place of Arthur Bagby. In 1850 he was chosen President *pro tem.* of the Senate, Vice-President Fillmore having succeeded to the Presidency. He was considered one of the champions of Southern State rights. His residence was at Selma, on the Alabama River, and he never was married.

William Larned Marcy, the new Secretary of State, was a native of Massachusetts, and in his sixty-seventh year at this time. On the organization of that potent and secret association called "the Albany Regency," Mr. Marcy became one of the most trusty and confidential members and advisers of its head,

Martin Van Buren. He was Secretary of War under Mr. Polk, and his ability as a writer, tactician and statesman was generally admitted. Robert McClelland, the Secretary of the Interior, was a native of Pennsylvania, but resided in Michigan, of which State he was elected Governor in 1851. Jefferson Davis, the Secretary of War, was a native of Kentucky, but removed in early life to Mississippi. His military education was received at West Point. In 1847, he was elected United States Senator. In person he was of medium size. He was forty-five years of age, and the last man one would imagine a "fire-eater," being prim and smooth-looking, with a precise manner, a stiff, soldierly carriage, and an austerity at first forbidding. As a speaker he was clear, forcible and argumentative; his voice clear and firm. Caleb Cushing, Attorney-General, was the author of "Reminiscences of Spain," and "Historical and Political Review of the Revolution in France," which appeared in 1830. He commenced public life as a friend of John Quincy Adams, was one of the Justices of the Supreme Court of Massachusetts, and was known as a distinguished politician and eminent scholar. Cushing, too, had served in the Mexican war, and won the rank of Brigadier-General. He was at this time fifty-three, and was tall and slender, with dark complexion. It created something of a sensation—the discovery that General Cushing was the only man in the cabinet who could speak another than his native language. At a diplomatic dinner given by M. de Bodisco, the Attorney-General surprised the distinguished party by conversing in French with M. Le Compte de Sartiges, in

Spanish with Don Calderon de la Barca, in Dutch with Baron Testa, in German with Baron von Gevolt, in Portuguese with De Figaniere, and in unexceptionable Tuscan with the representative of the two Sicilies. The Secretary of State figured in tolerable English only. Mr. John Slidell, of New Orleans, was nominated as minister to Central America. The last executive levee of the season was given on the 24th March.

On the death of Mrs. Fillmore—March 30th—the cabinet council was suspended, and all public offices were closed by order of the President. At the motion of Mr. Seward, the Senate adjourned. The President addressed a tribute of condolence to his bereaved predecessor. It was understood that the deceased lady would be taken to Buffalo for interment. The wife of Hon. Lewis Cass died in Detroit on the same day.

Major-General Scott went to New York, and in his absence the furniture of his house in Washington was advertised for sale. Dr. Kane of the Arctic exploring expedition, and G. P. R. James, the novelist, were also visitors to the capital, Dr. Kane preparing for his last Arctic expedition. The death of Vice-President King brought a gloom over Washington towards the last of April. He had reached his home in Alabama. Sergeant O'Neil's departure from the White House was a severe loss to the President, whom he relieved from much unnecessary annoyance. In November General Cass engaged a suite of apartments at Willard's, for the winter, intending to bring his daughter, keep a carriage, &c. This was a great change from the plain manner of life observed by the General for several years in Washington. In 1854, Lieutenant Bodisco, a nephew of the late M. de Bodisco, an attaché of the Russian Legation, was recalled to St. Petersburg by his government.

During the winter of 1854 diplomatic balls, though usually the most elegant and not the least numerous in Washington, had been discontinued till the 24th March, when the Brazilian minister gave the first entertainment of the season, in honor of the birthday of the Emperor of Brazil. Don Calderon de la Barca had given delightful soirées, at which all the beauty of Washington was gathered. M. de Sartiges, the French minister, previous to his marriage, had also given a large ball. But this season had seen no cards issued by the diplomatic corps. Fifteen hundred invitations were issued by "Le Ministre du Brézil et Mme. de Carvalho Moreira," and all the fashionable part of Washington was in a delightful state of excitement. Some dragons of propriety whispered that it was Lent, and Friday at that; but their murmurs were lost in the tumult of satisfaction. Was not the Brazilian minister a Catholic? and did he not know what was proper! The house was one that had been occupied by the Chilian minister, and afterwards by Mr. Crampton, the British minister; and was admirably adapted for an entertainment. All the rooms on the first floor were thrown open, forming an elegant suit of six, leading into each other. The halls and rooms were filled with exotics, and the whole house was brilliantly lighted with gas. At the door, servants in rich scarlet liveries ushered the guests into the disrobing apartments up stairs. Madame de Carvalho Moreira received her guests in the center parlor. She was dressed in blue and white brocade, with feathers in her hair. By her side stood the minister and his brother, Mr. Andrada, the Secretary of Legation, dressed in full court costume. The ball-room was farther on, running the whole length of the house. A long room was fitted up at the back of the house, communicating with all the others, and filled with tables where the waiters dispensed refreshments during the evening. Besides the Count de Sartiges and Mr. Crampton, General Almonte, the Mexican minister, was there; also Chevalier Halseman, the Austrian minister; Baron Grabon, the acting Prussian; Chevalier George de Sebbern, minister of Sweden and Norway; Señor Don José de Marcoleta, Nicaraguan minister; Señor de Coma, Peruvian, &c. But few Senators or members were present; among them Judge Douglas and Senator Brodhead; of the cabinet only Jefferson Davis and Dobbin. But the array of beauty was unrivalled. Mrs. McClelland was becomingly dressed in straw colored brocade. Madame Almonte wore blue brocade, sparkling with diamonds. Mrs. Aiken of South Carolina was superb as usual. It was the first time the appearance of Hon. James Buchanan's beautiful niece, Miss Lane, was publicly noticed.

While the social ascendency of Mrs. Roosevelt in Washington is noticed, justice requires the mention of her young friend and connection, Mrs. Henry Butterfield. This lady was Miss Mary Roosevelt Burke of New York. Her exquisite beauty, grace and accomplishments, youthful as she was, rendered her a belle whenever she appeared. After her marriage to Mr. Butterfield she went to reside in Paris, where she was a distinguished favorite in the court society. The portrait represents her in a dress arranged with her own artistic taste; the tiara of superb diamonds suiting well her style of loveliness. She died in Paris after some years' residence.

While residing in the executive mansion, Mrs. Pierce never made her own sorrows a reason for any change in the accustomed routine of public affairs, social or official. Although of course with no heart for such things during the early portion of the administration of her husband, she considered it her duty to do every thing in that regard, which had been done before, or which her social position required. For years the established routine of the White House had been a morning reception and an evening reception each week during the session of Congress. These were never intermitted, and Mrs. Pierce invariably "received" with her husband, unless too ill; often when few could have borne up against her physical suffering. In addition, during the session, General and Mrs. Pierce gave every week a state dinner to which thirty-six persons were invited. Besides, there was rarely a week-day that they dined alone; the guests averaging from three to twelve. Indeed, "public gayety" at the White House from 1853 to 1857, was never better known.

Superficial persons who attended the receptions at the White House might mistake the unrivalled grace, dignity and sweetness of Mrs. Pierce's manner, for the result of her great sorrow. But they were in

MRS. HENRY J. BUTTERFIELD.

error. The absence of everything like bustle or hurry, and the presence always of repose and gentleness in her bearing, were things innate and inbred, without which she would not have been the lady of refinement she was.

A letter dated in November, 1855, says that at the tea-tables in Washington the doings of the President and cabinet were anatomized, and hands were held up at the grandeur of an aristocratic democracy; ultra style prevailing at court ceremony and retinue beyond all that had gone before. "Strangers are crowding in already. The new Spanish minister and many others are making themselves comfortable for the winter. Escalante does not come from the old worn out families of Spain, from which have been hitherto chosen their representatives at foreign courts. He belongs to the new school. Our wealthy banker, Mr. Corcoran, will be here soon with his daughter; above all, Rachel will soon be here. The maids in hiring themselves for the season, require to be allowed time to attend to their French studies; and many of them, on being asked their names, answer 'Rar-char-el' with a sweeping curtsy." "They tell a good joke of Tucker, who is said to be clever at repartee. The 'little giant' one day, in one of his free and easy moods, marched up and affected to lean familiarly on Tucker's shoulder; saying to him jocosely; 'Bev. when I get to be President, what shall I do for you, old boy?' 'Do?' replied Tucker, 'why, put your arm on my shoulder in as kind a mood as you do now, and ask me the same question then.' Douglas laughed heartily."

A new minister from Mexico appeared in the place of General Almonte—Colonel Robles, a gentleman of accomplished and scientific education, of talents and ample fortune. Though not more than forty years of age, he held a deservedly high military rank. His appointment at this time to a responsible mission, indicated a fusion of all parties who opposed and were punished by Santa Anna.

The guests at a diplomatic dinner given early in the following season by the President, at which Mrs. Pierce presided, were Mr. Crampton and Secretary Lumley, representatives of England, M. and Madame Boileau of France, Mr. and Madame Stoeckl of Russia, Señor Almonte of Mexico, Mr. and Mrs. Marcoleta of Nicaragua, Mr. and Mrs. Sibbern of Sweden, Señor Escalante, Secretary of Legation of Spain, Don Adrada and wife of Brazil, M. de Gerelt and secretary of Prussia, M. Bochebencer of Belgium, Mr. Schleider of Bremen, Señor Osma of Peru, Mr. Molina of Costa Rica, Mr. Winsrea of Naples, Mr. Hulsemann of Austria, with General Thomas, Under Secretary of State, and Sidney Webster. At one of the President's levees, in January, Senator Hale of New Hampshire, who had taken occasion some time before to lampoon the President from his seat in the Senate, called with thousands of others to pay his respects to the Chief Magistrate. With his face wreathed in smiles and a lovely woman on his arm, he approached his Excellency in the blue room in the presence of a crowd of spectators. General Pierce received the lady with marked courtesy, and, having done so, he turned upon his heel, right-about face, presenting the New Hampshire Senator with a full view of his back. The tableau created not a little amusement.

In spite of political disorganizations, dancing and parties became more popular than ever this winter. The President's levees and receptions by the secretaries alternated with "hops" and "grand affairs" at the different hotels. Mr. Buchanan was expected to return from the mission to England in February, Mr. Dallas being appointed his successor. There were many "grand features" in the way of parties, brightened by elegant women from all parts of the Union. One at Mrs. Parker's was particularly noticed, the Misses Parker appearing among the most beautiful and accomplished. Another brilliant party was given by Mrs. Wood, the daughter of General Taylor. The Legislature of Maryland gave a grand ball at Annapolis, the 4th February. In quickness, fluency of speech, decision, firmness and dignity, Mr. Banks excelled, and was on the whole an admirable Speaker, sustaining the high reputation he had established in Massachusetts as a presiding officer.

The carnival season closed early in February with unusual brilliancy and gayety. A reception given by Mrs. Jefferson Davis was attended by the most elegant and fashionable of the court circle; the lady hostess appearing to great advantage, celebrated as she was for being one of the most superior women in the country. Mrs. Jefferson Davis was Miss Varina Howell, the daughter of a merchant of Natchez. She was married in that city. She was a brunette, with dark, fine eyes, and was very Spanish looking. Another superb party was given at Hon. A. C. M. Pennington's. At the great annual ball the wife of Senator Weller of California wore a black brocade silk, with flowers and diamonds. Mrs. Crittenden, ever the impersonation of gentle grace; the dark-eyed Miss Mechlin, exquisitely dressed, Mrs. S. P. Havens and her fair daughter Minnie of New York, and Mrs. George Parker, with two lovely daughters, drew general attention. The beautiful Mrs. Webb, daughter-in-law of James Watson Webb, attracted much attention. She was attired in white watered silk. The celebrated Mrs. Coventry Waddell, wearing white moire antique, with diamonds, was universally admired; also Mrs. Montgomery Blair; and Mrs. Coke, the daughter of Secretary Guthrie, and Mrs. Pope, his niece, the greatest favorites in Washington. Another niece was the lovely Miss Mary Tyler of Kentucky. She was the object of marked attention. Mrs. Reverdy Johnson and her two daughters were surrounded by distinguished statesmen and Senators. Miss Woodbury, daughter of Judge Woodbury of Massachusetts, received the homage accorded to a distinguished belle of Washington; also Miss Riggs of the same city; and the lovely blonde, Miss Beal, and the beautiful brunette, Miss Kecouver. Miss Belle Cass—the gifted and accomplished, the elegant and stately—was dressed in black silk, with trimmings of lace and jet, and diamond ornaments. The charming Mrs. Lindsay, a descendant of the author of the song "Auld Robin Gray," was there; with Mrs. Charles King, the wife of the President of Columbia College, New York, and her daughter Mrs. Gracie; the wife of Senator Trumbull of Illinois; the wife of Judge Gilchrist, and a host of others. Among the distinguished gentlemen were General Sam. Houston, Hon. Mr. Banks, Secretary Guthrie, Lieutenant Lowell, of the Arctic expedition, Sidney Webster, Marshal Hoover, Senator Toucey, Hon. Reverdy Johnson, Judge Gilchrist, of the court of claims, and others too numerous to mention.

A spectator found in each beauty the fit representative of her home. "Yonder flits the bland mannered Kentucky belle, her figure so embonpoint, her face so radiant; her gossamer skirts falling like spray from her white satin bodice, and looped with fresh flowers. Then floating with elastic step comes the fair Georgian, wearing a coronet studded with pearls and rubies. Here the lithe figure of a belle from Mississippi glows in the foreground. Tyrian dyes could not give a brighter tint to her skirts, which she manages with the grace of a Lady Constance; her dark auburn hair girded with a band of emeralds and diamonds. There is the vivacious and intelligent representative of Massachusetts, in white satin tastefully trimmed with gold blonde and looped with orange blossoms; and the placid one of Philadelphia, sensitive, modest and graceful; wearing a tiara of diamonds on her head, while her full shoulders are graced with a cape of Spanish point lace, disclosing in front a chain of diamonds that blaze in a stream of light about her neck; her dress a rich claret-colored silk trimmed with tulle, with white satin under-robe. Passing down the gay throng is the statuesque Baltimorian, her queenly form robed in green and white brocade, trimmed with white tulle and blonde; her dark hair parted in glossy waves over her brow, where rested a wreath of green and white May blossoms blended with emeralds and diamonds. There too was the bright-eyed Buckeye, than whom none was more coy, nor had a face more fair; the rustic, artless daughter of Down East; the buxom Green Mountain maid, her motion as crude as her cheeks were ruddy; the New Hampshire prude of some forty summers, lisping regardless of Murray; the flirting blonde of Washington; the gracious Virginian, with features classic and serene, and the daisy-like daughter of Connecticut, with mild and measured laugh. Then came the imperious Carolinian, with stately step, face of Grecian mould, dark languishing eyes and Ion-like expression. Nor must be omitted the matronly mother of the old school, and her two bouncing daughters, whose rich Dutch blood does now and then make riot at the round table."

Governor Aiken of South Carolina, gave a splendid party early in March; and the ball at the National hotel, was a grand affair. Senators Crittenden, Douglas, Hale, Jones, Weller, &c., were at the ball; also General Cass, General Houston, the Secretaries and Speaker Banks, with many other distinguished persons, and ladies of high repute in the fashionable world. One of the most interesting incidents was the début of Horace Greeley in a quadrille. His Terpsichorean feats were the theme of general admiration.

An amusing story went the rounds that Mr. Crampton, the British minister, had endeavored to satisfy the public mind as to his permanency in official position, by employing a perfect train of coal-carts, engaged all day in carting wood and coal to his residence on the heights of Georgetown. The great Presidential battle of this year resulted in the election of James Buchanan.

Judge Douglas came to Washington in November, 1856, to be united to a lady who had been for some time the belle of the city. Miss Cutts belonged to one of the oldest families in Virginia. She was a Catholic, and the marriage was appointed to take place in the Catholic church. Senators Slidell and Toucey were in the capital in November in fine health and spirits, and were looked on as members of the future cabinet, and treated with corresponding deference and courtesy. Harry Hibbard was also there, spending most of his time at the executive mansion, and in conference with President Pierce. A gay winter was anticipated; the short session preceding an inauguration being usually very brilliant in social matters.

It seems that a Buffalo hatter sent for the measure of Mr. Buchanan's head; also that some of the chivalry of Charleston had desired to make him a present of a grand carriage. But the President elect could not fail to remember that when certain public-spirited citizens of Boston got up a magnificent carriage, and presented it to Mr. Pierce,—almost every subscriber to that carriage put in for a fat office. On Thanksgiving evening, 1856, Washington presented a gay and stirring scene; the dwellings in the principal streets being illuminated, and the balustrades lined with spectators; the scene closing with fireworks, in honor of the victory in Buchanan's election. General Houston "ties his neck-cloth in a very clumsy bow, and wears a tiger-skin vest, as if for an Arctic expedition. His face is almost covered with menacing whiskers of iron gray; and such shaggy and threatening brows overhang his eyes, that one dreads to look what kind of eyes they are." A spectator in the gallery remarked, in January: "That small, delicate, and very youthful figure seated near the Senator from South Carolina, has, during the brief time he has been here, made a marked impression. His position, as he listens to the Speaker, with one hand behind his ear, indicates that his hearing is imperfect. Mr. Pugh is the youngest man in the Senate."

The opening reception of the season came off at the residence of Secretary McClelland, in January. The hostess, a very beautiful woman, with a manner of quiet elegance, was dressed in a rose-colored robe edged with white plush. Her niece was a fair girl with joyous eyes and heavy masses of chestnut ringlets shading her face. The radiant smile of Mrs. Slidell, wife of the Senator from Louisiana, attracted many admirers. Her plainly parted hair was encircled by brilliant diamonds. There was an animation, a fascination in her conversation rarely seen equalled. "The *abandon* with which she speaks, the grace of her gestures, excite a perpetual interest, and leave a delightful impression. About eleven, the silvery head of the Senator from South Carolina, Judge Butler, appeared. He seemed to infuse new life into the circles he passed through, and one might trace his progress by the livelier movements and more mirthful laugh that followed him like the bubbling wake of a ship." "There, too, might be seen the bachelor member from North Carolina in full dress, from kid gloves to French boots. How many smiles this gentleman has had wasted on him! and yet he contrives to dodge the whole artillery. Towering head and shoulders above all the world, we observed the witty member from Georgia, Mr. Cobb, who is expected to say what nobody else has a right to say, and it is all chargeable to a peculiar development of the organ of mirthfulness." Senator Andrew Pickens Butler was conceded to be the most unique and original intellect in the Senate. His face, though not handsome, was sturdily expressive, with massive features and "troubled, streaming, silvery hair, that looked as if it had been contending with the blasts of winter. His was the face of one difficult to lead and impossible to drive, with abilities which gave him a towering eminence. His power as a speaker stood acknowledged in the admiration of both Houses. Like all men of impetuous impulse, he was very restless; one moment pacing to and fro the space behind the Speaker's desk, another giving the grasp of his hand to some younger Senator, the next taking active part in the debates of the day. He seemed to hold the same preëminence in the Supreme Court as in the Senate. The moment a question was submitted to him, his mind instinctively applied all the great principles. He went through the most difficult processes of thought with the ease and familiarity of ordinary discourse. Venerable for his years and abilities, he possessed a dignity of mind that rendered him infinitely superior to mere party spirit. He was of a frank and generous temperament, an admirer of every kind of excellence, with heart as warm as his intellect was ample. Seated near Senator Butler is a slight, slender figure, a combination of the poet and politician in appearance. This is the young Senator from Alabama, Mr. Clay, known as a rising statesman. In debate he is noted for classic elegance, in contrast with the harsher style of the Senator from Illinois, as a Grecian temple to the grim bleakness of a Methodist chapel. State rights is Mr. Clay's political pet, and with it he is as closely amalgamated as a Smyrna fig to its fellow-fig in its drum. He cultivates it as a favorite plant—waters it, prunes it and supports it with sticks. Whenever this subject comes up, he seems inspired; 'State rights' is his department, as much as the 'Navy bill' is that of Mr. Mallory, or the 'Pacific railroad bill' of Mr. Gwin."

A noted reception of the season was given at the mansion of the Secretary of the Interior, Mr. Guthrie's. The elegant Mrs. McLean, wife of Judge McLean of the Supreme Court, was a prominent attraction. Conspicuous among the belles in the dancing-room was Miss Morgan of Kentucky, a queenly looking girl in black velvet and pearls, who walked through the figures like an empress. She was chaperoned by Mrs. Crittenden. Few men in the Senate made so distinct and definite an impression upon the public mind as Judge Douglas. A letter writer remarked: "His figure, short, stout and thick, would have been fatal to the divinity of the Apollo Belvidere. His features are rather stern and heavy, and if it were hinted that there was a vein of acrimony in his character, you imagine what expression that keen eye will take, that heavy eyebrow and that firmly set mouth, when he is belaboring the republican party. But when he rises to speak, you forget everything, except his ability. Bold and independent in utterance, he has the power of thrilling his hearers; rapidity and boldness of thought are his inseparable attributes. He strikes on all the hard, strong points of his subject till they ring again. His language is always sharp, clear, strong and knotty; never soft; seldom beautiful. With a whole storm of unpopularity roaring around him, he sternly pursues his course; breasting the storm, combating the surge." Mr. Hunter, the distinguished Senator from Virginia, "wears his garments in a fashion that shows his abhorrence of restraint; for his clothes would be an equally good fit for any other Senator. His neckcloth tied carelessly, leaves his throat half bare; and a lock of hair is always falling over his forehead, or tossed behind his ear. Though negligent, he is never slovenly."

General Cass struck one at first sight as a man of thoughtful and reflective habits. Amid the noise and confusion going on around him, he would sit calm and abstracted, listening benignantly to the business before the Senate, and patting his hands in unconscious approval. His looks showed no gayety, and he appeared absorbed in his own reflections. His life, said a lady who studied him, "substantiates in the clearest manner two principles of the highest importance to the aspiring statesman; that the nation eminently honors political integrity and private worth, and that no ability destitute of moral character can hold a permanent ascendency in the public mind. Lofty in character, honoring the moralities of private life, superior to the temptations of public gain, his life affords a useful lesson." An athletic figure, and features handsome and clearly cut, belong to Senator Toombs. His "thick black hair clusters in heavy masses above an expansive forehead and dark eyes. He takes rank as one of the best speakers in the Senate. His extempore remarks are quick, reasoning, and acute; and there is always an imposing vigor in his language, tones and gestures. His voice is sharp and high, sometimes shrill and dissonant, lacking the round, full, mellow tone. His warmth and nervous energy make him a most attractive speaker. His colleague, Judge Iverson, has a marked Scotch physiognomy, and a serious dignified expression. He is distinguished in the Senate for sound sense and accurate judgment. His argument is clear; his reply to objections rapid and conclusive; with little declamation, he is simple, searching, strong, seldom impassioned, always in earnest.

The most elegant party of the season was an elaborate entertainment given at the mansion of Governor Aiken, member from South Carolina, who, in the six years passed in Washington, had contributed largely to the entertainment of the fashionable world. It was known that he was about going abroad to reside some years, and this was his farewell fête. Mrs. Aiken, a graceful woman, with a form of perfect symmetry, draped in embroidered brocade which fell around it in heavy waves of silver, and splendid in diamonds, received the guests with her daughter, a young girl in white illusion with white lilies in her hair, with a quiet manner and air of gentleness. The walls of the ball-room were decorated with a profusion of evergreens and flowers, and the orchestra platform was almost hidden by festooned branches and laurel wreaths. One of the distinguished guests was George Peabody, the world-famed banker; and passing down the room with the air of a queen, with perfect features as if carved in marble, white and smooth as marble, too, with clear liquid eyes and shadowy lashes, was Mrs. Douglas, wife of the Senator from Illinois. Near her stood a sylph-like form, a lady with low white brow and wealth of golden curls, and sunny smile and fair cheek lightly tinted with crimson; the daughter of Major Smith, recently married to Mr. Holt, an eminent lawyer of Louisville, Kentucky. Seated upon a lounge, with a circle constantly around him, was a gentleman "with a superb head, and a face that wore a beaming smile as if he loved the whole world. He is not an old man, but there is a patriarchal pathos in his expression and manner." This was Mr. Henry Schoolcraft, the author of "Schoolcraft's Indian History." He was not in the habit of going out to entertainments, having long been helpless from paralysis of the limbs; he was at this party in compliment to his old friend Governor Aiken. His placid cheerfulness under affliction, the result of faith in God, had a better influence than all the compliments his learning won from literary societies, and the private letters from the great minds of Europe.

The season of Lent put a stop to the large dancing parties, substituting the more unpretending social reunions. One of the most agreeable was given by Mrs. Watterson, to enliven the retirement of her invalid daughter, one of the most cultivated and intellectual ornaments of society. The poet, Rufus Dawes, was one of the guests. A lady remarked "the repose in his manner which seemed to infuse into everything about him something serene and refining." The busts of Benton and Chief-Justice Taney, by Dr. Stone, said to combine the delicacy of Powers with the elaborate execution of Greenough, were so much admired, that the sculptor was commissioned by Congress to furnish a statue of John Hancock for the east wing of the capitol. Mr. Kingman, "the Napoleon of correspondents, the Talleyrand of admiring editors and bewildered politicians,—sitting in critical judgment upon governments, dynasties, presidents and cabinets"—was present, and also a distinguished artist, the son of Judge Cranch of the District Court; while among the ladies were conspicuous Miss Lea, the daughter of the former "Indian Commissioner," and Miss Fendall, a versatile and brilliant belle, a privileged wit in society; expected to say what no one else could, with face "full of a hundred laughing fancies." Her father was a leading lawyer.

A visitor to the Senate chamber was old Mr. Bradley, a veteran from Vermont. He was Senator for that State in 1812. Yet he looked younger than General Cass, who was at that time a young lawyer in Detroit. A number of Senators crowded round him, enjoying the jokes he dealt out with great liberality. His last visit before this had been in General Jackson's Presidency. "I went to see the General," said he, "and he set me down in his arm-chair, and giving me a slap on the leg, said: 'What a hearty old cock you are, Bradley! What makes you so fat?' 'I don't know, unless it is that I haven't got any office, and don't want any.' I ain't much of an idolater, but I've kept those pants till now that the General gave such a familiar slap." The jolly and venerable Senator weighed about two hundred and fifty.

Among the New Year's receptions the favorites were those of Senators Slidell, Seward, Fish, Douglas and Bright, Governor Aiken, Speaker Banks, Mr. Pennington, &c.

XVII.

BUCHANAN'S ADMINISTRATION.

The "Pilgrims" to Wheatland—Dan Dougherty—Fancy Characters assumed by the Ladies at a Ball in Washington—Excitement in the Federal City—Procession of Citizens to escort the President Elect—The Inauguration—The Mysterious Old Man at Capitol Hill—Sketch of Buchanan and Breckenridge—General Lewis Cass—Other Members of the Cabinet—Arrival of Lord and Lady Napier—Miss Harriet Lane's first Reception—First Dinner Party—Lord Napier's Hospitality—Mrs. Alexander Slidell—Mrs. Rose Greenhow—New Regime at the White House—Superb Entertainment at Governor Brown's—Sir William and Lady Ouseley—The Elite of Society at Secretary Thompson's—Ladies Described—The Charming Miss Ellen Woodbury—Lady Napier's Party—Scene in the Gallery to hear the Vote on the Kansas Question—Lord Napier's Party to Mr. Everett—Mr. and Mrs. Charles Eames—Mrs. Pickens.

AFTER the nomination of Mr. Buchanan at Cincinnati, Lancaster became a point of universal interest and importance; the Mecca to which the hopes of hungry office-seekers were turned. One day a personal friend, who wanted no office, finding him surrounded by fifteen or twenty "pilgrims," apologized for his intrusion. "My dear sir," cried Mr. Buchanan, "I shall be most happy at any time to see you, either here or in Washington, the more especially as I know you are not after an office. This office-hunting, sir, is a most miserable life." One Dan Dougherty, on a mission to Wheatland, found a score of "pilgrims," and drawing his chair close to the President, began to talk in an undertone. The ex-minister at the court of St. James did not relish this breach of politeness, and after manifesting his uneasiness in silence, rose and said: "Mr. Dougherty, I desire you to understand, my dear sir, that I will not receive suggestions from any man in regard to my appointments." That single shot winged the flock. It was understood that Mr. Buchanan's nephew was to be his private secretary; his niece doing the honors of the White House.

"The last hop of the season" was given in the parlors of Brown's hotel on the 26th February, and the lady guests agreed to appear "in character." Mrs. Bocock of Virginia, wore black, sprinkled with gold stars and a crescent on her forehead as "Night." Miss Bennett of Mississippi, as "Morning," was in white, with a long white veil. Mrs. Williams of Tennessee, was "The Goddess of Liberty," in silk of "red white and blue," with a miniature banner and crimson cap. Miss Faulkner, of Virginia, was "The Daughter of the Regiment," looking soldier-like with her little drum. Miss Patterson, daughter of General Patterson of Philadelphia, personated the Pompadour, in powdered hair and antique dress. Lady Macbeth was represented by Mrs. Hopkins of California, robed in maroon velvet edged with fur, and wearing a gold crown set with jewels. Miss Richardson of Kentucky was the Spanish Queen; Miss Benson the French peasant girl; Mrs. Richardson, of Boston, the Countess of Belmore, with dashing scarlet hat and feathers. Mrs. Burt, of Ohio, one of the most charming ladies in Washington, appeared as Lady Byron, in orange-colored silk covered with lace. Miss Disney, of Ohio, and Miss Zimmerman, of Baltimore, were attractive in their own beauty and sparkling wit, as was Miss Patterson of New York. The leading characteristic in the society of the capital was its continual change. Personal friendships and strong social ties were formed among those temporarily thrown together during the sessions of Congress, too often only to be severed at the adjournment.

Some Italian republicans sent to Mr. Buchanan a beautiful enamelled gold chronometer watch. On the front of the case was a finished likeness of the Emperor and Empress of Austria, painted on the blue enamel surrounded with a richly wrought wreath. The portrait of the Archduke Maximilian was on the back, similarly ornamented. It was to be presented before the inauguration, after which the President could not receive a gift from any foreign power or people.

Once more the Federal city was the scene of universal excitement. General Pierce's cabinet had their last meeting; the President and cabinet took possession of the Vice-President's room for the night, for the convenience of approving the bills passed by Congress; the Judges of the Supreme Court waited on Mr. Buchanan, at his rooms at the National; Mr. Breckenridge had arrived and was surrounded by his friends, and President Pierce gave his last reception to a committee of the city authorities and the citizens. At Wheatland a procession of citizens came to escort Mr. Buchanan to the railway station. All manner of public demonstrations evinced the respect and good wishes of the people.

On the 4th March, an aged man, apart from the crowd, might have been seen plodding his way towards Capitol Hill. He had witnessed many inaugurations, seated on a particular stone in the same spot; and when the first gun announced that the ceremonies were complete, he would always rise, and pronounce the name of the new President and his date in the order of succession of Chief Magistrates; then significantly ask: "What next?" and then take up his line of march for his home in Virginia. It was said this pilgrim had enjoyed the rare honor of taking by the hand, and breaking bread with, all the Presidents of the United States. His youth had been spent at the seat of government. On the inauguration of Mr. Madison in 1809, he took a somewhat remarkable part in the events of the day. When the President retired, the crowd rushed on, leaving the avenue nearly deserted; and then appeared, on horseback, and entirely alone, Thomas Jefferson. The old pilgrim pointed out this spectacle to two Revolutionary officers—Colonel Thomas Parker and Major Butler, saying: "See, gentlemen, how soon a great man becomes neglected, and his services forgotten in America, when he ceases to be the fountain of patronage and power! Whatever may be the Revolutionary patriot's and statesman's politics now, they were of the right sort in 1776, and led to the independence of his country. Honor to whom honor is due!" The Revolutionary veterans now begged to be introduced; and the small party falling into line, the retired Chief Magistrate was escorted down the avenue by a trio of his political opponents. The pilgrim's stone had been removed to make way for the improvement of the grounds; but people looked for the pilgrim near the ancient spot, and listened while the echoes of the artillery were sounding, for his impressive words: "James Buchanan, fifteenth President of the United States. What next?" On that morning the President and Vice-President elect took their seats in the carriage, and moved amid the cheers of the crowd to the capitol. Next to them was the Liberty car, surmounted by a pedestal on which stood the Goddess of Liberty, magnificently attired, supported by a liberty pole fifty feet high, and drawn by six horses. A full-rigged ship was drawn by horses; the sailors were seen engaged in the rigging, and on deck, in their various duties as if at sea. After Mr. Buchanan delivered his inaugural address, and took the oath of office, he was conducted to the executive mansion, at the door of which the ex-President left him. The inauguration ball was given in an immense building erected for the purpose on Judiciary Square. The list of managers included Senators and Representatives from almost every State in the Union, and fifteen thousand tickets were sold.

General and Mrs. Pierce took up their temporary abode at Governor Marcy's.

James Buchanan was a native of Pennsylvania, and born in 1791. In 1820, he was chosen to represent his district in Congress, continuing ten years in that body. In 1831, Jackson tendered to him the mission to St. Petersburg. In this post he rendered the country valuable services, and negotiated the first commercial treaty between the United States and Russia, securing to our commerce the ports of the Baltic and Black Seas. In 1845, he accepted the office of Secretary of State under President Polk. He was appointed minister to England by General Pierce after the return of Mr. Lawrence. At the time he became President he was in his sixty-fifth year. John Cabell Breckinridge, thirty-six when nominated for Vice-President, was the only son of a distinguished member of the legal profession, and a prominent politician of Kentucky. His mother was a daughter of Rev. Samuel Smith, President of Princeton College, New Jersey, and the grand-daughter of John Witherspoon, one of the signers of the Declaration of Independence, and a lineal descendant of the Scotch reformer, John Knox. General Lewis Cass, the Secretary of State, had been a prominent public man for half a century, occupying posts of high distinction, and, whether as a military man, an administrator, a diplomatist or a statesman, showing himself capable of filling the most eminent position. He was a native of New Hampshire, but studied law at Marietta, Ohio, whither his father had removed. In 1831 he was called by Jackson to the War department, and after his retirement accepted the mission to France. Though seventy-five years of age, he was younger than most men at sixty. The Secretary of the Treasury was Howell Cobb, of Georgia, who had been in Congress, the faithful and efficient advocate and defender of the rights and interests of his own section of the country. John Buchanan Floyd, of Virginia, Secretary of War, had long been a prominent politician in the western part of Virginia, and had been Governor of the State.

He was connected with the first families, facetiously called the "F. F. V's." He was a fluent speaker, and was between forty-five and fifty. Jacob Thompson, of Mississippi, Secretary of the Interior, was a mild looking man, about forty. He had been a member of the House, and an able Speaker. Aaron Venables Brown, was a Virginian, educated in North Carolina. He had been Governor, as well as member of Congress, and was said to be sixty-two. It was to him General Jackson had addressed his celebrated letter in favor of the annexation of Texas; and Mr. Adams, in reply to his speech, had miscalled his name, and dubbed him "Aaron Vail Brown." Senator Benton founded his famous joke on this mistake, and made him "Aaron Vicarious Brown." The Attorney-General was Nathan Clifford, of Maine, a portly gentleman of forty-five, who had been minister to Mexico.

Lord Napier, the new British minister, arrived in March, accompanied by Lady Napier, four children, their governess and tutor, and two men and two women servants. His lordship was only thirty-eight. He belonged to a noble Scotch family, tracing its lineal descent as far back as the fourteenth century to John de Napier. He had gained some literary celebrity by his "Sketches of Russia," and was a gentleman of refined and cultivated tastes. Lady Napier was a woman of remarkable beauty, with attractive and engaging manners, and an amiable character.

The obsequies of Mrs. Joseph Wilson, a lady of note in Washington society, took place in March. Mr. Buchanan's first reception was given on the 6th March, and was very largely attended. All the foreign legations were represented, and a great number of officers of the army and navy were present; while the rooms presented a splendid array of beauty. Miss Lane's first reception at the White House and the first executive dinner party were given late in March. When news arrived of the death of the President's nephew, Eskridge Lane, the White House was closed the day the despatch came.

Chevalier Hulsemann, ambassador from Austria, had some dispute with the master of a negro woman whom he had hired, and the master, meeting the slave in the street, bade her go home to his house. The woman obeyed; and the worthy Chevalier invoked the interposition of the State department, to defend his right as Minister Plenipotentiary against interference with his servants! General Cass wrote him a long letter on international law and the privileges of ministers; a humorous thing, it was said, which afforded no small amusement in social circles. Lord Napier's large family and intentions to give social entertainments, required a large house; and he preferred Senator Fish's house, in the center of the city. He was more given to hospitality than any foreign minister who had ever lived in Washington.

For eleven years Judge Andrew Pickens Butler of South Carolina had occupied his prominent position in the Senate, and all who heard him speak, recall the picturesqueness and vigor of his style. "There was a glow, a quick, expansive feeling in his speaking, like the outpouring of an improvïsatore; in his style of thought and utterance there was something vivid, heroic and generous. The qualities of his heart softened and checked the impulses of a fiery temper and vehement will."

One of the leaders of fashion was Mrs. Alexander Slidell. It was said of her: "Her influence in society is remarkable. Were she to appear attired in a tunic and zone, the ranks of fashion would swarm with Cordelias and Agrippinas. Were she to discover an eighth deadly sin in the vulgarity of robust health, chicken broth would become the rage." Mr. Buchanan tendered to F. W. Pickens of South Carolina, the post of ambassador to Russia. His high personal character and rare abilities well fitted him for so distinguished a position. Count de Sartiges, the French minister, was pronounced by Mr. Marcy, "a concentration of diplomatic tact." Some wags used to say that with him the decalogue was superseded by an eleventh commandment: "Thou shalt not be found out." "Judge Wayne, of the Supreme Court, passes along in dignified abstraction, looking like a portrait of St. Jerome by the tender pencil of Guido."

The name of Joseph Gales is inseparably connected with that of "The National Intelligencer." "Whether we view this venerable chief editor of the chief organ of the 'old line whig party,' as the acute critic, the fervid politician, or the high-minded and generous man—we have before us one of the ablest men of the day." Mr. Harris, the principal editor and proprietor of the "Union," was pronounced by the ladies "a fine specimen of a Virginia gentleman." The election of Judge Nicholson as Senator from Tennessee was heard of with pleasure in the capital, where he had lived four years as editor of the Union. The family of the Postmaster-General also made a charming addition to the society of the city. Mrs. Rose Greenhow, who was imprisoned as a rebel during the war, was a sister of Mrs. James Madison Cutts, and the aunt of Mrs. Stephen A. Douglas. A journalist called her "a bright and shining light in those gay secession circles which ruled the court and cabinet under the diluted rose-water administration of Mr. Buchanan." She was one of the brilliant coterie of which Mrs. Slidell and Mrs. Gwin were the ruling spirits. Mrs. Gwin was the widow Logan of Texas, and had rich lands in that country. The grandest masquerade ball ever given in Washington was at Senator Gwin's about this time. Mr. Kingman appeared as President Monroe, dressed by Mr. and Mrs. Gouverneur in the very court dress Monroe wore at the French court as ambassador. Miss Arabella Young—a belle of distinction, became the wife of Albert G. Brown of Mississippi. The opening of the new regime at the White House was very animated. But in most of the entertainments the Southern element of vitality was sadly missed. That spirit, vivacity, hilarity, and universal abandon to the enjoyments of the hour, which had so enlivened society, was found wanting. Studied propriety and cold formality ruled more decidedly; and the general expression was solemn rather than cheerful. The cabinet receptions of Buchanan's opening administration, it was understood, would commence much earlier than those of their predecessors. The known wealth and elegant style of living of the members, led to pleasing anticipations, and gorgeous preparations of costume. Mr.

Benton's health had improved since his severe illness; but his evident debility caused sad forebodings.

In January, 1858, a superb entertainment, said to be the most brilliant ever given in Washington, came off at the residence of the Hon. A. V. Brown of Tennessee. The ball-room was lined with mirrors extending from floor to ceiling; the drawing-rooms on the other side of the entrance-hall, richly furnished, were adorned with flowers from the White House conservatories. Mrs. Brown, an elegant looking woman, wore rose-colored brocade and point lace; her daughter white tissue embroidered with moss rose-buds with pearls and natural flowers. Among the distinguished guests was Sir William Gore Ouseley, whose massive head and waves of gray hair showed intellectual dignity suited to his majestic figure. Lady Ouseley, wearing a beautiful head-dress and diamonds, stood near Lady Napier, who was dressed in white, with a head-dress of scarlet honeysuckles. "She is winning all hearts by the sweet, womanly attributes of her character; lending a grace to her high position by never seeming to lose sight of her happy fireside and domestic pursuits." Dr. Charles Mackay, the English poet, was also present. He had a slight figure, and seemed inclined to avoid observation. A fine-looking man, whose dress glittered with foreign orders, was the Count de Sartiges, "a matchless diplomat, said to coquet with our negotiations." Madame de Sartiges was attired in white embroidered crape, with flowers of light green spray. The financial world was represented in Mr. Baring, the great London banker. The niece of Mr. Thompson, the

Secretary of the Interior, a lady from Mississippi, attracted attention by her delicate, spiritual face. Mrs. Slidell appeared in a Russian court dress—a crimson velvet cap trimmed with rich lace and ostrich feathers, and a black velvet dress, the small jacket trimmed with gray fur. In the center of the supper-table stood a bouquet of immense height, of japonicas and hot-house flowers. One ornament was a mammoth "nest," containing two harnessed swans driven by a man, made of sugar and snowy white. This party was followed by one at Governor Floyd's, of unusual splendor. Mrs. Floyd "was a type of the quiet, serene excellence of woman; one of that class who hold aching heads and bathe hot temples, and sit and watch" beside the couch of pain. She and her daughter, Mrs. Hughes, received the brilliant company. The central figure among the guests was the stately one of General Scott. He appeared in full uniform; his commanding mien and stern face indicating that what he says is law; "his very step has a quarter-deck brevity and decision." A young officer beside him was Major Calhoun, the son of the great statesman. The wife of Captain Goldsborough of the navy, the daughter of the distinguished William Wirt, was much noticed among the ladies. There, too, was the thin, slight, contracted figure and the striking face, with sharp, angular features, of William H. Seward. Lady Ouseley's expressive face and exceeding grace made her conspicuous; and near her could be seen the queenly form of the wife of the Russian minister, conversing in French. The nephew of the President elect was noticed, and Colonel Carpenter, an eminent lawyer from Kentucky, and a "rising man" as well as a ripe scholar.

Mr. Jefferson Davis was thus described by an eyewitness in the Senate chamber: "His first sentence was the signal for profound silence and attention. His keen eye literally blazed as he poured forth a torrent of withering sarcasm and crushing invective. This burst of eloquence, this torrent of oratory, sparkling and flashing, did not last more than thirty minutes. We think a cool criticism will place Mr. Davis nearer to Mr. Clay than any speaker in the Senate. He has much of Clay's purity and flow of style, richness of imagination, and graceful elocution."

The *élite* of Washington society was assembled at an entertainment given at Secretary Thompson's. The charming hostess had been a favorite from her first appearance for her gracious kindliness, and the piquant animation of her manners. There was the usual circle of Senators' wives, diplomats, and ladies of the cabinet; and the Secretary was seated in a small anteroom, in vain seeking freedom from state cares in the shape of applications for office. The "far-famed Benjamin Perley Poore," known as a ripe scholar and an able writer, and noted "for his conscientious payment of a wager on Mr. Fillmore's election—wheeling a barrel of apples a distance of thirty miles"—could be seen, with his wife, a daughter of Mr. Dodge. The ball given by Miss Saunders, on the 25th February, was supposed the closing one of the season. The fair hostess wore illusion over white silk, finished with rose-color quilling, and was aided by her mother in receiving the guests. Lord Napier, quiet and reserved as usual, was among them, with his gentle and accomplished wife; and Colonel Raslof, the Danish minister, with expressive face and light mustache; also General Hearney, the hero; and the violet-eyed Miss Lane, supported by Mr. Clingman, "the bachelor member from North Carolina;" General Ward, and the Texas ranger, Major McCullough; and one of the new administration belles, the niece of the Secretary of the Interior; and Miss Cass, with her striking intellectual face and melancholy eyes; and the host's beautiful niece, with oriental eyes and dress of point lace over canary-colored satin. A regal looking lady, with stately head crowned with raven hair and princely port, was a daughter of Duff Green, and a sister of Mrs. Calhoun. The new member from Charleston was noted for polish and courtly ease, "a South Carolinian to his finger tips." A graceful beauty with soft blue eyes and glowing complexion, was Miss McGuire; and Mrs. Crittenden wore a superb blue moire with point lace trimmings; beside her the wife of the Russian minister. The successor to the lamented Butler in the Senate, was "a noble-browed, middle-aged man, who maintains a species of dignity of all dignities the most imposing." At political dinners he was a courted guest; and he was marked as a gentleman of cultivated mind and extended intelligence. In speech he had the self-possession of an habitual debater. Not far from Mr. Hammond was the youthful form of one of the celebrities of the day—recognized by the fashionable eye; one who had lately left the House for the Senate chamber. He had taken his position in that body as one of its rising statesmen. Thomas L. Clingman was complained of by some as a cold and calculating politician; but his benevolent acts were known to all who knew him well.

The season of Lent, putting an end to crowded balls, replaced them by more agreeable reunions. One in March at the residence of Sir William Gore Ouseley, was remembered. The house was illuminated; but there was no confusion; no shouts of wrangling coachmen outside, nor clamor within when the Hungarian footman, in silver livery and crimson-topped boots, threw open the door. The names of guests entering the reception-room were announced by an English butler in a stentorian voice. Lady Ouseley's grace, elegance and self-possession were admirable as usual. One of a cluster of gentlemen in the drawing-room was the great orator, Mr. Everett; and Lord Napier could be seen talking to Mr. Seward of the beauties in the room. Not far off was seen "the mild face of the widow of Judge Woodbury. Thorwaldsen might have taken a model of her countenance for that of the mother of the Maccabees in his celebrated group." There, too, was her daughter, elegantly dressed without pretension, and the wife of the Senator from New Jersey; and Miss Cass, with her pale face and stylish air; and the soft-eyed daughter of the Attorney-General; and "the handsome nephew of our Delaware Senator, of whose family it is said—Before them the Deluge!" There was the Mexican minister "with his foreign face and the rich glow of a Titian's head;" the quiet and unpretending daughter of the Secretary of War; the wife of the Secretary of the Interior, surrounded by a host, to each of whom she seemed to have something brilliant to say; and the finished gentleman of the Virginia school, Mr. Harris, editor of the Union; and the youthful face of Mrs. Brown, the wife of the Postmaster-General, the fair representative of Tennessee. The daughter of Mrs. Brown was equally charming and lovely. Mr. Brown was said to have seriously impaired his fortune by his lavish hospitalities in Washington. The parties at his house were frequent and very brilliant. Mrs. Brown played the harp admirably.

Dinners were a prominent feature of Washington life, and the cards of invitation were sometimes issued two weeks beforehand. They were often given, as were evening parties, at "those brown-faced Babylons,"—the hotels. An elegant party came off at the National in March, and among the fair celebrities were the wife of General McQueen, with a head-dress of wondrous pearls, and the wife of Senator Brown of Mississippi, in crimson moire, with point lace trimmings; with other distinguished persons. At President Buchanan's levee the Turkish admiral created a sensation. He and his two attendants, one of which was the interpreter, were dressed like other people, except a conical red silk cap pressed down over brow and ear; while the chief wore the crescent with a splendid diamond star. In a little circle of gentlemen was noticed the Secretary of War, Governor Floyd.

Mr. A. V. Brown's figure was stout and portly; his face open and full of benevolent expression. His hair was threaded with silver, though he was scarcely beyond middle age. The dignity and purity of his life caused him to be respected, and his speeches indicated an elegant taste for literature as well as sound intellect. At a reunion at his house his daughter's music on the harp and piano formed a great attraction. The new Senator from Minnesota, Mr. Rice, and Governor Foote were present. Lord Napier gave one of the most elegant parties of this season. Coroneted carriages deposited their inmates at his door, and the pompous butler admitted many groups of distinguished citizens. The youthful belle selected by Lady Napier to open the festivities, was the daughter of Captain Dahlgren of the navy. The British minister gave another entertainment in May, to celebrate his Queen's birthday. Lady Napier had a wreath of water lilies in her hair, surmounted by a tiara of diamonds and emeralds. Lord Napier's costume glittered with gold lace elaborately wrought, and Baron Stoeckl, the Russian ambassador, appeared in a coat decorated with silver lace, and a drawing-room hat ornamented with a curled ostrich plume. The French minister wore a cherry-colored badge across a coat that blazed with imperial stars and orders. The stately form of Mr. Hope, secretary of the British embassy, was seen with left breast studded with medals, the Queen's gift for his bravery while an officer in the Crimea. His wife was a beautiful, gentle-looking woman. Among the American ladies, the wife of the Senator from Illinois was transcendent in beauty. Near at hand was M. Bantinetti, the Sardinian minister, in full court dress; with the wife of the distinguished member from Virginia, Mrs. Faulkner, in blue silk with flounces of

Mechlin lace; and the daughters in snow wreaths of illusion. The Speaker of the House, Mr. Orr, had there thrown off the toga of public life; and Mr. Breckinridge, called one of the best bred men in Washington, was there; with the nephew of Lord John Russell, speaking with fluency several languages; Mrs. Crittenden in pea-green moire with point lace bertha; Mrs. Pringle of Charleston, in superb attire; the eminent banker, Mr. Riggs, and General McQueen, prominent in society as an excellent husband, with the refined and agreeable Mr. Toucey, Secretary of the Navy, Commodore Breese, and Mr. Lamar of Mississippi.

A *soirée musicale* had been given by Lady Napier on the first of the month. Mrs. Gwin's fancy ball excited the fashionables to the highest pitch of enthusiasm; and scarcely less was awakened by the bridal party given at the residence of the Attorney-General, Judge Black, in compliment to his daughter. The celebrities of the diplomatic world, French, English, Spanish, Danish, Russian, Austrian, &c., were seen; and the superb Mrs. Slidell, in black velvet with bandeau of pearls, and the wife of the Secretary of the Interior, in blue silk and Mechlin lace flounces; Mrs. Crittenden, "with her perfect coiffure, her air of society, her easy manners," and the wife of the Secretary of the Treasury in a magnificent blue moire.

The deepest interest was excited in Washington by the announcement that the final vote on the Kansas question would be taken; and every corner was filled in the ladies' gallery of the Senate chamber, with an assemblage of the beauty and intelligence of the city. There was unusual excitement; Senators talked in knots and groups. On the southern side numbers were gathered round a pale, ghastly-looking person, his eye bandaged with strips of white linen, his whole aspect denoting feebleness. This was Mr. Jefferson Davis, come out for the first time since his illness, to vote on the measure. Governor Brown, with flushed and excited face, was pacing, with Senator Toombs, the space back of the Speaker's chair. Mr. Hale's jovial face was overcast with sombre expression. Mr. Seward wore a look of inscrutable thought.

This most brilliant of seasons became lively as it drew near its close. In June Lord Napier gave a delightful party to Mr. Everett, then on his way southward. Numerous celebrities, political and diplomatic, crowded around Mrs. Crittenden, to compliment her on the able speech of her husband in the Senate; and there was Sir William Gore Ouseley, and the bachelor, Colonel Keitt, of South Carolina, devoted to the ladies; and Mrs. Gwin, the wife of the Senator from California, most elegantly dressed; and General Hearney, leading Miss Pleasanton, a great social favorite; with Miss Saunders, and Madame Albeynerz, wife of the Brazilian minister; and Mrs. Zulee, daughter of Mr. Wickliffe, a former Postmaster-General; and the Attorney-General, Judge Black, whose daughter had so lately given her hand to her father's private secretary.

The summer heats now substituted small social gatherings for evening receptions. A very noticeable one was given in June by Mr. Evans, at which were Lady Ouseley and her beautiful sister Mrs. Roosevelt

MISS ELLEN WOODBURY.

Eng^d by H. B. Hall, N. Y.

of New York, and other distinguished persons elsewhere named, with the lovely wife of Senator Dickson from Connecticut, and the stately Senator from Texas, General Houston, whittling a heart for a charming lady from Texas, niece of the host. The past winter had been one of unprecedented brilliancy. Perhaps at no time before had a cabinet included so many examples of beauty and elegant taste, or had a Washington season boasted so many magnificent entertainments. To many a belle the season had been one long triumph; to many a political dinner-giver it brought pecuniary embarrassment. As early as the following October there was evidence of preparation for the season shortly to open.

On the 29th January, President Buchanan gave one of the largest and most brilliant levees that had been seen for years. Several members of the cabinet, all the leading republican Senators and Representatives, almost the entire diplomatic corps, a large number of army and navy officers, and a splendid array of ladies were in attendance. The President looked well, and was very talkative. One of the new arrivals was Dr. Middleton, a young physician who had not long before removed to Alabama, and settled there in the practice of his profession. For expressing his opinions he was expelled from the State with his family, on a notice so short that he had hardly time to pack his trunks, and was obliged to sacrifice his horse and carriage and other property.

At a levee where Miss Benton and the daughter of General Scott attracted much attention, the lovely Miss Woodbury of New Hampshire was surrounded by satellites. She was called "the most beautiful lady that graced the east room." Another report styles her *the* belle of the city, to whom "the palm is always given;" "very handsome and very popular, dancing well," and charming in conversation. At Newport and other summer resorts she was the reigning belle and the star of admiration, and always surrounded by a host of admirers. Her captivating style of beauty was always dwelt on with rapture. On one occasion her rich dress was described as corn-colored silk covered with lace, with a splendid necklace and six large bouquets which had been presented. "Bright and beautiful" ever, her presence was the ornament of every assembly. "A face so refined and sweet, a person so sylph-like, could only exist in harmony with a lovely soul." Her appearance as "Queen of the Gypsies," at a fancy ball in Washington, in a picturesque dress, dispensing fortunes to her numerous admirers, created a great sensation. One observer wrote: "As for her grace, we have seen a whole battalion of admirers surrender their senses at witnessing her movements in the waltz and polka."

During this administration, Mr. Charles Eames returned from Venezuela, where he had been minister four years, and Mrs. Eames, the daughter of Judge Campbell of New York, became a leader in Washington society. She gave informal receptions, and made her house exceedingly attractive as the resort of the most distinguished men and charming women. Her powers of mind, and quick perceptions, her brilliant wit and droll way of saying clever things, delighted every one. She had a dry quaint humor which is very rare, and adds a wonderful charm to conversation. After the death of her husband in 1867 she went to Europe.

The wife of Governor Pickens of South Carolina, was a native Virginian. Her maiden name was Lucy Holcombe, and she was born in Lynchburg. The family afterwards removed to La Grange, Tenn., fifty miles from Memphis, and subsequently to Marshall, Texas, where she was married to Governor Pickens immediately before his departure to St. Petersburg. Her first cousin was Professor Holcombe of the university of Virginia.

XVIII.

BUCHANAN'S ADMINISTRATION.

The Expected Visit of the Prince of Wales—His Arrival—General Cass introduced by Lord Lyons—The Prince at the White House—Visits the Capital—Reception in Honor of Him—Game at Ten-pins with Miss Lane—Diplomatic Dinner, and Evening Reception—The Prince at the Tomb of Washington—Dinner at Lord Lyons'—The Prince a "Heart-smasher"—Sketch of Harriet Lane—Her Marriage—Letter of Queen Victoria—Of the Prince of Wales—Political Excitement—Mr. Crittenden's Great Speech—His Dinner Party—Senator Toombs and General Scott—The President's last Levee—Display of Martial Preparation around Washington—The Peace Commissioners—Imposing Scene of Counting the Electoral Votes—Noted Men present and their Manifestations of Interest—Douglas and Lane—Abraham Lincoln declared President—Quiet dispersion of the People.

The Prince of Wales was expected to visit Mr. Buchanan as a private gentleman, and not in royal state. The well-bred citizens of Washington understood this, and arrangements were made accordingly. He was to arrive by a special train, on the 3d October, 1860, and proceed directly to the executive mansion; the company invited to meet him at dinner consisting of the members of the cabinet and their wives, with a few other ladies, the British minister and his first Secretary of Legation. Another dinner-party at the President's was to be attended by the Foreign Ministers, Senators, the Mayor of Washington, the Assistant

Secretary of State, and their wives, besides the Prince's suite. Lord Lyons was to give a dinner on the following day.

On the arrival of the royal train, awaited by a thousand spectators at the station, General Cass was introduced by Lord Lyons to the Prince, and with the minister and the Duke of Newcastle, accompanied him to the White House. General Cass presented His Royal Highness to the President, while Lord Lyons introduced the suite. The gates of the President's grounds, meanwhile, were closed against intrusion and guarded by the police. General Cass having been born before the treaty of peace—was born a British subject according to the theory of the British constitution. He had been present at the coronation of Queen Victoria.

The next day the Prince and suite visited the Capitol, and inspected the various halls, rooms, works of art, &c. At twelve the President gave a public reception in his honor, held in the east room; Mr. Buchanan and party standing in the center, the persons introduced entering at the left-hand door, and leaving by the large folding-doors on the right. There was a great crowd and rush, and many of the ladies were magnificently dressed, though full dress was not insisted on. The Prince wore his usual blue coat and gray pants, and with ungloved hands, stood on the right of the President—Lord Lyons near him—the royal guest bowing his head to those who were presented. Several of the ladies succeeded in shaking hands with him. A boy four years old, a lineal descendant of Robert Bruce, dressed in Highland garb, attracted his particular notice. In half an hour he was so much fatigued that the reception was closed, to the chagrin of many who were unable to effect an entrance. After luncheon the royal party went to see the public buildings. Accompanied by Miss Lane and Mrs. Thompson, the wife of the Secretary, the Prince and his party then visited Mrs. Smith's Institute for young ladies, remaining two hours, and expressing themselves delighted with the visit, especially to the gymnasium, where the royal guest enjoyed several games of ten-pins with Miss Lane, laughing heartily at the sport, and exercising himself in the gymnastics. The society of ladies seemed the more agreeable to him from his long deprivation of it, and though too tired for receptions he was never weary of going out with his charming hostess.

Mr. Buchanan's conversational powers attracted the admiration of his English guests at the dinner. It was rather a bore to the Prince, however, to attend the diplomatic dinner given the same evening at the President's—which was a splendid affair, though enjoyed but indifferently by him. Miss Lane sat between him and the Duke of Newcastle; Madame Gerolt and Mrs. Slidell sat on either side the President. At nine Miss Lane held her reception, for which only two or three hundred cards were issued, as the object was to give the favored guests an opportunity of observing the elaborate fireworks. The Prince, with the President and Miss Lane, appeared on the balcony, and was heartily cheered by the crowd.

The next morning the royal party, accompanied by the ladies of distinction, the President and Lord Lyons, went to Mount Vernon. Mrs. Riggs, Vice-Regent of the Mount Vernon Association, acted as chaperone on the grounds, and other visitors were excluded. The Prince stood reverently uncovered in the room where Washington died, and all expressed gratification at the taste and neatness displayed in the arrangements. The marine band, in a neighboring thicket, played a solemn dirge while the party stood before the tomb of Washington, the Prince, the President and the party grouped in front, and a cloud softening the sunlight. Royalty thus contemplated the last abode of one pronounced a rebel and a traitor by his ancestors, and now in rank above the kings of earth. The scene was indeed historical. At the request of the ladies, the Prince planted a young horse-chestnut tree on a little mound, in commemoration of his visit.

On their return the steamer went slowly up the Potomac; the deck was cleared for dancing, and the Prince danced with Miss Lane and Miss Slidell; also with Miss Gwin, Miss Riggs and Miss Ledyard. The party drove, on landing, to Lord Lyons' house and remained to dinner. Lord Lyons' magnificent service of plate was displayed to advantage. In the center of the table stood the large golden tray, with three ornamental gold vases, which, with the porcelain vases at the ends of the table, were filled with flowers. On the side-boards and rich beauffets more splendid plate appeared. On either side of the host were Miss Lane and the Prince. Opposite sat the President, with the cabinet and diplomatic corps.

The Prince remained at the White House that night, and on the 6th, proceeded to Acquia Creek, on the way to Richmond. He took an affectionate leave of his host and hostess, with mutual wishes for their future health and prosperity. When the royal party was gone, Washington again assumed its usual "recess" look, and the fashionable quarter its aspect of solitude. Sir Henry Holland remained till Monday, the guest of Mr. Buchanan. The ladies all agreed that the young Prince was a "heart-smasher,"—and many of the rough old fellows, too, were captivated. The diplomatic corps, according to etiquette, made no personal calls, but merely left their cards.

It will be but meager justice to Miss Lane, to give a brief sketch of her, which may be appropriate here.

Miss Harriet Lane is the youngest child of Elliott T. Lane and Jane Buchanan, and passed the earliest years of her life in the village of Mercersburg, in the midst of an intelligent and refined society. Left an orphan at nine years of age, though independent in fortune, she accepted a home with her uncle James, preferring his guardianship to that of any other relative. She attended school in Lancaster. When twelve years old she was sent with her sister to a select boarding-school in Charlestown, Va., where they remained three years. Afterwards, Harriet was sent to the convent in Georgetown, a justly celebrated seminary. In her visits every Saturday and Sunday to her uncle—then Secretary of State, she met the best society of the country.

Miss Lane was a blonde, with deep violet eyes, golden hair, classic features and bright expression, and a mouth of peculiar beauty. Her form had a statuesque majesty, and every movement was grace. She was noted for good taste in dress. At Wheatland she entertained her uncle's friends and foreign visitors, with lady-like courtesy and cordiality. She was in the habit of reading the newspapers to her uncle, and afterwards discussing with him the political and literary subjects of the day. Her domestic occupations were frequently interrupted by visits to the principal cities, and in Virginia.

She first met Mr. Johnston at Bedford Springs in 1849, during the annual visit made there by herself and Mr. Buchanan. In 1852 she accompanied her uncle on his mission to England. Her first appearance at the Queen's drawing-room, produced a marked impression; and on many occasions she received flattering attention from the Queen and other members of the Royal Family. The years spent by her in England were very happy ones, and she greatly enjoyed a tour in Europe and the months spent in Paris with Mr. Mason's family.

Jefferson Davis, who was not friendly to Mr. Buchanan, remarked to Dr. Craven at Fortress Monroe: "The White House under the administration of Buchanan, approached more nearly to my idea of a Republican Court, than the President's house has ever done before since the days of Washington." This brilliancy was in part owing to Miss Lane.

It was a memorable occasion when the Prince of Wales stood beside the President before the gateway of Washington's tomb; when the great grandson of George the Third paid homage to the memory of the chief who took away the brightest jewel in his imperial crown; when the heir to William the Conqueror's throne bowed his knee before the dust of the greatest rebel of all time!

After the Prince's return to England, the Queen sent the following autograph letter to the President:

"WINDSOR CASTLE, November 19th, 1860.

"*My Good Friend*,—Your letter of the 6th ult., has afforded me the greatest pleasure, containing as it does, such kind expressions with regard to my son, and assuring me that the character and object of his visit to you and to the United States, have been fully appreciated, and that his demeanor and the feelings evinced by him have secured to him your esteem and the general good-will of your countrymen.

"I purposely delayed the answer to your letter until I should be able to couple with it, the announcement of the Prince of Wales' safe return to his home. Contrary winds and stress of weather have much retarded his arrival; but we have been fully compensated for the anxiety which this long delay has naturally caused us, by finding him in such excellent health and spirits, and so delighted with all he has seen and experienced in his travels.

"He can not sufficiently praise the great cordiality with which he has been everywhere greeted in your country, and the friendly manner in which you have received him; and whilst, as a mother, I am most grateful for the kindness shown him, I feel impelled to express, at the same time, how deeply I have been touched by the many demonstrations of affection personally toward myself which his presence has called forth.

"I fully reciprocate towards your nation the feelings thus made apparent, and look upon them as forming an important link to connect two nations of kindred origin and character, whose mutual esteem and friendship must always have so material an influence upon their respective development and prosperity.

"The interesting and touching scene at the grave of General Washington, to which you allude, may be fitly taken as the type of our present feelings and I trust, of our future relations.

"The Prince Consort, who heartily joins in the expressions contained in this letter, wishes to be kindly remembered to you, as we both wish to be to Miss Lane. Believe me always your good friend,

"VICTORIA R."

The Prince of Wales sent the following note:

"JAFFA, March 29th, 1862.

"*Dear Mr. Buchanan,*—Permit me to request that you will accept the accompanying portrait as a slight mark of my grateful recollection of the hospitable reception and agreeable visit at the White House, on the occasion of my tour in the United States.

"Believe me, that the cordial welcome which was then vouchsafed to me by the American people and by you as their Chief, can never be effaced from my memory.

"I venture to ask you at the same time to remember me kindly to Miss Lane, and believe me, dear Mr. Buchanan, your very truly,

"ALBERT EDWARD."

The Prince also presented to Miss Lane a set of engravings of the Queen and other members of the Royal Family. He informed Lord Lyons that he had asked the young lady to accept them, and would send them through the minister from Portland. This was done: Lord Lyons placing them in the hands of the lady to whom they were addressed..

In January, 1866, Miss Harriet Lane was married to Mr. Henry Elliott Johnston. After spending a month or two in Cuba, they took up their residence in Baltimore.

Among the queens of society wherever she went, was the beautiful wife of Mr. Alexander Jeffrey, Rosa Vertner Jeffrey. In her visits, brief as they were, the impression she made was always abiding. This lady's literary fame—as one of America's most celebrated poets and prose writers, though endearing her to thousands who do not know her, has not lessened the influence of her personal merits. She deserves a more extended mention than this volume can afford.

On the last day of 1860, "The whole city is on the

tiptoe o. expectation in regard to the President's special message on South Carolina affairs. Not only politicians, but nearly all families accustomed to attend to public matters, took an early start this morning. Breakfasts were dispatched at a comparatively primitive hour, and with amazing celerity, and before eleven o'clock carriages and other private vehicles were competing with crowded omnibuses for the quickest arrival at the capitol, while the sidewalks of Pennsylvania avenue were densely filled with pedestrians of all ages and ranks and of both sexes, tramping through the snow-slush to the same point.

"The President's house was besieged all the forenoon by anxious inquirers; but Mr. Buchanan, quietly engaged in the library with his secretaries, was denied to all visitors. At a quarter before twelve the cabinet was summoned. Among the first arrivals were Secretaries Thompson and Thomas, thus putting a stop to the unfounded rumors respecting their resignations. No political news being within ear-shot of even the detectives, the inquisitive crowd was obliged to be content with observing the preparations by the workmen and servants for the New Year's day reception on the morrow.

"Miss Lane having returned on Saturday evening from Philadelphia, whither she had gone to attend as first bridesmaid the marriage of her friend Miss MacAlister to M. Berghmann of the Belgian Legation, will, by her presence, add to the attraction of the public reception to-morrow. At eleven o'clock the diplomatic corps will be received; they and the different attachés to the legations will appear in full court costume. Next in order will come the Chief-Justice and the associate judges of the Supreme Court; then the officers of the army and navy in uniform, preceded by Lieutenant-General Scott and the senior commodore now in Washington. As the wives and daughters of the members of the cabinet, of the Senators and Representatives, have the *entrée* about the same time, the blue and green parlors will present a dazzling show of brilliant and many-colored dresses and of distinguished men and lovely women. The general reception will begin at twelve. The President will receive his fellow-citizens in the blue parlor, whence they will pass to the green parlor, into the east room, and thence make their egress through the great front window, between which and the pavement a temporary bridge has been constructed."

"The feature at the capitol to-day, (January 3, 1861,) was the speech of Judge Douglas, who followed Senator Baker of Oregon. The 'Little Giant' was never in better voice, health or spirits, and his speech was almost Websterian in its power, logic and eloquence. The republicans do not like it, because he laid the present troubles at the doors of the politicians of their party; and the secessionists do not speak favorably of it, because denied the right of secession; but the great mass of the middle-men, the center and heart and main dependence of the country in the hour of danger, applaud it as one of the greatest speeches delivered in the Senate since the days of Henry Clay. The galleries were again crowded to suffocation."

A few days later: "The affairs of the country are every day getting into a more critical condition.

Wave succeeds wave, and the ship of state labors fearfully in an angry sea. Mr. Crittenden's glorious speech, delivered during the morning hour of the Senate to-day, is the topic of eulogy in every circle to-night. The venerable Senator had an interview of two hours with the President on Saturday. Mr. Toombs is willing to stand by Mr. Crittenden's proposition, and in this he speaks for the whole South. Why will not the North meet the South on these terms of accommodation? Can either section expect anything better? The universal sentiment among the Union members of Congress and the most influential circles in Washington is in favor of this proposition. The President elect is understood distinctly to favor it. Here, then, is a ground on which all parties may meet and save the Union, and preserve the country from the disasters which are about to be brought upon it by short-sighted politicians.

"Senator Crittenden gave a dinner party at the National to about thirty of his personal friends, among whom were Lieutenant-General Scott, Judges Nelson, Campbell, Clifford and Catron of the Supreme Bench, several Senators and Representatives of all parties, and prominent citizens of Washington. The brother of Major Anderson, who had returned from a visit to Fort Sumter, was also among the guests.

"Senator Seward has had a late dinner party at his residence to-night, at which many conservative men of all parties were present, and not a few that were at Senator Crittenden's dinner. There was considerable excitement among the extremists North and South, consequent upon the belief that the two Senatorial dinner parties given by Crittenden and Seward are intended to sell them out. The subject has been discussed to-night by the strict Chicago platform republicans, and the result will be a stern resistance in the Senate and House against any compromise." It was plain that a broad and satisfactory compromise must be initiated within ten days, or the country must choose between the recognition of an independent southern confederacy or the suicidal folly of a civil war. "The defeat of Crittenden's compromise creates intense feeling. Nearly every moderate democrat declares that 'now the thing is up, and we must prepare for the worst.'"

Ex-President Tyler, one of the commissioners from Virginia to consult with the Executive on the state of the country and advise some measures of adjustment, arrived in January. He was in precarious health. He had an interview with the President, at which several prominent gentlemen were present. Mr. Tyler was invited to sojourn at the White House.

Such extracts may show the effect of the times upon the aspect and feeling of social circles. It is no part of the design of this book to touch on political matters.

"At a private dinner party yesterday, high words passed between Senator Toombs and Lieutenant General Scott. According to relations in Congressional circles, the conversation turned on the sending of troops to Charleston, when Senator Toombs expressed the hope that the people there would sink 'The Star of the West,' by which reinforcements were sent. The General, with much earnestness, asked whether it was possible that he, as an American, desired such an event. Mr. Toombs replied affirmatively, and said that those who sent the vessel there should be sunk with her. General Scott thereupon remarked that he was responsible for what he said, and Mr. Toombs responded, 'You have known me for twenty-five years, and are aware that I too am responsible.' The matter here ended; but the subject, it is said, is in the hands of friends."

"The President's levee was held on the 15th January, an elegant affair. Probably a similar scene never occurred in the White House before. With very few individual exceptions, the party that elected Mr. Buchanan to the office he now holds, was absent. The party that opposed him and has increased in numbers every day since it did so, was represented by its best men now in Washington. One of the officers of the White House remarked at the close of the levee, that he never saw so many republicans there before.

"Mr. Buchanan was warmly greeted by the republicans, and he conversed pleasantly with each of them. Lieutenant General Scott was absent on business, but several of his staff were present; also General Harney and a number of other army and naval officers. Colonel Hayne, who comes here claiming to represent South Carolina as a separate confederacy, approached the President at the White House to-day; but the President promptly disposed of him by not recognizing him as anything else than a citizen of another State. The interview was exceedingly brief."

Mr. Buchanan gave his last levee on the 12th February, 1861. It was most largely attended, and the most brilliant of all during his administration; and it was stated that five thousand were in attendance; amid the throng the venerable heads of the Peace Congress being prominent, and all the leaders of the incoming administration who were in the city. Governor Chase of Ohio was there; and the representatives of the army and the navy were attired in their gorgeous warlike trappings.

The President seemed well satisfied that the end of his office drew near, and Miss Lane never did the honors more gracefully. She was dressed in pure white, and was surrounded all the evening with hosts of friends and admirers, each of whom had a parting word to say. The number of ladies present was unusually large, and everybody seemed to be merry. The band played "Away down in Dixie," and closed with "Yankee Doodle."

The display of martial preparation about Washington gave rise to rumors that caused many persons to regard it as in a most perilous position. Yet matters in the Federal city continued to go on pretty much in the old style, and the scenes were similar to others just prior to inauguration day in the more staid and secure times of the republic. In social matters there was little change. Fashionable "hops" were less frequent, but the deficiency was made up in dinner parties and other more private entertainments. The occasional appearance on the avenue of small squads of the uniformed "regulars" brought to mind the startling stories about the seizure of the capital: but the very air and faces of those guardians of the public peace tended to satisfy one that nothing was further from them than the idea of actual service in that locality. The jolly darkies and "gemmen" of leisure moved carelessly about, whistling "Yankee Doodle," "The Star Spangled Banner," and other national melodies, as though peace had just been declared with some hostile foreign power; and all seemed very odd to those who came expecting to elbow their way through fields of bayonets and revolvers, instead of white kids, white vests and rustling silks.

"The Peace Commissioners, after adjournment, sit long at table, drink their wine with gusto for men who come on such a solemn errand, and 'coerce' the best of Havanas in great profusion, looking remarkably wise, and saying but little when inquired of as to the probable result of their labors of love and patriotism. Last evening a large number of them, including the Rhode Island and other peace delegations, had a jolly old time at the house of Governor Corwin. Friend Cheever, by the bye, the dashing representative from 'Nyatt,' is assisting Mr. Corwin this winter in doing the honors of his hospitable mansion. The throngs about the hotels and the capitol are immense. Members are button-holed about most unmercifully, and from the occasional sentences overheard in passing, it is very evident that visitors here do not contemplate the destruction of the offices if they do that of the government. Thurlow Weed is here, doing his best to get some kind of temporary or permanent fastening about the bodies of the border States. His idea is that if Uncle Sam is not rich enough to keep

ROSA VERTNER JEFFREY.

house alone, he could get along, perhaps, for awhile by taking boarders."

The scene of counting the electoral votes was thus described: "The Senators having appeared in the hall of the House of Representatives, and the Vice-President of the United States having assumed the chair of the Speaker, the committee appointed to count the electoral votes, and the other officials being properly disposed of about the Speaker's and Clerk's desks, let us look down upon the unique and imposing throng, and observe who compose it. Directly in front of the gallery, and facing the Vice-President whose duty it is to declare the result of the vote, is Stephen A. Douglas of Illinois. He is at once the center of all eyes as well as seated in the center. On his right is the Premier of the incoming administration—William H. Seward; on his left General Lane. Beside Seward is Senator Cameron of Pennsylvania. The familiar and easy manner of these men towards each other is believed to be indicative of their warm and intimate relations, political as well as personal. Sweeping around a gentle curve, still to the right facing the chair, are Senators Foot of Vermont, Doolittle of Wisconsin, Grimes of Iowa; and close beside each other are Daniel Clark of New Hampshire, and Charles Sumner of Massachusetts, looking quietly on with apparent indifference, as if feeling that his hour of triumph had arrived in the election of a republican President. Just beyond these twain we catch a glimpse of the bushy gray head of the unwearied Senator from Rhode Island, J. F. Simmons.

"On the left of Judge Douglas, we find, calm as a

June morning, the erudite Judge Collamer, Senator from Vermont; the brilliant-minded and silver-tongued Fessenden of Maine; the industrious and able Powell of Kentucky; the clear-headed Fitch of Indiana; the go-ahead and self-willed Ten Eyck of New Jersey; and beside him, in deep contemplation profoundly wrapped, is the new Senator from 'away down East,' Morrill of Maine. Hard by, looking as if he had not more than his share of care on his mind, is K. S. Bingham of Michigan. In the second aisle of seats is the patriotic, self-sacrificing, Union-loving, and indefatigable laborer for his whole country, the venerable Senator from Kentucky, John J. Crittenden. To the right and left we have Senator Pearce of Maryland, Senator Andrew Johnson of Tennessee, in confidential confab with the spirited and talented Etheridge of the same State. There, too, is Senator Baker of Oregon, looking a little more gray and bald than he did twenty-five years ago, when he and Colonel John J. Hardin used to crack jokes together in Jacksonville, Illinois. The worthy Senator looks a little more bald than when he first came to Washington this session, having probably worn a good deal of his hair off in rubbing through the Pacific Railroad bill, of which great project he is a firm and steadfast friend. That queer, rough, but intelligent looking man with Bahn is old Senator Wade of Ohio, who doesn't care a pinch of snuff whether people like what he says or not. He is a patriot who believes he could pass the gates of St. Peter whether entitled to or not, if he was only wrapped in the American flag. Near Wade are Senators Bigler of Pennsylvania, and Bragg of North Carolina; the former bearing his usual steady, careful, thoughtful front. Not far off you see the smooth face and marble brow of Senator Wilson of Massachusetts, with the honest features and sturdy frame of Chandler of Michigan. You may ask: 'Who is that burly-framed individual talking to Representative Spaulding of New York?' 'Do you mean him with the Atlas shoulders?' 'No, he can't be an Atlas man—not the "Albany Atlas," at any rate; for those men have not that amount of girth.' 'Ah, I see! That is Preston King of New York, who has as much weight in the Senate, and probably will have as much in the next administration as any other man.' Then come before your vision the faces of Senators Rice of Minnesota, and Latham of California. Near them sits Senator Hale of New Hampshire, talking to Mr. Hamilton of Texas. They pause in their conversation to hear Representative Phelps declare the vote of Illinois. It goes for Lincoln. Douglas smiles faintly but good-humoredly, and twitches his cane closer between his legs. Lane, sitting beside Douglas, does not care to hear how his State, Oregon, has gone; and proposes to leave. 'No, no, General,' says Douglas, laying his hand pleasantly on Lane's shoulder: 'You have heard how my State has gone, now let us hear about yours.' Lane subsides into his seat, and shortly afterwards Senator Trumbull, who alternated with Phelps in announcing the vote, declared that even his State—his beloved Kentucky—had gone against her favorite son. It is a somewhat remarkable fact that not one of the States to which two of the Presidential and one of the Vice-

Presidential candidates belong, cast its electoral vote for either. Douglas lost Illinois, Breckenridge Kentucky, and Lane Oregon.

"When at twenty minutes before two o'clock, Vice-President Breckinridge declared in a distinct and audible voice, that Abraham Lincoln, of Illinois, was elected President of the United States for four years from the 4th of March next, there was in that immense throng of five thousand people, a breathless and almost deathly silence of a moment, as if every one was expecting the occurrence of some long hidden and dreadful catastrophe. But the stillness of the moment was only disturbed by the clear voice of the Vice-President, announcing the election of 'Hannibal Hamlin, of Maine, as Vice-President of the United States for four years from the 4th of March next.'

"And then the people, without a cheer, without a murmur of dissatisfaction; without the firing of artillery or the rattling of musketry, quietly dispersed to their homes, thankful in their hearts that at least one threatening ordeal in our country's history had been passed through peacefully and happily."

XIX.

LINCOLN'S ADMINISTRATION.

Dangers ahead for the New President—Visitors to him in Springfield—The Delegates to the Washington Conference—Farewell Party given by Mr. and Mrs. Lincoln—Sketch of Mrs. Lincoln—Progress to Washington—The President's Military Escort—Gorgeous Reception in New York—Ladies of Mrs. Lincoln's Party—General Doniphan and "Old Abe"—Notices of Lincoln and his Cabinet—Gorgeous Scene of the Inauguration—Attendance at the Ball—Appearance of Mrs. Lincoln and other Ladies—The first Levee a "Monster Gathering"—An English Tourist's Description of Lincoln—Other Prominent Men—Mr. Sumner—Mr. Stanton—Wendell Phillips—Alexander H. Stephens—Lincoln's humorous Advice to Lord Lyons—Crowded New Year's Reception—Hon. James W. White—Mrs. Farragut—Hon. Judge Brewster—Financial Movements.

AMBITIOUS souls might now have looked with envy on Abraham Lincoln; but there was danger that the very tide of fortune that carried him to the highest place might whelm the inexpert steersman. Shoals and rocks without number were ahead, and the chances for utter wreck were equal to those for safe landing. Few mortals ever carried a heavier load than that likely to rest on his shoulders. Nor could it be concealed that the burden already felt was beginning to tax to the utmost his patience and power of endurance. The grandeur of the mission he was called on to fulfil, as head of a nation of thirty millions, caused him more anxiety and embarrassment than hope and exultation. He was now chiefly occupied in receiving visitors at his home in Springfield, Illinois, conducting negotiations for the completion of his cabinet, and attending to his correspondence. The general crowd of place-seekers had to content itself with one hour a day of audience, and they were admitted in mass, not separately. His correspondence had so increased that his servant was met in the vestibule of the post-office carrying a large market-basket full of letters. They were opened by the private secretary, who determined their importance from the signatures, those coming from obscure sources, and petitions for office, being consigned to the fire.

The delegates to the Washington conference, to assemble by invitation of Virginia, were James S. Wadsworth, a wealthy gentleman of the western part of the State of New York; Greene C. Bronson, an eminent lawyer of New York; Erastus Corning, a well-known democrat, financier, railroad manager and politician—the member of Congress elect from the Albany district; William M. Evarts, a New Englander by birth but a resident of New York, where he pursued the legal profession with ability and profit; he early linked his political influence with the republican party; David Dudley Field, a New Englander by birth, a lawyer, and a republican politician; William Curtis Noyes, a celebrated lawyer and republican politician. Salmon P. Chase was one of the bright and shining lights of the republican party. Born in New Hampshire in 1808, he removed early to Ohio, and finally qualified himself for the legal profession in Washington, D. C., was admitted to the bar there in 1829, and returned to practice in his adopted State. He took but slight part in politics till 1841. In 1848 he was elected to the United States Senate, and became Governor of Ohio in 1855. Thomas Ewing had been Secretary of the Treasury in the Harrison administration. He was an old-line whig. David Wilmot was the author of the celebrated proviso bearing his name. Governor Charles S. Olden of New Jersey was sixty-two, and in mercantile life had acquired a fortune. Richard F. Stockton, a native of New Jersey, had risen to the highest rank in the navy, and in 1851 was elected to the United States Senate, where he displayed splendid talents. He was possessed of wealth. Alexander Duncan was one of the wealthiest men in Rhode Island, and father of the senior member of the firm of bankers, Duncan, Sherman & Company. James Guthrie had been Secretary of the Treasury in Pierce's administration. After his retirement from public political life, he devoted his time to railroad enterprises, and to the enjoyment of social and domestic intercourse. James B. Clay, the son of Henry Clay, was an ex-member of Congress. Charles Wickliffe had been in Harrison's cabinet, and was afterwards Governor of Kentucky. William O. Butler was one of the early settlers of Kentucky, and had taken an active part in the Indian wars in the early history of that State, and in the war of 1812. John Tyler, ex-President of the United States, was the chairman of the Virginia delegation. He was Governor of that State in 1826, and subsequently in the Senate, till, on a difference of opinion between General Jackson and himself, he resigned his seat and went into voluntary retirement, not making his appearance again in public life till 1840, when he was nominated for Vice-President by the whig party. After the expiration of his term of office, he lived in retirement, and was at this time seventy-one years of age. George W. Summers was distinguished as a literary character. Ex-Judge Brockenbrough was one of the most distinguished jurists in Virginia, and a descendant of a high family. William C. Rives was an eminent lawyer, who had represented Virginia in the United States Senate. He was minister to France under the Harrison administration. David S. Reed was ex-Governor of North Carolina. Mr. Morehead was ex-Governor and ex-Senator. Thomas Ruffin was ex-Chief-Justice of the State. D. M. Barringer was appointed minister to Spain by President Taylor. Reverdy Johnson of Maryland was a distinguished lawyer, and an ex-member of the United States Senate and House of Representatives. He was Attorney-General in the Fillmore administration. Alexander William Doniphan of Tennessee had some celebrity as colonel of the Tennessee regiment of volunteer cavalry in the Mexican war. All these had been prominent in the society of the capital.

It was arranged that the President elect and his suite should leave Springfield on the 13th February, the party consisting of fifteen persons. Mr. and Mrs. Lincoln gave a party to their friends at their house in Springfield on the 6th. Seven hundred ladies and gentlemen, composing the political *élite* of the State, and the beauty and fashion of the town and its vicinity, were present, while the host and hostess did the honors with dignity and affability. A splendidly ornamented sewing-machine was presented to Mrs. Lincoln.

Mrs. Lincoln is the daughter of Hon. Robert Todd, of Lexington, Ky., who had held high places of trust in the State, and was universally esteemed. Clay and Crittenden were his intimate friends, and were often entertained at his hospitable mansion. His wife was a niece of Governor Porter of Michigan and Pennsylvania. Their eldest daughter married a son of Governor Edwards, the first United States Senator from the then territory of Illinois. Mary Todd, early bereaved of her mother, spent much time with her sister in Springfield. The last four years of her school days were passed at Mde. Mentelle's select establishment, opposite Mr. Clay's house in Lexington, where a near relative, Margaret Wickliffe, afterwards Mrs. William Preston, was her room-mate. The young ladies continued intimate friends till the civil war; and during that, Mrs. Preston often sought Mrs. Lincoln's help, to be permitted to join General Preston. Miss Todd returned from school to Springfield, when only seventeen, and was soon admired in a select society of gentlemen, of whom many became distinguished. Judge Douglas was one of her persistent suitors. Abraham Lincoln paid his addresses three months after the first meeting with the lovely and accomplished girl, who alone of all her sex had ever touched his heart. He had never sought any other woman's society. He courted her devotedly for three years, and during the twenty-two or three years of married life that followed, he remained the fond lover as well as the affectionate husband and father; never absent from his wife more than a day without sending daily letters; sharing with her the joy of every success; finding no happiness so great as that of the home brightened by her. She shared with him the anxieties that accompanied his elevation to the Presidency, as well as the affliction of losing his gifted son; seeking relief from sorrow in visits to the hospitals where her kind ministrations to the suffering soldiers might do them good, and bathing eyes swollen with weeping when duty called her to the drawing-room reception. Mrs. Ann S. Stephens, the distinguished novelist, often accompanied her on these visits of mercy, and described the scene as most interesting—to see the wife of the President walking for hours through the wards to say cheering words of hope and encouragement to the wounded and sick; laying fresh flowers on their pillows, and offering them delicacies brought from the White House. Her carriage would be laden with flowers and baskets of dainties, fruits, &c., for these hapless ones. In strawberry time her gardens would be stripped for their benefit. She often assured Mrs. Stephens that but for these humane employments, her heart would have broken when she lost her child. No one who knew her could doubt Mrs. Lincoln's possession of a feeling and noble heart.

The progress of the President elect was a continued ovation. Mrs. Lincoln, with her sons and party, joined him at Indianapolis and the united family proceeded through Indiana. The reception at Cincinnati was an era in the history of the Queen City. His handshaking exertions made the poor man somewhat stiff;

and his voice was slightly hoarse from speaking in the open air at the different stopping-places. His good humor, however, was unimpaired, and Mrs. Lincoln conversed in a lively manner with the ladies and gentlemen around her. At Albany the Governor proposed to entertain the honored guest at his own residence, but was censured for his wish to monopolize Mr. Lincoln. At this time Mrs. Lincoln had two married sisters on a visit at Montgomery, Ala. One was from Kentucky, and visiting her sister who resided at Selma, Ala. Both were secessionists, and opposed to the government of their brother-in-law; of course they attracted much attention, and were the toast of Southerners.

Of Lincoln's military escort, Colonel E. V. Sumner had served forty years in the army, and spent most of his life in the saddle, west of the Mississippi, participating in the whole of the Mexican war. His form was erect and his faculties were unimpaired, the result of an active, temperate life. He was one of the most efficient officers and brightest ornaments of the army. Major D. Hunter had served also with distinction in the Mexican war. Mrs. Hunter was a native of Illinois. The family was wealthy, and celebrated for hospitality and cultivated taste. Captain George W. Hazard was a hero of the Mexican and Florida wars, and of many skirmishes with the Indians, being an excellent officer and a cultivated gentleman. Captain John Pope, a son of Judge Pope, was a soldier and a gentleman of profound scientific attainments. Those four had been detailed by the War department to escort the President elect to Washington. Colonel Ward Hill Lamon, a lawyer of high standing, was with the party as a personal friend to Mr. Lincoln. Colonel E. E. Ellsworth, of United States Zouave Cadets fame, excited general admiration for the manner in which he managed to protect the President from the importunities of curious crowds. Among the civilians N. B. Judd of Chicago, a lawyer of great ability, and an old and tried friend of Mr. Lincoln, was prominent. He was of middle size, rather heavy set, with florid countenance and flowing gray hair and beard; and was often recognized by an unlighted cigar protruding from his lips. Judge David Davis of Illinois, probably attracted more attention than any other member of the suite, by virtue of his rotund figure, the humor of his broad good-natured face, and the roars of laughter in which he almost constantly indulged. Without his mirthfulness, the trip would have been a dull affair. He was a distinguished republican leader of his State, an intimate friend and former partner of the President, a man of judgment and discretion, of great talent, penetrating mind, and first-class acquirements.

The private Secretary of the President was John George Nicolay, a German by birth but educated in America. He was of slender figure and pale but handsome features, wearing a mustache and goatee, and was remarkable for intelligence, industry and discretion. John M. Hay, assistant Secretary, was an Illinois lawyer, of splendid talent and high culture, though a very young man. His handsome form and noble presence were said to have deeply impressed the belles of Springfield, and awakened no little emotion among those of Washington. Dr. W. S. Wallace, the brother-in-law of Mr. Lincoln, accompanied him as his physician. He had lived in Springfield a quarter of a century. His manner was quiet, but his even temper and good humor made him an agreeable companion. Lockwood M. Todd was a cousin of Mrs. Lincoln, and had come from California to see the family safe to Washington. George Latham was a college chum of "Bob," and had all the gay and easy ways of the "Prince of Rails." Lastly, a useful member of the party was the mulatto William, who took care of the company with untiring vigilance.

The reception of the President elect in New York was a gorgeous one, and detailed with a great variety of incident by the reporters. Mr. Lincoln remarked, in favor of his lady visitors, that "their hands did not hurt him." Five gentlemen and six ladies formed the party at dinner. Mrs. Hamlin had been received at the entrance of the Astor House, and given in charge to Mrs. Follansbee, who had the care of the Presidential and Vice-Presidential ladies. The little boys went to Laura Keene's theater, showing great anxiety to be off before the nurse was ready to go, and expressing fears that "it will be all over before we get there, if we do not make haste." Another time the family visited Barnum's Museum with Mrs. Lincoln, described as "a handsome, matronly lady." She received calls from the ladies stopping at the hotel, in company with Mrs. Edwards and Mrs. James Watson Webb. Her dress was steel-colored silk, made high in the neck, with trimming of box-plaited satin ribbon, a small lace collar fastened with a diamond brooch, diamond ear-drops, and black chenille and gold head-dress. Mrs. Webb wore a dark-colored merino, cashmere shawl and black velvet bonnet; Mrs. Edwards a dark-colored silk, sprigged with small bright flowers. The ladies carried bouquets, and Mrs. Lincoln had a small ivory fan with which she occasionally fanned some of the gentlemen who paid their respects to her, playfully telling them "not to get too warm in the cause." Mrs. Webb introduced the ladies to Mrs. Lincoln, whose smile was a pleasant and amiable one, with a frank and lady-like manner. All agreed that she would fill her high position with ease and dignity. In two hours about a hundred ladies were presented. During the evening a delegation from the Young Men's Central Campaign Club was presented to Mrs. Lincoln by General Webb. Mrs. Lincoln's sister and niece arrived from Boston, to accompany her to Washington and assist in inaugurating the hospitalities. Miss Lane had sent an invitation to Mrs. Lincoln to come directly to the White House on her arrival—an act of courtesy highly appreciated by all intelligent classes. The party, however, went to Willard's, where a suite of five elegantly furnished rooms had been appropriated to their use.

When the tall General Doniphan of Missouri was introduced, "Old Abe" had to look up to catch his eye. He immediately asked: "Is this the Doniphan who made that splendid march across the plains, and swept the swift Camanches before him?" "I commanded the expedition across the plains," modestly responded the General. "Then you have come up to the standard of my expectation," rejoined Mr. Lincoln. Democrats as well as republicans were pleased with the new President; and the ladies, who at first thought him awkward, changed their opinion and declared him "a very pleasant, sociable gentleman, and not bad looking by any means."

A brilliant dinner party was given by Mr. Spaulding to the President and Vice-President elect on the 28th February, attended by distinguished and intellectual guests. After returning from the dinner, Mr. and Mrs. Lincoln held a levee at Willard's, receiving a vast number of ladies and gentlemen. The music of the marine band brought an immense crowd to the front, and Mr. Lincoln appeared on the balcony. Mr. and Mrs. Hamlin also had an ovation at their hotel. The lady had become exceedingly popular among the élite of the metropolis.

Abraham Lincoln was born in Kentucky, in 1809. He was educated in Indiana, and in 1830 removed to Illinois. Elected to Congress in 1846, he served three years, distinguishing himself by his pertinacity in sustaining the Wilmot Proviso, and his opposition to the Mexican War. He was first brought into public notice by his memorable campaign against Douglas for the Senatorship. Hannibal Hamlin was a native of Maine; of about the same age as Mr. Lincoln, and a lawyer by profession. He was a Senator of the United States, and Governor of Maine. William H. Seward, the Secretary of State, had a large and lucrative practice as a lawyer. Early in his public life he had traveled in the Southern States, and was supposed then to have formed his opinions hostile to slavery.

In some respects he was among the foremost of American statesmen, and was said to have "the best and clearest head in America." Salmon Portland Chase, Secretary of the Treasury, had studied law in Washington under the celebrated William Wirt, then Attorney General. General Simon Cameron, Secretary of War, was a native of Pennsylvania. To no single man within her borders was Pennsylvania more indebted for her great systems of public improvement and public instruction. Maryland was represented in the Lincoln cabinet by Judge Montgomery Blair. His father was Francis P. Blair, well known in General Jackson's time. He was in the prime of life and mental vigor, and was very popular with the republicans of the North and West. He was the son-in-law of Levi Woodbury. His wife is a brilliant and charming woman. Gideon Welles, of Connecticut, had been for thirty years a leading politician. Edward Bates, Attorney General, was a native of Virginia, and considerably advanced in years. He was a shrewd, quiet lawyer, and was made a judge, and had been complimented by two colleges with the honorary degree of LL.D.

As of old, the scene of the inauguration was a gorgeous pageant, witnessed by assembled thousands. The two Presidents went to the ceremony in the same carriage, which was so closely surrounded by marshals and cavalry as to hide it from view. No shot could have been aimed at Mr. Lincoln through such a dense military enclosure, and the apprehensions of a murderous plot were quieted. When he left the carriage, Mr. Lincoln walked slowly to the threshold of the capitol, leaning on the arm of his predecessor, and looking pale, fatigued and anxious. His vivacity appeared to have deserted him, and the instant he passed the portals, he hung his head and looked fixedly upon the marble tiles. He proceeded to the President's room on the Senate floor. The line of procession to the portico was formed, and when they reached the platform, Senator Baker of Oregon introduced Mr. Lincoln to the assembly. He was received with cheers. Laying down his manuscript, he pulled from his pocket a pair of steel-bowed spectacles, and proceeded to read the address in a clear and distinct voice. The oath of office was then administered by Chief Justice Taney, who seemed agitated with emotion. It was the eighth ceremony of the kind at which he had officiated. The President was then escorted to the White House, where Mr. Buchanan took his leave of his successor, and retired to the residence of District Attorney Ould.

General Scott had made the most extensive arrangements for the preservation of order. His officers were continually passing to and fro, and he was heard to utter a devout expression of thanks to the great Ruler of events, that everything was going on peaceably. When a portion of the crowd came to pay their respects to him, the appearance of the gigantic form of the Commander-in-Chief upon the porch of his house was a signal for a burst of the wildest enthusiasm. Standing erect in noble dignity, in a voice half choked with emotion, he congratulated his "friends" that one of the great saturnalias of the nation was safely passed. He announced himself "the oldest servant of this mighty republic, of which we are all pillars and supporters. He had labored fifty years to serve the country." At eleven that night the President and Mrs. Lincoln, attended by a numerous suite, and followed by Mr. and Mrs. Hamlin, entered the room of the Inauguration Ball. Five thousand were said to be present. The distinguished guests were welcomed by enthusiastic applause, and a fearful quantity of handshaking ensued. All eyes were turned on Mrs. Lincoln, whose exquisite toilet and admirable ease and grace, won compliments from thousands. Several of the new Cabinet, the English, French and Russian ambassadors, Senators, Members of Congress, the Army, Navy, &c., were present.

In entering the room, Mrs. Lincoln followed her husband, leaning on the arm of the self-possessed Senator Douglas. He reminded her of a playful prediction that her husband would be President, years before. Some one in the crowd observed that "she would have made a better match for Judge Douglas than 'Old Abe,'" probably because they were more nearly of the same hight. Vice-President Hamlin had a very dark complexion, with a pleasant face that wore no marks of care. An eye-witness said: "Mrs. Lincoln, always amiable and dignified, was to-night more charming than ever. Mrs. Baker, her sister-in-law, was escorted by Governor Yates of Illinois. Mrs. Yates wore white silk, with cherry-colored double skirt. Mrs. Berghmann, wife of the Belgian minister, was dressed in white watered silk. Mrs. Hoover, one of the most agreeable ladies adorning Washington society, was dressed with perfect taste in violet-colored brocade silk with heavy flounces; a wreath on her head. Miss Helen Green wore the Union costume. Miss Alice Green was greatly admired in her dress of blue tarletan flounced to the waist, with a bertha of Honiton lace. Mrs. Parker, a leader of the *ton*, wore stone-colored silk with black lace; Miss Fanny Parker white tarletan with gold trimmings. She was one of the most engaging and accomplished young ladies seen. Mrs. Stone, wife of the celebrated Dr. Stone of Boston, wore white brocade silk. Mrs. Samuel A. Way of Boston, an attractive and interesting lady, was attired in a rich black velvet, with diamonds to the value of at least eight thousand dollars. Her sister, Mrs. Cutting, a lovely, bright-eyed, graceful young widow, wore, also, plain black velvet, with a pearl necklace and other jewels. Mrs. Fenton had on a rich brown silk with velvet arabesque; her majestic mien showed her a woman of intellect and cultivation. Her daughter Josephine was in pure white, and beautiful as a just-opened lily." This was called "The Union Ball;" but, alas! with the true Union severed, many sad associations were called up. The South was unrepresented, and many citizens of Washington were absent.

Mr. Lincoln's first levee at the White House on the 8th March, was a "monster gathering." From eight till half-past ten Mr. Lincoln had not one minute's rest from shaking hands; often shaking a gentleman's with his right hand and a lady's with his left at the same time, to facilitate the movements of the multitude. Colonel Lamar, one of his suite, stood on his left, and introduced with dispatch and courtesy those who desired to be presented by name. Mrs. Lincoln, in magenta colored brocade, with diamonds, stood next to her husband on his right, the observed of all observers; while Dr. Blake introduced people to the Queen of the occasion. Distinguished among the guests were Mr. and Mrs. Douglas. The members of the new cabinet were all present except Mr. Seward. Charles Sumner appeared for the first time in six years, in the most approved style of English evening dress. In the gay throng, as usual, mingled the diplomatic corps and the officers of the army and navy, their uniforms flashing in the light of the chandeliers, and only excelled by the brilliant costumes of the ladies, splendid with diamonds and other precious gems. Not only was the élite of Washington society represented; but the wealthy and fashionable circles of nearly every State, from Maine to Louisiana, from the Atlantic to the Pacific. One of the most admired belles was from the Golden State, the wife of an officer in the army.

Dicey, an English tourist, wrote: "If you take the English stock caricature of the typical Yankee, you have the likeness of President Lincoln. Fancy a man six foot high, and thin *out* of proportion, with long bony arms and legs, large rugged hands, which grasp you like a vice when shaking yours; with a long scraggy neck, and a chest too narrow for the great arms hanging by its side; add to this figure a head somewhat too small for such a stature, covered with rough, uncombable, lank, dark hair, a face furrowed, wrinkled and indented; a high, narrow forehead, and sunk deep beneath bushy eyebrows, two bright, somewhat dreamy eyes, that seem to gaze through you without looking at you; a few irregular blotches of black, bristly hair in the place where beard and whiskers ought to grow; a close set, thin-lipped, stern mouth, with two rows of large white teeth, and large nose and ears. Clothe this figure in a long, tight, ill-fitting suit of black; creased and puckered at every salient point—and every point of this figure is salient; put on large boots, gloves too long for the bony fingers, and a fluffy hat, covered to the top with puffy crape, and then add to all this an air of strength, physical as well as moral, and a strange look of dignity, coupled with all this grotesqueness, and you will have the impression left on me by Abraham Lincoln."

"Some of the party began smoking; and Mr. Seward, who was present, remarked laughingly, 'I have always wondered how any man could ever get to be President of the United States with so few vices. The President, you know, neither drinks nor smokes.' 'That,' answered the President, 'is a doubtful compliment. Once, outside a stage in Illinois, a man sitting by me offered me a cigar. I told him I had no vices. He smoked for some time, and then grunted out, It's my experience in life that folks who have got no vices have plaguy few virtues.'"

A gentleman present mentioned a friend who had been expelled from New Orleans as a Unionist, *made* to go of his own free will. Mr. Lincoln said, "It reminded him of a hotel-keeper in St. Louis, in cholera time, who boasted that he had never had a death in his hotel. No more he had; for when a guest was dying, he had him carried out in the street in his bed, to die." Talking of the Missouri compromise, Mr. Lincoln remarked: "It used to amuse me some to find that the slave-holders wanted more territory because they had not room for their slaves; and yet they complained of not having the slave-trade because they wanted more slaves for their room!" "Unless you could give the dry chuckle with which the President's stories were repeated, and the gleam in his eye, as, with the action habitual to him, he rubs his hand down the side of his long leg, you fail in conveying a true impression of their quaint humor."

Mr. Sumner he noticed as "that great, sturdy, English-looking figure, with the broad, massive forehead, over which the rich mass of nut-brown hair, streaked here and there with gray, hangs loosely; with the deep blue eyes, and the strangely winning smile, half bright, half full of sadness. Sitting in his place in the Senate, leaning back in his chair, with his head stooping slightly over that great broad chest, and his hands resting upon his crossed legs, he looks, in dress, attitude and air, the very model of an English country gentleman." Mr. Stanton, Mrs. Stowe says, "is one of those men built on the lion pattern; a man who never knew what fear was; a man also, awful and tremendous in powers of wrath and combativeness." He was appointed Secretary of War in January, 1862. When Mr. Lincoln announced his selection, some one objected to Mr. Stanton's impulsive temper; and Lincoln replied: "Well, we may have to treat him as they are sometimes obliged to treat a Methodist minister I know of out West. He gets wrought up so high in his prayers and exhortations that they are obliged to put bricks in his pocket to keep him down. We may be obliged to serve Stanton the same way; but I guess we'll let him jump awhile first!"

Dicey described Wendell Phillips; "a spare, slight man, with scanty grayish hair, dressed in colors of almost quaker-like sombreness. My first impression was that he looked like a cross between a dissenting minister and a country doctor. The one sign of genius was the high, narrow forehead, and the one attractive feature the wonderful sweetness of his smile."

Alexander H. Stephens, of Georgia, was known throughout the Union as one of the most prominent of Southern politicians and eloquent orators. He was born in Georgia in 1812. A stranger judging by looks, would never have selected him as the John Randolph of our time, more dreaded as an adversary and more prized as an ally in a debate than any other member of the House of Representatives. His voice was sharp and shrill at the beginning of a speech, but as he warmed with his subject, the clear tones and vigorous sentences rolled out with a sonorousness that found its way to every corner of the building. He was witty, rhetorical and solid, with a dash of keen satire that put an edge on every speech. He possessed hosts of warm friends, and was regarded as an enlightened Christian and a man of inflexible integrity.

Upon the betrothal of the Prince of Wales to the Princess Alexandra, Queen Victoria sent a letter to each of the European sovereigns, and also to President Lincoln, announcing the fact. Lord Lyons, her ambassador at Washington,—(a bachelor,)—requested an audience of Mr. Lincoln that he might present this important document. At the time appointed he was received at the White House, in company with Mr. Seward. "May it please your Excellency," said Lord Lyons, "I hold in my hand an autograph letter from my royal mistress, Queen Victoria, which I have been commanded to present to your Excellency. In it she informs your Excellency that her son, his Royal Highness the Prince of Wales, is about to contract a matrimonial alliance with her Royal Highness the Princess Alexandra of Denmark." After continuing in this strain for a few minutes, Lord Lyons tendered the letter to the President and awaited his reply. It was short, simple and expressive, and consisted simply of the words:—"Lord Lyons, go thou and do likewise."

The New Year's reception at the Presidential mansion in 1865, was said to have been more crowded than ever before. Among the Generals were Halleck, Hitchcock, Hunter, Doubleday, Fessenden, Terry, Farnsworth, Thomas and others. Admiral Smith and Commodore Goldsborough headed the Naval Delegation. At Mrs. Lincoln's first drawing-room reception, the élite of the metropolis was in attendance. Admiral and Mrs. Farragut were conspicuous. This lady is a Virginian, and has the frank, easy manner and impulsive grace of the Southern ladies.

One of the most valued confidential friends of President Lincoln, as he had been for years of most prominent statesmen, was Judge James W. White of

HON. F. CARROLL BREWSTER.

Eng'd by H. B. Hall, N. Y.

New York. At all hours he was received by the President and Cabinet; his advice and aid were frequently sought, and his influence was great. This eminent man deserves more than a cursory and feeble tribute. He was of an ancient Irish family, noted for the virtues as well as the talents of its members. He was a nephew of Gerald Griffin. At a navy-yard ball given this winter, one of the stars of attraction was the daughter of Judge White, then only seventeen. Her singing created a furore of admiration in the select circles of that time. All the family of Judge White had great talent for music, and their abilities were highly cultivated. Mrs. Mack and Mrs. George Walker of New York are still celebrities in society for their vocal powers and for many other attractions.

In November, 1865, an interesting case was argued before the Supreme Court at Washington, concerning the act authorizing a bridge over the Schuylkill. This had excited great public attention, because the decision in the Wheeling Bridge case had been adverse to the right to bridge a navigable river. The right of Philadelphia to bridge the Schuylkill was maintained by Mr. Frederick Carroll Brewster, and many thousand inhabitants of the city had a vital interest in his able argument. The case was fiercely contested before the Supreme Court; but the argument on behalf of the city carried it against opposi tion, and received the rare compliment of a congratulation from the bench. When the constitutionality of the "Bounty Act" was called in question, it was argued by the same distinguished gentleman before a full bench. The cause involved upwards of thirty millions of dollars, and was said by the court to be "beyond comparison the most important ever brought before it since the formation of the government." When the Girard will case, involving millions of property and questions as to charitable uses, was before the Supreme Court, Mr. Brewster argued it on behalf of the city of Philadelphia, and procured a reversal of the judgment entered against the city. The eminent reputation of this gentleman, acknowledged to be at the head of the Philadelphia bar, and—since his successful management in 1856 of the famous contested election case of Mann vs. Cassidy, where he gained the cause though opposed by the flower of the bar—regarded as the great legal champion of the cause which cherishes the purity of the ballot-box—renders a brief notice proper. Born in 1825, he graduated at the University of Pennsylvania at the age of sixteen; studied law with his father, Francis E. Brewster, and was admitted to the bar when only nineteen. In a few years he rose to the head of the criminal bar, being engaged in most important cases. His defence of a medical practitioner from the charge of homicide of a patient by mal-practice, was proof of the old saying, "the lawyer must be master of all sciences."*

Mr. Brewster's reputation in civil cases is equally

* His defence of Lenairs, who shot a Jersey farmer while attempting to arrest him, was a most eloquent effort, and pronounced by the press "the speech of the trial." Though the highest talent of the New Jersey bar was invoked for the prosecution, the life of the accused was saved. A masterly defence by Mr. Brewster also secured the discharge of Kirkpatrick and his wife, in one of the longest criminal trials that ever occupied the attention of a Philadelphia jury. His defence of Mr. Alibone, charged with conspiracy to defraud the Pennsylvania bank, in an important and protracted trial, triumphed

eminent. For years prior to his elevation to the bench he had more cases upon trial and argument lists than any other member of the bar. In the conduct of contested election cases he was particularly distinguished. Several were argued before the Committee on Elections of the House of Representatives at Washington. In important constitutional questions his aid was eagerly sought. The constitutionality of the act allowing soldiers to vote, of the act of Congress making greenbacks a legal tender, and others —were all argued and gained by Mr. Brewster.

In 1862, he was elected City Solicitor by a large vote, and re-elected in 1865 by an increased majority. In 1866 he was nominated for Judge of the Court of Common Pleas, and received a greater majority in his county than the governor polled. During the time he has occupied the bench, his decisions have been marked by clearness of judgment and great industry in the examination of authorities. These decisions of important questions have won him the highest name as a jurist, and secured universal confidence and commendation. Some cases have bristled with perplexing points, having to be decided almost upon the moment. Mr. Brewster was ever known to be a "whole-souled Union man," and a fearless patriot. His cheerful, cordial and frank manner inspires confidence, and is peculiarly agreeable in society. He

over the popular prejudice. In other celebrated cases his labor triumphed. Ebon Lane, who was captured by the Confederates with a New England vessel, had been compelled by them to navigate "The Enchantress." He did so in such a way as to get her overhauled by the United States steamer "Albatross." It needed the skill of his distinguished counsel to rid him of the suspicion naturally attaching to such association.

has the scorn of all crooked ways innate in a high-toned gentleman, and his rich mental culture is evident in conversation. As a speaker he is equalled by few, and the natural advantages of a clear and finely modulated voice, noble features and an elegant person, aid the effect of his oratory.

The financial question was one of so great importance during the administration of Mr. Lincoln, that it brought into prominent positions many gentlemen who had not previously been much in the habit of frequenting the "salons" of the capital. Many brought with them their wives and daughters, usually well-educated, refined, intelligent ladies, often more dignified and retiring than showy. Among them were the wife and daughter of Mr. J. U. Orvis of New York. He had established a national bank in that city, and managed it so successfully as to have drawn from Secretary Chase at Providence, R. I., the remark, that he considered the bank of which Mr. Orvis was president a model of what he intended those financial institutions to be. Secretary Fessenden also complimented Mr. Orvis publicly on "having done his duty;" and an assistant Secretary of the Treasury said that he did "as much as any banker in the country to promote the sale of government bonds in the time of the country's necessity."

The peculiar great financial movements of those days can now scarcely be understood. The daily doings of the various agents were chronicled in the journals, and the great public heart vibrated as with electric shocks, when reports came in of the almost fabulous amounts transferred to the public treasury.

In one case we heard of an ordinary carriage driven down Broadway to the Sub-Treasury, conveying four millions of dollars in greenbacks. In another, of a messenger carrying four hundred thousand dollars on his back in a bag, being jostled in a crowd, and relieved by a pickpocket of eight dollars which was in his vest pocket. Mr. Orvis has been connected as originator, director or chief officer, with some of the best and most successful institutions in the country. As the originator and president, from 1864 to 1867, of the Ninth National Bank of New York, which, under his direction, furnished the government with the money for over one-twentieth part of the entire 7-30 loan, Mr. Orvis achieved the crowning success of his financial career. In one day he obtained a subscription exceeding five millions of dollars.

An English visitor said of Lincoln: "There are women about whom no one ever thinks in connection with beauty; and there are men to whom the epithet of 'gentlemanlike' or 'ungentlemanlike' appears utterly incongruous; and of such is the President. Still, there is about him a complete absence of pretension, and an evident desire to be courteous to everybody, which is the essence, if not the outward form, of high breeding. There is a softness, too, about his smile, and a sparkle of dry humor about his eye which redeem the expression of his face. You cannot look upon his worn, bilious, anxious countenance, and believe it that of a happy man. In private life his disposition, unless report and physiognomy both err, is a sombre one; but, coupled with this he has a rich fund of dry, Yankee humor."

"My first reflection, at meeting Mr. Seward, was one of wonder that so small a man should have been near creating a war between two great nations; a man, I should think, little over five feet and a half in height and some sixty years of age, with small, delicate hands and feet, and a spare, wiry body, scanty, snow-white hair, deep-sunk, clear gray eyes, a face clean shaven, and a smooth, colorless skin. He was in his office when I first saw him, dressed in black, with waistcoat half-unbuttoned, one leg over the side of his arm-chair, and a cigar stuck between his lips. You are at your ease with him at once; there is a frankness and *bonhomie* about his manner which renders it very pleasant. A glance at that spare, hard-knit frame, and that clear, bright eye, shows that no pleasure has been indulged in to excess throughout his long, laborious career. Probably the most striking looking of the ministers is Mr. Chase, the Secretary of the Treasury. His lofty, spacious forehead, his fresh, smooth countenance, his portly figure and his pleasant, kindly smile, seem to mark the philanthropist. Mr. Blair, though a Maryland man, is the only one of the ministers who has what we consider the characteristic Yankee type of face—the high cheek-bones, sallow complexion and long straight hair. Mr. Gideon Welles, the Secretary of the Navy, wears a long white beard and a stupendous white wig, which cause him to look like the heavy grandfather in a genteel comedy. Mr. Bates of Missouri, the Attorney-General, is a lawyer, very much like elderly legal authorities in other parts of the world."

Mrs. Lincoln seemed to have impressed foreigners

most favorably. A visitor said: "She performed her part of the honors in response to the ovation paid to her as well as to her husband, with that propriety which consistently blends all the graces with an unreserved dignity, and is much more becoming the wife of a republican President, than any attempt to ape the haughty manner of European courts." Her spirit was equal to any emergency. Before the inauguration some impudent South Carolinians had sent to Mrs. Lincoln by express a scandalous painting upon canvass, representing her husband with a rope round his neck, his feet chained, and his body covered with tar and feathers. Many of her lady friends took up the newspaper rumors of intended attacks upon him while on his way to the Federal capital, and entreated her to delay her removal to Washington till he was safely installed in the White House. But the courageous lady met all these well-meant propositions with scorn, and made the spirited declaration that she would see Mr. Lincoln on to Washington, danger or no danger! Her self-possession at all times showed that she had readily adapted herself to the exalted station to which she had been so strangely advanced from the simple social life of the little capital of Illinois.

XX.

JOHNSON'S ADMINISTRATION.

Social Reaction from the Depression caused by the War—The fashionable Season a Carnival—Changes in Society—Andrew Johnson and his Family—New Years, 1866—Prominent Ladies—The French Minister's Party—Marriage of Mrs. Douglas—Madame Le Vert and her Daughters—Opening Receptions of the next January—Mrs. Sprague — Receptions at Chief-Justice Chase's — Celebrities and Beauties—Hon. Alex. W. Randall—Mrs. Randall—Mrs. Grant's Dress and Receptions—A new Feature at the White House—The Foreign Ministers — Fashionable Gayety at its toppling Height —Party at Admiral Lee's—Splendid Party at General Butler's—At Senator Morgan's, &c.—Last Reception of the President—Mrs. Dahlgren's Reunions—Mrs. Pomeroy—Mrs. Henderson—Mrs. Williams—Mrs. Gaines—Rush to the Capital.

The long social depression and privations caused by the war, were followed by a reaction in the first year of the term of Andrew Johnson. Even the shock of President Lincoln's assassination and the mourning of the Nation, had no abiding effect in checking the gayety resumed when a few months had passed. The fashionable season of 1866 was almost a carnival. Washington seemed to have gone wild. The accession to society of many families suddenly grown rich, and their display of splendor in entertainments, the unparalleled influx of visitors to the capital, the emulation of ladies anxious to become leaders of the ton, the general love of pleasurable excitement consequent on a long season of terror and distress, the exultation of victory and the joy of deliverance, the expansion of good feeling and the aspirations of ambition, all contributed to a whirl of festivity and good cheer. The older residents complained of the mixed character of these assemblages; averred that the "scum" had all risen to the top, and that Washington had lost its pride and boast in the indiscriminate admission of "everybody" to its once brilliant circles, and its confusion of "shoddy" and parvenu elements with solid respectability. But little heed paid the pleasure-loving crowd to such carping strictures. The city overflowed with gayeties, and those who liked them not were welcome to seclude themselves.

Andrew Johnson, it will be remembered, was born in Raleigh, N. C., in 1808. He and his wife traveled on foot across the mountains, and set up a business establishment in Greenville, Tenn. He was Governor of that State in 1853, and afterwards United States Senator. Elected Vice-President, he succeeded to the Presidency by the death of Abraham Lincoln in April, 1865. Mrs. Johnson was an invalid, unable to undergo the fatigues of receiving company; the task, therefore, devolved upon her daughters, one of whom—Mrs. Stover—was a widow; the other—Mrs. Patterson—the wife of a Senator. On the 1st January, 1866, the gates were opened to the public at twelve, Among the visitors were Sir Frederick Bruce, the British minister, Mayor Wallach, and all the public officers and diplomatics. Mr. McCulloch for the first time opened his house for New Year festivities. Mrs.

McCulloch was assisted in receiving by her sister, Mrs. Meyers of New York. At the Postmaster-General's, Mr. Dennison welcomed his guests. Mrs. Welles received with cheerful grace, assisted by Miss Mary Morgan. General Grant received company at his own house in Georgetown; Mrs. Dent, the wife of General Dent, and Mrs. Porter, wife of Colonel Horace Porter of Grant's staff, welcoming the guests. During the season the ladies of the President's family had receptions every Tuesday evening and every Friday from one to three, exclusive of the President's levees. The wife of Secretary Stanton received on Saturday evenings, as did Admiral and Mrs. Dahlgren. Party divisions were ignored, and asperities were forgotten in the cordiality of social intercourse. Mrs. Harlan, wife of the Secretary of the Interior, also held weekly receptions. At those of Schuyler Colfax, his mother, Mrs. Mathews, and Miss Mathews, received the visitors. The parties at Secretary Welles' were noted for overflowing hospitality, reviving the memory of old times. The wife of General Ramsey—Miss Gales—was a celebrity. The Marquis de Montholon, French minister, who resided in the house of Cocheron the banker, gave receptions. At one of his regal parties the guests remained till morning, partaking of a sumptuous breakfast before the gentlemen departed to their several places of business. Some of the ladies attended morning receptions the same day without changing the costume worn at the ball; thus keeping up festivities for twenty-four hours without interruption. In January, 1866, the distinguished Madame Le Vert, with her lovely daughters, Miss Octavia and

Miss Cara Netta, came to spend some weeks in Washington. The city was thronged with the most notable of society from the North and West, and such a winter had not been known for eight years. Madame Le Vert frequently attended six receptions during the day, and four or five parties the same evening. Mrs. George W. Riggs gave a splendid party the same evening she arrived, at which the charming lady met numerous old friends from whom she had been separated during the gloomy years of the war. Her reception in Washington circles was most cordial. Her daughters were admired belles wherever they appeared.

On the 23d January, General Robert Williams was wedded to Mrs. Douglas, formerly Miss Cutts, the widow of the noted Senator. She gave four superb receptions after her marriage; at the first, the Right Rev. Archbishop Spalding and Chief-Justice Chase were present, with many distinguished persons, and a representation from Baltimore. Mrs. Grant gave several balls and some of the largest receptions of the season. Mrs. Sprague's was a *matinée* with dancing and Senator Sherman's was attended by an immense crowd. Mrs. Sherman's quiet grace and womanly sweetness were greatly admired. She was assisted by her niece, Mary Sherman. The Bachelor's Ball called to mind the departed glories of the Washington assemblies. Party-givers were at a loss to find an evening disengaged. At the British embassy, Lady Elma Thurlow received with winning grace and cordiality. The French minister had married Miss Victoria Gratiot, daughter of General Gratiot, and a belle in the most distinguished circles. Conspicuous in society were Mrs. Charles Knapp and Governor and Mrs. Smythe of New Hampshire. After Lent a brilliant reception was given by General and Mrs. Grant, at which the President and his daughters were seen, with Sir Frederick Bruce, Mr. and Lady Elma Thurlow, Alexander H. Stephens, etc., among the notables. In January 1867, Mr. O. H. Browning was Secretary of the Interior, and led the way in receptions; also Mrs. and Miss Mathews at those of Mr. Colfax. Select receptions were given by General Grant, with dancing, and by Mayor and Mrs. Wallach. Mrs. Sprague's morning receptions were given at the house of her father, Chief-Justice Chase. The engaging manners of Mrs. Sprague gave her an ascendency in society. Her slender form became a rich and ornamented style of dress, and her eyes, fringed with dark lashes, lighted her intellectual face with expression. The Senator had lustrous eyes, with small features and long hair rather carelessly worn. His manner was gentle, but he was said to possess a striking element of greatness—tenacity of purpose. The presence of the Chief-Justice would grace a palace; his face expressed the most bounteous benevolence. At this time Mrs. Alexander W. Randall, one of the brightest ornaments of Washington society, had recently arrived from Europe with her husband, the Postmaster-General. Mr. Charles Eames, recognized as, in his specialty—the Admiralty jurisprudence—one of the most accomplished and able members of that bar, was struck down by sudden illness and removed from this world. The best society suffered a great loss in the withdrawal of his widow, who went to Europe. The daughter of General Morris Miller, and grand-daughter of Major-General Macomb, who had been Commander-in-Chief under John Quincy Adams and Jackson, was this winter married to Major-General Frank Wheaton of Rhode Island. Mrs. Stanbery, the wife of the Attorney-General, and Mrs. Reverdy Johnson, were noted on many occasions. Card receptions were given in February by the secretaries, and a party at the house of Senator Pomeroy of Kansas, where the delighted guests enjoyed "the wee sma' hours ayont the twal'."

On New Year's Day, 1868, the chief celebration was, of course, at the White House. At eleven the member of the cabinet and foreign ministers, the Judges of the Supreme Court, Senators and Representatives in Congress and the Judges of the District and Court of Claims were received, followed by army, navy and marine officers. Then came the soldiers of the War of 1812, and the "Oldest Inhabitants' Association of the District;" and at noon the citizens were admitted. The black suits of statesmen and jurists, and the splendid toilets of the ladies, were contrasted with the court dresses of the foreign ministers and their attachés, and the full dress uniforms of officers in service. General Sherman's daughter wore light buff grenadine over a green silk skirt gored and with full train; Mrs. Rives lavender-colored silk trimmed with folds of black velvet, a black velvet cloak and white bonnet; Mrs. Freeman, wife of the Secretary of the British legation, a pearl-colored silk and black lace shawl, with white bonnet; Mrs. Long, sky-blue silk trimmed with folds of white satin, with white cloak and bonnet; Mrs. Michler black moire antique with white furs, and black velvet bonnet. A very old gentleman, Mr. Noble Hurdle, residing in Georgetown, took President Johnson by the hand, and said: "God bless you, Mr. President! I have shaken the hand of every President from Washington's time, and now, Sir, I am happy to shake yours." The mansion of Secretary Seward was also a central point of interest; as was that of General Grant, Secretary McCulloch, the Secretary of the Navy, Postmaster-General Randall, and Chief-Justice Sprague. Senator Reverdy Johnson, too, received a large number of friends, entertaining them with hospitality.

Hon. Alex. W. Randall is a native of Ames, Montgomery County, N. Y.; a son of Judge Phineas Randall, a gentleman of great legal ability. At the age of twenty he set off for Wisconsin, alone and without means. He resided at Waukesha, where he lived a score of years. His advancement being very rapid, he became identified with the interests of the State, and filled many important offices. His profession was that of the law. He was Governor of Wisconsin in 1857 and 1858, re-elected triumphantly by the citizens, who were justly proud of his fame and honorable character. He did honor to the chair of state by his firm and decided discharge of duties; and his wise and vigilant course gave entire satisfaction to his political friends. He was a most eloquent speaker, unexcelled as an orator in debate; clear, forcible and conclusive. His eminent ability and acknowledged integrity, with his indomitable energy, fitted him for the highest responsible office. He resigned the Governorship to accept the post of United States Minister to the Papal Court at Rome, afterwards returning to take the office of First Assistant Postmaster-General; succeeding Mr. Dennison of Ohio as Postmaster-General at the restoration of the Union, and holding that office more than three years. While First Assistant, he was married at Elmira to Miss Helen M. Thomas, formerly of Wisconsin. This beautiful young girl had been for many years an orphan, and a ward of Governor Randall. Her life had been in great part passed at school; for some time at the Rockford Female Seminary and the Elmira College; her education having been completed under private professors. After she became Mrs. Randall, she resided six years in Washington, and was universally admired for beauty, grace and intellectual gifts, while her gracious and winning manners were the true indication of a gentle and generous nature. Few, if any ladies were ever more popular, or more beloved by her own sex. Mrs. Randall's form is slender and symmetrical; her features have classic regularity, and her complexion is of that pearly paleness so exquisite in a faultless face, varying in color with every shade of feeling. She always had perfect taste in dress, and her presence gave a charm to every circle. Her loss was deeply felt and deplored when she left Washington. "She is *lovely!*"—was the emphatic phrase of every tongue; and all felt as if one dearly prized had been removed from their midst.

In January, 1868, at a reception by the ladies of the executive mansion, among the guests were Hon.

R. S. Spofford and his wife—Harriet Prescott Spofford. Receptions were regularly given by General and Mrs. Grant, and the members of the cabinet. Mr. Edward Thornton, the newly appointed British minister, had the advantage over his old bachelor predecessors, Sir Frederick Bruce and Lord Lyons, in being a married man. Mrs. and Miss Matthews were noted at Grant's; also Miss Smythe of New York; the secretaries and Postmaster-General Randall with his young wife. Conspicuous, too, were Generals Sheridan, Hearney, Ord, Thomas, Carr, Washburne, Dent, Badeau, McCook, Senators Cole and Corbett, Clark Mills, a few of the foreign ministers, and a delegation of Indian chiefs. Sheridan's brisk and jovial manners seemed to infuse increased animation through the company, and there was much standing on tiptoe to catch a glimpse of his compact little figure. Mr. Johnson introduced into the social life of the White House a hitherto almost unknown feature—children's parties. One given in December was a highly enjoyed entertainment. The President's grandchildren invited over three hundred juveniles to a party in which there was dancing and a supper. The supper table had in the center a large cake inscribed with Mr. Johnson's name, presented to him as a birthday gift, he having just completed his sixtieth year.

At the New Year's reception immediately following, Secretary Seward introduced M. Berthemy, the French minister, wearing the cross of the Legion and a tri-colored sash; Baron Gerolt, the Prussian ambassador, with heavy gold embroidered pocket lappets and collar; and Blacque Bey, the Turkish minister, with his crimson fez, gold mounted scimiter and gorgeous oriental costume. Baron Stoeckl, the Russian minister, Le Baron de Frankenstein, the Austrian Chargé d' Affaires, Baron de Wetterstedt of Sweden, and Señor Don Colonel Domingo F. Sarmiento, of the Argentine Republic, followed; afterwards Don Alberto Gava, of the Chilean Legation, M. de Bille, Danish minister, Chevalier Marcee Cerrutti, Italian, and others of the Spanish, Russian, and Grecian Legations; with the Peruvian minister and Consul General of Switzerland, &c.

During January and the first ten days of February, 1869, the fashionable gayety was at its toppling height, and improved with a rush. A thousand cards of invitation were sent out for a bridal party by Admiral and Mrs. Lee. The bride was a daughter of Montgomery Blair. Mrs. Blair, the daughter of Mrs. Levi Woodbury, has been mentioned as a leader in society. Miss Woodbury, her sister, was as much admired as ever, and even more beautiful. The Presidential receptions seemed to become more popular as the time approached for their discontinuance. The dresses of the ladies were pronounced less gorgeous than last year, but were of singular variety. A few ladies came in bonnets and shawls; and sometimes a long cloth cloak and fur cape moved among a bevy in airy ball costume. The most marked contrast in colors was observable. One remarkable looking middle-aged lady, with a winning and lively grace, was Mrs. Judge Merrick.

The party at Admiral Lee's was said to be, in point of the number and distinction of the guests, the brilliancy of the scene, and the general "success," the most magnificent given in the capital for the last twenty years. It was, in fact, historical, if we consider the number of generals, statesmen and scholars present, and given in compliment to the bridal pair —General and Mrs. Comstock. The rooms were filled at ten o'clock, with a gaily dressed crowd. General Meade was there, and Senator Sherman was for a few moments conspicuous. The Secretaries were seen as they passed, and the next moment lost in the flutter of lace and silk. The three Misses Blair were among the bridesmaids. The procession was continually pressing along towards the veranda, which was enclosed and draped with flags for the supper-room. The venerable Frank P. Blair, Sr., was seen; a thin, fragile looking man. Generals Delafield, Woodruff, Schofield, Eaton, Parker, Miller, Dent, Babcock, Ramsey, and many others, Secretary Welles, Mayor Wallach, General Humphreys, etc., all escorted ladies, and all were intent on the banquet. It was elegantly set out, under hanging baskets of flowers.

The greatest celebrity of the evening, was Mrs. Levi Woodbury, the mother of Mrs. Montgomery Blair. This lady came from Portland to spend the winter, about the 1st of January. Still very handsome, she brought back, like a dream, recollections of the days when, in General Jackson's second term, she was the hostess in many a brilliant party at the Secretary's residence. She has a highly intellectual countenance, with graceful self-possession, and the most winning, cordial kindness beams from her eyes and speaks in her voice. A noted guest was Mrs.

Fremont. The daughter of Senator Benton and the wife of so distinguished a man as General Fremont, she is always a celebrity, besides being one of the most brilliant women in conversation in America. "How changed she is!" ejaculated a gentleman. But her gray hair was a mark of honor; her locks having changed from a dark brown to their present frosted aspect, in three days, during the troubles of the war.

Attorney-General and Mrs. Evarts gave a card reception the same evening; many of the guests going there first. The season was closed by a party at General Butler's, where all of beauty, brilliancy, fashion and official dignity that Washington sends forth to scenes of gayety, was gathered. The staircases to the dressing-rooms on the third floor were adorned with pots of flowers and green flowering vines that wreathed the banisters. In front of every large mirror in the parlors were suspended immense baskets of flowering and fragrant plants; also from the doors and window cornices, while wreaths of fern and bright autumnal leaves surrounded the pictures. The effect was unique and splendid. Mrs. Butler was dressed in a "Turkey red" silk with train and panier, and low corsage. A white point lace scarf, fastened on the left shoulder, crossed the panier, looped under the right arm, and half way down the skirt. Her hair was arranged in a thick heavy coil on the top of the head with several long ringlets floating down the back of the neck. At her right stood the General, and on her left a fairy vision of loveliness—Miss Blanche Butler; tall, graceful and elegant, with a wealth of rippling auburn hair, having the golden sheen so much prized, floating down behind, and coils on the top of the head; attired in a flowered silk robe with white ground, with long train and high and large panier; the underskirt, white tarletan with fluted flounces. The ladies were generally dressed with great magnificence. Speaker Colfax was lively; his wife was dressed in corn-colored silk, much gored, and plain in front, with black lace trimmings. There was also General Ramsey, of the War department, a jovial-looking gentleman with white locks, and a frequent and pleasant smile; with General George H. Thomas, the hero of the battle of Nashville; Generals Harvey and Heintzel, General McCook, and many others. Mrs. McCook was pointed out as the handsomest lady in the room—short and in misty white, with brilliant complexion, and bright, black eyes.

The evening before there had been a brilliant party at Senator Morgan's. Mrs. Morgan was dressed in blue satin, with a flounce of white lace, and a handsome lace shawl. She wore superb diamonds. The entertainment was in compliment to Mrs. Beach of Philadelphia, who wore a lemon-colored satin robe, trimmed with point lace, over a white illusion skirt, with flounce of point lace, the necklace pearls and diamonds. The bouquets were very numerous; baskets and globes of flowers were in every available spot, and a wreath of japonicas hung from the ceiling of one of the parlors, supporting a basket full of rich, fragrant blossoms and trailing vines.

The last Presidential evening reception but one was crowded, though enjoyable. Mrs. Patterson received in a handsome black silk dress, low in the neck, with short sleeves, puffed lace covering the neck and arms. The wife of the British minister wore pink silk, with train and panier, and over it a low-necked basquine of black velvet, with very long points and profusely trimmed with bugles. Mrs. Gaines, just arrived from New Orleans, radiant as ever, wore a pearl-colored satin trimmed with black lace, with a light dress bonnet decorated with a large aigrette of costly diamonds. "She must have been successful in her ejectment suits," said one. "Oh," replied another, "every now and then they send her a million as a sop to keep her quiet!" Mrs. Gaines is of the medium height, slender, but well rounded and symmetrical in form. Her brown hair is thick, and clusters in short curls; her eyes are dark and brilliant; her complexion is fair and clear; her features are regular, and she is beautiful beyond criticism. Full of life and animation, fresh in feeling and impulsive, with a store of information and a mind well cultivated, possessing rich humor and spirit, with manners cordial, piquant and winning, she was a universal favorite in society, and had a court of gentlemen about her wherever she moved.

Mrs. Dahlgren's Saturday evening parties were continued through Lent, and were often numerously attended. Something of sadness prevailed in the receptions of the ladies of the cabinet, as the time of parting drew near. At Mrs. Randall's last, she wore mauve silk, becoming to her fair and delicate beauty. Among her visitors was the wife of Senator Ramsey of St. Paul, Minn. The luxuriant tropical style of loveliness was exemplified in her handsome face and majestic form. A tall, regal looking woman, dressed in dark silk, was Mrs. Chandler, whose husband was the Senator from Michigan. Mrs. Samuel C. Pomeroy, whose husband was Senator from Kansas, is a queenly looking woman. Her features are massive, but expression lights them up into splendor of beauty. Her eyes are blue, and her complexion is fair. Mrs. Henderson, the wife of the Senator from Missouri, is recently married, and is a highly intelligent and cultivated woman, fluent in conversation and piquant in wit.

Mrs. Williams—Mrs. Douglas that was—is a queen who has abdicated; she never appears in general society. Her residence is a beautiful villa a little out of the compact part of the city. One of the curiosities of the capitol is the model of the statue of Lincoln, for which Congress has appropriated ten thousand dollars. There were many competitors for this commission; the successful candidate being a young woman, in appearance hardly over twenty, who presented her model, and bore away the palm. Her name is Miss Vinnie Ream. She presents an instance of the triumph of genius over difficulties, almost unprecedented in the history of art. Sculptors who have devoted half a lifetime to study, might be proud of the model, which she is said to have completed after two years of labor. She is short and slight, usually seen in her working dress, and is very pretty, with fawn-like dark eyes.

As the 4th of March approached, the city became full to overflowing. The hotels were crammed, and in the evening their parlors presented a gorgeous appearance; the elder ladies appearing in gold colored or mauve satin, with long trains, trimmed with black lace or white point, with the costliest lace shawls, and diamonds worth a duke's ransom. The ladies of the South and West often dress in this ornate style in hotels.

XXI.

GRANT'S ADMINISTRATION.

Last Reception of the retiring President—Ladies' Dresses—Mrs. Thomas—Inauguration Day—The Procession and Pageants—Surviving Soldiers of the War of 1812—The Ship of State—The crowded Ball—Dresses of the Ladies—The Generals present—Too crowded for Comfort—Incident in New Orleans—General Gaines' gallant Defense of his Wife—The partial Judge—The Advocate of "Women's Rights"—Mrs. Gaines' Interview with her, and sensible Reproof of her Conduct—Olé Bull again—The Cabinet—Mrs. Walworth—Mrs. Gates—Sketch of Mrs. Grant—Her first Reception in the White House—Dresses of the Ladies—Second Reception—Reception of Applicants for Office, &c., at the White House—Mrs. Dix's Reception to Mr. Washburne—Mrs. Robb—Mr. Philp's Entertainment.

THE last reception of the retiring President was a crush that rendered the ten thousand who gained admission uncomfortable, and disappointed the thousands unable to get even to the doors. Many ladies lost their wrappings and were compelled to return home in aerial costume without protection from the night air. Yet the dresses were magnificent almost beyond precedent. The fashion prevalent of loading one skirt above another with trimmings, and the bright contrasts of colors, were abundantly exhibited. Mrs. Patterson received in black velvet with a lace shawl. Mrs. Ann S. Stephens wore black velvet with low corsage and lace shawl; her daughter-in-law, white

MRS. ULYSSES S. GRANT.

Engd by H. B. Hall. N. Y.

satin, with panier looped up with heavy bands of green satin, and a necklace of pearls. Mrs. Sprague was dressed in blue silk with a pink tunic, and pink convolvuluses in her hair; Mrs. Randall in white silk with black lace trimming and pearl ornaments. The "New York Times" remarked: "The belle of the evening was recognized in the person of Mrs. Joseph T. Thomas of Philadelphia, by far the most elegantly dressed and queenly-looking woman present." Indeed, at every assemblage and on every festive occasion of this season, Mrs. Thomas had been noted for beauty, superior bearing, and her rich and tasteful attire.

Mrs. Thomas is a native of the valley of Virginia, and was educated in Richmond, where her piquant and graceful manners and her excellent qualities of heart won hosts of admirers and lasting friends. She was married at the elegant country-seat of her uncle, Colonel Tuley of Virginia, to Mr. J. T. Thomas, a member of the Philadelphia bar; they reside on Rittenhouse Square, in that city.

Mrs. Thomas possesses the peculiar charm of Southern women, a blending of grace and dignity, of cordial frankness, and winning ease. Her true hospitality has been proved by many visitors.

The morning of the 4th of March opened with a pouring rain, but as the time approached for the inaugural procession, the sun parted the clouds, and all looked sunny and hopeful. Mr. Johnson remained till twelve at the capitol, where he was said to have been all night signing bills. For three or four days the streets of Washington had been full of bustle and noise of words and works, every hour bringing hundreds of new comers, all the hotels overflowing, and every private house crammed with visitors. The streets through which the procession passed, were lined with persons standing, and the windows of hotels and shops were filled with spectators. The President elect passed in his carriage with his private secretary, taking off his hat and bowing to either side continually. There was great enthusiasm when the omnibus passed bearing "the surviving soldiers of the War of 1812," and the Ship of State well manned and rigged,—a representative pageant that always seems to please the populace. The colored military turned out in force. The Inauguration Ball, or reception, took place in the new wing of the Treasury department. Telegraphic machines were set on the different floors to start the dancing sets; but there was little dancing. The committee had made insufficient provision for the accommodation of those to whom they sold tickets. The surging masses of humanity swelled and swayed, to the utter destruction of all comfort. A larger number was brought together than since the close of the war, and crowd jostled crowd; vast numbers unable to proceed finding their energies taxed to effect an egress. The President, Vice-President and their ladies had a small reception room in another part of the building, and were supported by Generals Sherman, Terry, Kilpatrick, Pleasanton, Webb and Thomas, with General Grant's staff, and Admirals Farragut and Goldsborough—all in full uniform. Mrs. Grant was dressed in pearl-colored satin with long train, point lace fichu and pearl ornaments; a wreath of leaves and flowers on her hair; Mrs. Colfax in pink satin with an over-dress of white tulle caught up with pink flowers; the bodice á la Pompadour, and pearl ornaments. The wife of General Griffin was there, with Mrs. and Miss Pendleton, the last in white silk with pink satin tunic. Mrs. Gaines wore black and gold lama with gold fringe and embroidery, blue bonnet and diamonds. Mrs. Vielé appeared in white valenciennes lace, with blue ribbons and roses; the wife of General Webb in lavender silk; Miss Spinner in pink tulle; the widow of General Greene of North Carolina in heavy black silk brocaded with gold, with diamonds in her head-dress; Mrs. Christmas, the daughter of Mrs. Gaines, in white alpaca with blue satin train, and gold jewelry; the daughter of Governor Ward of New Jersey, in pale silk with point lace panier; the wife of Attorney-General Robson of New Jersey in blue velvet with overskirt of thread lace; hair à la Marie Antoinette. Secretary McCulloch escorted a lady in puffed tarletan, with pink satin panier, and pearls and jewelry, with natural curls. The mother-in-law of Fernando Wood appeared in rich costume and loaded with diamonds; and one of the most elegant women seen was Mrs. T. M. Pomeroy. Miss Phillips, a stately blonde, accompanied Miss Barry, an elegant brunette, wearing corn-colored silk, with a profusion of diamonds. Miss Blanche Butler wore pale pink silk with long train, panier of point appliquée, diamonds and pearls. Miss McCorcklin, a niece of Mrs. Morgan, Mrs. McClure, Miss Danbery, Miss Sands and Miss Bean, a niece of the wife of Senator Harlan, were all at this time prominent in the gay circles of Washington. The foreign ministers, as usual, came in full court costume.

Notwithstanding such splendors, and the presence of numerous belles and distinguished men, most of the ladies voted the assemblage horrible as far as comfort was concerned, and were mortified to confess that they had been a portion of the struggling and suffering mass. Mrs. Gaines commanded as usual, a very large share of attention. Her devotion, patience, heroic hopefulness and dauntless courage, her untiring defense of the right, were so admiringly appreciated by all, that it may be truly said there was not so popular a woman in Washington. Everywhere she was surrounded, and was stopped every moment, if walking out, by friends delighted to recognize her. Some of them remembered an incident that occurred in New Orleans, when a suit was brought against her, claiming damages for asserting her title to a certain portion of her father's property. Mrs. Gaines appeared in court with her counsel and her gallant and veteran husband, "the hero of Fort Erie," who came in his uniform, wearing his sword. In the progress of the trial the counsel fell into a wrangle with the judge, and withdrew from the court-room; whereupon General Gaines rose and announced to the court that he was the husband of the defendant, and as an admitted member of the bar of the United States, he might claim the right to represent his wife's interests. Unfortunately, however, he had studied law in Virginia under a very different system of jurisprudence, and as he felt out at sea in the courts of a civil law State he would ask that the lady defendant, who was better acquainted with the remarkable facts of her history than any one else, should be allowed to address the jury in her case. The judge replied that the lady had the right to argue her own case. Then the General, with that grand dignity for which he was so distinguished, led forward Mrs. Gaines, who proceeded to address the jury at length, reading documents bearing upon her case. The judge at length interfered, alleging that the documents were not in evidence. The lady still persisting, he again interfered, and a disagreeable contest arose, in the midst of which Mrs. Gaines charged the judge with having an interest against her. Judge Buchanan retorted with temper, and notified General Gaines that he was expected to control his wife in court, where no persons were privileged. Whereupon the stately old General arose to his full altitude of six feet three, and assuming the position of a commander of grenadiers, and gracefully touching the belt of his sword, responded; "May it please your honor, for everything that lady shall say or do, I hold myself personally responsible in every manner and form known to the laws of my country or the laws of honor."

This reply and the accompanying action, and the appearance of the General in his military garb, aroused to a still higher pitch the Irish fire of the judge, who quickly answered: "General Gaines, this court will not be overawed by the military authorities."

"Rest assured, your honor, that when an attempt of that sort is made, the sword which I wear in conformity to the regulations of the service, and out of respect to this honorable court, will be quickly unsheathed to defend the rights and dignity of your honor, and of all the civil tribunals of my country."

After these explanations, peace and order were restored, but the judge considered it his duty to note the charge of Mrs. Gaines that he was sitting in a case in which he was interested. He should, therefore, reduce it to an exception of recusation, and require the evidence to be produced to sustain it. It had chanced that years before, in some proceedings in which Mrs. Gaines' rights were involved, Judge Buchanan had made a motion for a brother lawyer who was retained against Mrs. Gaines. This, it was decided, did not justify his recusation, and the case proceeded, and was, we believe, in the Supreme Court at least, determined in favor of Mrs. Gaines.

This was the first appearance of Mrs. Gaines as her own advocate in court. Afterwards she advocated her case in and out of court to the judges, in public and private, in every place and under all circumstances, and in every form and with every agency and appliance, maintaining all the while her confidence, her equanimity, her earnest zeal and unflagging energies, and exhibiting to the world the most remarkable example of courageous devotion and resolute persistency, which can be found in the history of the severest of all trials of human patience and endurance, tedious, complicated and exciting lawsuits. This undoubted right to claim the possession of qualities usually assigned to the sterner sex, gave point to her reproof of the fanatical pretensions of an advocate of women's rights, who was exhibiting herself at this time in Washington as an illustration of the superior healthfulness of masculine attire. Twenty or thirty gentlemen in the employ of the government were witnesses of the curious interview between Mrs. Gaines and "Mrs. Dr. Walker," as the former came out of the patent office. As she came near the "Doctor" in her peculiar dress, Mrs. Gaines stopped, asked her name and permission to give her a little advice, and then said:

"Please discard those pantaloons."

"Why should I do so?"

"Because it shocks the moral sentiment of the whole people. You have no right to do this; the world is not made alone for you or me. We are only part and parcel of the whole. Again, you place my sex in a false position, in a light to be ridiculed and treated with contempt by the other sex. Had I assumed your garb, I should have failed to obtain the sympathy of the virtuous and good throughout the country, in this great struggle for my rights. If your object is imitation, then do not, I pray, imitate that which God has not made half so perfect as woman; that is—man."

Mrs. Walker then said:

"Why do you dress in this gay style of lace and flowers?"

To which Mrs. Gaines replied:

"If told that my dress was repugnant to the public taste, I would instantly change it. I admit that it looks more youthful than my years would warrant; but, feeling young, I dress according to those feelings. When I feel old, I will dress suitable to age."

At this stage of the conversation Mrs. Walker asked—

"Who are you, madam?"

"I am Mrs. Gaines."

"Oh! I am very happy to know you. I was not prepared to see so young a looking woman. I expected to see a lady at least twenty years older than you appear to be. What is the secret of your looking so much younger than you really are?"

"This is the secret, madam: I feel kindly towards every human being. There should not be a sorrowing heart within my knowledge if I could prevent it. I look upon life thus: That we are placed here by our Heavenly Father to assist each other and do every possible good in our power. Money is merely a loan to effect that object. Though I have had one of the severest battles of life for nearly thirty-seven years, persecuted and wronged out of my estate since childhood, yet notwithstanding all this, I entertain no feelings of revenge or bitterness towards any one, and the world to-day looks to me as bright and beautiful as though I had never passed through such terrible scenes of grief and sorrow; and in all these trials I have never for a moment ceased to entertain an everlasting, undying faith in my God, upon the principle that so long as I was true to myself He would be true to me. My life has been devoted to duty. A fashionable woman I never was. God has blessed me with a remarkable constitution, and these probably are the reasons, madam, why they say I look so many years younger than I really am. Now permit me to renew my request that you change that unseemly garb. I am told that you are advocating woman's suffrage, but be assured that by your appearance in this improper apparel, you are doing that cause more injury than the strongest argument of its enemies. What can be the object of your wearing this dress, madam?"

"My health."

"Your health! That can not be, for I—continually exposed to all weathers—enjoy the best of health, and look younger to-day than you do. Pardon me for saying that I fear your only motive proceeds from a vulgar love of notoriety, to which none of our sex should ever descend."

The auditors expressed their approval of these sentiments by repeated plaudits.

At this time Olé Bull was again in Washington, and in great favor with lady visitors; his form still erect and majestic, his face serene, and his spirits excellent. At one of the hotels frequented by southerners were the widows of two prominent generals: Mrs. Greene of North Carolina, and Mrs. Gates of New York.

The roughest kind of prose followed the poetry of inauguration festivities. The White House was undergoing a renovation as to cleaning, refurnishing, &c., and the President's family did not occupy it for several days, though General Grant received those who waited on him, and there was a continual procession of strangers to see the apartments. Those on the floor above the public reception rooms were every day filled with eager applicants for boons from the Executive. Many waiting for an audience were women. General Dent, the private secretary, introduced them as fast as business could be despatched. The rooms of the new officials were equally besieged—and they were going through a purgatory of office-seekers. General Grant's cabinet seemed to be selected with reference to the competency of the members to discharge their duties and second the President in the course of reform and retrenchment, and the press generally expressed approbation. At present, it stands as follows: Hamilton Fish of New York, Secretary of State; George S. Boutwell of Massachusetts, Secretary of the Treasury; John A. Rawlins of Illinois, Secretary of War; George M. Robeson of New Jersey, Secretary of the Navy; Jacob D. Cox of Ohio, Secretary of the Interior. Mr. Cresswell, the retiring Maryland Senator, was named a worthy successor to Mr. Randall in the office of Postmaster-General; Mr. E. Rockwood Hoar, an able jurist and learned scholar, was appointed Attorney-General. The cabinet represents different sections of the country, and is composed of men of culture and energetic in action.

Mrs. Chancellor Walworth (the widow of Colonel Harden, who was killed at Buena Vista), is residing in Washington, and one of her intimate friends, the widow of General Gates (who served in the war of 1812, and in that of Florida and Mexico), was there for the purpose of getting a bill passed. She is yet young, and a handsome and elegant woman, with a voice of rich melody, and remarkably pleasing in conversation. These two ladies got up the farewell *fête* given at the National to Senator and Mrs. Crittenden, which has become historical. The distinction and beauty of Washington graced that party. Mrs. Walworth and Mrs. Gates received the company, supported by the Italian minister and Mr. Lovejoy. Mrs. Gates wore white silk with cherry silk tunic and pearl ornaments; Mrs. Walworth, buff satin trimmed with lace, and diamonds; Mrs. Crittenden, black velvet. The Cabinet, Senate and diplomatic corps were represented, and a farewell address was delivered to Mrs. Crittenden. That was one of the last of those chivalric festivals—as different from the taste of the present day as the baronial feasts of the middle ages from our modern political gatherings. Now the complaint is that the rabble have overflowed and permeated everything social, at least where the masses can obtain access, and vulgar self-assertion rules the day.

Four miles west of Jefferson barracks, near St. Louis, in a house pleasantly situated on the Merrimack, lived Colonel Frederick Dent, the father of Mrs. Grant. He had settled in Missouri in 1815, purchasing land on Gravor's Creek, ten miles south-west of St. Louis, and calling his estate Whitehaven. It comprised a pretty variety of wooded hills and grassy valleys. Julia was the fifth child and the eldest daughter. She was comely, sprightly, amiable and lovely, well-bred and attractive in her manners. She received her education in St. Louis at Colonel Moreau's school. Her father's house and estate were tended by some thirty slaves, and the hospitality exercised was Southern in its liberality. When Grant joined his regiment in the neighborhood, he became a welcome visitor, though the family were not altogether pleased when the young lieutenant won the affections of the eldest daughter. All opposition ceased, however, after he had saved her brother's life in Mexico. On the 22d of August, 1848, Miss Julia Dent was married to Ulysses S. Grant in St. Louis. It was a merry wedding, and the dancing was kept up till midnight. The company consisted of the numerous friends of the Dent family and Grant's military comrades. General and Mrs. Grant resided at Detroit, near the garrison, and she often made visits to her father's house. When Mrs. Grant found the demands of society exacting, she fulfilled them with grace, and in a spirit of kindliness.

Ever since the close of the war she had lived in some measure in public; had resided for years in Washington, and mingled in its social circles, giving many receptions and parties, and accompanying the General on his visits to other cities where an ovation was tendered to him. Thus she had experience to qualify her for a leader in the best society. Her first reception in the White House was given early in April. The visitors were ushered into the red drawing-room, and presented by General Michler. Mrs. Grant wore lavender silk trimmed with white lace; her hair slightly crimped in front, and three heavy curls falling over her left shoulder. Mrs. Morgan, the wife of the Governor, stood on her right, and the wives of Senators Morton and Williams on the left; the latter in crimson silk trimmed with white quilling; Mrs. Morgan in purple silk. Mrs. Butler, Miss Blanche Butler, Mrs. Wilson and other noted ladies, represented New England. General Grant was not present on this occasion. The second weekly reception was on Tuesday from two to four, when Mrs.

Grant took her place in the blue room, supported by the wife of Senator Sherman, Mrs. Fish, the Secretary's wife, and Mrs. Hoar. Her dress was blue silk, dotted with white roses, with an elaborate train trimmed with white lace, displaying an underskirt striped with lace.

In New York the wife of General Dix gave a superb reception to Mr. Washburne, just before he sailed for Europe to replace General Dix as minister. Mr. Washburne stood beside the hostess, with Mrs. Blake, her daughter. Mr. and Mrs. James Robb were among the distinguished guests. Mrs. Robb was Mrs. Stanard, formerly an admired leader of society in Richmond, Va., and since the war a resident of Baltimore. Her beauty, grace, and winning manners, with her Southern warmth of heart, gained hosts of friends. She is now very popular in New York society.

A memorable entertainment was given in Washington by Franklin Philp, at the opening of his elegant house, and most of the celebrities were present. Mrs. Philp's dress was white moire, trimmed with green tarletan. The walls were covered with a large collection of water color drawings.

Mrs. Sprague's receptions continue to be a prominent feature of society in Washington during every session. Gifted with beauty and brilliant mental qualities, her reign is undisputed. Her lovely sister, Miss Chase, assists her in receiving the visitors.

The impression produced on intelligent strangers is always worth notice. An English tourist, who visited Washington during the civil war, said: "Washington has not the one merit of American architecture—symmetry. The whole place looks run up in a night, like the card-board cities which Potemkin erected to gratify the eyes of his imperial mistress on her tour through Russia; and it is impossible to remove the impression that, when Congress is over, the place is taken down and packed up again till wanted. Every body is a bird of passage at Washington." This impression was created by the number of buildings run up for temporary occupation. "The diplomatic corps is transitory by its very nature. The Senators, Representatives and ministers reside there for two, four, possibly six sessions, as the case may be; the clerks, officials and government employés are all, too, mere lodgers. Hence none of these, with a few exceptions, has a house of his own. The wives and families of the married members come to Washington for a few months or weeks during the session, and for the time of their stay a furnished house is taken. In consequence there is little style about the mode of living. The number of private carriages is comparatively few, and people are afraid of bringing good horses to be ruined by the rut-tracks that serve the purposes of streets in Washington. Even according to the American standard there is not a decent hotel in the whole place. Willard's and the National are two large rambling barracks, where some incredible number of beds could be run up; but it is hard to say which is the shabbiest internally. At all times Willard's is the house of call for everybody who has business in Washington. From early morning till late at night its lobbies and passages are filled with a motley throng of all classes and all nations. With the exception of the President, there is not a statesman or a general, or man of note of any kind in Washington, whom I have not come across at different times, in the passages of Willard's. Soldiers in every uniform, privates and officers thrown together in strange confusion; congressmen and senators, army contractors and Jews; artists, newspaper writers, tourists, prize-fighters and gamblers, were mixed up with a nondescript crowd of men who seem to have no business except to hang about. In the parlors there was a like confusion. Half a dozen rough-looking common soldiers, with their boots encased in deep layers of Virginia mud, would be dozing with their feet hoisted on the high fenders before the fire. At the tables gentlemen dressed in the mouldy black evening suits American are so partial to, would sit all day writing letters. Knots of three or four belonging apparently to every grade of society, would be standing about the room shaking hands constantly with new comers, introducing everybody to everybody, and adjourning at intervals in a body to the bar. On the floor above, splendidly dressed ladies were strolling at all hours about the passages, chatting with friends, working, playing, and flirting with smartly bedizened officers and gay young diplomatists."

"On a fine bright spring day, when the wooded banks that line the south side of the Potomac were in their early bloom, I have thought the city looked wondrously bright; but on nine days out of every ten, the climate of Washington is simply detestable. When it rains, the streets are sloughs of liquid mud; even in the paved streets the stones sink into the ground and the mud oozes up between them. In a couple of hours from the time the rain ceases, the same streets are enveloped in clouds of dust."

An anecdote related of Governor Randall illustrates his unostentatious kindness. One dark evening an old man who had been carrying the mail from the post-office to the railway station, drove his horse to the side-walk. "I say, stranger," he called out, "open that gate for me!" "Certainly," replied Mr. Randall, and he immediately pushed the gate open. "Now," said the old man, "please to shut the gate and fasten it." "Certainly," again answered Mr. Randall, suiting the action to the word.

Judge Mason, who was American minister to Paris, had taken for his residence, a house in a beautiful spot facing the Champs Elysées. He employed a tall colored man, of the true Virginia type, who had been brought out fifteen or twenty years before by an American minister, and had remained in Europe ever since, in the service of American ambassadors, either in Paris, St. Petersburgh or Germany. He spoke French, Russian and German, and his manner combined the grace and politeness of a French dancing-master with the faithful devotion of a well-trained Virginia servant. It did his countrymen good to see his honest black face in the ante-chamber of Mr. Mason, giving them an agreeable impression of home.

Mrs. Wolcott's niece, (page 30) a daughter of General Collins of Guilford, resided with her, and was called "the belle of Connecticut," so distinguished was she for her beauty. She married Mr. Edward Jessup, a cousin of the General of that name. A great grand-daughter of this lady, who has inherited some of her charms of person, is now one of the court circle at Stockholm. One of the court officials writing from that city to a friend in New York, says: "The young Countess Rosen shines like a star in Stockholm society. She is beloved by all for her grace, affability and charm of manner, even as she attracts all by her beauty of face and form." She is a daughter of Mrs. Bloomfield Moore of Philadelphia.

The social prospects of Washington have been much discussed, and rather in a spirit of despondency. It seems, to many, unlikely that so brilliant a period as the administration of Buchanan, or those of some of his predecessors, will again enliven the capital. They maintain that where a society is so widely spread, it follows the law of fluids, and becomes the shallower the more it is diffused; also, that the intelligence, high culture, and fastidious taste that formerly marked the best circles, have of late given place to the mere love of display, pride of wealth and sensuous apprehension, that form the claim of "the newly enriched" or elevated, to superior consideration. There is no doubt of the tendency of society at the present time to this kind of deterioration. The example of New York and other commercial cities shows the danger. It may not be long, some aver, before Washington, too, may be an arena merely for the exhibition of vulgar wealth, and extravagance in dress and entertainments may become a test of aristocratic refinement. There are a few conservative elements at work, however, and the leaven may suffice to prevent the whole lump from settling into a sluggish mass. The influence of foreigners has a beneficial effect; and when the Union is fully restored, and the South represented as it should be, completely and harmoniously, the balance will be so preserved as to lessen the peril now dreaded. There has never been in Southern communities, a tendency to undue honoring of riches and empty show; the ancient English prejudice in favor of blood, remains, and among the old families, a gentle bearing and careful mental cultivation are held essential to the breeding of those who lead in the highest sphere. An infusion of this spirit will do good. And how know we what may be done by the influence of individuals! If the days of Clay, Webster, Calhoun and Mrs. Madison are gone by—are we certain that we ne'er shall look upon their like again! May we not hope that other royal intellects may lift the sceptre now idle or profaned; that other gracious and benign creatures may teach women their true power! that the society of our capital may again be what it has been, a nursery for the noble qualities of our nature, and for the training of gifted minds, where greatness mav be achieved without the sacrifice of principle!

www.ingramcontent.com/pod-product-compliance
Lightning Source LLC
LaVergne TN
LVHW021224110826
845150LV00002B/239

* 9 7 8 1 4 2 5 5 6 4 0 5 6 *